天天读英语

感动一生的美文全集

（英汉对照）

青 闰⊙主 编

蒋 铮⊙副主编

台海出版社

图书在版编目(CIP)数据

英汉双语感动一生的美文全集 / 青闰主编 . -- 北京：
台海出版社 , 2018.5

ISBN 978-7-5168-1881-7

Ⅰ . ①英… Ⅱ . ①青… Ⅲ . ①英语—汉语—对照读物
②散文集—世界 Ⅳ . ① H319.4：I

中国版本图书馆 CIP 数据核字 (2018) 第 092500 号

英汉双语感动一生的美文全集

主　　编：青　闰	
责任编辑：高惠娟　贾凤华	装帧设计：同人内文化传媒·书装设计
版式设计：同人内文化传媒·书装设计	责任印制：蔡　旭

出版发行：台海出版社

地　　址：北京市东城区景山东街 20 号　　邮政编码：100009

电　　话：010 — 64041652（发行，邮购）

传　　真：010 — 84045799（总编室）

网　　址：www.taimeng.org.cn/thcbs/default.htm

E－mail：thcbs@126.com

经　　销：全国各地新华书店

印　　刷：香河利华文化发展有限公司

本书如有破损、缺页、装订错误，请与本社联系调换

开　　本：710mm × 1000mm		1/16	
字　　数：370 千字		印　　张：21.5	
版　　次：2018年9月第1版		印　　次：2018年9月第1次印刷	
书　　号：ISBN 978-7-5168-1881-7			
定　　价：39.80 元			

前　　言

　　《感动一生的美文全集》是让人获得幸福的心灵密码，是按摩情感的心灵圣经，也是温暖千万心灵、改变千万人生的传世宝典。本书所选篇章以英汉对照形式编排，原汁原味，新颖独特，系统全面，贴近实际，贴近时代，贴近生活，所选内容发人深省、引人入胜、耐人寻味、励人奋进。

　　《感动一生的美文全集》分为幸福像阳光一样、快乐是一首自由的歌、让心灵充满阳光、春天在你的心里、放飞心灵的翅膀、予人玫瑰手留余香、从梦想之火到最后胜利、让生活充满阳光和克服忧虑的快乐生活等九卷，涉及心态、宽容、尊重、亲情、爱情、友谊、善良、感恩、幸福、做人、做事、挫折、成功等一系列人生课题。这些文章既可以使读者感到心灵震撼，又可以从容自信，端正人生态度，找到生活方向，成就美满人生。

　　朋友，每当华灯初上，白天的喧哗与骚动渐渐平息，伴着明月清风，和着舒缓旋律，携一卷美文，品一杯香茗，坐在属于自己的空间，体验文字带给你的优美、睿智、灵动与流畅，感受时间从指缝间飘然而去，体味一种纯净、充实和有趣的生活，是何等美妙和惬意！

　　我们奉献给你的正是这样一种精神享受。她们像一只只神奇灵动的手拨动着你的心弦，使你如沐春风、如逢甘霖。她们就像鲜花一样芬芳，月色一样柔和，微风一样清新，春雨一样滋润。

　　朋友，请走进我们营造的精神家园，这里有你的青春，有你的记忆，有你的梦想，还有你的爱情和希望。让我们在此相会，让我们的人生得到心灵的滋润，提升人生的品位。

本书由焦作大学青闰主编、翻译和统稿，西安电子科技大学外国语学院蒋铮副主编并参与部分翻译。

目　　录

第一卷　幸福像阳光一样

第二卷　快乐是一首自由的歌

第三卷　让心灵充满阳光

第四卷　春天在你的心里

第五卷　放飞心灵的翅膀

第六卷　予人玫瑰，手留余香

第七卷　从梦想之火到最后胜利

第八卷 让生活充满阳光

第九卷　克服忧虑的快乐生活

第一卷

幸福像阳光一样

The Direction of Happiness

A young man was walking by the lakeside when he suddenly saw a piece of gold glittering in the water. He was so happy that he jumped into the water to fish for it. But he couldn't reach it on matter how he tried his best. Being wet, dirty and tired, he had to disembark for a rest. Unexpectedly, after the water became placid, the gold appeared again.

He jumped into the water again unwillingly, but in vain, so he had to disembark again to sit beside the lake. He thought, "Where is the gold coin in the water on earth? I have seen it clearly, why can't I find it even though I have tried so hard?" After the water became placid, the gold coin appeared once again. So once again he jumped into the water to fish for it. He did it again and again, but in vain, which made him really unwilling to accept.

At that moment, his father came to look for him. Seeing his son wet and dirty, he asked, "What happened in the world? Why are you so embarrassed?"

His son answered, "I see a piece of gold coin in the water clearly, but I can't get it anyway!"

His father saw a gold coin seemed on the placid water, so he looked up at the tree and said to his son, "Look! It's not a gold coin but the reflection of the sheet metal that is hung on the tree."

Ordinary people are always busy running about honorary and illusory things while all these just consist in greed, which eclipses our ability of telling right from wrong. Some people think life is hard and we must find a way of releasing at once! So they turn to seek for religious belief; but if religious belief has no right understanding, suggestions or ideas, you will go astray. So we should choose the right direction of life, get rid of evil and cultivating good and comprehend truth.

Worldly substance is illusory like the reflection of the water, so we should often have a contented mind and can understand, tolerate and thank everything, which will reach perfection. In this way, you'll be even-tempered and good-humored every day and have a happy life.

幸福的方向

一位年轻人走到湖边散步，突然看到水中有一块闪闪发亮的金币。他很高兴，就赶快跳进水里捞取。但是，无论怎么努力，他都捞不到金币。他浑身又湿又脏，非常疲倦，只好上来坐在岸边休息。没想到湖水平静之后，金币又显现了出来。

他很不甘心地又跳下水，结果还是没捞到，只得再上来坐着。他心想："水中的金币到底在哪里呢？我明明看到了，为什么费了这么大劲儿还捞不到呢？"等水面又恢复平静后，金币再次出现。于是，他又跳下去捞，如此反复都徒劳无功，他实在很不甘心。

这时，父亲出来找他。看到儿子全身湿淋淋、脏兮兮的，就问他："到底发生了什么事？你为什么会如此狼狈？"

儿子回答说："我明明看到水中有金币，可怎么捞都捞不到！"

父亲看到平静的水面上好像真有一个金币，又抬头看看树上，就对儿子说："你看！哪是什么金币，那是挂在树上的金属片，投射在水中呈现的幻影罢了！"

凡夫总是为名利、空幻的东西在奔波、辛劳，而这一切都只在于一贪念，而贪念往往会蒙蔽我们辨别是非的能力。有的人认为，人生很苦，要赶快找解脱的方法，因此转而寻求宗教信仰；但是，如果信仰没有正知、正见、正念，路就会走偏了。所以，我们应该要选择正确的人生方向，断恶修善，领悟真理。

世间的事物不过如水中倒影般虚无，因此要常怀知足之心，对人生事物能善解、包容、感恩，凡事就能圆融，这样就能天天过得心平气和，拥有一个幸福的人生。

The Uncared-for Happiness

In a painter's house, I saw a very special painting, which was a piece of mounted white paper, on the left middle of which there was a black stain.

I didn't understand what gifted pen such a black stain was that the painter hung it on the most prominent position right in the middle of the wall. I kept pondering for a long time, but my mind was still a complete blank.

I asked the artist for advice.

The painter said, "This painting of mine is called 'Happiness.'"

"Happiness? I don't understand." In my memory, no artist could paint happiness.

The painter said, "The black stain in the middle stands for pain. When every person sees this painting of mine, he or she only sees this painful black stain, but can't see the happiness in the background. Isn't our life in this way? How much happiness we turn a blind eye to, but we are shut out by the minimal pain."

I said, "In your mind, this painting should be a piece of white paper."

He said, "Without pain, we won't even more see happiness."

I come to see that we always focus on the pain while the happiness is often the part we have overlooked.

被忽略的快乐

在一位画家的屋里，我见到了一幅非常特别的画。那是一张被装裱起来的白纸，在中间偏左上的位置有一块黑渍。

我不明白这块黑渍到底算什么妙笔生花，被画家挂在了墙壁正当中最为显眼的位置上。我琢磨了很长时间，头脑里仍然是一片空白。

我向画家请教。

画家说："我的这幅画叫'快乐'。"

"快乐？我不明白。"在我的记忆中，没有哪个画家能画出快乐来。

画家说："中间这块黑渍是痛苦，每个人看到我的这幅画时，都是只看到这块痛苦的黑渍，却看不到背景里的快乐。我们的生活不是这样吗？多少快乐，我们都视而不见，却被微小的痛苦遮住了双眼。"

我说："按照你的说法，这张画应该是一张白纸。"

他说："没有痛苦，我们更见不到快乐。"

我明白了，我们总是盯着痛苦，而快乐常常是被我们忽略的那部分。

The Catalogue of Happiness

"On my head pour only the sweet waters of serenity. Give me the gift of the untroubled mind."

Once, as a young man full of exuberant fancy, I undertook to draw up a catalogue of the acknowledged happiness of life. As other men sometimes tabulate lists of properties they own or would like to own, I set down my inventory of earthly desirable: health, love, beauty, talent, power, riches and fame.

When my inventory was completed, I proudly showed it to a sage who had been the mentor and spiritual model of my youth. Perhaps I was trying to impress him with my precocious wisdom. Anyway, I handed him the list. "This," I told him confidently. "is the sum of mortal happiness. If a man could possess them all, he would be as a god."

"An excellent list," he said thoughtfully. "But it appears, my young friend, you have omitted the most important element of all. You have forgotten the one ingredient, lacking which each possession becomes a hideous torment."

"And what," I asked, "is that missing ingredient?"

With a pencil stub he crossed out my entire tabulation and wrote down: peace of mind. "This is the gift God reserves," he said.

"Talent and beauty he gives to many. Wealth is commonplace, fame not rare. But peace of mind—that is his final guerdon of approval, the fondest insignia of his love. Most men are never blessed with it; others wait all their lives—yes, far into advanced age—for this gift to descend upon them."

人生幸福的目录

"只将宁静蜜汁醍醐灌顶，赐我以无忧心境。"

我年轻时曾充满丰富的幻想，着手起草了一份被公认为人生幸福的目录。就像他人有时会把他们拥有或想拥有的财产列成表那样，我把世人想要的东西——健康、爱情、美丽、才能、权力、财富和名誉——列了一个详细目录。

我列完这个详细目录后，自豪地让一位智者过目，他曾是我少年时代的辅导老师和精神楷模。也许我是想以自己早熟的智慧给他留下深刻印象。总之，我把那张目录递给了他。我充满自信地对他说："这是人类幸福的总和。一个人能拥有所有这些，就和神一样了。"

他若有所思地说："是一张出色的目录。可是，我年轻的朋友，你遗漏了最重要的一个要素。你忘记了一个因素，缺少了它，每项财产都会变成可怕的痛苦。"

我问道："那遗漏的这个因素是什么？"

他用铅笔头划掉了我的整张表格，写下了：心静。"这是上帝保留的礼物。"他说。

"他把才能和美丽赐予许多人。财富是平凡的，名望也不稀罕，但心静才是他恩准的最后赐赏，是他最温柔的爱的象征。多数人从来没有这种福气，有些人则等了一辈子——是的，一直等到了老态龙钟，才等到这个赏赐降临到他们身上。"

Don't Keep Happiness away from Us

A college student once told me, "I don't need to be happy—just successful."

It's an odd juxtaposition. She needn't be happy, "just successful." She places one in opposition to the other.

Students are today's expressions of tomorrow's practices.

I remember from my own undergraduate years of a headline in my campus newspaper, "Why Aren't We Happy?" As the headline suggested, we fell short of leading joyful lives. Yet at least we are still looking for happiness. Like my success-seeking student, why do many of us want to give up happiness?

I've often failed to enjoy Sunday because of my schedule on Monday. At bottom, it was simply anticipatory anxiety over the work of the week ahead—I fear that there would be unexpected complications or that I would fail to measure in some way. Usually, when Monday came, I did quite well. Much of what I worried about never happened.

Happiness has its own underpinning. There's completeness to happiness that does not allow us to exclude our sense of the person we should be. Pleasure is certainly possible in less-than-honorable actions. But the experience of happiness requires more; it is pleasure taken in worthy things.

True happiness requires choices that develop into habits that evolve into character. And that's work we can't delegate.

So the essential first step is trying to lessen the anxiety—one that can avoid it. It requires us to brave everything unexpected and face all the annoyances of life calmly.

别让幸福远离我们

一名大学生曾告诉我说："我不需要幸福，只要成功。"

这是一个奇怪的交叉对比。她不需要幸福，"只要成功"。她把这两者对立了起来。

学生今日之言就是明日之行。

我记得上大学时，校报上有一篇文章的标题是："为什么我们不幸福？"这个标题是说：我们缺少快乐的生活。然而，我们至少仍在寻找幸福。为什么我们中的许多人像那个追求成功的学生一样要放弃幸福呢？

我常常不能去享受星期天，是因为星期一的工作进度。实际上，这仅仅是提前对未来一周的工作感到忧虑，我担心会发生难以预料的麻烦，要么是担心自己在某些方面无法进行估量。通常，星期一来临时，我做得还不错。我担心的很多事情从来没有发生过。

幸福自有其道德基础。幸福的完整性让我们不得不考虑自己应该做什么样的人。当然，一些不怎么光彩的行为也可能会产生快乐。但要想体验幸福，需要付出更多；正是快乐让我们体会到事物的价值。

真正的幸福需要作出选择，这些选择可以形成习惯，从而发展成为性格。这是我们无法越俎代庖的工作。

因此，获取幸福的首要一步就是尽量减少忧虑，这关键的第一步能让我们避开忧虑。它要求我们勇于接受毫无预想的一切，坦然面对生活中的一切烦恼。

The Secret of Happiness

There was a businessman, who sent his son to the most wise man in the world to ask for the secret of happiness. After going through all hardships for 40 days, this boy finally found the wise man's beautiful castle.

When he entered the castle, the boy didn't meet a saint, but witnessed an unusually lively scene: business people came in and out, in every corner people were talking with each other and a small band was playing gentle music. The local delicacies was placed on a table. The wise man was talking with all the people one by one, so the boy had to wait for two hours for his turn.

The wise man attentively listened to the boy's reason for the visit, but he said at this point he didn't have time to explain the secret of happiness to him. He suggested the boy go around the palace and returned to see him after two hours.

"At the same time I ask you to do one thing," the wise man said as he handed a spoon to the boy and dripped two drops of oil into it, "When you walk, take this spoon and do not let the oil spill."

The boy began walking up and down the steps of the palace, his eyes always focusing on the spoon. Two hours later, he returned to the wise man.

"Have you seen the Persian carpets of my restaurant? Have you seen my garden the gardening master spent 10 years creating? Have you noticed those beautiful sheepskin volumes of my library?" the wise man asked.

The boy was very embarrassed, admitting he didn't see, for what he was only concerned about was the thing the wise man entrusted to him—namely, not to let the drops of oil in the spoon spill.

"Then you go back to see all kinds of rare things in here," the wise man said, "If you don't know a person's home, you won't be able to trust him."

Feeling more easily, the boy picked up the spoon and walked back into the palace. This time, he noticed all the artworks hung on the ceiling and walls, viewed the garden and the surrounding mountain scenery and saw the delicate flowers. When he returned to the wise man again, the boy dwelt on all he saw.

"But where's the two drops of oil I gave you?" the wise man asked.

Looking at the spoon, the boy found the oil had all been spilled.

"So this is the only warning I want to give you," the wise man said, "the secret of happiness lies in enjoying all the wonders of the world and at the same time never forget the two drops of oil in the spoon."

幸福的秘密

有位商人把儿子派往世界上最有智慧的人那里，去讨教幸福的秘密。这个男孩历尽艰辛，走了40天，终于找到了智者的美丽城堡。

男孩走进城堡，没有遇到一位圣人，却目睹了一个热闹非凡的场面：商人们进进出出，每个角落都有人在交谈，一支小乐队在演奏轻柔的乐曲。一张桌子上摆满了当地的美味佳肴。智者正一个个同所有的人谈话，所以男孩必须要等两个小时才能轮到。

智者认真地听了男孩所讲的来访原因，但说此刻他没有时间向男孩讲解幸福的秘密。他建议男孩在他的宫殿里转上一圈，两个小时后再来找他。

"与此同时，我要求你办一件事，"智者边说边把一个汤匙递给男孩，并在里面滴进了两滴油，"当你走路时，拿好这个汤匙，不要让油洒出来。"

男孩开始沿着宫殿的台阶上上下下，眼睛始终盯着汤匙不放。两小时后，他回到了智者面前。

"你看到我餐厅里的波斯地毯了吗？看到园艺大师花了10年心血创造出来的花园了吗？注意到我图书馆那些美丽的羊皮卷文献了吗？"智者问道。

男孩感到十分尴尬，承认他什么也没看到，他当时唯一关注的只是智者交付给他的事，也就是不要让汤匙里的两滴油洒出来。

"那你就转回去见识一下我这里的种种珍奇之物吧，"智者说道，"如果你不了解一个人的家，你就不能信任他。"

男孩轻松多了，他拿起汤匙重新回到宫殿里漫步。这一次，他注意到了天花板和墙壁上悬挂的所有艺术品，观赏了花园和四周的山景，看到了娇嫩的花儿。当他再回到智者面前时，男孩仔细地讲述了他所见到的一切。

"可是，我交给你的两滴油在哪里呢？"智者问道。

男孩向汤匙望去，发现油已经洒光了。

"那么，这就是我要给你的唯一忠告，"智者说，"幸福的秘密在于欣赏世界上所有的奇观异景，同时永远不要忘记汤匙里的两滴油。"

The Law of Happy Life

It is okay to make mistakes. Making mistakes is something we all do, and I'm still a fine and worthwhile person when I make them. There is no reason for me to get upset when I make a mistake. I am trying, so even if I make a mistake, I am going to continue trying. I can handle making a mistake. It is okay for others to make mistakes, too. I will accept mistakes in myself and in others.

Everybody doesn't have to love me. Not everybody has to love me or even like me. I don't necessarily like everybody, I know, so why should everybody else like me? I enjoy being liked and being loved, but if somebody doesn't like me, I will still be okay. I cannot make somebody like me, as somebody cannot get me to like them. I don't need approval all the time. If someone does not approve of me, I will still be okay.

I don't have to control things. I will survive if things are different than what I want them to be. I can accept things the way they are, people the way they are and myself the way I am. There is no reason to get upset if I can't change things to fit my idea of how they ought to be. There is no reason why I should have to like everything. Even if I don't like it, I can't live with it.

I'm responsible for my day. I'm responsible for how I feel and what I do. Nobody can make me feel anything. If I have a rotten day, I'm the one who allows it to be that way. If I have a great day, I'm the one who deserves credit for being positive. It is not the responsibility of other people to change so that I can feel better. I'm the one who is in charge of my life.

I can handle it when things go wrong. I don't need to watch out for things to go wrong all the time. Things usually go just fine, and when they don't, I can handle it. I don't have to waste my energy worrying. The sky won't fall in; things will be okay.

I can do it. I don't need someone else to take care of my problem. I can do it. I can take care of myself. I can make decisions for myself. I can think for myself. I don't have to depend on somebody else to take care of me.

I can play to the score. There is more than one way to do something. More than one person has had good ideas that will work. There is no one and only"best" way. Everybody has ideas that are worthwhile. Some may take more sense to me than others, but everyone's ideas are worthwhile while everyone has something worthwhile to contribute.

幸福生活的定律

犯错误也没什么大不了的。我们都会犯错误。就算犯错误,我还是一个恪尽职守的人才。我犯错误后，完全没有理由忐忑不安。因为我一直在努力，所以即使犯了错误，也会继续努力。我能正确对待犯错误。别人犯错误也没关系。我会接受自己犯错误，也会接受别人犯错误。

并不是人人都得爱我。不是每个人都得爱我或喜欢我。我不一定喜欢我认识的每一个人，所以为什么其他每个人都应该喜欢我呢？尽管我乐意被人喜欢或被人爱，但如果有人不喜欢我，我仍会好好的。我无法迫使某个人喜欢我，就像某个人也不能迫使我喜欢他一样。我不需要时时刻刻得到认可。如果有人不认可我，我仍会好好的。

我不必事事都控制。就是事情和我想的不一样，我也照样活着。我能接受事情本来的样子，接受人们本来的面貌，接受本真的我。如果我不能让事情成为我想要的样子，也没有什么理由忐忑不安。我没有理由要喜欢世间的一切。即使不喜欢，我仍能忍受。

我对自己的每一天负责。我对自己的感觉和自己的所为负责。没有人能强迫我对一切事情的感觉。如果我一天过得很糟，那是我对自己的放任自流。如果我一天过得很棒，那是我态度积极，应该受到赞扬。其他人没有责任为了让我感觉更好而改变。我是掌握自己人生的主人。

出了问题，我能处理。我不必时刻担心事情会出错。事情常常会顺利进行，就算不能顺利进行，我也能处理好。我不必浪费时间去杞人忧天。天不会塌下来，一切都会好起来。

我能行。我不需要别人来处理我的问题。我能行。我能照顾好自己，能自己作出决定，能自己思考。我不必依靠别人来照顾我。

我能随机应变。做事方法不止一种。不止一个人有奏效的妙方。也没有哪一种方法"无懈可击"。每个人都有值得一试的主意。有些可能对我更有帮助，但每个人的主意都有可取之处，每个人都能想出一些好办法。

The Ways of Happiness

I live in the land of Disney, Hollywood, where the sun shines all the year. You may think people in such a glamorous place brimming over with fun are happier than others. If so, you have some mistakes about the nature of happiness.

Many intelligent people still equate happiness with fun. The truth is that fun and happiness have little or nothing in common. Fun is what we experience during an act. Happiness is what we experience after an act. It is a deeper, more abiding emotion.

The way people firmly believe that life full of joy and away from pain equaling happiness actually diminishes their chances of ever attaining real happiness. If fun and pleasure are equated with happiness, pain must be equated with unhappiness. But in fact, the opposite is true: more times than not, things that lead to happiness involve some pain.

As a result, many people avoid the very endeavors that are the source of true happiness. They fear the pain inevitably brought by such things as marriage, raising children, professional achievement, religious commitment, civic or charitable work and self-improvement.

Ask a bachelor why he resists marriage even though he finds dating to be less and less satisfying. If he's honest, he will tell you that he is afraid of making a commitment. For commitment is in fact quite painful. The single life is filled with fun, adventure and excitement. Marriage has such movement, but they are not its most distinguishing features.

Similarly, couples who choose not to have children are in favor of painless fun over painful happiness. They can dine out whenever they want, travel wherever they want and sleep as late as they want. Couples with infants are lucky to get a whole night's sleep or a three-day vacation.

But couples who decide not to have children never experience the pleasure of hugging them or tucking them into bed at night. They never know the joy of watching a child grow up or of playing with a grandchild.

But these forms of fun do not contribute in any way to my happiness. Writing, raising children, creating deep relationship with my wife and trying to do good in the world will bring me more happiness.

Understanding and accepting that true happiness has nothing to do with fun is one of the most liberating realizations we can ever come to. It liberates time: now we can devote more hours to activities that can genuinely increase our happiness. It liberates money: buying that new car or those fancy clothes won't increase our happiness now. And it liberates us from envy: we now understand that all those rich and glamorous people we were so sure are happy because actually they are not be happy at all.

The moment we understand that fun doesn't bring happiness, we will begin to lead our lives differently. The effect can be surely life-transforming.

幸福的方式

我住在好莱坞的迪士尼乐园，那里一年四季阳光普照。你也许以为生活在那样富有魅力、充满乐趣的地方一定比别的地方的人幸福。假如这样的话，你就对幸福的真谛有些误解。

很多聪明人仍把幸福和乐趣相提并论。其实，乐趣和幸福几乎或根本没有共同之处。乐趣是我们行为过程中的体验。幸福是我们行为过后的体验。它是一种更深刻、更持久的感情。

人们坚信充满欢乐、远离痛苦的生活方式就等于幸福，其实减少了他们获得真正幸福的机会。如果欢乐和愉快等同幸福，那痛苦就一定等同不幸。但事实上恰恰相反：多数情况下，能带来幸福的事物常常包含一些痛苦。

因此，许多人避开的那些努力正是真正幸福的源泉。他们害怕那些肯定会带来痛苦的事情，比如结婚、抚养子女、专业成就、承担宗教义务、社会或慈善事业及自我改善。

即使一个单身汉对约会越来越不满意，你问他为什么不想结婚时，如果他诚实，也会告诉你，他害怕承担义务。因为承担义务确实非常痛苦。独身生活充满乐趣、冒险和激情。尽管婚姻也有这样的活动，但大为逊色。

同样，选择不要孩子的夫妇都赞成没有痛苦的快乐，而不要痛苦的幸福。他们可以随时出去吃饭，随便到什么地方旅游，想睡多晚就睡多晚。有小孩子的夫妻能睡一晚上或有三天假期，算是幸运的了。

可是，决定不要孩子的夫妇绝不会体会到拥抱孩子或晚上给孩子掖被子时的乐趣。他们绝不会明白看着孩子长大或逗弄孙子孙女的喜悦。

不过，这些形式的乐趣无论如何都不是我说的幸福。写作、抚养孩子、加深和妻子的感情与尽力做善事会给我带来更多的幸福。

理解并接受真正的幸福和娱乐无关，我们却能获得最大限度的解放。它解放时间：现在，我们可以把更多时间用于那些能真正增加我们幸福的活动。它解放金钱：买那辆新车或那些时尚衣服现在不会增加我们的幸福。而且它把我们从嫉妒中解放出来：我们现在理解了那些我们确信幸福、令人向往的富人，因为他们其实根本不幸福。

我们懂得了娱乐不会带来幸福，就会开始以不同的方式生活。其效果肯定会改变人生。

The Door to Happiness

Happiness is like a pebble dropped into a pool to set in motion an ever-widening circle of ripples. As Stevenson said, "Being happy is a duty."

There is no exact definition of the word—happiness. Happy people are happy for all sorts of reasons. The key is not wealth or physical well-being, for we find beggars, invalids and so-called failures are extremely happy.

Being happy is a sort of unexpected dividend. But staying happy is an accomplishment, a triumph of soul and character. It is not selfish to strive for it. It is, indeed, a duty to us and others.

Being unhappy is like an infectious disease; it causes people to shrink away from the sufferer. He soon finds himself alone, miserable and embittered. There is, however, a cure that seems ridiculous but simple: if you don't feel happy, pretend to be!

It works. Before long you will find that instead of repelling people, you attract them. You will discover how deeply rewarding it is to be the center of wider and wider circles of goodwill.

Then the make-believe becomes a reality. You possess the secret of peace of mind and can forget yourself in being of service to others.

Being happy, once it is realized as a duty and established as a habit, opens door into mysterious gardens thronged with grateful friends.

幸 福 之 门

幸福就像掉进池塘里的一枚鹅卵石，渐渐荡起一圈圈涟漪，不断向外扩散。就像史蒂文森所说："幸福是一种责任。"

"幸福"这个词没有确切的定义，幸福的人之所以幸福，有各种各样的理由。关键不在财富或健康，因为我们发现乞丐、残疾人和所谓的失败者都特别快乐。

幸福是一种意想不到的红利。但保持幸福是一种成就，是灵魂和品格的成功。追求幸福并不是自私，其实是对自己和他人的一种责任。

郁郁寡欢就像传染病，这使人们常常对郁郁寡欢的人退避三舍。他很快会发现自己孤独、痛苦和难过。然而，有一种治疗方法看似荒唐，其实简单：如果你觉得不幸福，就假装幸福！

这很管用。不久，你会发现，自己会吸引他人，而不是令人不快。你会发现以善意为中心、越来越宽广的交际圈是多么有益，深得人心。

于是，假装的幸福就成了一种事实。你拥有内心平静的秘诀，就能在帮助他人时忘记自我。

一旦意识到保持幸福心境是一种责任并形成一种习惯，就能打开神秘花园的门，那里聚集着满怀感激的朋友们。

Happiness Doesn't Need a List

A man and his girlfriend were married. It was a large celebration.

All of their friends and family came to see the lovely ceremony and to partake of the festivities and celebrations. All had wonderful time.

The bride was gorgeous in her white wedding gown and the groom was very dashing in his black tuxedo. Everyone could tell that the love they had for each other was true.

A few months later, the wife came to the husband with a proposal, "I read in a magazine, a while ago, about how we can strengthen our marriage. Each of us will write a list of the things that we find a bit annoying with the other person. Then, we can talk about how we can fix them together and make our lives happier together."

The husband agreed. So each of them went to a separate room in the house and thought of the things that annoyed them about the other. They thought about this question for the rest of the day and wrote down what they came up with.

The next morning, at the breakfast table, they decided that they would go over their lists.

"I'll start," offered the wife. She took out her list. It had many items on it. Enough to fill three pages, in fact. As she started reading the list of the little annoyances, she noticed that tears were starting to appear in her husband's eyes.

"What's wrong?" she asked.

"Nothing," the husband replied. "Keep reading your list."

The wife continued to read until she had read all three pages to her husband. She neatly placed her list on the table and folded her hands over the top of it.

"Now, you read your list and then we'll talk about the things on both of our lists," she said happily.

Quietly the husband stated, "I don't have anything on my list. I think that you are perfect the way that you are. I don't want you to change anything for me. You are lovely and wonderful and I wouldn't want to try and change anything about you."

The wife, touched by his honesty and the depth of his love for her and his acceptance of her, turned her head and wept.

In life, there are enough times when we are disappointed, depressed and annoyed. We don't really have to go looking for them. We have a wonderful world that is full of beauty, light and promise. Why waste time in this world looking for the sad, disappointing or annoying when we can look around us, and see the wondrous things before us?

幸福不需要列单子

一个男人和他的女朋友喜结连理，举行了一场盛大庆典。

所有的亲朋好友都来亲眼见证这场迷人的典礼，同喜同贺，大家都非常开心。

新娘一袭雪白婚纱，光彩照人；新郎一身黑色礼服，英气逼人。大家都能看出来，他们彼此相爱是出于真心。

几个月后，妻子向丈夫提出了一个建议："我刚才在杂志上看到一篇文章，说的是我们如何能巩固我们的婚姻。我们各自列出使对方有点儿生气的事情，然后可以商量一下看如何一起解决，这会使我们的生活更加幸福。"

丈夫表示同意。于是，他们各自到自己的房间里想使对方生气的事情。那天剩下的时间，他们都在想这个问题，并把想起来的事情写了下来。

第二天早上吃早饭时，他们决定仔细看了一下对方写的。

"我先来吧。"妻子主动说道。她拿出自己列的单子，上面写了满满三页。她开始念丈夫那些小毛病时，注意到丈夫的眼里涌出了泪水。

"怎么了？"她问道。

"没什么，"丈夫答道，"继续念你的单子吧。"

妻子接着念，直到向丈夫念完三张纸后，才把单子整齐地放在桌子上，两手交叉放在上面。

"现在，你念自己的单子吧。你念完后，我们来谈谈双方单子上列的那些事情，"妻子开心地说道。

丈夫平静地说："我在单子上什么也没写。我认为你现在非常完美。我不想让你为我改变什么。你可爱迷人，我不想设法改变你所有的一切。"

丈夫的诚实、深爱和容忍感动了她。她转过头，哭了起来。

生活中，很多时候，我们都会感到失望、沮丧和苦恼。我们不必较真去寻找它们。我们拥有一个充满美丽、光明和希望的奇妙世界。我们环顾四周，就可以看到这些奇妙事情，为什么要把时间浪费在寻找伤心、失望和苦恼上呢？

Happiness Lights Your Life

Ten things are necessary for happiness in this life, the first being a good digestion, and the other nine—money; so at least it is said by our modern philosophers. Yet the author of *A Gentle Life* speaks more truly in saying that the Divine Creation includes thousands of superfluous joys which are totally unnecessary to the bare support of life.

He alone is the happy man who has learned to extract happiness—not from ideal conditions, but from the actual ones about him. The man who has mastered the secret will not wait for ideal surroundings; he will not wait until next year, next decade, until he gets rich, until he can travel abroad, until he possesses everything, but he will make the most of life today.

Paradise is everywhere, but you must take your joy, or you will never find it.

It is after business hours, not in them, that people relax themselves. When finishing their work, people must, like Philip Amour, unlock the doors of some wholesome recreation at once. Dr. Lyman Beecher used to divert himself with a violin, relieving the great strain put upon him.

"A man," says Dr. Johnson, "should spend part of his time laughing."

Humor was Lincoln's life-preserver, as it has been of thousands of others. "If it were not for this," he used to say, "I should die." His jests and quaint stories lit the gloomy hours of the nation.

"Next to virtue," said Agnes Strickland, "the fun in this world is what we can least spare."

"I have fun from morning till night," said the editor Charles A. Dana to a friend who was growing prematurely old. "Do you read novels, play billiards and walk a great deal?"

Gladstone early formed a habit of looking on the bright side of things and never lost a moment's sleep by worrying about public business.

There are many out-of-door sports, and the very presence of nature is to many a great joy. How true it is that, if we are cheerful and contented, all nature smiles with us-the air seems more balmy, the sky more clear, the earth has a brighter green, the trees have a richer foliage, the flowers are more fragrant, the birds sing more sweetly, and the sun, moon and stars all appear more beautiful. "It is a grand thing to live—to open the eyes in the morning and look out upon the world, to drink in the pure air and enjoy the sweet sunshine and to feel the pulse throb; it is a good thing to be alive simply, and it is a good world we live in in spite of the abuse we're fond of giving it."

Each of us has joy mines that aren't prospected. And he who goes "prospecting" to see what he can daily discover is a wise man, who is training his eyes to see beauty in everything and everywhere.

"One ought, every day," said Goethe, "at least to hear a little song, read a good poem, see a fine picture, and, if it were possible, to speak a few reasonable words."

And if this be good for one's self, why not try the song, the poem, the picture and good words on someone else?

Shall music and poetry die out of you while you are struggling for that which can never enrich the character, nor add to the soul's worth? Shall a disciplined imagination fill the mind with beautiful pictures? He who has intellectual resources to fall back upon won't lack daily recreation most wholesome…

It is a remark of Archbishop Whateley that we ought to cultivate the cornfields of the mind, but the pleasure grounds also. A well-balanced life is a cheerful life; a happy union of fine qualities and unruffled temper, a clear judgment, and well-proportioned faculties. In a corner of his desk, Lincoln kept a copy of the latest humorous work; and it was frequently his habit, when fatigued, annoyed or depressed, to take this up and read a chapter with great relief. Honesty, sagaciousness or wit—anything to provoke mirth and make a man jollier—this, too, is a gift from heaven.

幸福点亮人生

这一生要幸福，必须具备十个条件，首先要有良好的消化能力，其他九个则都是金钱。至少这是我们当代的哲学家这样说的。不过，《温柔生活》的作者说得更为现实，他说这种神圣产物包含成千上万的多余快乐。这对毫无生活能力的人来说完全是多此一举。

他自己就是一个幸福的人，他已经学会了如何找到幸福，不是来自理想的状态，而是来自身边的实际生活。领悟了这个秘密的人，就不会等待理想的环境，不会等到下一年、下一个十年，不会等到自己成为富人，不会等到自己能去国外旅行，也不会等到自己拥有一切，而是充分利用今天。

天堂无处不在，但你必须带着快乐，否则你将永远找不到。

人们应在上班时间后，而不应在上班时间内，放松自己。人们必须像菲利普·阿穆尔那样，在完成工作时，马上打开有益于健康的娱乐之门。莱曼·比彻博士经常用一把小提琴自得其乐，以此来缓解巨大的紧张感。

约翰逊博士说："一个人应花一部分时间欢笑。"

和成千上万的人一样，幽默是林肯的人生秘诀。他常常说："要不是因为这样，我就应该死。"他的笑话和有趣故事点亮了处于低潮时期的国家。

"除了美德，"艾格尼丝·斯特里克兰说，"乐趣也是世界上我们能分享的最少东西之一。"

"我一天到晚都很快乐，"编辑查尔斯·达纳问一个未老先衰的朋友，

"你看小说、打台球、经常散步吗？"

英国首相格拉德斯通很早就养成了一种乐观看待事物的习惯，从来没有因担心公务而失眠过。

许多户外活动和自然景象都可以让人获得许多快乐。确实，如果我们愉快满足，大自然都会同我们微笑——空气似乎比平常更加和煦，蓝天更加晴朗，大地更加翠绿，树木更加茂盛，鲜花更加芬芳，小鸟唱得更加甜美，太阳、月亮和星星更加美观。

"活着的感觉真棒——清晨睁开眼睛，望着窗外的世界，呼吸着纯净的空气，享受着可爱的阳光，感受着脉跳；简单地活着就是一件好事；尽管我们动不动就骂这个世界，但我们仍然生活在一个美好的世界里。"

我们每个人身上都有"尚未开采的快乐宝藏"。

每天都去"采矿"并能有新发现的人才是真正的智者，因为他让自己的眼睛训练有素，从每件事和每个地方中看到美。

歌德说："一个人应该每天至少听一首小曲、咏一首好诗、赏一幅美画，而且如果可能的话，说几句有道理的话。"

如果这对一个人有益的话，何不试着去听歌、咏诗、赏画，对他人说有道理的话呢？

当你为既不能充实性格又不能增添心灵价值的东西奋斗时，音乐和诗歌会从你的心中消失吗？循规蹈矩的想象力怎能让你的脑海里充满美丽的画面？一个心智健全的人每天都不缺少有利身心健康的娱乐活动……

惠特利大主教说，我们应该耕种心灵的麦田，也应该培养精神的游乐场。意识健全的生活是一种愉快的生活；是优秀品质、温和性情、清晰判断和适当能力的一种幸福结合。林肯总是在桌角放一册最近的幽默作品，每当疲乏、烦恼或沮丧时，他就常常习惯地拿起这册书，带着极大安慰看上一章。诚实、睿智或风趣都能带来欢笑，使人更加开心，这也是上天赐予的礼物。

Where Is Happiness

A bird went to look for its happiness in the distance.

It flew and flew when it suddenly saw a little wilting flower, whose face was full of smile. Not knowing why, the bird asked the little flower, "You're going to die. Why are you still so happy?"

"Because my dream will come true," said the little flower.

"What kind of dream do you have?"

"To bear luscious fruit."

Then the little bird saw it: happiness is a hope in the heart.

The little bird kept flying; it flew and flew when it suddenly saw a lame duck, which was singing a song. Not knowing why, it asked the duck, "The fate treats you so unfairly. Why are you still so happy with yourself?"

"Because I saw a little duck fall," said the duck.

"So are you happy because you saw it trip over itself?"

"No, I'm happy because I help it stand up again."

Then the little bird saw it: happiness is a love in the heart.

The bird kept flying; it flew and flew when it suddenly saw a spider climbing up a slippery wall. The spider fell off the wall midway, but it kept climbing again and fell off again. This didn't discourage the spider; it kept climbing over and over again. Not knowing why, the little bird asked the spider, "You failed again and again, why don't you have pain but happiness on your face?"

"As long as I keep making my efforts, there is still hope to climb up it. Because of this, I'm so delighted," said the spider.

The little bird saw it: happiness is a faith in the heart.

So the little bird pursued happiness no longer because it had seen the truth: happiness is not in the distance but in your own heart.

幸福在哪里

一只小鸟去远方寻找幸福。

它飞啊飞，突然看到了一朵快要枯萎的小花，但小花笑容满面。小鸟不解何故，便问小花："你快要死了，为什么你还这样开心呀？"

"因为我的梦想就要实现了。"小花说。

"什么梦想？"

"长出甜美的果实。"

小鸟明白了：幸福是心中的一个希望。

小鸟向前飞；它飞啊飞，突然看到了一只瘸腿鸭。鸭子正哼着歌儿。小鸟不解何故，便问鸭子："命运对你这样不公，为什么你还这样开心呀？"

"因为我看到一只小鸭摔倒了。"鸭子说。

"你是见到小鸭摔倒而开心吗？"

"不是。我开心，是因为我帮小鸭站了起来。"

小鸟明白了：幸福是心中的一份爱。

小鸟继续向前飞；它飞啊飞，突然看到了一只蜘蛛正在爬一面滑溜溜的墙。蜘蛛中途摔了下来，但它又向上爬，爬到中途，又摔了下来，但蜘蛛一点也不泄气，继续向上爬。小鸟不解何故，便问蜘蛛："你一次次失败，为什么你的脸上没有痛苦而是快乐呢？"

"只要我不断努力，总有希望爬上去。正因为这样，我非常开心。"蜘蛛说。

小鸟明白了：幸福心中的一种信念。

于是，小鸟不再去远方寻找幸福，因为它已经开始懂得，幸福不在远方，而在自己心里。

I Choose to Be Cheerful

At the beginning of my 8：00 a. m. class one Monday at college, I cheerfully asked my students how their weekend had been. One young man said that this weekend had not been very good. He'd had his wisdom teeth extracted. The young man then proceeded to ask me why I always seemed to be so cheerful.

His question reminded me of something I'd read somewhere before, "Every morning when you get up, you can have a choice about how to spend that day." I said to the young man, "I choose to be cheerful."

"Let me give you an example," I continued. The other students in the class ceased their chatter and began to listen to our conversation. "In addition to teaching here at college, I teach at the community college, about seventeen miles down the freeway from where I live. One day, a few weeks ago, I drove those seventeen miles to that college. I exited the freeway and turned onto College Drive. I only had to drive another quarter-mile down the road to the college. But just then my car died. I tried to start it again, but the engine wouldn't turn over. So I put my flashers on, grabbed my books and marched down the road to the college.

"As soon as I got there I called AAA and asked them to send a tow truck. The secretary in the Provost's office asked me what had happened. 'This is my lucky day,' I replied, smiling.

"'Your car breaks down and today is your lucky day?' She was puzzled. 'What do you mean?'

"'I live seventeen miles from here,' I replied. 'My car could have broken down anywhere along the freeway. It didn't. Instead, it broke down in the perfect place: off the freeway, within walking distance of here. I'm still able to teach my class, and I've been able to arrange for the tow truck to meet me after class. If my car was meant to break down today, it couldn't have been arranged in a more convenient fashion.'

"The secretary's eyes opened wide, and then she smiled. I smiled back and headed for class."

After ending my story to the students, I scanned the sixty faces in the lecture hall with a smile. Obviously, my story had touched them.

我选择快乐

星期一早上8点，我在大学授课时，兴高采烈地问学生们周末过得怎么样。一位年轻人说这个周末过得不很好，因为他拔掉了智齿。年轻人随后问我为什么总是看起来这样快乐。

他的问题使我想起了以前在什么地方看过的一句话："每天早上起床时，你可以选择如何度过这一天。"我对年轻人说："我选择了快乐。"

"我给你举个例子，"我接着说。班上其他同学也不再叽叽喳喳说话，开始听我们谈话。"除了在这里授课，我还在社区学院授课。顺着高速公路，距离我住的地方有17英里车程。几周前的一天，我开车去那个学院授课。我下了高速公路，拐到学院快车道上。我再开四分之一英里就到那个学院了。但就在这时，我的车熄火了。我试着重新发动车子，但发动机没有起动。于是，我打开闪光灯，一把抓起书，大步流星朝学校走去。

"我一到那里，就给美国汽车协会打电话，让他们派一辆拖车来。教务处的秘书问我发生了什么事儿。我面带微笑地回答说：'今天是我的幸运日。'

"'你的车坏了，今天是你的幸运日？'她迷惑不解，'你是什么意思？'

"我回答说：'我住的地方离这里有17英里。我的车子本可能坏在高速公路上的任何地方，但它并没有，而是坏在了一个非常理想的地方：下了高速公路，刚好可以步行到这里。我仍能授课，而且我已经安排好拖车下课后来接我。如果我的车子今天想坏，它安排的方式是再方便不过了。'

"秘书睁大了眼睛，然后露出了微笑。我也对她微笑了一下，就上课去了。"

讲完故事后，我面带微笑扫视着报告厅里的60张面孔。显然，我的故事已经打动了他们。

The Mystery of Happiness

In Jerusalem, I met such a young man, who was extraordinarily optimistic, so

I asked him what the secret of his happiness was. He said to me, "At the age of 11, I accidentally received a thing.

"That day I rode a bicycle in the street when a gust of wind blew me to the center of the street. An approaching truck from the opposite direction knocked me down and rolled my leg.

"When the blood kept oozing, I realized I would live for the rest of my lifetime with only one leg. I was extremely frustrated, but I quickly realized my sadness and frustration couldn't exchange my lost leg, so I decided that I could never waste my time in sorrow and grief in the future.

"When my parents rushed to the hospital, they were both shocked and saddened.

"I told them, 'I have adapted to all this. It's time for you to adapt to the situation that I spare one leg.'

"From then on, seeing my friends feel sad and dismayed at some trifles, I will tell them to smile on life and enjoy life."

At the age of 11, this young man has understood that it is a waste to put time and energy on things that have lost, whereas the secret of happiness is to enjoy and cherish what we have now owned.

幸福的奥秘

我曾在耶路撒冷遇到这样一个年轻人，他有着非同寻常的快乐性格，因此我问他快乐的秘密是什么，他对我说："11岁时，我意外地收到了一样东西。

"那天，我在街上骑着自行车，一阵大风把我吹到街中央。这时，迎面驶来一辆大货车，把我撞倒在地，轧伤了我的一条腿。

"血不断地流，那时我意识到，我的下半生将会在只有一条腿的情况下度过。当时，我沮丧万分，但我很快意识到，悲伤与沮丧都无法换回失去的那条腿。因此，我决定，以后绝不能把时间浪费在悲伤、难过中。

"我父母赶到医院时，他们既惊愕又难过。我对他们说：'我已经适应了这一切，这次轮到你们来适应我只剩下一条腿的境况。'

"从此以后，看到我的朋友们因一些小事而难过、沮丧时，我都会告诉他们要笑对人生、享受生活。"

这个年轻人11岁时就已经明白把时间和精力用在已经失去的事物上是一种浪费，而快乐、幸福的秘密就是享受并珍惜现在拥有的。

The Power of a Smile

I placed the items on the moving belt. Slowly, my packages moved towards the cash register.

The cashier was tired. I could see it on her face. It was towards the end of her shift. She had no doubt been standing and ringing the cash register all day. I know the cash registers don't ring anymore, for they are computerized, but when I worked as a cashier, they rang.

My two-year-old son, Josees, was with me.

She performed her job with all her weary spirit she could summon.

Josees stood in front of her across the belt. His tiny frame was inches below the top of the moving belt. I don't know what made him move away from me and stand there. Children can at times move more on instinct than logic.

He stood there looking up.

Sensing something, she looked down. "Oh thank God, look at that smile!" she exclaimed.

She changed. The tiredness left. The dreariness left. She appeared as fresh as if she had just walked through the door.

Josees continued standing and smiling. She continued to revive.

I saw not the power of a child, but the power of a pure smile.

Remember, you have the same power.

Each day you will meet someone who is tired, weary and dreary. For many, the tired, weary, dreary person you meet will be in the mirror.

Even in the mirror, the power of a smile still works.

When you smile, the muscles of your face contract on a special gland in the brain which release a hormone in the brain that eases stress and causes a slight euphoric high.

Smile right now and see if that gland is in your brain, too.

She was still bubbling as we walked out of the store.

Josees never said a word. He only smiled.

Remember Josees when you meet your weary person each day. Remember someone needs smile.

微笑的力量

我把要买的商品放在传送带上。慢慢地，我那些东西移向收银员。

收银员一脸倦容，我从她的脸上看得出来，她轮班的时间要到了。她肯定一直在那里站着按了一天的收银机。我知道收银机不再响铃了，因为它们都电脑化了，但我做出纳时，收银机都响铃。

两岁的儿子乔西斯和我在一起。

收银员强打精神工作着。

乔西斯随着传送带站在她面前，他矮小的身材离传送带顶还有几英寸（1英寸＝2.54厘米）。我不知道是什么让他离开我站在了那里。孩子们有时更多的是依靠本能，而不是逻辑，进行活动。

他站在那里，仰起头。

收银员感觉到了什么，低下头。"噢，天哪，看那微笑！"她惊叫道。

她像变了个人，疲倦和低落一扫而光，看上去就像刚开始工作似的神采奕奕。

乔西斯继续站在那里微笑着。她继续精神抖擞。

我明白那不是一个孩子的力量，而是一个纯真微笑的力量。

记住，你也拥有这样的力量。

每天你都会遇到某个疲惫、厌烦和低落的人。对许多人来说，镜子里的那个疲惫、厌倦、低落的人正是自己。

即便是在镜子里，微笑的力量仍会发生作用。

你微笑时，面部肌肉会因大脑里的某个特定的腺体而收缩，分泌荷尔蒙来减轻压力，产生一种轻微的快感。

马上微笑吧，看你的大脑里是否也有这样的腺体。

我们走出商店时，收银员还是喜气洋洋。

乔西斯一句话没说，只是微笑。

每天当你遇到疲惫的人时，记住乔西斯。记住有人需要微笑。

第二卷

快乐是一首自由的歌

What Does Happiness Come from

This story is about a beautiful, well-dressed lady who complained to her psychiatrist that she felt her whole life was empty and meaningless.

So the doctor called over the old lady who cleaned the office floors, and then said to the rich lady, "I'm going to ask Mary here to tell you how she found happiness. All I want you to do is to listen."

So the old lady put down her broom and sat on a chair and told her story, "Well, my husband died of malaria and three months later my only son was killed by a car. I had nobody…I had nothing left. I couldn't sleep; I couldn't eat; I never smiled at anyone; I even thought of taking my own life. Then one evening a kitten followed me home from work. Somehow I felt sorry for that kitten. It was cold outside, so I decided to let the kitten in. I got it some milk, and it licked the plate clean. Then it rubbed against my leg, and for the first time in months, I smiled. Then I stopped to think: if helping a kitten could make me smile, maybe doing something for people could make me happy.

"So the next day I baked some biscuits and took them to a neighbor who was sick in bed. Every day I tried to do something nice for someone. It made me so happy to see them happy. Today, I don't know of anybody who sleeps and eats better than I do. I've found happiness, by giving it to others."

When she heard that, the rich lady cried. She had everything that money could buy, but she had lost the things which money couldn't buy.

幸福来自什么

这个故事说的是一个衣着华贵的美丽女士。她对心理医生抱怨说她感到生活空虚、毫无意义。

于是，医生叫来负责打扫办公室地板的老太太，然后对这个富有的女士说："我让玛丽告诉你她是怎样发现快乐的。我要你做的就是好好听。"

于是，老太太放下扫帚，坐在一张椅子上，讲起了她的故事："噢，我丈夫死于疟疾。三个月后，我唯一的儿子也被汽车撞死了。我失去了亲人……我一无所有。我睡不好，吃不下，对谁也没有个笑脸，甚至想寻短见。后来有一天晚上，我下班时，一只小猫跟我回了家。不知怎么的，我很可怜那只小猫。外面很冷，所以我决定让小猫进屋。我给了它一些牛奶，它把碟子舔得一干二净，然后蹭起了我的腿。几个月里，我第一次露出了笑脸。于是，我就停下来想，如果帮助一只小猫就可以让我微笑，也许帮助别人会让我快乐。

"于是，第二天我烤了一些小点心，送给一位卧病在床的邻居。每天，我都试着为别人做一些好事。看到别人快乐，我也非常开心。今天，我不知道还有谁会比我吃得好、睡得香。通过奉献他人，我找到了幸福。"

听了老太太的话，富有的女士哭了。尽管她拥有钱能买到的一切东西，却失去了钱无法买到的那些东西。

Happiness Is a Flow of Air

A merchant prince collected many precious antiques, calligraphy and paintings, various pearls, emeralds and the like. In order to prevent theft, he installed a tight security system and rarely went to enjoy them every day, only as part of his personal wealth to show off.

One day, seized by a whim, the rich merchant decided to let the building dustman widen his view. When he entered, the dustman didn't reveal his envy, but slowly looked through them one by one and enjoyed them carefully. Out of the thick steel door, the businessman couldn't help flaunting, "What about them? Having seen so many good things, aren't you well worth your lifetime?"

The dustman said, "Yes, I now feel myself as rich as you, and happier than you."

The businessman was extremely puzzled, looking unhappy.

"I have seen all your treasures, so am I not rich as you? And I don't have to worry about those things, so am I not happier than you?"

To appreciate is often happier than to possess.

快乐是一种流动的空气

一位富商花费巨资收藏了许多珍贵的古董、字画，以及各种珍珠、翡翠等。为防失窃，他安装了严密的保安系统，平日很少进去欣赏，只当成个人财富的一部分用来炫耀。

一天，富商忽然心血来潮，决定让大厦的清洁工进去开开眼界。清洁工进去后，并未流露出艳羡之色，只是慢慢地逐一浏览，细细欣赏。待步出厚厚的铁门时，富商忍不住炫耀说："怎么样？看了这么多的好东西，不枉此生了吧？"那个清洁工说："是啊，我现在自觉与你一样富有，而且比你更快乐。"

那富商大惑不解，面露不悦。

"你所有的宝贝我都看过了，不就是与你一样富有了吗？而且我又不必为那些东西担心，岂不比你更快乐？"

能够欣赏，常常比实际拥有更快乐。

The Source of Happiness

Life is like a heavy truck, so happiness and sorrow are like the two wheels. No cross, no crown. No pain, no joy. There are two different minds. One is that to live a day is to leave a day. The other is that to live a day is to enjoy a day. Just one word difference, it has reflected the complete reverse state of psychology. Life is like the course that is investing all the time. Therefore, in a sense, life is the capital.

Life is like a book. There are two pens that can write this book. One is writing growth while the other is writing caducity. One is describing success while the other is describing failure. In other words, one is depicting happiness and the other is showing sorrow as well.

When you have it, you should utilize it well and make it develop great actions. Please remember, the active attitude creates wonderful life while the negative attitude waste lifetime.

One noon, a rich lady went to visit a poor but happy family. When she was about to knock at the door, she heard someone speaking in the room.

A little girl said, "Would you like some braised pork today?"

Another girl said, "No. I would like some toasted chicken."

Following the words, the lady knocked at the door and went into the room. She saw them sitting at a table. Surprisingly, there were only some pieces of thin and dry bread, two cold potatoes and a jar of water on the table. The lady asked them what the matter was. They said that they imagined that, so poor food was turned into many kinds of delicious food.

One girl said, "When you consider it as pancakes, the bread will be very tasty."

Another girl said, "If you consider bread as ice-cream, it will be more delicious."

When the lady left the family, she had a new understanding of happiness. She found that the source of happiness is not substance, but human's heart. Where is the happiness in our life? It is in our heart.

幸 福 之 源

生活就像一辆载重卡车，喜与悲有如两个车轮。没有苦难，就没有王冠；没有痛苦，就没有欢乐。有两种不同的思想：一种过一天少一天，另一种是过一天享受一天。仅一字之差，就反映出了截然不同的心态。生活就像不断投资的过程。因此，就某种意义来说，生活就是资本。

生活如同一本书，谱写这本书可以有两支笔。一支描写成长，另一支描写衰老；一支描写成功，另一支描写失败。换句话说，一支在描述幸福，另一支在表现悲伤。

当你拥有生命时，就应该好好利用它，使之变成伟大的行动。请记住，积极的态度创造精彩的人生，而消极的态度虚度人生。

一天中午，一位富有的女士去拜访一个贫穷但幸福的家庭。她正要敲门时，听到屋里有人在说话。

一个小女孩说："今天你想吃炖肉吗？"

另一个女孩说："不，我想吃烤鸡肉。"

听到这里，那位女士敲门，进了屋里。她看到她们坐在桌边。让她吃惊的是，桌子上只有几片又薄又干的面包、两个凉土豆和一罐水。那位女士问她们这是怎么回事。她们说她们是那样想象的，这样可怜的食物就变成了各种各样的美食。

一个女孩说："当你把这面包想成薄煎饼时，它就会美味可口。"

另一个女孩说："如果你把这面包想成冰激凌，它就会更香甜可口。"

那位女士离开这家人时，对幸福有了新的理解。她发现幸福的源泉不在物质，而在人心。我们生活中的幸福在哪里呢？它在我们的心里。

The Light of a Smile

About ten years ago I was stuck in an abusive relationship. The relationship lasted 10 years and during that time all my thoughts were negative and circled around how I was going to get out of that relationship alive and with my children. The negativity had pulled me so far away from the truth that I was blind towards anything good.

Then one day I went to the bank. I was standing in line and as usual I was totally caught up in my thoughts about survival. I suddenly had the feeling that someone was watching me. I looked up and saw a man with his son standing in line in front of me. The man and the child were looking at me, then looking at each other and looking at me again. Both of them had a light around them that I had never seen before, they did not say a word, but smiled. I don't recall but I probably did not smile back. I was too stunned. I forgot everything around me, my life, the bank and all happenings. As soon as I was done with my transaction at the bank I ran outside to see where they were heading. But they were gone. But the smile was deeply imbedded into my soul. I found the strength to leave the relationship and start a new life. For me those two"visitors" were angels.

When I think back at this beautiful experience that helped me to change my life, I feel blessed for all it took was a smile and I have plenty of them now to give away.

An old saying goes, "If you don't have something positive to say, don't say anything at all." I would like to rephrase that saying to, "If you don't have something positive to say, at least smile." The truth is not what is said in words, but the words unsaid in a smile.

微笑的光芒

大约10年前，我处在受到虐待的家庭关系中。这种关系持续了10年。在此期间，我所有的想法都很消极，整天思来想去的都是如何带着孩子们摆脱这种关系。这种消极的想法已经让我远离现实，所以我对一切美好的事情也都熟视无睹。

后来，有一天，我去银行办事。我站在那里排队时，和平常一样全神贯注地想着如何生存下去。我突然感觉仿佛有人在目不转睛地看着我。我抬起头，看到一个男人带着儿子排在我前面。那人和孩子正在看着我，然后他们相互看了看，又看着我。他们俩周围有一种我以前从未见过的光，他们一言不发，只是微笑着。我现在想不起来了，但我可能没有对他们微笑。我当时目瞪口呆，忘记了周围的一切，包括我的生活、银行和所有正在发生的事情。我一办完事，就跑出银行，去看他们朝哪里去了。可是，他们已经不见了踪影。那种微笑却深深地嵌入了我的脑海。我找到了离开那种虐待关系的力量，开始了一种新的生活。对我来说，那两个"客人"就是天使。

我回想这段帮助我改变人生的美好经历时，感到非常幸运，尽管得到的仅仅是一个微笑，但我现在把很多微笑送给他人。

一句古话说："你若不知该说什么好，就什么也别说。"我想可以改为："你若不知该说什么好，至少微笑一下。"其实，不在于说了什么，而在于微笑不语中。

The Essence of Happiness

There was a man who tried his best to make money in youth, finally attained his goal in middle age and became a millionaire. But the rich substance didn't make him happy for his attained dream. Instead, one of his senior high school classmates who ran a vanilla garden lived an ordinary but happy life, always with a smile on the face. He was very puzzled about it.

One day, he was reluctant to ask his classmate, "My money can buy 100 vanilla gardens, but why am I not as happy as you?"

Pointing to the window next to them, his classmate asked, "From the window what have you seen?"

The rich man said, "I've seen many people strolling in the garden."

The classmate asked again, "What have you seen in the mirror?"

Seeing he was so haggard in the mirror, he said, "I only see myself."

The classmate asked, "Which landscape is vaster?"

The rich man said, "Of course it is through the window."

The classmate said with a smile, "Just because you live in the world of a mirror! When you try to take off the quicksilver on the back of the mirror, you will see the world."

Happiness comes from share and devotion. The essence of the meaning of life does not lie in the possession, but in the share. The one who shares happiness with others will always enjoy the countless happiness.

幸福的本质

有个人年轻时拼命赚钱，中年时终于实现了自己的梦想，成为一个富翁。可是，物质丰富的他并没有因为达到梦想而感到幸福。他的一个经营香草园的高中同学反而过着平凡而幸福的生活，时常可以看见他那愉快的笑脸。对此，他十分不解。

有一天，他很不甘心地请教这位同学："我的钱可以买100个香草园，可为什么我没有你幸福？"

同学指着旁边的窗户问："从窗外你看到了什么？"

富翁说："我看到很多人在逛花园。"

同学又问："那你在镜子前又看到了什么呢？"

富翁看到镜子里憔悴的自己说："我看到了我自己。"

同学问："哪一个风景更辽阔呢？"

富翁说："当然是通过窗户看得远了。"

同学微笑道："就因为你活在镜子的世界里！当你试着将镜子后面的那层水银剥掉，你就会看到全世界。"

幸福来自分享与付出。生命意义的本质不在于拥有，而是分享。与人分享幸福的人，永远都有享不尽的幸福。

He Who Can Be Moved Will Be Happy

"We can be moved everywhere, as if spring is the nourishment of life, but we always hurry on, suffering from thirst."

Going to work every day, I cross the zebra crossing at the east entrance of the university and go on eastwards to my office building. Most of the time when I just come to the junction, the red light at the crosswalk lights up and I have to wait. It was the same that day that I occasionally turned around when I suddenly saw beside the enclosure of the expansion site of the campus remaining the two old willow trees, whose huge green crowns glitter in the morning sun and undulate with the breeze, perfectly beautiful.

At that moment, I was deeply moved.

That night, I wrote in the diary, "It was an intolerable red light when I rushed to work, but surprisingly, an occasional turning round gave me one whole day's happiness, or even the sense of happiness reviving the memory of the willow trees any time in my lifetime."

In this world sometimes we are mentally tired, sometimes we are physically tired, and sometimes life seems a hard journey faraway. However, the sudden pigeon whistle passing overhead surprise us, and this is the advent of being touched unexpectedly. As if the pure cotton protecting our body and mind, being moved makes us dwell in the homes of considerate happiness.

Whether the natural beauty of the survived willow trees, or the minor details of a child growing up, or the conscientious assistance that human suffering arouses, is all the branches that the flower that we are moved blooms and bear the fruit of happiness for us.

He who can be moved will be happy.

人能感动，就能幸福

"感动无处不在，仿佛泉水，是滋养生命的。但是，我们匆匆走过，忍受着干渴。"

每天上班，我都要在大学东门过斑马线，再往东走到单位。多数时候，都是刚到路口，人行横道的红灯就亮起来，我只有等待。那天也一样，只是我偶然回了一下头。我忽然看到大学校园扩建工地围墙边被留存下来的两棵老柳树，那巨大的绿色树冠在朝阳下熠熠闪光，随着微风荡漾，美到了极致。

那一刻，一种感动深深袭击了我。

那天晚上，我在日记中写道："本是匆忙上班时一次难耐的红灯，偶然的回头，给我的竟是一整天的幸福，甚至是一生中任何时候对柳树的回忆重复唤起的幸福感觉。"

在这个世界上，有时心累，有时身累，有时人生仿佛就是天涯苦旅。但是，头顶的鸽哨突然掠过，让人顿感一丝惊喜，这就是意想不到的感动。感动，仿佛纯棉呵护我们的身心，让我们常住在体贴入微的幸福家园之中。

无论是幸存柳树的自然之美、一个幼儿长大成人的细枝末节，还是人间辛酸唤起的良知援助，都是感动之花开放的枝丫，都为我们结出幸福的果实。

人能感动，就能幸福。

Happiness of Saying Thanks

In our life, we have rarely expressed our gratitude to the one who'd lived those years with us. In fact, we don't have to wait for anniversaries to thank the ones closest to us—the ones so easily overlooked. If I have learned anything about giving thanks, it is this:give it now! While your feeling of appreciation is alive and sincere, act on it. Saying thanks is such an easy way to add to the world's happiness.

Saying thanks not only brightens someone else's world, it brightens yours. If you're feeling left out, unloved or unappreciated, try reaching out to others. It may be just the medicine you need.

Of course, there are times when you can't express gratitude immediately. In that case don't let embarrassment sink you into silence—speak up the first time you have the chance.

Once a young minister, Mark Brian, was sent to a remote parish of Kwakiutl Indians in British Columbia. The Indians, he had been told, did not have a word for thank you. But Brian soon found that these people had exceptional generosity. Instead of saying thanks, it is their custom to return every favor with a favor of their own, and every kindness with an equal or superior kindness. They do their thanks.

I wonder if we had no words in our vocabulary for thank you, would we do a better job of communicating our gratitude? Would we be more responsive, more sensitive, more caring?

Thankfulness sets in motion a chain reaction that transforms people all around us—including ourselves. For no one ever misunderstands the melody of a grateful heart.

感谢的快乐

在我们的生活中，我们很少向和我们共同生活了多年的人表达感激之情。事实上，我们不必去等待周年纪念去感谢那些最亲近却又容易被我们忽略的人。如果说我学到了表达感谢的东西，那就是现在就去感谢！当你仍然存在感激之情并出自真心时，要马上行动。道谢是一种非常容易给世界增添幸福的方法。

道谢不仅能点亮他人的世界，也会点亮你的世界。如果你觉得失落、不被关爱、不被欣赏，那就试着向他人敞开你的心灵，也许这正是你需要的良药。

当然，有时你无法及时表达感谢。在这种情况下，不要让困窘使你陷入沉默，用你抓住的第一次机会大声说出来。

从前，有一位年轻的牧师，叫马克·布赖恩，他被派到加拿大不列颠哥伦比亚省夸丘特尔印第安的一个遥远的教区。有人告诉他，这些印第安人的语言中没有一个词用来表达"谢谢你"。但是，布赖恩不久便发现，这些印第安人非常慷慨。他们不去道谢，而是习惯通过帮助别人来回报每一个帮助自己的人，而且每一个善行都会得到同等或更多的回报。他们是以行动来感谢。

我不知道，如果我们的词汇里没有道谢的词语，我们会在相互传达感谢时做得更好吗？我们会更有责任感、更能善解人意、更体恤他人吗？

表达感激会产生一连串反应，改变我们周围的人，包括我们自己，因为没有人会误解来自感激之心的悦耳音调。

Keeping Pleasant

"He is a fool who cannot be angry, but he is really a wise man who won't."

The habit of keeping pleasant is indeed better than an income of a million dollars a year. The life without cheerfulness is like the severe winter without the sun.

We all love cheerful company, but we are apt to forget that cheerfulness is a habit which can be cultivated by all.

We find it very difficult to be gay when we are in distress. It requires great courage. We should never forget that to be cheerful when it is not easy to be cheerful shows greatness. Thorny may be our way, but how happy is the conqueror's song!

The perfection of cheerfulness consists in the happy frame of mind. It is displayed in good temper and kind behavior. It arises partly from personal goodness and partly from belief in the goodness of others. It can make people see the glory in the grass and the sunshine on the flower. It encourages happy thoughts, and lives in an atmosphere of peace. It costs nothing, and yet it is invaluable. It blesses its possessor, and affords a large measure of enjoyment to others.

To light up other's heart, one's own heart must be lit first.

保 持 快 乐

"不会生气的人是笨蛋，但不生气的人是真正的智者。"

保持快乐的习惯确实比年薪百万美元的收入强。生活没有快乐，就像严冬没有阳光。

我们都喜欢快乐的伙伴，但我们容易忘记快乐是每个人都可以培养的一种习惯。

我们发现，悲伤时很难快乐起来，那需要有极大的勇气。我们永远也不要忘记，不快乐时能够快乐起来是一件了不起的事儿。也许前方的道路充满荆棘，但胜利者的歌是多么快乐！

快乐的极致在于快乐的心境。它表现在良好的性情和得体的举止上。它一部分来自个人的善良，一部分来自对他人善良的信赖。它能使人看到绿草间的美丽光辉和花朵上的灿烂阳光。它可以促进快乐的思想，然后生活在和平的氛围中。它分文不花，却是无价之宝。它会祝福其所有者，并会给别人带来无穷的快乐。

要照亮别人的心，首先必须照亮自己的心。

Happiness Is like the Sunshine

"There's the dearest little old gentleman," says James Buckham, "who goes into town every morning on the 8∶30 train. I don't know his name, and yet I know him better than anybody else in town. He just radiates cheerfulness as far as you can see him. There is always a smile on his face, and I never heard him open his mouth except to say something kind, courteous, or good-natured. Everybody bows to him, even strangers, and he bows to everybody. If the weather is fine, his jolly compliments make it seem finer; and if it is raining, the merry way in which he speaks of it is as good as a rainbow."

"The inborn geniality of some people," says Whipple, "amounts to genius." There are those whose very presence carries sunshine with them wherever they go; a sunshine which means pity for the poor, sympathy for the suffering, help for the unfortunate and benignity toward all.

Everybody loves the sunny soul. His very face is passport anywhere. All doors fly open to him. He disarms prejudice and envy, for he bears good will to everybody. He is as welcome in every household as the sunshine.

"He was quiet, cheerful, genial," says Carlyle in his "Reminiscences" concerning Edward Irving's sunny helpfulness. "Irving's voice was to me one of blessedness and new hope."

And to William Wilberforce the poor Southey paid his tribute, "I never saw any other man who seemed to enjoy such perpetual serenity and sunshine of spirit."

When Goldsmith was in Flanders he discovered the happiest man he had ever seen. At his toil, from morning till night, he was full of song and laughter. Yet this sunny-hearted being was a slave, maimed, deformed, and wearing a chain. How well he illustrated that saying, if there is no bright side, to polish up the dark one!

The first prize at a flower show was taken by a pale, sickly little girl, who lived in a close, dark court in the east of London. The judges asked how she could grow it in such a dingy and sunless place. She replied that a little ray of sunlight came into the court; as soon as it appeared in the morning, she put her flower beneath it, and, as it moved, moved the flower, so that she kept it in the sunlight all day.

"Water, air and sunshine, the three greatest hygienic agents, are free, and within the reach of all. Twelve years ago," says Walt Whitman, "I came to Camden to die. But every day I went into the country, bathed in the sunshine, lived with the birds and squirrels and played in the water with the fishes, I received my health from nature."

"It is the unqualified result of all my experience with the sick," said Florence Nightingale, "that second only to their need of fresh air is their need of light; that, after a close room, what most hurts them is a dark room; and that it is not only light, but direct sunshine they want."

The sun, making all living things grow, exerts its happiest influence in cheering the mind of man and making his heart glad. If a man has sunshine in his soul, he will go on his way to happiness, content to look ahead under a cloud, not bating one jot of heart or hope if for a moment cast down, and not only happy himself, but giving happiness to others.

幸福像阳光一样

詹姆斯·巴克汉说："有一位非常可爱的老先生，他每天早上坐八点半的火车进城。我不知道他的名字，但我比城里任何人都熟悉他。无论离多远，只要你能看到他，他就会露出快乐的神情。他的脸上总是带着微笑，他只要一开口，所说的话都是那样亲切、谦恭、愉快。所有人都向他鞠躬致敬，就连陌生人也是这样；他也向所有人鞠躬致敬。如果天气晴好，他那令人愉快的问候会使天气显得更加晴好；如果是雨天，他讨论天气时的乐观语气则像彩虹一样美丽。"

惠普尔说："有些人具有天生的亲切感。"那些人无论走到哪里，都会带来阳光；这里所说的阳光是指对穷人的怜悯，对痛苦者的同情，对不幸者的帮助和对所有人的善行。

每个人都喜欢快乐的人。他那张脸就是前往各地的通行证，所有的大门都对他敞开。他常常消除偏见和嫉妒，因为他总是把好意带给每个人。他像阳光一样受到所有家庭的欢迎。

卡莱尔在他的《回忆录》里说到了爱德华·欧文乐观助人的性格："他平静、乐观、亲切。欧文的话语对我来说就是一种充满幸福和新希望的声音。"

绍迪对威廉·威尔伯福斯这样赞美道："我从来没有见过其他任何人能像他这样享受永久的平静和精神的阳光。"

戈德史密斯在佛兰德斯时，发现了一个他所见过的最快乐的人。这个人干活时，从早到晚，歌声和笑声不断。然而，这个性情乐观的人是一个奴隶，残疾、丑陋、戴着脚镣。他充分证明了那句话：如果没有光明的一面，就去改善阴暗的一面！

在一次花展上，一个苍白病弱的小女孩夺得了一等奖。她住在伦敦东区的一个狭窄、阴暗的庭院里。评委问她是怎样在这样一个肮脏、阴暗的地方种出了如此美丽的花。她回答说，是一小缕阳光照进了庭院，每天早上太阳一出现，她就把花放在这缕阳光下。随着光线移动，她移动花盆。这样，她就可以让花儿一整天在阳光下。

"水、空气和阳光这三种最有益健康的因素是免费的，人人都能得到，"沃尔特·惠特曼说，"12年前，我来到卡姆登想死。但我每天走进乡村，沐浴在阳光下，和小鸟、松鼠共同生活，和那些鱼儿在水里嬉戏时，我从大自然中得到了健康。"

弗洛伦斯·南丁格尔说："在我照顾病人的所有经历中，有一种观点说病人对灯光的需要仅次于对新鲜空气的需要，这是一个不合格的结论。在一个封闭的房间里，对病人伤害最大的是房间的阴暗；他们需要的不仅是灯光，而且他们需要阳光的直射。"

太阳使万物生长，同时发挥着最令人愉快的影响，使人精神振奋、心情愉快。如果一个人心里拥有阳光，他就会走上幸福之路；在压力下也愿意向前看，即使有片刻沮丧，也不会减少一丝精神或希望；不仅自己幸福，而且把幸福送给他人。

Pleasure Is a Freedom Song

Pleasure is a freedom song, but it is not freedom. It is the blossoming of your desires, but it is not their fruit;it is a depth calling unto a height, but it is not the deep or the high;it is the caged bird taking wing, but it is not space encompassed. Ay, in very truth, pleasure is a freedom song. And I fain would have you sing it with fullness of heart;yet I would not have you lose your hearts in singing.

Some of your youth seek pleasure as if it was all, and they are judged and rebuked. I would not judge nor rebuke them. I would have them seek, for they shall find pleasure, but not her alone;seven are her sisters, and the least of them is more beautiful than pleasure. Have you not heard of the man who was digging in the earth for roots and found a treasure?

And some of your elders remember pleasures with regret like wrongs committed in drunk. But regret is the beclouding of the mind and not its chastisement. They should remember their pleasures with gratitude, as they would the harvest of a summer. Yet if it comforts them to regret, let them be comforted.

And there are among you those who are neither young to seek nor old to remember;and in their fear of seeking and remembering they shun all pleasures, lest they neglect the spirit or offend against it.

But even in their foregoing is their pleasure. And thus they too find a treasure though they dig for roots with quivering hands.

But tell me, who is he that can offend the spirit?Shall the nightingale offend the stillness of the night, or the firefly the stars? And shall your flame or your smoke burden the wind?

You think the spirit is a still pool which you can trouble with a staff. Oftentimes in denying yourself pleasure you do but store the desire in the recesses of your being.

Who knows but that which seem omitted today, waits for tomorrow? Even your body knows its heritage and its rightful need and won't be deceived.

And your body is the harp of your soul, and it is yours to bring forth sweet music from it or confused sounds.

And now you ask in your heart, "How shall we distinguish that which is good in pleasure from that which is not good?" Go to your fields and your gardens and you shall learn that it is the pleasure of the bee to gather honey of the flower, but it is also the pleasure of the flower to yield its honey to the bee, for to the bee a flower is a fountain of life, and to the flower a bee is a messenger of love, and to both, bee and flower, the giving and the receiving of pleasure is a need and an ecstasy.

Be in your pleasures like the flowers and the bees.

快乐是一首自由的歌

快乐是一首自由的歌，但它不是自由。它是你欲望的绽放，但不是果实；它是深谷对高峰的呼唤，但它既不深沉也不高耸；它是囚禁在笼里的展翅的小鸟，但不是环抱的空间。哎，快乐的确是一首自由的歌。我希望你全心全意地歌唱它，而不是在歌唱时丧失信心。

你们年轻人中有些人追求快乐，好像它是所有的一切，他们遭到了判决和谴责。我不会判决他们，也不会谴责他们。我会让他们去寻找，因为他们要找到快乐，而不仅仅是快乐；快乐有七个姐妹，她们中最小的也比快乐美。你没听说过有人在刨树根时发现了宝藏吗？

你们中有些老年人遗憾地回忆快乐，就像酒醉时做的错事。但遗憾会让心灵蒙上阴影，而不是惩罚。他们应以感恩之心回忆自己的快乐，就像回忆夏天的收获。然而，如果遗憾能给他们安慰，那就让他们得到安慰吧。

你们中的一些人既不是追寻的年轻人，也不是回忆的老年人；他们在追寻和回忆的恐惧中避开一切快乐，唯恐自己忽视或冒犯了灵魂。

但是，他们在前行中也有快乐。所以，尽管他们用颤抖的双手挖掘树根，也会找到宝藏。

可告诉我，谁敢冒犯灵魂？是夜莺会扰乱夜的宁静，还是萤火虫会冒犯繁星？你的火焰或烟雾会给风增加负担吗？

你以为灵魂是用一根木棍就能搅乱的一潭静水。你通常拒绝快乐，只是把快乐的欲望藏在心间。

谁知道今天忽略的事情会等到明天吗？就连你的身体也知道它的本性和合理需求，不会受到欺骗。

你的身体是灵魂的竖琴，它或奏出甜美的乐曲，或发出杂音，全都在你。

现在，你扪心问一下："我们将怎样区别快乐中的善与恶？"去田野和花园，你会认识到蜜蜂的快乐在于采集花蜜，对花朵来说，给蜜蜂提供花蜜就是快乐。因为对蜜蜂来说一朵花就是生命之泉；对花朵来说，一只蜜蜂就是爱的使者；对蜜蜂和花朵两者来说，给予和接受的快乐是一种需要和狂喜。

像花朵和蜜蜂那样享受快乐吧。

World of Smiles

About ten years ago when I was in college, I was working as an intern at my University's Museum of Natural History. One day while working at the cash register in the gift shop, I saw an elderly couple come in with a little girl in a wheelchair.

As I looked closer at this girl, I saw that she was kind of perched on her chair. I then realized she had no arms or legs, just a head, neck and torso. She was wearing a little white dress with red polka dots.

As the couple wheeled her up to me I was looking down at the register. I turned my head toward the girl and gave her a wink. As I took the money from her grandparents, I looked back at the girl, who was giving me the cutest, largest smile I have ever seen. All of a sudden her handicap was gone and all I saw was this beautiful girl, whose smile just melt me and almost instantly gave me a completely new sense of what life was all about. She took me from a poor, unhappy college student and brought me into her world: a world of smiles, love and warmth.

That was ten years ago. I'm successful person now. And whenever I get down and think about the troubles of the world, I think about that little girl and the remarkable lesson about life that she taught me.

微笑的世界

大约10年前，我上大学时，在学校的自然历史博物馆当实习生。有一天，我正在礼品店的收银台工作，看到一对老夫妇推着一个坐轮椅的小女孩走进店里。

我贴近看时，只见她坐在轮椅上有点儿不稳。随后，我意识到，她没有手臂和双腿，只有脑袋、脖子和躯干。她穿着一身雪白的红色圆点小连衣裙。

当那对夫妇推着她向我走来时，我正低头看着收银机。我把头转向那个女孩，向她眨了眨眼。我接过老夫妇的钱时，回头看那个女孩，只见她正朝我微笑，那是我有生以来见过的最可爱、最灿烂的微笑。突然间，她的缺陷消失了，我所看到的是一个美丽的女孩。她的微笑感化了我，几乎马上给了我一种生命的全新感觉。她把我这样一个郁郁寡欢的穷大学生带进了她的世界：一个充满微笑、爱和温暖的世界。

那是10年前的事了。如今，我功成名就。每当我萎靡不振，想起世间的种种烦恼时，就会想起那个小女孩和她教给我的人生的非凡一课。

The Value of Smile

You must have a good time meeting people if you expect them to have a good time meeting you.

I have asked thousands of people to smile at someone every hour of the day for a week and then come to class and talk about the results. How did it work? Let's see… here is a letter from William B. Steinhardt, a New York stockholder. His case isn't isolated. In fact, it is typical of hundreds of cases.

"I have been married for over eighteen years," wrote Mr. Steinhardt, "and in all that time I seldom smiled at my wife or spoke two dozen words to her from the time I got up until I was ready to leave for business. I was one of the worst grouches who ever walked down Broadway.

"When you asked me to make a talk about my experience with smiles, I thought I would try it for a week. So the next morning, while combing my hair, I looked at my glum mug in the mirror and said to myself, 'Bill, you are going to wipe the scowl off that sour puss of yours today. You are going to smile. And you are going to begin right now.' As I sat down to breakfast, I greeted my wife with a 'Good morning, my dear,' and smiled as I said it.

"You warned me that she might be surprised. Well, you underestimated her reaction. She was bewildered. She was shocked. I told her that in the future she could expect this as a regular occurrence, and I kept it up every morning.

"This changed attitude of mine brought more happiness into our home in two months since I started than there was during the last year.

"As I leave for my office, I greet the elevator operator in the apartment house with a'Good morning'and a smile; I greet the doorman with a smile. I smile at the cashier in the subway booth when I ask for change. As I stand on the floor of the Stock Exchange, I smile at people who until recently never saw me smile.

"I soon found that everybody was smiling back at me, I treat those who come to me with complaints or grievances in a cheerful manner, I smile as I listen to them and I find that adjustments are accomplished much easier. I find that smiles are bringing me dollars, many dollars every day.

"I share my office with another broker. One of his clerks is a likable young chap, and I was so elated about the results I was getting that I told him recently about my new philosophy of human relations. He then confessed, when I first came to share my office with his firm he thought me a terrible grouch—and only recently changed his mind. He said I was really human when I smiled.

"I have also eliminated criticism from my system. I give appreciation and praise now instead of condemnation. And these things have literally revolutionized my life. I am a totally different man, a happier man, a richer man, richer in friendships and happiness—the only things that matter much after all."

You don't feel like smiling? Then what? Two things. First, force yourself to smile. If you are alone, force yourself to whistle or hum a tune or sing. Act as if you were already happy, and that will tend to make you happy. Everybody in the world is seeking happiness—and there is one sure way to find it. That is by controlling our thoughts. Happiness doesn't depend on outward conditions. It depends on inner conditions.

It isn't what you have or who you are or where you are or what you are doing that makes you happy or unhappy. It is what you think about it. For example, two people may be in the same place, doing the same thing; both may have about an equal amount of money and prestige—and yet one may be miserable and the other happy. Why? Because of a different attitude. I have seen just as many happy faces among the poor peasants toiling with their primitive tools in the devastating heat of the tropics as I have seen in air-conditioned offices in New York, Chicago or Los Angeles.

"There is nothing either good or bad," said Shakespeare, "but thinking makes it so."

Abe Lincoln once remarked, "Most folks are about as happy as they make up their minds to be." He was right.

Whenever you go out-of-doors, draw the chin in, carry the crown of the head high; drink in the sunshine; greet your friends with a smile, and put soul into every handclasp. Do not fear being misunderstood and do not waste a minute thinking about your enemies.

Try to fix firmly in your mind what you would like to do; and then, without veering off direction, you will move straight to the goal. Keep your mind on the great and splendid things you would like to do, and then, as the days go sliding away, you will find yourself unconsciously seizing upon the opportunities that are required for the fulfillment of your desire. Picture in your mind the able, earnest, useful person you desire to be, and the thought you hold is hourly transforming you into the particular individual…Thought is supreme. Preserve a right mental attitude—the attitude of courage, frankness, and good cheer. To think rightly is to create. All things come through desire and every sincere prayer is answered.

Some years ago, a department store in New York City, in recognition of the pressures its sales clerks were under during the Christmas rush, presented the following homely advertisement:

THE VALUE OF A SMILE AT CHRISTMAS

It costs nothing, but creates much. It enriches those who receive, without impoverishing those who give. It happens in a flash and the memory of it sometimes lasts forever. It brings the rest to the weary, the daylight to the discouraged and the sunshine to the sad. Yet it can't be bought, begged, borrowed, or stolen, for it is something that is no earthly good to anybody till it is given away. And if the last-minute rush of Christmas buying some of our salespeople should be too tired to give you a smile, may we ask you to leave one of yours? For nobody needs a smile so much as those who have none left to give!

微笑的价值

如果你希望别人愉快接见你，你必须愉快会见别人。

我曾要求数千人时刻对某人微笑，持续一周后，到班里来说说结果。它会起怎样的作用呢？我们来看一下……这是纽约股票经纪人威廉·B.斯坦因哈特写的一封信。他的情况并不是孤立的。事实上，它在数百个案例中具有代表性。

"我已经结婚18年多了，"斯坦因哈特先生写道。"在此期间，我从起床到准备去上班，很少对妻子微笑，也很少说二十几个词。我是那些走在百老汇大街的人当中最糟糕的一个。

"当你要我谈一下自己微笑的经验时，我认为我要尝试一星期。所以，第二天早上梳头时，我看看镜子里自己哭丧着脸，就对自己说：'比尔，你今天要把脸上的愁容一扫而光。你要微笑，马上就开始。'当我坐下来吃早饭时，我向太太招呼说：'早安，亲爱的，'而且一边说，一边对她微笑。

"你曾提醒过我，她可能大吃一惊。噢，你低估了她的反应。她不知所措，大为震惊。我告诉她说，她以后可以把这看成平常的事情，而且我每天早上都要这样做。这种改变的态度两个月里给我们家带来的快乐比去年一年的还要多。

"我离开家去办公室时，会对公寓大楼的电梯员微笑说'早上好！'我还微笑着和看门人打招呼。我在地铁售票处兑换零钱时，也会向出纳员微笑。我站在证券交易所时，向那些从未见过我微笑的人微笑。我发现每个人也都对我微笑。我用一种愉快的方式对待那些向我抱怨或诉苦的人。我一边微笑一边听他们说，我发现调解起来要容易得多。我发现微笑给我带来金钱，每天都财源滚滚。

"我和另一位经纪人共用一间办公室。他的一个职员是个可爱的小伙子。我为自己取得的成效扬扬得意，最近把自己人际关系的新人生观告诉了他。后来，他承认说，我起初和他的公司共用办公室时，他还以为我是一个郁郁寡欢的人，直到最近才改变了看法。他说，我微笑时的确有人情味。

"我也改掉了批评别人的习惯。现在，我总是欣赏和赞扬，而不是指责。而且这些东西实际上已经彻底改变了我的生活。我完全变成了另一个人，一个更快乐、更充实的人——毕竟这才是真正重要的东西。"

你不想微笑吗？那怎么办？做两件事。首先强迫自己微笑。如果你一人独处，就强迫自己吹口哨、哼小曲或唱歌，装作自己非常快乐的样子，这样就会让你快乐起来。世界上每个人都在追求快乐，找到快乐只有一个可靠的方法，那就是控制我们的思想。快乐并不依靠外在条件，而是依靠内在条件。

决定你快乐不快乐的不是你有什么、你是谁、你在何处或你正在做什么，而是你有什么想法。比如，两个人也许在同一个地方做同样一件事，两个人也许拥有同样多的金钱和声望，但其中一个也许很痛苦，另一个则很快乐。为什么？因为想法不一样。我曾看到贫穷的农夫在热带酷热难当的地方用原始的工具辛苦劳作，但他们的笑脸和我在纽约、芝加哥或洛杉矶的办公室里看到的笑脸一样多。

"事情没有好坏之分，"莎士比亚说，"只是思想不同。"

亚伯·林肯说过："大多数人的快乐是因为他们决定快乐。"他说得对。

无论何时你出门，要收下巴，头抬高，吸收阳光，用微笑来问候朋友们，每一次握手都要注入灵魂。别怕误解，别浪费一分钟去想自己的敌人。

尽力下定决心去做你喜欢做的事情，然后不要偏离方向，直达自己的目标。聚精会神做你喜欢做的伟大美好的事情。然后，随着岁月流逝，你会发现自己不知不觉抓住了实现自己心愿所需要的机会。你在心里把自己想象成你渴望做的干练、认真、有用的人，你心里的想法每时每刻都在把你变成你所希望的那种不同寻常的人……思想至高无上。保持一种正确的人生态度，一种勇敢、坦率和乐观的态度。思想正确就是创造。一切事情都源于希望，每个真诚的祈祷都会实现。

几年前，纽约市一家百货商店为缓解圣诞节高峰期店员们的压力，展出了下面这个亲切的广告：

圣诞节微笑的价值

它分文不花，却创造多多。它让得到者富有，付出者也不会贫穷。它在瞬间发生，有时却给人留下永恒的回忆。它给疲惫者带来休息，给沮丧者带来光明，给悲伤者带来阳光。但它买不到，讨不来，借不了，偷不走，因为你把它送给别人才会有好处。在圣诞节最后一分钟的高峰期，如果我们的售货员太累没有向你微笑，请你留下一个微笑好吗？因为那些无法给予微笑的人更需要微笑！

Smile at Strangers

Have you ever noticed or thought about how little eye contact most of us have with stranger? Why? Are we afraid of them? What keeps us from opening our hearts to people we don't know?

I don't really know the answers to these questions, but I do know that there is virtually always parallel between our attitude toward strangers and our overall level of happiness. In other words, it's unusual to find a person who walks around with her head down, frowning and looking away from people, who is secretly a peaceful, joyful person.

I'm not suggesting it's better to be outgoing than introverted, that you need to expend tons of extra energy trying to brighten others' days, or that you should pretend to be friendly. I'm suggesting, however, that if you think of strangers as being a little more like you and treat them not only with kindness and respect, but with smiles and eye contact as well, you'll probably notice some pretty nice changes in yourself. You'll begin to see that most people are just like you—most of them have families, people they love, troubles, concerns, likes, dislikes, fears, and so on. You'll also notice how nice and grateful people can be when you're the first one to reach out. When you see how similar we all are, you begin to see the innocence in all of us. In other words, even though we often mess up, most of us are doing the best that we know how with the circumstances that surround us. Along with seeing the innocence in people comes a profound feeling of inner happiness.

对陌生人微笑

你曾注意到或想到我们中的大多数人和陌生人的目光接触是多么少吗？为什么？是我们害怕他们吗？是什么阻挡了我们向陌生人敞开心扉的呢？

我确实不知道怎样回答这些问题，但我知道，其实在我们对待陌生人的态度和我们总体幸福水平之间总有一种类似的东西。换言之，发现一个低头皱眉、眼望别处的人内心安详而又快乐，是不同寻常的。

我并不是说，性格外向就比性格内向好，为了使别人生活得更愉快，你需要浪费额外的精力，或者说，你必须要假装友好。我是说，如果你把陌生人看成你自己的一个影子，然后不仅用善意和尊重对待他们，还用微笑和目光接触，你也许会注意到一些非常美好的变化会发生在你身上。你会开始看到多数人都和你一样——他们多数人都有家庭、烦恼、忧虑、喜恶、恐惧等。你还会注意到，当你第一个伸出援手时，他们是多么友好和感激。当你看到他们都是多么相似时，你会开始看到我们所有人身上的单纯率直。换言之，即使我们常常陷入困境，我们多数人会竭尽全力去应对我们周围的环境。看到人们的单纯率直，随之而来的则是来自内心深处的一种幸福感。

Where the Sun Always Rises

"Get up! Get up!" my mother whispers. My eyes flash open in the predawn gray. Sleepily, I look around the screened-in porch of our family's log cabin, where we spend our summer weeks.

I take in the dock-green porch swing, the birch-leg table, the twin bed where my sister sleeps, the smoky gloss of the kerosene lantern. My face feels the coolness of the early-morning air.

I relax and curl deeper beneath the blankets' warmth. "Get up!" my mother whispers again. "The sunrise is glorious!" Careful not to let the screen door slam, she sets off down to the lake.

Get up to see the sunrise? The last thing this 14-year-old wants to do is leave a warm bed to see the sun rise. It's freezing out there.

My 17-year-old sister pushes back her covers and sits up. I make a supreme effort and struggle out too. We grab my father's World War II army blankets and wrap them tightly around our cotton nighties. Our pace is quick. One of us misses catching the screen door. It slams.

Carefully, we pick our way over slippery rocks and prickly pine needles, down 49 dew-covered log steps to the shore. We catch our breath and look up. Across the lake, a sliver of brilliant red crests the top of the shadowed forest. It outlines our mother on the lakeshore, the first light catching the soft red of her hair.

Hues of purplish, rose and amber begin to pulsate in the sky. High above, in the soft blue, a lone star still sparkles. Silver mist rises gently from the lake. All is still.

Suddenly, the curve of a brilliant sun bursts through the dark forest. The world begins to awaken. A blue heron rises from a distant shore and gently fans its way over the water. Two ducks make a rippled landing near our dock, while a loon skims along the edge of a nearby island, hunting its morning food.

Breathing the chill air, the three of us draw our blankets closer. At last, the soft hues of dawn turn bright with the new day. The star fades. My sister and I took one more look and race back to bed.

My mother is reluctant to leave the sunrise amphitheater. It is a while before I hear her reach the top step and gently close the porch door.

太阳总在那里升起

"起床喽！起床喽！"母亲低声喊道。我一下子睁开眼睛，闪现在眼前的是黎明前的灰暗。我睡眼惺忪地环顾着我们家小木屋的那个安着屏风的门廊。这里就是我们度过数周夏日时光的地方。我欣赏着草绿色的门廊秋千、白桦木腿桌、姐姐睡的成对单人床，还有那烟黑的煤油灯罩。我感到脸上掠过凉爽的晨风。

我伸了伸腰，又往温暖的毛毯里拱了拱身子。"起来吧！"母亲又小声喊道，"日出多么壮观！"母亲小心翼翼，不让屏门发出任何响声，然后向湖边走去。

起床就为了看日出？对一个14岁的孩子来说，最不想做的就是离开暖被窝去看日出。外面冻死人了。

17岁的姐姐掀被坐起，我也一鼓劲儿钻了出来。我们俩一把拽起父亲"二战"时用过的军用毛毯，紧紧地裹在棉睡衣外面，匆匆跑了出去。我们俩都忘了带上门。门"砰"的关了上去。

我们小心翼翼地走过滑溜溜的岩石，绕过那些山地松针，沿着露水打湿的49级木台阶向湖岸走去。我们喘了口气，抬头望去。只见在湖对岸，一抹耀眼的红色爬上了树影婆婆的林梢，映衬出了母亲在湖岸的身影；第一缕阳光照在了她柔红色的头发上。

淡紫色的、玫瑰色的和琥珀色的光波开始在天空中微微颤动起来。苍穹之上，柔蓝之中，一颗孤星仍在闪烁。银雾从湖面上冉冉升起。四周万籁俱寂。

突然，一道灿烂的阳光射过黑黝黝的森林。整个世界开始苏醒。一只蓝苍鹭从远处的湖岸振翅飞起，在湖面上轻轻抖动着向前飞去。在我们的码头附近，两只鸭子荡起涟漪上了岸。一只潜鸟掠过附近一个小岛的边缘，在猎食早餐。

我们仨呼吸着习习凉气，将毛毯裹得更紧了。终于，黎明时那种朦胧的色调随着新的一天的到来变得明亮。那颗孤星退隐而去。我和姐姐又看了一眼，便又飞快地钻进了被窝。

母亲舍不得离开那蔚为壮观的日出美景。过了好一会儿，我才听到她迈上门前最高一级台阶，轻轻合上了门廊的门。

Keep Walking in Sunshine

I hadn't walked across our old farm in fifteen years. Yet the sensations came flooding back. I could smell the freshness of new mown alfalfa. I could feel the sun's sudden warmth on my wet shoulders when it reappeared after a brisk July thunderstorm.

Rain or shine, I used to walk this path each day to see Greta. She always made me smile, even after Sis and I had just had a big squabble. I would help Greta with her chores. Then we would visit over a generous helping of her delicious homemade chocolate cookies and ice cream. Being confined to a wheel chair didn't stop Greta from being a fabulous cook.

Greta gave me two of the greatest gifts I've ever received. First, she taught me how to read. She also taught me that when I forgave Sis for our squabbles, it meant I wouldn't keep feeling like a victim. Instead, I would feel sunny.

Mr. Dinking, the local banker, tried to foreclose on Greta's house and land after her husband passed away. Thanks to Pa and Uncle John, Greta got to keep everything. Pa said that it was the least he could do for someone talented enough to teach me to read!

Soon folks were coming from miles around to buy Greta's homemade cakes, pies, bread, cookies, cider, and ice cream. Hank, the grocery store man, came each week to bring Greta supplies and stock his shelves.

Greta even had me take a big apple pie to Mr. Dinking who became one of her best customers and friends. That's just how Greta was. She could turn anyone into a friend!

Greta always said, "Dear, keep walking in sunshine!"

No matter how terrible my day started, I always felt sunny walking home from Greta's house—even beneath the winter starlight.

I arrived at Greta's house today just after sunset. An ambulance had stopped a few feet from her door. When I ran into the old house, Greta recognized me right away.

She smiled at me with her unforgettable twinkling blue eyes. She was almost out of breath when she reached out and softly touched my arm. Her last words to me were, "Dear, keep walking in sunshine!"

I'm sure that Greta is walking in the brightest sunshine she's ever seen. And, I'm sure that she heard every word I read at her memorial service.

I chose a beautiful verse by Leo Buscaglia. It's one that Greta taught me to read many years ago.

"Love can never grow old.
Locks may lose their brown and gold.
Cheeks may fade and hollow grow.
But the hearts that love will know,
Never winter's frost and chill,
Summer's warmth is in them still."

常常走在阳光里

我已经15年没有走过我们的老农场了。然而，那些感情又潮水般涌来。我可以闻到新割的紫花苜蓿的清新气息，可以感觉到7月的一场清新的暴风雨过后，阳光突然暖暖地照在湿湿的肩膀上。

无论雨天还是晴天，我每天沿着这条小路去看格丽塔。即使我刚和姐姐大吵了一架，她也总让我露出微笑。我常常帮格丽塔做家务。然后，我们常常放开肚子，吃她亲手做的巧克力饼干和冰激凌。坐轮椅并不能阻止她成为一名出色的厨师。

格丽塔送给我两件有生以来最了不起的礼物。首先，她教会了我念书。她还教会我，我们争吵时要原谅姐姐，这意味着我不再感到委屈，而会感到快乐。

格丽塔的丈夫去世后，当地银行家丁金先生曾想取消她抵押给银行的房产的赎回权。幸亏爸爸和约翰叔叔帮忙，格丽塔才保住了所有的一切。爸爸说，他对一位能教会我念书的人只能这样尽他所能帮忙了！

很快，方圆几英里（1英里≈1.6千米）的人们都来买格丽塔做的蛋糕、馅饼、面包、饼干、苹果酒和冰激凌。食品杂货店老板汉克每周都会给格丽塔送来供应品并从她这里进货。

格丽塔甚至让我给丁金先生送去一个大苹果馅饼。他也成了她最好的顾客和朋友。格丽塔就是这样做的。她可以把任何人都变成朋友！

格丽塔总是说："亲爱的，要经常走在阳光里！"

无论每天开始时多么糟糕，从格丽塔的小屋走回家时，即使是披着冬夜的星光，我总会感觉心情愉快。

今天太阳刚下山，我就来到了格丽塔家。一辆救护车已经停在她门前几英尺（1英尺≈0.3米）的地方。我跑进老房子时，格丽塔立刻认出了我。

她那双令人难忘的蓝眼睛闪动着向我微笑。当她伸手轻抚我的手臂时，她几乎上气不接下气。她最后对我说的话是："亲爱的，要常常走在阳光里！"

我相信格丽塔正走在她所见过的最明媚的阳光里。而且，我也相信她听到了我在她的追悼仪式上念的每一个字。

我选的是利奥·巴斯卡格里亚的一首优美的诗。这正是格丽塔多年前教我念的一首诗。

"爱从来不会衰败。

秀发会失去原有的光彩。

脸颊会日渐黯淡消瘦。

但有爱的心中，

从来没有冰霜寒冬，

夏天的温热永远依旧。"

Sunshine on a Rainy Day

Have you ever had a day when everything seemed to go wrong? Not too long ago I was having one of those days. I was discouraged, weary and sad. My focus was on me, me, me. After all, no one else was experiencing the same trials as I was.

I expressed my downcast state to my mother, hoping for some pity. Instead, she said, "I heard Jamie was having a difficult day, too. Why don't you make her some cookies and we will take them to her this afternoon?" I didn't really want to, but I decided that I didn't want to go back to my other problems just yet. I made the cookies and arranged them on a little plate. Then I made a card with a sunflower on it and wrote a small note of comfort.

That afternoon we dropped by my friend's house. I went to the door and rang the bell. Soon, Jamie came to the door and looked at me in surprise for my unexpected visit. Before she could say anything, I rushed, "I heard you were having a hard day and decided to bring you something. I hope your day goes better." The look that came over Jamie's face was one that I could never put into words. It was as if a darkened sky was suddenly lit with the golden rays of the sun;it was as if in that small act her day was brightened.

I got back into the car and for some amazing reason, I felt a lot better myself. That day I experienced the truth that James Barrie attempted to describe. "Those who bring sunshine to the lives of others cannot keep it from themselves."

雨天的阳光

你曾有过事事不顺的一天吗？不久以前，我就过了这样一天。我感到沮丧、厌倦和伤心，一门心思想的都是自己。毕竟，没有人经历过和我这样的磨难。

我把自己沮丧的心情告诉了母亲，希望得到一些同情。可是，她说："我听说杰米也过了艰难的一天。你何不给她做一些饼干，今天下午送给她呢？"我真不想做，但我决定不再去想其他问题，所以就去做饼干了，把做好的饼干摆在一个小盘子上，然后做了一张画着太阳花的卡片，在上面写了一句安慰话。

那天下午，我们去我的朋友家拜访。我去按门铃。很快，杰米来到门口，吃惊地望着我，没想到我会来看她。还没等她开口说话，我马上说道："我听说你今天很难过，就决定送你一些东西。我希望你这一天好起来。"当时，杰米的表情让我难以言表，就像是阴暗的天空突然被一道道金色的阳光照亮一样，也像是我那个小小的举动照亮了她的一天。

我回到车里，惊奇地发现自己的心情也好多了。那天，我体会到了詹姆斯·巴利试图描述的一条真理："给别人的生活带去阳光的人，也会给自己带来阳光。"

第三卷

让心灵充满阳光

The Gold Watch in the Barn

A farmer carelessly lost an expensive gold watch in the barn on the farm, where he searched for everywhere but in vain.

So he put a notice on the gate of the farm: whoever finds the gold watch will be rewarded 100 dollars.

Facing the temptation of the handsome reward, people tried their best to look for everywhere. However, the grain was piled like a hill along with bales of straw, so if they wanted to find the gold watch, it would be like fishing for a needle in the ocean.

When the sun set, the gold watch was not found yet. They took pains but found nothing. So they began complaining the watch was too small, the barn was too large and the straw was too thick. It was getting dark that they were still unable to find it. So they gave up the temptation of 100 dollars one by one.

But only a small boy in shabby clothes was still not discouraged but kept looking for it in the grain. He had nothing to eat throughout the day. In order to solve the family problem, he was eager to find the gold watch and let his parents, brothers and sisters have a full meal.

The night was already getting late; the boy was also tired. He was lying in the straw to have a rest when he heard a strange "tick-tock".

He immediately held his breath and listen attentively.

It was quieter in the barn while "tick-tock" sounded clearly. The boy followed the sound, found the gold watch buried in the depths of the grain and finally got the 100 dollars.

Like the gold watch in the barn, success has existed around us and spread in every corner of life. Only we are calm and firmly look for it can we find it.

谷仓里的金表

一个农场主不慎将一只名贵的金表丢失在了农场的谷仓里。他到处搜寻，结果毫无踪迹。

于是，他在农场门口贴上了一条告示：凡是找到金表的，奖赏100美元。

面对重赏的诱惑，人们竭尽全力四处寻找，无奈谷仓内谷粒成山，还有成捆成捆的稻草，想在其中找回金表如同大海捞针。

太阳落山了，金表还是杳无踪迹。大家费尽心机，一无所获，开始抱怨金表太小了，谷仓太大，稻草太厚。天渐渐暗了下来，更是无法寻找。于是，一个个放弃了100美元的诱惑。

但是，只有一个衣衫褴褛的小男孩依然毫不气馁，继续在谷堆里寻找。

他已经整整一天没有吃饭了。为了解决家庭的困难，他渴望能找到金表，能让父母和兄弟姐妹吃上一顿饱饭。

夜已深了，男孩也累了。他躺在稻草堆里想歇一会儿，突然他听见了一个奇特的"嘀嗒嘀嗒"声。

他顿时屏住了呼吸，认真倾听。

谷仓更加安静了，"嘀嗒"声更加清晰了。男孩循着声音找到了埋藏在谷堆深处的金表，最终得到了100美元。

成功如同谷仓内的金表，早已存在我们周围，散布在人生的每个角落，只有我们静下心来，执着地去寻找，才能发现。

A Definite Goal

A father went to hunt for hares with his three sons to the grassland. Upon arrival at the destination, all well prepared, before they took action, their father asked three sons a question, "What do you see?"

The eldest son replied, "I saw the shotguns in our hands, the hares running on the prairie and the endless stretch of grassland." His father shook his head and said, "You're wrong."

The second son answered, "I saw our father, eldest brother, younger brother, shotguns, hares and the boundless grassland." The father again shook his head and said, "You're wrong."

The youngest only answered, "I can only see hares." Then their father said, "You're right."

Only can a definite goal point out the right direction of action and less detour on the road to achieving the objective. In fact, the indiscriminate or excessive goals will impede our progress, so in order to achieve what we have in our mind, if unrealistic, we may ultimately accomplish nothing.

明确的目标

父亲带着三个儿子到草原上猎杀野兔。在到达目的地、一切准备得当、开始行动之前，父亲向三个儿子提出了一个问题："你看到了什么？"

老大回答道："我看到了我们手里的猎枪、在草原上奔跑的野兔还有一望无际的草原。"父亲摇摇头说："不对。"

老二回答："我看到了爸爸、大哥、弟弟、猎枪、野兔，还有茫茫无际的草原。"父亲又摇摇头说："不对。"

而老三的回答只有一句话："我只看到了野兔。"这时，父亲才说："你答对了。"

只有有了明确的目标，才会为行动指出正确的方向，才会在实现目标的道路上少走弯路。事实上，漫无目标或目标过多都会阻碍我们前进，要实现自己的心中所想，如果不切实际，最终可能一事无成。

Do One Thing Every Day

There was a painter, who held over a dozen of painting shows. Regardless of the number of visitors, he always smiled.

I once asked him, "Why are you have so happy every day?"

He told me one thing, as a boy, I had a lot of interests and was very eager to excel. Painting, playing the accordion, swimming or playing basketball, I must be the first. This, of course, was impossible. So I felt so depressed that my learning plummeted.

When my father learned about it, he took a funnel and a handful of corn seeds, let me put my hands under the funnel to take, picked up one seed and threw it into the funnel, when the seed slipped down the funnel and dropped on my hands. My father threw more than 10 times, so my hands had more than 10 seeds. Then, my father grasped a full handful of corn seeds and put them into the funnel. The seeds jostled each other and no one dropped.

My father said to me, "This funnel represents you; if you can finish one thing every day, you will harvest a seed and happiness. But when you want to hold everything together to do, you won't harvest one seed."

每天做好一件事

有一位画家，举办过十几次个人画展。开始无论参观者多少，他脸上总是挂着微笑。有一次，我问他："你为什么每天都这么开心呢？"

他给我讲了一件事："小时候，我兴趣非常广泛，也很要强。画画，拉手风琴，游泳，打篮球，必须都得第一才行。这当然是不可能的。于是，我心灰意冷，学习成绩一落千丈。父亲知道后，找来一个漏斗和一捧玉米种子，让我双手放在漏斗下面接着，然后捡起一粒种子投到漏斗里面，种子便顺着漏斗滑到了我的手里。父亲投了十几次，我的手中也就有了十几粒种子。然后，父亲一次抓起满满的一把玉米粒放在漏斗里面，玉米粒相互挤着，竟然一粒也没有掉下来。

"父亲对我说：'这个漏斗代表你，假如你每天都能做好一件事，你就会有一粒种子的收获和快乐。可是，当你想把所有的事情都挤到一起来做时，反而连一粒种子也收获不到了。'"

Another Secret to Success

A sculptor got a marble with very fine texture. He felt the marble was so suitable for carving a portrait. So he picked up the chisel. Not knowing the tension or excessive force, only a chisel, he knocked off a large chunk of debris. The sculptor stopped immediately. After three days' thought, he decided to abandon the sculpture he had designed because he realized he was hard to manage this valuable material. Later, this marble was presented to the sculptor Michelangelo, who used this marble to carve the unparalleled masterpiece—David Statue.

The careful viewers pointed to an obvious streak of scar on David's back, slightly regretted for its not 100% perfection and sighed for the former previous sculptor's temerity in a sort of way.

Michelangelo corrected, "The gentleman has been very careful. If he's temerarious and hasty, this special material has been long gone, and my David Statue will never come into being."

"So, would you also like to thank the sculptor?" some people were puzzled.

"Yes, I would like to thank him for his rare seriousness, because his sculpture and abandon are extremely serious. Furthermore, I would like to thank him for the scar he left. It always reminds me that I must be extremely careful of each of my carving and chiseling, without any slightest carelessness."

Michelangelo told another secret to highlight his success with respect—learn from the lessons of others and accomplish everything at hand with the greatest seriousness.

成功的另一个秘诀

一位雕塑家得到一块质地非常精美的大理石。他觉得大理石非常适合雕刻一个人像。于是，他拿起了凿子。不知是因为紧张还是用力过重，只那么一凿，他就敲掉了一大块碎屑。雕塑家立刻停下来，经过3天思索，他决定放弃构思好的雕塑，因为他意识到自己难以驾驭这块宝贵的材料。后来，这块大理石被赠送给雕塑家米开朗琪罗。米开朗琪罗用这块大理石雕刻出了旷世杰作——《大卫像》。

细心的观赏者指着大卫背上的一道明显的伤痕，为其不能百分之百的完美而略感惋惜，并慨叹先前的那位雕塑家有些冒失。

米开朗琪罗纠正道："那位先生已经相当慎重了，如果他冒失草率的话，这块特别材料早就不复存在了，我的大卫像也就无从产生了。"

"这么说，你还要感谢那位雕塑家？"有人困惑不解了。

"是的，我要感谢他难得的认真，他的雕刻和放弃都是极其认真的。另外，我还要感谢他留下的那块伤痕，它总是在提醒着我，让我的每一刀、每一凿都千百倍细心，不能有丝毫疏忽大意。"

米开朗琪罗充满敬意地道出了他获得成功的另一个秘诀：汲取别人的教训，以最大的认真去做好手头的每一件事。

I Can Make It Happen

History abounds with tales of experts who were convinced that the ideas, plans and projects of others could never be achieved. However, success favored those who believed, "I can make it happen."

The Italian sculptor Agostino D'Antonio worked diligently on a large piece of marble. Unable to produce his desired masterpiece, he lamented, "I can do nothing with it."

Other sculptors also worked on this piece of marble, but to no avail.

Michelangelo discovered the stone and visualized the possibilities in it. His "I-can-make-it-happen" attitude resulted in one of the world's masterpiece—David.

Even the great Thomas Edison discouraged his friend, Henry Ford, from pursuing his rudimental idea of a motorcar. Convinced of the worthlessness of the idea, Edison invited Ford to come and work for him.

However, Ford tirelessly pursued his dream. Although his first attempt resulted in a vehicle without reverse gear, Henry Ford knew he could make it happen. And, of course, he did.

Let's not forget our friends Orville and Wilbur Wright. Journalists, friends, armed forces specialists, and even their father laughed at the idea of an airplane.

"What a silly and insane way to spend money. Let the birds fly in the sky," they jeered.

"Sorry," the Wright brothers responded. "We have a dream, and we can make it happen."

You can also make it happen.

我 能 做 到

历史上有很多深信别人的想法、计划和方案根本无法实现的专家的故事。然而，成功青睐那些相信"我能做到"的人。

意大利雕刻家阿高斯提诺·丹东尼奥对一块巨大的大理石上勤奋雕刻。当他无法雕刻出理想的作品时，悲叹道："我对它无能为力。"

另一些雕刻家也在这块大理石上费了一番工夫，但无济于事。

米开朗琪罗发现了这块巨石，并使其中的所有可能性都显现了出来。他的"我能做到"的态度最终成就了世界名作——《大卫像》。

就连伟大的托马斯·爱迪生也劝阻他的朋友亨利·福特放弃制造汽车的初步想法。爱迪生深信这个想法没有任何价值，邀请福特过来为他工作。

然而，福特不屈不挠地追求自己的梦想。尽管初次尝试的结果是一辆没有倒车挡的汽车，但亨利·福特知道他能做到。而且，他的确取得了成功。

我们不要忘记我们的朋友奥维尔·怀特和威尔伯·怀特。新闻记者、朋友们、军事专家，甚至他们的父亲都嘲笑他们对飞机的构想。

"这样花钱真是愚蠢疯狂！让小鸟在天空飞吧。"他们嘲笑说。

"对不起，"怀特兄弟回答说，"我们有一个梦想，而且我们能让它实现。"

你也能把梦想变成现实。

The Danger of Success

A young novice climber prepared to climb the Alps in the border of Swiss. This was the first time he would climb the mountains in the true sense, so he invited the two experienced guides to keep company.

That was a very dangerous steep mountain road, but protected by the two excellent guides around him, he did not feel any danger.

They climbed a long road, and when they were out of breath exhausted, the summit was close at hand. The guide walking ahead was willing to let the novice first stand on the peak and enjoy the feeling of"seeing the mountains around and below are wee," so he moved aside and let the young climber walk ahead.

At this moment, charmed by the honor, the young climber who had climbed up the peak forgot the strong gust that would blow on the peak at any time and excitedly jumped up cheering his victory.

Just at this moment, the guide caught up with him and pulled him down to the ground.

"Kneel on the ground quickly!" he snapped, "For the position you are now on, no gesture is safe, unless kneeling on the ground!"

There are too many times we want to stand up tall and enjoy the success and glory that belong to us. But it is in these moments that we most easily disappear in the gale.

成功的危险

有一位年轻的登山新手，准备去攀登瑞士境内的阿尔卑斯山。这是他第一次攀登真正意义上的高山，所以他邀请了两名经验丰富的向导陪同。

那真是一段危险陡峭的山路，但有一前一后两名优秀向导的保护，他并没有觉得自己有什么危险。

他们攀登了很长的山路，就在他们筋疲力尽气喘吁吁之时，顶峰到了眼前。走在前面的向导愿意让新手第一个站到山巅，享受"一览众山小"的感觉，于是挪向一边，让年轻的登山者走在了前面。

这时，在荣誉的魔力下，爬到峰顶的年轻登山者，竟然忘记了山峰上随时可能刮起猛烈的阵风，他兴奋地跳起来，欢呼自己的胜利。

就在这时，向导赶上前来，一把将他拉倒在地。

"跪到地上，快！"他厉声说道，"你现在所处的这个位置上，没有什么姿势是安全的，除非跪在地上！"

我们有太多的时刻，想要高高站起，享受属于我们的成功与荣耀。可就是在这些时刻，我们最容易消失在狂风之中。

Will Inspired Life

The little country schoolhouse was heated by an old-fashioned pot-bellied coal stove. A little boy had the job of coming to school early each day to start the fire and warm the room before his teacher and classmates arrived.

One morning they arrived to find the schoolhouse engulfed in flames. They dragged the unconscious little boy out of the flaming building more dead than alive. He had major burns over the lower half of his body and was taken to a nearby county hospital. From his bed the semi-conscious little boy faintly heard the doctor talking to his mother. The doctor told his mother that her son would surely be dead, for the terrible fire had devastated the lower half of his body.

But the brave boy didn't want to die. He made up his mind that he would survive. Somehow, to the amazement of the physician, he did survive. When the mortal danger was past, he again heard the doctor and his mother speaking quietly. The mother was told that since the fire had destroyed so much flesh in the lower part of his body that he was doomed to be a lifetime cripple.

Once more the brave boy made up his mind. He would not be a cripple. He would walk. But unluckily from the waist down, he had no motor ability. His thin legs just dangled there, all but lifeless. Ultimately, he was released from the hospital.

Every day his mother would massage his little legs, but there was no effect. He was either in bed or confined to a wheelchair. Yet his determination that he would walk was as strong as ever.

One sunny day his mother wheeled him out into the yard to get some fresh air. This day, instead of sitting there, he threw himself from the chair. He pulled himself across the grass, dragging his legs behind him. He worked his way to the white picket fence bordering their lot. With great effort, he raised himself up on the fence. Then, stake by stake, he began dragging himself along the fence, resolved that he would walk.

He started to do this every day until he wore a smooth path all around the yard beside the fence.

Ultimately, through his daily massages, his persistence and his resolute determination, he did develop the ability to stand up, first to walk haltingly, then to walk by himself—and then—to run.

He began to walk to school, then to run to school, to run for the sheer joy of running. Later in college he made the track team. Still later in Madison Square Garden this young man who was not expected to survive, who would surely never walk, who could never hope to run—Dr. Glenn Cunningham, ran the world's fastest mile!

意志激励人生

小乡村校舍靠一个老式大肚煤炉取暖。小男孩负责每天一早在师生到校前赶来生起炉火、温暖教室。

一天早晨，师生们发现校舍被大火吞没了。他们把昏迷的小男孩从燃烧的房子里拽出来时，他已经九死一生，下半身严重烧伤，被送到了附近的一家县医院。半昏迷的小男孩在病床上模糊听到了医生对他妈妈的谈话。医生对小男孩的母亲说，她的儿子肯定会死，因为可怕的大火已经烧坏了他的下半身。

但勇敢的小男孩不想死。他下定决心要活下来。不知何故，让医生惊愕的是，他真的活了下来。致命的危险过后，他又听到医生在低声对母亲说话。医生告诉男孩的母亲说，大火已经烧坏了他下半身的大部分肌肉，所以他注定要终生残疾。

勇敢的小男孩又一次下定了决心，他不会残疾，他要走路。但不幸的是，他腰部以下根本没有了运动神经能力，细腿只是在那里摇晃，几乎毫无知觉。最后，他终于出院了。

每天，妈妈都会按摩他的双腿，但毫不见效。他每天不是待在床上，就是坐在轮椅上。然而，他想行走的决心仍是那样坚强。

一个阳光灿烂的日子，妈妈把他推进院子里呼吸新鲜空气。这天，他没有坐在那里，而是从轮椅上扑下来，拖着双腿爬过草地，努力爬到那个地方边界的白色尖桩篱栅边，用了很大劲儿扶着篱笆站了起来。随后，他开始顺着篱笆的一个个木桩向前拖行，下定决心一定要行走。

渐渐地，他每天都这样做，直至把院子里沿着篱笆的部分磨出了一条平滑的小路。终于，通过每天按摩、坚持不懈和坚定决心，他确实养成了站起来的能力，起初步履蹒跚，后来独立行走，最后竟跑了起来。

他开始步行上学，然后跑步上学，跑步成了他的一大乐趣。后来上大学时，他参加了田径队。再后来，这个曾被认为不能活下来、再也不会行走、更没有希望跑步的年轻人格伦·坎宁汉博士，在麦迪逊广场花园跑出了世界上最快的速度！

A Creed to Live by

Don't determine your worth by comparing yourself with others because each of us is special.

Don't set your goals by what other people deem important. Only you know what is best for you.

Don't take for granted the things closest to your heart. Cling to them as you would your life, for without them life is meaningful.

Don't let your life slip through your fingers by living in the past or the future. Treasure each day in your life and you will have all the days of your life.

Don't give up before you try your best. Nothing is really over until the moment you stop trying.

Don't be afraid to admit that you are less than perfect. It is this fragile thread that binds us to each other.

Don't be afraid to encounter risks. It is by taking chances that we learn how to be brave.

Don't shut love out of your life by saying it's impossible to find. The quickest way to receive love is to give love; the fastest way to lose love is to hold it too tightly; and the best way to keep love is to give it wings.

Don't abandon your dreams. To be without dreams is to be without hope; to be without hope is to be without purpose.

Don't run through life so fast that you forget not only where you've been, but also where you're going. Life is not a race, but a journey to be savored each step of the way.

人生的信条

不要通过和他人比较来确定自己的价值，因为我们每个人都与众不同。

不要以别人认为重要的来确立自己的目标。只有你知道什么对你最好。

不要想当然地对待最贴近你心灵的东西。要像对自己的生命一样紧紧地抓住它们，因为没有它们，生命就毫无意义。

不要生活在过去或未来而让生命从指尖溜走。珍视生活中的每一天，你就会拥有生命的全部日子。

不要在竭尽全力之前就放弃。直到你停止努力，一切才会真正结束。

不要害怕承认自己还不完美。维系我们之间关系的正是这根脆弱的细线。

不要害怕遭遇风险。只有抓住这种机会，我们才能学会如何勇敢。

不要说找不到爱而把生命中的爱拒之门外。得到爱的最快方式就是付出爱；失去爱的最快方式就是把爱抓得太紧；保持爱的最佳方式就是给爱一双翅膀。

不要放弃自己的梦想。生活没有梦想，就没有希望；没有希望，就没有意义。

不要让生命的脚步跑得太快，这样你不仅会忘记自己曾到过什么地方，而且会忘记自己要去什么地方。人生不是一次赛跑，而是一段旅程，途中的每一步都要细细品味。

The Secret of Becoming Rich

Ayer lived a rich life, so his friends wanted to know the secret of his wealth. One day, Ayer would go to the market to handle affairs, when one of his friends happened to go the same way. So they went along.

It was terribly sultry. When they went halfway, they were so tired and thirsty that they stopped and sat down under a big tree by the roadside.

Ayer took out two bowls from his backpack, placed before them, then untied the water bag and filled the bowls with water.

They carried the bowls and were about to drink off when a gust of wind suddenly blew, making them not open their eyes.

After the wind stopped, his friend found a lot of sand dropped in his bowl, even with some leaves on it. The friend frowned, poured away the water in the bowl without hesitation, picked up Ayer's water bag conveniently, poured himself another bowl and drank off without a break.

When he put down his bowl, he found Ayer's bowl was also muddy, but Ayer only carefully picked up the fallen leaves, threw them off and put the bowl on the ground.

After a while, the water was gradually clean and clear, when Ayer carried the bowl and drank slowly.

His friend laughed at his misery, for he even regarded a bowl of water as a treasure.

After hearing that, Ayer said with a smile, "Each bowl of water is drawn by me from the well, which I took pains to dig. How can't I regard it as a treasure?"

When sand and leaves dropped into a bowl, what Ayer's saw was still the water, but what his friend was nothing but the sand and leaves. Maybe it was the secret of Ayer's wealth.

致富的秘诀

阿伊尔生活富裕，朋友们很想知道他致富的奥秘。有一天，阿伊尔要到集市上办事，他的一位朋友正好同路。于是，两人结伴而行。

天气十分闷热。走到半路，两人又累又渴，就停下脚步，在路边的一棵大树下坐了下来。

阿伊尔从随身携带的背囊里取出两只碗，摆放在两人面前，然后解下水囊，向碗里倒满了水。

他们端起碗，刚要一饮而尽，突然刮来了一阵风，吹得人睁不开眼。

风停后，朋友发现碗里落了不少沙子，水面上还多了几片树叶。朋友皱了皱眉，没多想，就把碗里的水倒了，顺手拿起阿伊尔的水囊，给自己重新倒了一碗，一口气就喝干了。

等他放下手中的碗时，发现阿伊尔的碗里也是一片浑浊，但阿伊尔只是小心地拈起碗里的落叶扔掉，再把碗放到地上。

过了一会儿，水渐渐澄清了，阿伊尔这才端起碗，慢慢地喝了起来。

朋友笑阿伊尔吝啬，连一碗水都当成宝贝似的。

阿伊尔听完，微微一笑说："每碗水都是我从井里打上来的，而井又是我辛辛苦苦亲手挖的。我怎么能不把它当成宝贝呢？"

一碗水落进了沙子和树叶，在阿伊尔的眼中，看到的还是水，而在朋友的眼里，看到的只是沙子和树叶，这或许就是阿伊尔致富的奥秘。

Life Lies in Believing in Yourself

There may be days when you get up in the morning and things aren't the way you had hoped they would be.

That's when you have to tell yourself that things will get better. There are times when people let you down.

But those are the times when you must remind yourself to trust your own judgments and opinions, to keep your life focused on believing in yourself.

There will be challenges to face and changes to make in your life, and it is up to you to accept them.

Constantly keep yourself headed in the right direction for you. It may not be easy at times, but in those times of struggle you will find a stronger sense of who you are.

So when the days come that are filled with frustration and unexpected responsibilities, remember to believe in yourself and all you want your life to be.

Because the challenges and changes will only help you to find the goals that you know are meant to come true for you.

人生在于相信自己

你或许会有这样的日子：早晨起来，却发现事情并不像自己原来希望的那样。

这个时候，你必须告诉自己：情况一定会好起来。总会有人们让你失望和沮丧的时候。

但这个时候，你必须提醒自己，要相信自己的判断和看法，提醒自己一生都要始终相信自己。

生活中总会要面对挑战，总会要发生改变。你要接受挑战和改变。

始终让自己朝适合自己的正确方向前进。也许时有不易，但一次次奋斗，你都会更强烈地意识到自己是谁。

因此，当充满沮丧和意外责任的日子来临时，要记住相信自己，要记住你想要的人生是什么样。

因为，挑战和改变只能帮你找到对你来说一定会实现的目标。

Life Lies in Choosing

When he was still young, everything was possible, for the world was just before him.

One morning, God came to him, "What wish do you have? Tell me and I can make it come true for you, for you're my pet. But remember, you can only tell one."

"However," he said unwillingly. "I have a lot of wishes."

God slowly shook his head, "There're too many beautiful things in the world, but life is limited, so no one can possess all. Once you make a choice, you will give up others. Come on, choose carefully, with no regrets."

Surprised, he asked, "Will I regret?"

God said, "Who knows. Choose love and you will have to put up with the emotional torment; to choose wisdom means pains and loneliness; choose money and you will have the trouble it brings along. There're too many people who regret that they should virtually take another way after they've gone one way. Think about it carefully, what do you really want in your lifetime?"

He thought and thought, all desires pouring in and fluttering around him. Which one was the one he couldn't give up? Finally, he said to God, "Let me think, let me think."

God said, "But you should be quick, my son."

Since then, his life was filled with the constant comparisons and balances. He used half the time of his life to make lists and the other half to tear them up because he always found himself to leave out something.

Day after day, year after year, he was no longer young. God came to him again. "My child, haven't you decided your wish yet? But you only have five minutes left."

"What?" he exclaimed. "Over the years, I haven't enjoyed the joy of love, I haven't accumulated wealth and haven't received wisdom; I haven't gotten all I want. My God, how can you take away my life at this time?"

Five minutes later, no matter how painfully he pleaded, God couldn't help but take him away.

Life is like this: everywhere is alive with choices. Since it is impossible to have everything, you should learn to make a choice; if you're greedy for everything, perhaps you can only achieve nothing in the end.

人生在于选择

那时，他还年轻，凡事都有可能，世界就在他面前。

一个清晨，上帝来到他的身边。"你有什么心愿吗？说出来，我都可以为你实现，你是我的宠儿。但你记住，你只能说一个。"

"可是，"他不甘心地说。"我有许多的心愿啊。"

上帝缓缓地摇了摇头。"这世间的美好实在太多，但生命有限，没有人可以拥有全部，有选择就有放弃。来吧，慎重选择，永不后悔。"

他惊讶地问："我会后悔吗？"

上帝说："谁知道呢。选择爱情就要忍受情感的煎熬；选择智慧就意味着痛苦和寂寞；选择钱财就有钱财带来的麻烦。这世上有太多的人走了一条路后，懊悔自己其实该走另一条路。仔细想一想，你这一生真正要什么？"

他想了又想，所有的渴望都纷至沓来，在他周围飞舞。哪一件是他不能舍弃的呢？最后，他对上帝说："让我想想，让我再想想。"

上帝说："但要快一点啊，我的孩子。"

从此，他的生活就是不断比较和权衡。他用生命中一半的时间来列表，用另一半的时间来撕毁这张表，因为他总发现自己有所遗漏。

一天又一天，一年又一年，他不再年轻了。上帝又来到他的面前。"我的孩子，你还没有决定自己的心愿吗？可你的生命只剩下5分钟了。"

"什么？"他惊叫道。"这么多年来，我没有享受过爱情的快乐，没有积累过财富，没有得到过智慧，我想要的一切都没有得到。上帝啊，你怎能在这个时候带走我的生命呢？"

5分钟后，无论他怎么痛苦求情，上帝还是无奈地带走了他。

人生就是这样，无处不是在选择。既然无法拥有一切，那就学会有所取舍；如要贪全，恐怕最后只能是一无所得。

第四卷

春天在你的心里

The Love of a Hunchback

Moses Mendelssohn, the grandfather of the well-known German composer, was far from being handsome. Along with a rather short stature, he had a grotesque hunchback.

One day he visited a merchant in Hamburg who had a lovely daughter named Frumtje. Moses fell hopelessly in love with her. But Frumtje was repulsed by his misshapen appearance.

When it was time for him to leave, Moses gathered his courage and climbed the stairs to her room to take one last opportunity to speak with her.

She was a vision of heavenly beauty, but caused him deep sadness by her refusal to look at him. After several attempts at conversation, Moses shyly asked, "Do you believe marriages are made in heaven?"

"Yes," She answered, still looking at the floor. "And do you?"

"Yes I do," He replied. "You see, in heaven at the birth of each boy, the Lord announces which girl he will marry. When I was born, my future bride was pointed out to me. Then the Lord added, 'But your wife will be humpbacked.'"

"Right then and there I called out, 'Oh Lord, a humpbacked woman would be a tragedy. Please, Lord, give me the hump and let her be beautiful.'"

Then Frumtje looked up into his eyes and was stirred by some deep memory. She reached out and gave Mendelssohn her hand and later became his devoted wife.

驼背的爱情

德国著名作曲家门德尔松的祖父摩西·门德尔松一点儿也不英俊。他不仅身材非常矮小，而且长着奇形怪状的驼背。

有一天，他去汉堡拜访一位商人。这个商人有一个可爱的女儿，名叫弗鲁姆叶。摩西无可救药地爱上了她。但因为他相貌丑陋，弗鲁姆叶一口拒绝。

快要离开时，摩西鼓起勇气，爬上楼梯，来到她的房间，想利用这最后一次机会和她说说话。

她美若天仙，却让他非常伤心，因为她连看都不看他一眼。摩西连试了几次，才畏畏缩缩地问道："你相信婚姻是天作之合吗？"

"相信，"她回答说，眼睛仍然看着地板，"你呢？"

"是的，我也相信，"他回答说，"你明白，天堂里每个男孩出生时，上帝便宣布他要娶哪个女孩。我出生时，上帝也为我指出了未来的新娘。接着，上帝补充道：'但你的妻子会是一个驼背。'"

"我当场就大声叫道:'噢,上帝,一个驼背女人将是一场悲剧。上帝,求求您,把驼背给我,让她变漂亮吧。'"

于是,弗鲁姆叶抬起头,望着他的眼睛,她被深深地打动了。她伸出手,答应了门德尔松的求婚,后来成了他忠诚的妻子。

View in the Heart

There was a temple at the foot of the mountain and an old banyan was in front of the temple.

One morning, a young monk got up to clean the courtyard and saw the fallen leaves from the old banyan were everywhere, when he couldn't help feeling sad and looking at the tree with a sigh.

He couldn't hold back his sorrow, threw down the broom, rushed to his master's room and knocked on the door to plea for an interview.

On hearing the knocking, his master opened the door. When he saw the disciple's worried look, he thought something must have happened. So he hurried to ask him, "My disciple, why are you worried so much in the early morning?"

The disciple told his master doubtfully, "Master, you always admonish us to work hard, cultivate our moral character, grasp the truth and seize the hour. But even if I understand this truth, it is impossible to escape death. Till that time, won't I or so-called Dao be just like the fallen leaves in autumn or the deadwood in winter? Won't they be alike to be buried by a heap of loess?"

After hearing it, the old monk pointed at the old banyan and said to the young monk, "My disciple, you needn't worry about this. In fact, the fallen leaves in autumn and the deadwood in winter will climb back to the trees silently, become the flowers in spring, grow into the leafy profusion in summer, dance in the wind in autumn and return to the earth with the snowflakes of cold winter."

"Why don't I see it?"

"Because you haven't any view in your heart, you can't see their beautiful youth."

Fixing on the withered fallen leaves and imagining they will be in bud in the earth, your daily life will be sunny and full of vitality.

As long as you have the view in your heart, are you still hard to enjoy the path full of fragrance of flowers?

心 中 有 景

山脚下有一座庙,庙前有一棵老榕树。

一天早晨,一个小和尚起床后开始打扫庭院,看见满地都是榕树的落叶，禁不住开始伤感起来，望着榕树直叹气。

小和尚的伤心越发无法控制，干脆扔掉扫帚冲向师父的房间，叩门恳求师父召见。

师父闻声打开门，看到徒弟一脸忧虑，知道一定发生了什么事情，就急忙问道："我的徒儿，一大早的什么事情让你如此着急呢？"

徒弟充满疑惑地对师父说："师父，你总是告诫我们要勤奋努力、培养品德、掌握真理、只争朝夕。可是，即使我懂得了这个道理，也是无法避免死亡。到了那个时候，无论是我，还是所谓的道，不就像秋天的落叶和冬天的枯枝吗？它们不是一样会被一堆黄土埋葬吗？"

听完这番话，老和尚指着那棵老榕树对小和尚说："我的徒儿，对此，你不必担心。事实上，无论秋天的落叶还是冬天的枯枝，会悄悄爬回树干，春天成为花朵，夏天枝繁叶茂，秋天随风舞动，最后伴着寒冬的雪花又回到土地。"

"为什么我没有看到呢？"

"因为你的心中没有任何风景，当然就看不到它们美丽的青春了。"

凝望枯萎的落叶，想象着它很快又会在泥土中萌芽，每一天的生活都会充满阳光和蓬勃的朝气。

只要心中有景，要欣赏到花香满径还会难吗？

The Old Man Who Planted Oak Trees

A young traveler was exploring the Alps. He came upon a vast stretch of barren land. It was desolate. It was the kind of place you hurry away from.

Then, suddenly, the young traveler stopped dead in his tracks. In the middle of this vast wasteland was a bent-over old man. On his back was a sack of acorn. In his hand was a four-foot length of iron pipe.

The old man was using the iron pipe to punch holes in the ground. Then from the sack he would take an acorn and put it in the hole. Later the old man told the traveler. "I've planted over 100,000 acorns. Perhaps only tenth of them will grow." The old man's wife and son had died, and this was how he chose to spend his final years. "I want to do something useful," he said.

Twenty-five years later the now-not-as-young traveler returned to the same place. What he saw amazed him. He could not believe his own eyes. The land was covered with a beautiful forest two miles wide and five miles long. Birds were singing, animals were playing, and wild flowers perfumed the air.

The traveler stood there recalling the desolation that once was; a beautiful oak forest stood there now—all because someone cared.

种橡树的老人

一个年轻的旅行者在阿尔卑斯山探险。他来到一块一望无际的不毛之地。那里荒无人烟，是一种让人急欲离开的地方。

后来，年轻的旅行者突然停住了脚步。只见辽阔的荒地中央，一位老人正在弯腰播种。他背着一大袋橡子，手里拿着一根4英尺长的铁管。

老人用那根铁管在地上打洞，然后从袋子里掏出一颗橡子，放进洞里。后来，老人告诉那个旅行者："我已经种了10万颗橡子。大概只有十分之一的橡子能够成长。"老人的妻儿都已经死去，这是他选择度过晚年的一种方式。"我想做一些有用的事儿。"他说。

25年后，那个已不再年轻的旅行者又故地重游。眼前的景象让他惊叹不已。他无法相信自己的眼睛。那块土地覆盖上了5英里长、2英里宽的美丽森林。那里，小鸟歌唱，动物嬉戏，野花飘香。

旅行者站在那里，回忆着它以前的荒凉；一片美丽的橡树林现在之所以耸立在那里，都是因为某个人的关心啊。

The Pavilion in the Heart

For his honesty and trustworthiness, Mexican President Vicente Fox, was respected by the people. The principle he conducted himself all his life was honesty. It was the personality that made him a country's president from an ordinary salesman.

Once, Fox was invited to a university to give a lecture. A student asked him, "The political arena is always filled with fraud. In your experience in politics have you lied?"

Fox said, "No, never."

The students whispered among themselves and some of them were chuckling because every politician always expresses himself. They always vow, saying he has never lied.

Fox wasn't angry. He said to the college students, "Boys and girls, in this society, perhaps it is very hard to prove that I'm an honest man, but you should believe that, in this world there's honesty, which is always around us. I want to tell you a story. Perhaps after hearing it, you will forget it, but this story means a lot to me.

"There was a father who was a farmer. One day, he felt the pavilion in the garden was too worn-down, so he had it dismantled. His son was so interested in dismantling the pavilion that he said to his father, 'Daddy, I want to see how you have the pavilion dismantled, so can you have it dismantled until I come back from the boarding school to take a vacation?'

"His father agreed.

"However, after the boy left, the workers quickly dismantled the pavilion.

"After the boy returned from school, he found the old pavilion had disappeared. He said in low spirits to his father, 'Dad, you told me a lie.'

"His father looked at the boy in surprise. The boy went on, 'You said the old pavilion would be dismantled until I came back.' His father said, 'My boy, I'm wrong, and I should keep my promise.'

"The father called in the workers again and had them re-build a pavilion in the shape of the old one. After the pavilion made, he called in his son and said to the workers, 'Now, please dismantle it.'

"I know the father, who was not rich, but kept his promise in front of his child."

Hearing this, the students asked, "What's the father's name, please? We hope to know him."

Fox said, "He has died, but his son is still alive."

"Then, where's his son? He should be an honest man."

Fox said calmly, "His son is now standing here. It's me. I want to tell you is I'd like to treat this country and everyone of it like my father treating me."

A storm of applause thundered in the audience.

Dismantling and building a pavilion twice won't only satisfy a boy's wish, but also the moral requirement of an adult's self-improvement.

Dismantling a pavilion in the garden will build a pavilion in the heart of a boy. This pavilion is a faith-in trustworthiness.

心中的亭子

墨西哥总统福克斯以诚实守信的品德受到国人的尊重，他一生做人的原则就是两个字：诚实。正是这样的人格品质，使他从一个普通的推销员成为一个国家的总统。

一次，福克斯受邀到一所大学演讲，一个学生问他："政坛历来充满欺诈，在你从政的经历中有没有撒过谎？"

福克斯说："不，从来没有。"

大学生在下面窃窃私语，有的还轻声笑出来，因为每一个政客都会这样表白。他们总是发誓，说自己从来没有撒谎。

福克斯并不气恼，他对大学生说："孩子们，在这个社会上，也许我很难证明自己是个诚实的人，但你们应该相信，这个世界上还有诚实，它永远都在我们的周围。我想讲一个故事，也许你们听过就忘了，但这个故事对我很有意义。

"有一位父亲是农场主。有一天，他觉得园中的那座亭子已经太破旧了，就安排工人们准备将它拆掉。他的儿子对拆亭子这件事很感兴趣，于是对父亲说：'爸爸，我想看看你们怎么拆掉这座亭子，等我从寄宿学校放假回来再拆好吗？'

"父亲答应了。

"可是，等孩子走后，工人们很快就把亭子拆掉了。

"孩子放假回来后，发现旧亭子已经不见了。他闷闷不乐地对父亲说：'爸爸，你对我撒谎。'

父亲惊异地看着孩子。孩子继续说：'你说过的，那座旧亭子要等我回来再拆。'父亲说：'孩子，爸爸错了，我应该兑现自己的诺言。'

"这位父亲重新叫来工人，让他们按照旧亭子的模样在原来的地方再造一座亭子。亭子造好后，他把孩子叫来，然后对工人们说：'现在，请你们把它拆掉。'

"我认识这位父亲，他并不富有，但他在孩子面前兑现了自己的承诺。"

学生们听后问问道："请问这位父亲叫什么名字？我们希望认识他。"

福克斯说："他已经过世了，但他的儿子还活着。"

"那他的孩子在哪里？他应该是一位诚实的人。"

福克斯平静地说："他的孩子现在就站在这里，就是我。我想告诉大家的是，我愿意像父亲对我一样对待这个国家，对待这个国家的每一个人。"

台下掌声雷动。

将一座亭子拆建两次，绝不仅仅为了满足一个孩子的愿望，更是为了满足一个成人自我完善的道德要求。

在园子里重新拆掉一座亭子，就在孩子的心里重建了一座亭子，这座亭子就是一个信念——对诚信的信念。

Spring Is Coming and I Cannot See It

One day there was a blind man with a hat at his feet and a sign that read, "I am blind. Please help."

A man was walking by him and stopped to observe—he only had a few coins in his hat. The man dropped a few more coins in his hat and without asking for his permission took the sign, turned it round, and wrote another announcement. He placed the sign by the blind man's feet and left. That afternoon the man passed by the blind man again and noticed that his hat was full of bills and coins. The blind man recognized his footstep and asked if it was him who had rewritten his sign and he wanted to know what he wrote on it.

The man responded, "I just rewrote your sign differently." He smiled and went on his way.

The sign read, "Spring is coming and I cannot see it."

春天就要来了，我却无法看到

一天，有一个盲人，脚边放了一顶帽子和一个告示，上面写道："我是盲人。请帮帮我。"

一个人经过他身边，停下来观看，看见他的帽子里只有几枚硬币。那人又向帽子里丢了几枚硬币，然后未经允许就拿起告示，翻过来，又写了一张告示，放在盲人的脚边，就离开了。那天下午，这个人又路过盲人的身边，注意到帽子里放满了钞票和硬币。盲人听出了他的脚步声，问是不是他又写了告示并想知道他在上面写了什么。

这个人回答说："我只是用不同的方式写出了你的告示。"他微微一笑，就走了。

告示上写的是："春天就要来了，我却无法看到。"

The Oasis in the Heart

A young man called Cindy came to an oasis, where he met an old man.

Cindy asked, "What about here?"

The old man asked, "What about your hometown?"

Cindy replied, "It's horrible! I loathe it."

The old man went on, "Well, hurry away. It's as horrible as your hometown."

Later came a young man called Rockery. He asked the same question and the old man also countered with the same question.

Rockery replied, "My hometown is so good. I miss its people, flowers and things…"

The old man said, "It's equally good here."

The listener was so surprised that he asked the old man why his answer was different from the first one.

The old man said, "What you want to look for is what you will find!"

If you're enterprising, you will live in the oasis. If you reach for what's beyond your grasp and reap without sowing, the oasis of life will become the desert.

心里的绿洲

一个名叫辛迪的青年来到一片绿洲。他碰到一位老人。

辛迪问：“这里如何？”老人反问说：“你的家乡如何？”辛迪回答：“糟透了！我很讨厌。”老人接着说：“那你快走，这里同你家乡一样糟。”

后来又来了一个名叫罗加瑞的青年，他问了同样的问题，老人家也是同样的反问。

罗加瑞回答说：“我的家乡很好，我很想念家乡的人、鲜花和事物……”

老人便说：“这里也是同样的好。”

旁听者觉得诧异，问老人为什么前后说法不一致。

老人说：“你要寻找什么，你就找到什么！”

如果有进取心，生活则处处是绿洲。如果好高骛远、不劳而获，生活中的绿洲就会变成沙漠。

Spring Is Always Within

This past April while visiting my parents on the farm I'd grown up on, I wandered outside to drink in the feel of "home", a comfort I really needed right then. I was used to sunny Southern Californian mornings, and the brisk early-morning Iowan air nipped at my nose, ears and bare hands.

With my father's fleece-lined jacket wrapped around me, and my hands snuggled deep in its well-worn pockets, I meandered around the spacious homestead when the unexpected sweet scent of lilacs suddenly called to me. Turning toward the bountiful hedge of lilacs in the distance, I spotted what looked like blooms. I hurried over.

The lavender lilacs were indeed in glorious bloom! I pulled a plentiful clump to my face and inhaled the intoxicating scent, as I had done every spring throughout my childhood. A warm delight seeped through my chilled bones, and I smiled at the thought that spring had arrived!

Strolling back to the house, the promise of springtime-warmth, renewal and beauty-journeyed right along with me.

My father sat at the kitchen table, poring over the morning market reports.

"It's spring! The lilacs are in bloom!" I announced joyously.

"Lilacs in bloom or not, it isn't spring until winter is gone," he contradicted. "We'll get a bit of cold weather yet."

But my heart refused to let the optimism that the lilacs had brought to me fade. Immediately, I recalled the card my mother had sent me just that past week—one that had subconsciously inspired this trip home. My mother knew that I was feeling down. On the cover of the card she sent me was a photo of a single flower emerging from a desolate barren slope of rock. The exquisite flower willed itself to have life, in spite of the conditions around it. Inside were the words"In the midst of winter, I found within me an eternal spring," followed by my mother's words:

"Spring has always been your favorite time of year. As always, it's within."

These are words that my mother, ever the optimist, lives by. Even in the midst of winter, she finds spring.

"It's pouring rain!" Dad once said.

"Everything smells so fresh after a rain!" Mom responded.

"But I'd wanted to get the yards mowed today," he replied, obviously disappointed.

"We need the rain," she countered. "Now everything will be greener."

"But the forecast is rain for the entire day," Dad moaned.

"Then we should go to the movies this afternoon," Mom smiled.

"It's so expensive," he retorted.

"That's precisely why we should go to the matinee," she countered. "Three of the kids can get in free, and it's only half-price for the rest of us."

Recalling this Rockwell scene of a Sunday afternoon when I was twelve, I'm reminded that for my mother torrential rains produced a rainbow.

Throughout my childhood and over the course of my adult years, when I met with success, my mother presented me with a bouquet of lilacs. And on the days when the lemons were so bitter they simply couldn't be made into lemonade, no matter how much sugar was added, like the day a good friend passed away; like the day when a long-standing love relationship ended…lilacs arrived from my mother with a note of understanding to match their beauty and sweet fragrance.

"Spring has always been your favorite time of year," she always reminded. "As always, it's within."

Even so, it was the lilacs made her words ring true. With the sight and fragrance of that April morning's came the realization of why a trip home was necessary. I needed to assuage my sadness, my feelings of loneliness and melancholy. I was pining. My dear daughter, now an adult, had moved into a place of her own. She now lives many states and many miles away. While happy for her, I mourn the loss of her nearness…

That morning, the sight of the lilacs brought my mother's words back to life. They reminded me that in the midst of an internal winter, a winter that is within, I must recall the beauty of springtime and the scent of the lilacs. So I won't see her as having gone away, but rather as taking part in new and wondrous experiences in a world that has as many springs as winters.

"Dad, the lilacs are in bloom. It's spring!" I assured my father that day.

"Hmm," he said, glancing at me, his expression skeptical. Noting my frown, his features softened. "Of course it's possible that spring has arrived," he placated, smiling. "After all, like you said, the lilacs are in bloom."

Oh, for the every renewing beauty of springtime! And the sweet and irrepressible scent of the lilacs to remind us that spring is found within.

春天总在心里

过去的这个4月，我去自己从小在那里长大的那个农场探望父母亲。我漫步在屋外，沉浸在"家"的感觉中，我当时确实需要家的慰藉。我习惯了加州南部阳光明媚的早晨，艾奥瓦州清晨凛冽的空气刺痛了我的鼻子、耳朵和没戴手套的双手。

我将父亲的一件羊毛衬里夹克裹在身上，两手深深地插进破破烂烂的口袋里，在宽阔的农场上溜达。突然，紫丁香的芬芳出乎意料地向我袭来。我转向远处一丛丛茂密的紫丁香，注意到好像是花朵。我匆匆跑了过去。

淡紫色的丁香花确实在漂亮地怒放着！我将一大丛拉到面前，吮吸着那醉人的花香，就像我童年时每年春天做的那样。一股暖暖的喜悦之情穿过了我冰冷的身体。一想到春天已经来临，我露出了微笑。

我信步回到房里，春天的希望——温暖美丽、万物复苏——一路伴随着我。

父亲坐在餐桌边，仔细看着早晨行情报道。

"春天来了！紫丁香花开了！"我欢快地宣布道。

"紫丁香开不开花，只有等冬天过去，才是春天，"他反驳说，"冷天还要持续一阵。"

但我的内心不愿让紫丁香带给我的乐观消失。我马上想起上周母亲刚送给我的一张卡片，正是那张卡片促使我这次下意识地回了家。母亲知道我情绪低落。她送给我的那张卡片的正面是一张照片，照片上是一朵花从一块岩石荒芜贫瘠的斜面上露出来。尽管周围环境恶劣，这朵精美的花朵却努力活着。卡片里写着："在隆冬季节，我在自己的内心找到了永恒的春天。"后面还有母亲的一句话："春天总是你最爱的季节。春天总在心里。"

这就是我一向乐观生活的母亲的话语。即使是在隆冬季节，她也总能找到春天。

"大雨倾盆了！"有一次，爸爸说。

"雨后的一切都是那样清新好闻！"妈妈回答说。

"可我今天本来想割院子里的草。"父亲回答说，显然感到失望。

"我们需要这场雨，"她反驳说，"现在一切都会更加青翠。"

"可预报说，一天都有雨。"爸爸抱怨说。

"那我们今天下午就去看电影。"妈妈笑着说。

"太贵了。"他反驳道。

"那正是我们应去看日场的原因，"她反驳说，"3个孩子可以免票入场，我们其他人只需半价。"

回忆起我12岁那年一个星期天下午的这种罗克韦尔画风的情景，我想到，在母亲看来，倾盆大雨过后会出现一道彩虹。

在我童年时期和成年历程中，每当我取得成功时，母亲都会送给我一束紫丁香。而在柠檬苦涩，无论加多少糖也做不成柠檬汁时，比如好友去世那天，长久爱情关系结束那天……母亲也会送来紫丁香，上面写着一张与紫丁香的美丽芬芳相媲美的默契的纸条。

"春天总是你最爱的季节，"她总是提醒说，"春天总在心里。"

虽然如此，还是紫丁香让我感到她的话是真的。我从那个4月的早晨看到的紫丁香和闻到的芳香意识到，这次回家为什么必要。我需要缓解悲伤、孤独和忧郁。我在思念。我的爱女现在已经长大成人，搬到了一个属于自己的地方。她现在住的地方与我相隔好多州，离我有好多英里。我为她感到高兴的同时，也为她不在身边而忧伤。

那天早晨，看到那些紫丁香，使我又想起了母亲的话。它们提醒我，即使内心处在隆冬季节，我也必须记起春天的美丽和紫丁香的芳香。所以，我不再把她看成是远走高飞，而宁愿看成是进入了一个富有精彩体验的新世界。那个世界，春天和冬天一样多。

"爸爸，紫丁香开了！春天来了！"我那天对父亲断然说道。

"嗯，"说着，他瞥了我一眼，一副怀疑的神情。他看到我皱眉，表情变得温和起来。"当然，有可能春天已经来了，"他微笑着安抚说，"毕竟，像你说的那样，那些紫丁香已经开了。"

噢，为春天每年回归的美丽而喝彩！而且紫丁香抑制不住的芬芳提醒我们，春天在我们心里就能找到。

Courage

A father was worried about his son, who was sixteen years old but had no courage at all. So the father decided to call on a Buddhist monk to train his boy.

The Buddhist monk said to the boy's father, "You should leave your son alone here. I'll make him into a real man within three months. However, you can't come to see him during this period."

Three months later, the boy's father returned. The Buddhist monk arranged a boxing match between the boy and an experienced boxer. Each time the fighter struck the boy, he fell down, but at once the boy stood up; and each time a punch knocked him down, the boy stood up again. Several times later, the Buddhist monk asked, "What do you think of your child?"

"What a shame!" the boy's father said. "I never thought he would be so easily knocked down. I needn't have him left here any longer."

"I'm sorry that that's all you see. Don't you see that each time he falls down, he stands up again instead of crying? That's the kind of courage you wanted him to have."

勇　气

一位父亲为儿子担心。儿子16岁了，却没有一点勇气。于是，父亲决定去拜访一位禅师，请他训练儿子。

禅师对男孩的父亲说："你应该让他单独留在这里。不出3个月，我要让他成为一个真正的男子汉。不过，在这段时间，你不能来见他。"

3个月后，男孩的父亲又来见禅师。禅师安排这个男孩和一位经验丰富的拳师进行拳击比赛。拳师每次一出手，男孩就倒在地上，但男孩马上站起来；每次将他击倒，他就又站起来。几个回合后，禅师问道："你认为自己的孩子怎么样？"

"真丢人！"男孩的父亲说，"我绝没想到他这样不堪一击。我不需要他再留在这里了。"

"很遗憾，你只看到这一点。难道你没看到他每次倒下后并没有哭泣，而是重新站起来了吗？这才是你想要他拥有的那种勇气。"

Gifts from the Heart

A young man while roaming the desert came across a spring of delicious crystal-clear water. The water was so sweet he filled his leather canteen so he could bring some back to a tribal elder who had been his teacher. After a four-day journey he presented the water to the old man who took a deep drink, smiled warmly and thanked his student lavishly for the sweet water. The young man returned to his village with a happy heart.

Later, the teacher let another student taste the water. He spat it out, saying it was awful. It apparently had become stale because of the old leather container. The student challenged his teacher: "Master, the water was foul. Why did you pretend to like it?" The teacher replied, "You only tasted the water. I tasted the gift. The water was simply the container for an act of loving-kindness and nothing could be sweeter."

I think we understand this lesson best when we receive innocent gifts of love from young children. Whether it's a ceramic tray or a macaroni bracelet, the natural and proper response is appreciation and expressed thankfulness. After all, gifts from the heart are really gifts of the heart.

来自内心的礼物

一个小伙子途径沙漠偶遇一泓泉水：水晶般清澈，甘甜可口。于是，他灌了满满一皮水壶，以便能给做过他老师的同族中的一位长者捎些回去。经过4天跋涉，他将水呈给了那位老人。老人畅饮了一口，衷心地笑了，同时大大感谢他这位学生为他捎来这甘甜的泉水。年轻人心情愉快地返回了自己的村子。

老师让另外一名学生品尝这水。这名学生一口吐了出来，说难喝死了。显然，由于那个皮水壶的缘故，水已经变了味。学生去问老师："老师，那水明明是馊的，你为什么假装喜欢呢？"老师回答道："你尝的只是这水。我尝的是份礼物。那水只不过是表达爱的载体，没有什么比这更甘甜的了。"

我想，当我们收到小孩子们表达爱的无恶意的礼物时最能理解老人的话。无论收到的礼物是一只陶盘还是一只通心面做的手镯，自然而恰当的反应是欣赏和致谢。毕竟，来自内心的礼物才是真正的礼物。

The Precious Stone Within

A wise woman who was traveling in the mountain found a precious stone in a stream.

The next day she met another traveler who was hungry, and the wise woman opened her bag to share her food. The hungry traveler saw the precious stone and asked the woman to give it to him. She did so without hesitation.

The traveler left, rejoicing in his good fortune. He knew the stone was worth enough to give him security for a lifetime.

But a few days later he came back to return the stone to the wise woman. "I've been thinking," he said. "I know how valuable this stone is, but I give it back in the hope that you give me something even more precious. Give me what you have within you that enabled you to give me this stone."

Sometimes it's not the wealth you have but what's inside you that others need.

内心的宝石

一个聪明的女人在山里旅行时在山涧里发现一颗宝石。

第二天，她遇到了另一个饥饿的旅行者。聪明女人打开包，和他分享自己的食物。饥饿的旅行者看到了那颗宝石，让那女人把宝石送给他。她毫不犹豫就送给了他。

那个旅行者离开后，对自己的好运乐不可支。他知道那颗宝石足够他一辈子高枕无忧。

但几天后，他又回来把宝石还给了这个聪明的女人。"我一直在想，"他说，"我知道这颗宝石是多么珍贵，但我把它归还，希望你给我更珍贵的东西。我想要你把宝石给我时你内心拥有的那种东西。"

有时，别人需要的并不是你的财富，而是你内心拥有的东西。

The Real Meaning of Peace

There once was a king who offered a prize to the artist who would paint the best picture of peace. Many artists tried. The king looked at all the pictures. But there were only two he really liked, and he had to choose between them. One picture was of a calm lake. The lake was a perfect mirror for peaceful towering mountains all around it. Overhead was a blue sky with fluffy white clouds. All who saw this picture thought that it was a perfect picture of peace.

The other picture had mountains, too. But these were rugged and bare. Above was an angry sky, from which rain fell and in which lightning played. Down the side of the mountain tumbled a foaming waterfall. This did not look peaceful at all.

But when the king looked closely, he saw behind the waterfall a tiny bush growing in a crack in the rock. In the bush a mother bird had built her nest. There, in the midst of the rush of angry water, sat the mother bird on her nest—in perfect peace. Which picture do you think won the prize? The king chose the second picture. Do you know why?

"Because," explained the king, "peace does not mean to be in a place where there is no noise, trouble, or hard work. Peace means to be in the midst of all those things and still be calm in your heart. That is the real meaning of peace."

宁静的真谛

从前有一个国王，悬赏能画出最好的宁静画的画家。很多画家都进行了尝试。国王看了所有的作品，但他真正喜欢的只有两幅，他必须进行选择。一幅画中是一片宁静的湖，四周群山环绕，湖泊就是一面完美的镜子，蓝天之上白云飘飘，每个看到这幅画的人都认为这真是一幅完美的宁静画。

另一幅画也有山脉。但这些山脉崎岖不平，光秃秃的。上面是乌云滚滚的天空，大雨如注，闪电雷鸣，一条飞瀑从山的一侧倾泻而下。这看起来一点都不宁静。但国王仔细看时，看到瀑布后面在岩石的一条裂缝中长着一个小小的灌木丛。灌木丛中，一只母鸟极其安静地卧在巢上。你认为哪幅画能赢得悬赏呢？国王选择了第二幅。你知道为什么吗？

国王解释说："这是因为宁静并不是指这个地方没有噪音、烦恼和辛劳。宁静就是置于所有那些东西之中，你心里仍然平静。这才是宁静的真谛。"

I Have a Dream

I say to you today, my friends, that in spite of the difficulties and frustrations of the moment, I still have a dream.It is a dream deeply rooted in the American dream.

I have a dream that one day this nation will rise up and live out the true meaning of its creed: "We hold these truths to be self-evident: that all men are created equal."

I have a dream that one day on the red hills of Georgia the sons of former slaves and the sons of former slave owners will be able to sit down together at a table of brotherhood; I have a dream that one day even the state of Mississippi, a desert state, sweltering with the heat of injustice and oppression, will be transformed into an oasis of freedom and justice.

I have a dream that my four children will one day live in a nation where they won't be judged by the color of their skin but by the content of their character.

I have a dream today.

I have a dream that one day the state of Alabama, whose governor's lips are presently dripping with the words of interposition and nullification, will be transformed into a situation where little black boys and black girls will be able to join hands with little white boys and white girls and walk together as sisters and brothers.

I have a dream today.

I have a dream that one day every valley shall be exalted, every hill and mountain shall be made low, the rough places will be made plain, and the crooked places will be made straight, and the glory of the Lord shall be revealed, and all flesh shall see it together.

This is our hope. This is the faith with which I return to the South. With this faith we will be able to hew out of the mountain of despair a stone of hope. With this faith we will be able to transform the jangling discords of our nation into a beautiful symphony of brotherhood. With this faith we will be able to work together, to pray together, to struggle together, to go to jail together, to stand up for freedom together, knowing that we will be free one day. This will be the day when all of God's children will be able to sing with a new meaning, "My country,'tis of thee, sweet land of liberty, of thee I sing. Land where my fathers died, land of the pilgrim's pride, from every mountainside, let freedom ring." And if America is to be a great nation, this must become true.

So let freedom ring from the prodigious hilltops of New Hampshire. Let freedom ring from the mighty mountains of New York. Let freedom ring from the heightening Alleghenies of Pennsylvania! Let freedom ring from the snowcapped Rockies of Colorado! Let freedom ring from the curvaceous peaks of California! But not only that; let freedom ring from Stone Mountain of Georgia! Let freedom ring from Lookout Mountain of Tennessee! Let freedom ring from every hill and every molehill of Mississippi. From every mountainside, let freedom ring.

When we let freedom ring, when we let it ring from every village and every hamlet, from every state and every city, we will be able to speed up that day when all of God's children, black men and white men, Jews and Gentiles, Protestants and Catholics, will be able to join hands and sing in the words of the old Negro spiritual, "Free at last! Free at last! Thank God Almighty, we are free at last!"

我有一个梦想

朋友们，今天我对你们说，尽管我们会遇到种种困难和挫折，但我仍有一个梦想，它深深地扎根在美国人的梦想中。

我梦想有一天，这个国家会站立起来，真正表现出其信条的真谛："我们信奉的真理不言自明：人人生而平等。"

我梦想有一天，在佐治亚州的红山上，奴隶的后代与奴隶主的后代能兄弟般坐在一起；我梦想有一天，甚至密西西比这个正义匿迹、压迫成风、热浪逼人的地方，也将变成自由与公正的绿洲。

我梦想有一天，我的四个孩子将在一个不是根据他们的肤色，而是根据他们的品行来衡量他们的国度里生活。

今天，我有一个梦想。

我梦想有一天，种族歧视行为泛滥的亚拉巴马州能有所改变，尽管该州州长仍然满口异议反对联邦法令，但有朝一日，那里的黑人男孩和女孩将能和白人的男孩和女孩亲密无间、携手并进。

今天，我有一个梦想。

我梦想有一天，幽谷上升，高山下降，崎岖之路变成通途，圣光披露，满照人间。

这就是我们的希望。我怀着这种信念回到南方。有了这个信念，我们将能从绝望之巅劈出一块希望之石。有了这个信念，我们将能把这个国家种族不和的喧嚣变成一曲展现兄弟情义的优美乐章。怀着这个信念，我们将能共同努力、共同祈祷、共同斗争、共同坐牢、共同维护自由；因为我们知道，终有一天，我们会自由。在自由到来的那一天，上帝的所有儿女们将以全新的意义共同歌唱这支歌："我的祖国，美丽的自由之乡，我为你歌唱，你是我父辈逝去的地方，你是最初移民的骄傲，让自由之声响彻每一座山峦。"如果美国要成为一个伟大的国家，就必须实现这个梦想。

让自由之声从新罕布什尔州的巍巍山顶上响起来！让自由之声在纽约州的茫茫群山上响起来！让自由之声从宾夕法尼亚州高耸入云的阿勒格尼山上响起来！让自由之声从科罗拉多州白雪覆盖的落基山上响起来！让自由之声从加利福尼亚州崎岖不平的山地上响起来。不仅如此，还要让自由之声从佐治亚州的石山上响起来！让自由之声从田纳西州的瞭望山上响起来！让自由之声在密西西比州的每一座丘陵响起来！让自由之声从每一个山坡响起来！

当这一天来临，当我们让自由之声回响，让自由之声从每一个大大小小的村落、每一个州和每一座城市响起来时，我们将能够加速这一天的到来。到那时，上帝的所有儿女们，黑人和白人，犹太人和异教徒，新教徒和天主教徒，都将携手合唱古老的黑人灵歌："终于自由了！终于自由了！感谢万能的上帝，我们终于自由了！"

The Gold in the Orchard

There was once a farmer who had a fine olive orchard. He was very hardworking, and the farm always prospered under his care. But he knew that his three sons despised the farm work, and were eager to make wealth, through adventure.

When the farmer was old, and felt that his time had come to die, he called the three sons to him and said, "My sons, there is a pot of gold hidden in the olive orchard. Dig for it, if you wish it."

The sons tried to get him to tell them in what part of the orchard the gold was hidden; but he would tell them nothing more.

After the farmer was dead, the sons went to work to find the pot of gold; since they did not know where the hiding-place was, they agreed to begin in a line, at one end of the orchard, and to dig until one of them should find the money.

They dug until they had turned up the soil from one end of the orchard to the other, round the tree-roots and between them. But no pot of gold was to be found. It seemed as if someone must have stolen it, or as if the farmer had been wandering in his wits. The three sons were bitterly disappointed to have all their work for nothing.

The next olive season, the olive trees in the orchard bore more fruit than they had ever given; when it was sold, it gave the sons a whole pot of gold!

And when they saw how much money had come from the orchard, they suddenly understood what the wise father had meant when he said, "There is gold hidden in the orchard. Dig for it, if you wish it."

果园里的金子

从前有一个农民，他有一座漂亮的橄榄园。他非常勤劳，而且农场在他的照管下蒸蒸日上。可他知道自己的三个儿子瞧不起农活，都迫不及待想通过冒险发家致富。

这个农民上了年岁，感到死期快要来临时，将三个儿子叫到身边说："儿子们，橄榄园里藏有一罐金子。想要就去挖吧。"

儿子们想让父亲告诉他们金子藏在果园的哪一块地方，可他什么也没再给他们说。

那个农民死后，三个儿子就开始挖地，想找到那罐金子；因为他们不知道金子藏在什么地方，所以他们一致同意排成一行从果园的一头开始挖起，直到其中一人挖到金子为止。

他们挖啊挖，从果园的一头一直挖到了另一头，果树周围和果树之间也都挖到了，可还是没有找到那罐金子。看来一定是有人已经把那罐金子偷走了，要么就是他们的父亲一直在异想天开。三个儿子对他们白干了一场，感到大失所望。

到了第二年的橄榄季节，果园里的橄榄树结出的果子比以往的都多；卖完果子后，三个儿子赚了整整一罐金子！

他们从果园里得到这么多钱后，突然明白了聪明的父亲所说的"果园里藏有金子，想要就去挖吧"这句话的含义。

Four Seasons of a Tree

There was a man who had four sons. He wanted his sons to learn to not judge things too quickly. So he sent them each on a quest, in turn, to go and look at a pear tree that was a great distance away. The first son went in the winter, the second in the spring, the third in summer, and the youngest son in the fall.

When they had all gone and come back, he called them together to describe what they had seen. The first son said that the tree was ugly, bent, and twisted. The second son said no. It was covered with green buds and full of promise. The third son disagreed. He said it was laden with blossoms that smelled so sweet and looked so beautiful, it was the most graceful thing he had ever seen. The last son disagreed with all of them. He said it was ripe and drooping with fruit, full of life and fulfillment.

The man then explained to his sons that they were all right, because they had each seen but one season in the tree's life.

He told them that you cannot judge a tree, or a person, by only one season, and that the essence of who they are and the pleasure, joy, and love that come from that life can only be measured at the end, when all the seasons are up.

If you give up when it's winter, you will miss the promise of your spring, the beauty of your summer, and fulfillment of your fall. Don't let the pain of one season destroy the joy of all the rest.

树 的 四 季

从前，一个人有四个儿子。他想让儿子们学会不对事情匆匆作出判断，就让儿子们轮流去远方观察一棵梨树。大儿子冬天去，二儿子春天去，三儿子夏天去，小儿子秋天去。

当他们都已看过回到家时，父亲把他们叫到一起，让他们描述一下看到的情形。大儿子说那棵树很难看，弯弯扭扭的。二儿子说不是这样，树上满是绿芽，充满了希望。三儿子意见不一，说那棵树开满了花，芳香扑鼻，非常漂亮，那是他见过的最美的东西。小儿子不同意他们三人的看法，他说梨树成熟了，上面缀满了果实，充满了生机和成就感。

父亲向儿子们解释说他们说的都对，因为他们每人看到的只是那棵树一生中的一个季节。他告诉他们，不要仅凭一个时段来判断一棵树或一个人，他们的本质生命中的快乐、喜悦和爱只能到最后，当所有的季节都结束时才能去评判。

如果你在冬天就放弃，那将会错过春天的希望、夏天的美丽和秋天的收获。不要让一个季节的痛苦毁掉一年所有其他的欢乐。

The Upwind Fragrance

One day, Ananda sat quietly alone in the garden when he suddenly smelled the scent of flowers wafting with the evening wind.

When the wind usually blows the scent of flowers, you can't always smell the fragrance because you're unsteady in mood. While you calm down, the wind doesn't necessarily come, so you can't smell any scent.

Then one evening, Ananda was particularly quiet in mind, and it was spring—the season with the most fragrant flowers, and spring breeze was slowly wafting along. So with so many concerted reasons, Ananda smelt the most beautiful floral scent in his lifetime.

The fragrance encircled Ananda, running through him, and then flowing to an unknown distance. These scent kept him sit still from leaving from dusk to night and made him so moved.

In such a sensation, Ananda felt his heart wafting up with the scent; he thought of some problems that had never been considered: plants are fragrant when they are in bloom; are there the fragrant plants even without blossoming? Flowers are restricted to a short-lived karma and are there flowers often fragrant? Even if the spring flowers waft so far, they also have an extension and are there scents pervading all over the world? All flowers all waft downwind and are there fragrance that can be wafted upwind?

Thinking about these problems, Ananda was so enthralled that he couldn't be calm in the next few days. One day, Ananda sat spellbound in the fragrance of flowers when Buddha passed by where he sat quietly and asked, "Why are you not at ease?" Ananda asked his teacher of the abstruse questions that puzzled him.

Buddha replied, "The one who keeps to mitzvah is not necessarily fragrant in bloom and fruit and who will be also fragrant even without the flower of wisdom. The heart lost in Buddhist meditation needn't seek for fragrance in the karma, for he forever keeps merry fragrance within himself. The one who blooms wisdom will permeate his fragrance all over the world, not to be confined by seasons. A person who develops sila, meditation and prajna through his own heart can waft the fragrance of his personality even in adversity."

At this, Ananda was so moved.

Buddha said affably, "Not only do devotees smell the fragrance of the garden but also blossom in their hearts—the fragrance with virtue. Thus no matter where he lives, in the city or in the mountains, all the people will smell his scent!"

If our mind is a garden, isn't any day in our life the most beautiful blooming season?

If our hearts are filled with spring breeze, isn't anytime in our life the best spring?

逆风飘香

有一天，阿难独自在花园里静坐，突然闻到了随着黄昏吹来的风飘过来的一阵阵花香。

平常有风吹着花香时，心绪波动，不一定能闻到花香。当心静下来时，又不一定有风吹来，所以也闻不到花香。

那个黄昏，阿难的心情特别宁静，又是春天——花朵最香的时节，正好春风缓缓吹送。在这么多原因的配合下，阿难闻到了有生以来最美妙的花香。

花香围绕着阿难，花香穿流过他的身心，然后流向不可知的远方。这些花香使阿难从黄昏静坐到夜里舍不得离开，这些花香也使得阿难非常感动。

在感动中，阿难宁静的心也随花香飘动起来，他想到了一些从未想过的问题：草木都是开花时才会香，有没有不开花就会香的草木呢？花朵送香都限定在一个短暂的因缘里，有没有经常芬芳的花朵呢？春花的香再远也有一个范围，有没有弥漫全世界的香呢？所有的花都是顺风飘送，有没有逆风飘香呢？

阿难想着这些问题，想到入神，竟然使他在接下来的几天无法静心。有一天，阿难又坐在花香中出神，佛陀走过他静坐的地方，就问他："你的心情波动，到底是为了什么呢？"阿难就把自己苦思而难解的问题请教了老师。

佛陀说："守戒律的人，不一定要开花结果才有芬芳，即使没有智慧之花，也会芳香。有禅定的心，就不必要在因缘里寻找芬芳，他的内心永远保持喜悦的花香。智慧开花的人，他的芬芳会弥漫整个世界，不会被时节范围所限制。一个透过内在培养戒、定、慧的品质的人，即使在逆境里也可以飘送人格的芬芳！"

阿难听了，感动不已。

佛陀和蔼地说："修行人不只要闻花园的花香，也要在自己的内心开花——有德行的香。这样，不管他居住在城市或山林，所有的人都会闻到他的花香！"

如果我们的内心就是一个花园，人生的哪一天不是最美的花季呢？

如果我们的内心春风洋溢，人生的哪个时候不是最好的春天呢？

The Moon Still Shines

Shirley worked in Chicago. Every day she commuted between the suburban home and the office. She noticed the driver was a particular man. Whenever the passengers got on the bus, he would smile at them. All the people smiled back at him wonderfully.

However, Shirley also noticed there was a passenger never smiled back at the driver. He wore a bushy beard;he often coughed rudely as he got on the bus and forced the other to offer the seat to him in a loud voice.

All this didn't make the driver stop his smile at the passengers. Instead, the"bearded" man seemed never to see the smile.

This aroused Shirley's interest. Once, she asked the driver, "Sir, may I ask why don't you throw that damned 'bearded' man out of the bus?"

The driver looked at Shirley and said, "He's my guest."

"Then you take back your smile at least. Don't be so kind to him!"

"Let me tell you about my puppy," the driver said patiently, "each time the moon shines, the puppy would bark at it incessantly."

Hearing this, Shirley was puzzled and asked, "What can this dog and the moon account for?"

The driver said, "It keeps barking, but the moon still shines."

月光依然照耀

雪莉在芝加哥工作。每天，她搭乘公共汽车往返于工作单位和城郊的家。她注意到司机是个很特别的人，每当有乘客上车，他都朝他们微笑。大家都回敬那位司机一个个美好的笑容。

然而，雪莉也注意到，有一个乘客始终没有朝司机笑过。他留着浓密的大胡子，常常一边上车一边粗鲁地咳嗽，还大着嗓门强迫别人给他让座。

这一切都没让司机停止送上他的微笑。相反，"大胡子"男人似乎从来看不见那笑容。

这引起了雪莉的兴趣。有一次，她问司机："先生，请问您为什么不把那讨厌的'大胡子'男人扔出车外？"

司机望着雪莉，说："他是我的客人。"

"那您至少收回您的笑容，别对他那么和善呀！"

"让我来告诉您我家小狗的事吧，"司机很有耐心地说，"那小家伙每次有月光照耀，都会对月亮吠个不停。"

雪莉听了很疑惑，问："这狗和月亮的事又能说明什么呢？"

司机说："虽然它一直吠叫，但月光依然照耀啊。"

Looking for the Gold

At one time Andrew Carnegie was the wealthiest man in America. He came to America from his native Scotland when he was a small boy, did a variety ofodd jobs, and eventually ended up as the largest steel manufacturer in the United States. At one time he had forty-three millionaires working for him. In those days a millionaire was a rare person;conservatively speaking, a million dollars in those days would be equivalent to at least twenty million dollars today.

One reporter asked Carnegie how he came to hire forty-three millionaires.

Carnegie responded, "You got to remember that those men have not been millionaires when they started working for him but have become millionaires only as a result."

The reporter's next question was, "Well, how did you develop these men to become so valuable to you that you paid them that much money?"

Carnegie replied, "People are developed the same way gold is mined. When gold is mined, several tons of dirt and stone must be moved first to get an ounce of gold;but one goes into the mine not looking for dirt but gold."

Like everything else, the more good qualities we look for in our people, the more good qualities we are going to find.

寻 找 金 子

安德鲁·卡内基曾是美国最富有的人。他小时候从故乡苏格兰来到美国，打过各种零工，最终成为全美最大的钢铁制造商。43名百万富翁曾为他工作。当时，百万富翁如凤毛麟角。保守来说，当时的一百万美元至少相当于今天的两千万美元。

一名记者问卡内基是怎样雇用43位百万富翁的。

他回答说：“你要记住，那些人开始为我工作时并不是百万富翁，但为我工作后就成了百万富翁。”

记者又问道：“那你是怎样培养这些人，使他们成为有用之才，并付给他们那么多钱的呢？”

卡内基回答说：“培养人才就像淘金。淘金时，先要洗去几吨泥石，才能淘到一盎司金子。但到矿山要找的不是污泥，而是金子。”

像所有其他事情一样，我们从自己身上寻找的优良品质越多，找到的优良品质就越多。

Do You Have a Lighthouse in Your Heart

It was a dark and stormy night. The officer on the bridge came to the captain and said, "Captain, Captain, there is a light in our sea and they won't move."

"What do you mean they won't move? Tell them to move. Tell them to starboard right now."

The signal was sent out, "Starboard, starboard." The signal came back, "Starboard yourself."

"I can't believe this. What's going on here? Let them know who I am."

The signal was sent out. "This is the mighty Missouri, starboard." The signal came back, "This is the lighthouse."

My friends, correct principles are lighthouses, they do not move. They are natural laws. We cannot break them. We might as well learn them, accommodate them, utilize them and be grateful for them. Then it enlarges us, emancipates us and empowers us.

Eliot once said, "We shall never cease striving, and the end of all our striving will arrive where we began and know the place for the first time."

你心中有灯塔吗

那是一个漆黑的暴风雨之夜。驾驶台上的驾驶员走到船长身边说："船长，船长，我们的海道上有一个发光物，他们不愿移开。"

"你说'他们不愿移开'是什么意思？告诉他们移开。告诉他们马上右偏。"

信号发了出去："右偏，右偏。"信号返回："你自己右偏。"

"我无法相信。这里是怎么了？告诉他们我是谁。"

信号又发了出去："这是'密苏里'号巨轮，右偏。"信号返回："这是灯塔。"

我的朋友们，正确的原则就像灯塔，它们不会移动。它们是自然法则。我们无法打破。我们不妨去学习它们、适应它们、利用它们、感激它们。然后，它们会让我们扩展、解脱，并使我们得到使用的能力。

艾略特曾说过："我们将永不停止奋斗，经过全力以赴的奋斗后，我们将到达出发地，并第一次认识这个地方。"

第五卷

放飞心灵的翅膀

The Flowers That Can Speak

A 6-year-old girl asked her mother, "Can flowers speak?"

"Oh, my dearie, if flowers can't speak, how lonely the spring is, who will look around it?"

The little girl smiled with satisfaction.

At the age of 16, the girl asked her father, "Can the stars in the sky speak?"

"Oh, my daughter, if the stars can speak, the sky will be noisy, who will yearn towards the serene paradise?"

The little girl smiled with satisfaction again.

At the age of 26, the girl had become a full-blown female. One day she asked in private her husband, a diplomat, "At the banquet of the previous evening, was the way I behaved and spoke appropriate?"

"Great!" the diplomat had no intention of flattering, "When you spoke, it was like the tinkling spring or the melodious music; though you spoke so much, it was not unnecessary; when you were silent, you were like a fragrant lotus or an elegant crane; though quiet, it involved everything…' sweetheart, can you tell me how you cultivate yourself?"

His wife said with a smile, "At the age of , I learned from my mother as a teacher how to dialogue with Nature. At the age of 16, I learned from my father as a writer when to speak and when not. Before I saw you, I learned from historians, philosophers, writers, musicians, painters and diplomats what kind of speech I should make when I meet different kinds of people. Honey, I have also received thoughts, wisdom, courage, views and love from you!"

会说话的花儿

一个6岁的小女孩问妈妈："花儿会说话吗？"

"噢，孩子，花儿如果不会说话，春天该是多么寂寞，谁还对春天左顾右盼呀？"

小女孩满意地笑了。

小女孩长到16岁，问爸爸："天上的星星会说话吗？"

"噢，孩子，星星若能说话，天上就会一片嘈杂，谁还会向往天堂静穆的乐园呢？"

小女孩又满意地笑了。

女孩到了26岁，已是一个成熟的女性。一天，她悄悄地问做外交官的丈夫："昨晚宴会上，我的举止言谈合适吗？"

"棒极了！"外交官毫无吹捧之意，"你说话时，像叮咚的泉水、悠扬的乐曲，虽千言而不繁；你静处时，似浮香的荷、优雅的鹤，虽静音而传千言……亲爱的，能告诉我你是怎样修炼的吗？"

妻子笑道："6岁时，我从当教师的妈妈那里学会了和自然界对话。16岁时，我从当作家的爸爸那里学会了什么时候该说话、什么时候不该说话。见到你前，我从史学家、哲学家、文学家、音乐家、画家、外交家那里学会了和什么样的人谈什么样的话。亲爱的，我还从你那里得到了思想、智慧、胆量、看法和爱！"

The Flowers on the Ruins

A long time ago, in order to open up new streets, many old buildings were pulled down in London. However, owing to various reasons, new roads couldn't start working and the ruins of the old buildings were exposed to the sun and rain.

One day, a group of natural scientists came here and found weeds and wild flowers even grew on the ruins. Amazingly, some of the plants had never been seen in Britain, for they usually grow in the countries bordering the Mediterranean. These buildings pulled down were mostly built when the ancient Romans attacked Britain along the Thames.

It was mostly at that time when the seeds of these plants were taken here. They were wedged under the heavy stones and tiles year after year, losing the chance to grow and sprout. Once they saw the sunshine, they immediately resumed their vitality and bloomed beautiful flowers.

In fact, so is life. On the journey of life, we often encounter all kinds of setbacks and failures. At this time, don't be disappointed or give up easily. As long as you have a firm belief in your heart and try to look for it, you will always find"a ray of sunshine" that helps you pull through.

废墟上的花朵

很久以前，为了开辟新街，伦敦拆除了许多旧楼房。然而，因为种种原因，新路久久没能开工，旧楼房的废墟晾在那里，任凭日晒雨淋。

有一天，一群自然科学家来到了这里，发现在这一片废墟上竟长出了一片野花野草。令人惊奇的是，其中有一些花草在英国从来没有见到过的，它们通常只生长在地中海沿岸国家。这些被拆除的楼房大多都是在古罗马人沿着泰晤士河进攻英国时建造的。这些花草的种子多半就是那个时候被带到了这里的，它们被压在沉重的石头砖瓦下，一年又一年，丧失了生长发芽的机会。而一旦见到阳光，它们就立即恢复了勃勃生机，绽开了一朵朵美丽的鲜花。

其实，人的生命也是如此。在生命的旅途中，我们常常遭遇各种挫折和失败。这时，不要心灰意冷，不要轻易言败。只要心中有一个坚定的信念，努力去找，总会找到帮助自己渡过难关的"一缕阳光"。一旦有了阳光照耀，一定能萌发出新的生机，绽放出新的美丽。

A Boy and Flowers

On a country road, a small boy was bending to talk with the roadside flowers. I couldn't follow what he was talking. I asked him, "What are you talking to the flowers?" He couldn't hear me clearly, so I had to squat down to say again.

He said, "I told the flowers, how beautifully you're blooming!"

He also told me:if I want to talk to the flowers, I must squat down to whisper in their ears so that they can hear me.

What the boy said made me stand at the roadside for a long time, thinking:if we can't squat down to look at the same level, you can neither understand the boy nor see the roadside flowers, just as we will never know its temperature if we don't put our bare feet into the stream.

男孩与鲜花

乡路上，一个小男孩正低下身子，和路边的花说着一些我听不明白的话。

我问他："你对花说些什么呢？"

他听不清，我只好蹲下来对他又说一次。

他说："我对花说：'你今天开得真好看！'"

他还告诉我说，如果我要对花说话，一定要蹲下来在花边耳语，花才能听见。

小孩的话使我在路边呆立了很久，想着：如果我们不能蹲下平视，就不能了解孩子，也不能看清路旁的花；如同我们不赤足踏进溪水，就永远不会知道溪水的温度。

The Flower Never Minds

Recently I visited a friend who had a greenhouse. As she showed me her flowers, I came to the most beautiful one of all, a golden chrysanthemum in full bloom. But to my great surprise, it was growing in an old, dented and rusty bucket.

I thought to myself, "If this were my plant, I'd put it in the loveliest flowerpot I had!"

My friend changed my mind. "I ran short of pots," she explained, "and knowing how beautiful this one would be, I thought it wouldn't mind starting out in this old pail. It's just for a little while, till I can put it out in the garden."

Aren't we the same as flowers? The important is not where we are from or what position we are in now, but where we are going.

花儿不会介意

最近，我拜访了一位有花房的朋友。她带我参观她那些花儿，我来到一株最美丽的花儿前，那是一株盛开的金菊。但让我大为吃惊的是，它长在一个坑坑洼洼、锈迹斑斑的旧桶里。

我暗自想道："如果这是我养的花儿，我会把它种在最漂亮的花盆里！"

朋友的话改变了我的想法。"种花的罐子用完了，"她解释说，"而且我知道这株金菊肯定会艳压群芳，就想着它不会介意在这个旧桶里开始成长。过一阵子，我就能把它移到花园里了。"

我们和花儿不是一样吗？重要的不是我们来自哪里，也不是我们现在的位置，而是我们将去何方。

The Rose Root

There's life underground and on the ground, where there're a group of creatures knowing love and hate.

One day, the streamlet encountered the rose and said, "My root neighbor, I've never seen anyone as ugly as you. Whoever meets you will say it must a monkey inserted its long tail into the earth, threw it down and left. It seems that you want to imitate the earthworm, but you didn't learn its elegant and round movement, only learned to drink my blue juice. As soon as I met you, I was half drunk by you. Ugly, you say, what are you doing?"

The lowly root said, "Yes, my streamlet brother, in your eyes I certainly have no appearance. The long touch with the soil made me dark gray; the overtiredness deformed me, as a worker's deformed arm. I'm also a worker, who work for my extension to the sun. I absorbed juice from you, transmitted it to her and made her fresh and lovely; after you left, I would go afar to look for the juice to sustain life. My streamlet brother, one day, you will go to the place where the sun shines. Then, you can go to see how beautiful my part in the sunlight is."

The streamlet didn't believe that, but out of caution, he didn't say anything, thinking to himself, wait and see.

When his trembling body gradually grew up into the light, the first thing he did was to look for the extension the root had said. Gosh! Everywhere he could see the radiant and enchanting spring scenery while where the root took, a rose graced the land more beautiful.

On the branches hung the heavy flowers, whose intoxicating fragrance was filling the air.

The streamlet flowed across the grass with the blooming flowers, "My God, I haven't thought such an ugly root even stretching such a beauty!"

玫 瑰 花 根

地下同地上一样有生命，有一群懂得爱憎的生物。

有一天，细流遇到玫瑰花根，说："花根邻居，像你这么丑的，我从来没有见过呢。谁见了你都会说，准是一只猴子把它的长尾巴插在地里，扔下不管，径自走了。看来你想模仿蚯蚓，但没有学会它优美圆润的动作，只学会了喝我的蓝色汁液。我一碰上你，就被你喝掉了一半。丑八怪，你说，你这是干什么？"

卑贱的花根说："不错，细流兄弟，在你眼里我当然没有模样。长期和泥土接触，使我浑身灰黑；过度劳累，使我变了形，正如变形的工人胳臂一样。我也是工人，我替身体见到阳光的延伸部分干活。我从你那里吸取了汁液，就是输送给她的，让她新鲜娇艳；你离开后，我就到远处去寻找维持生命的汁液。细流兄弟，总有一天，你会到太阳照耀的地方。那时候，你去看看我在阳光下的部分是多么美丽。"

细流并不相信，但出于谨慎，没有作声，暗忖道：等着瞧吧。

当他颤动的身躯逐渐长大，到了亮光下时，他干的第一件事就是去寻找花根所说的延伸部分。天哪！他看到了到处是一派明媚的春光，花根扎下去的地方，一株玫瑰把土地装点得分外美丽。

沉甸甸的花朵挂在枝条上，在空气中散发着醉人的芳香。

细流穿过了鲜花盛开的草地。"天哪，想不到丑陋的花根竟然延伸出美丽！"

Flowers and Hope

When World War II ended, there were ruins everywhere. American sociologist David Popenoe visited a German family living in the basement.

After leaving there, one of the people going the same way asked Popenoe, "Do you think they can rebuild their home?"

"Surely!" Popenoe answered verily.

"Why did you answer so surely?"

"What did you see they put on the table in the basement?"

"A vase of flowers."

"Right," Popenoe said, "any nation in such a plight that has not yet forgotten the love of beauty must be able to rebuild her homes on the ruins."

This story tells us how admirable and inspiring the people in despair who could still pursue the flower of hope were!

鲜花与希望

第二次世界大战结束，到处是一片废墟。美国社会学家戴维·波普诺去访问一户住在地下室里的德国居民。

离开那里之后，同行的人问波普诺："你看他们能重建家园吗？"

"一定能！"波普诺肯定地回答。

"为什么回答得这么肯定呢？"

"你看到他们在地下室的桌上放着什么吗？"

"一瓶鲜花。"

"对，"波普诺说，"任何一个民族，处在这样困苦的境地，还没有忘记爱美，那就一定能在废墟上重建家园。"

在绝望中仍能追寻希望之花的人，是多么令人敬佩与振奋！

A Young Flower in the Desert

There was a young flower in the desert where all was dry and sad-looking. She grew there alone, enjoyed every day and said to the sun, "When shall I grow up?"

The sun would say, "Be patient—Each time I touch you, you will grow a little."

She was so pleased because she would have a chance to bring beauty to this corner of sand…and this was all she wanted to do—to bring a little bit of beauty to this world.

One day the hunter came by and stepped on her. She was going to die—and she felt so sad. Not because she was dying but because she would not have a chance to bring a little bit of beauty to this corner of the desert.

The great spirit saw her and heard her. Indeed, he spoke it out. She should be alive…and he reached down, touched her and gave her life.

Later, she grew up to be a beautiful flower. This corner of the desert became so beautiful because of her.

沙漠里的一朵小花

遍地干旱、满目凄凉的沙漠中有一朵小花。她独自生长在那里，享受着每一天，对太阳说："我什么时候才能长大呀？"

太阳总是说："要耐心。我每次抚摸你，你都会长大一点。"

她非常开心，因为她也有机会为沙漠的这个角落带来美丽……而且这是她唯一想做的事情，为这个世界带来一点美丽。

有一天，一位猎人经过，正好踩在她身上。她快要死了，感到非常伤心。并不是因为她即将死去，而是因为她再没有机会为沙漠的这个角落带来一点美丽了。

伟大的精灵看到了她，并听到了她的心声。事实上，他说了出来。她应该活着。于是，他俯下身，抚摸着她，给了她生命。

后来，她长成了一朵美丽的花。沙漠的这个角落因她而变得非常美丽。

The Rose Within

A man planted a rose and watered it faithfully and before it blossomed, he examined it.

He saw the bud that would soon blossom, but noticed thorns upon the stem and he thought, "How can any beautiful flower come from a plant burdened with so many sharp thorns?" Saddened by this thought, he neglected to water the rose, and just before it was ready to bloom it died.

So it is with many people. Within every soul there is a rose. The noble qualities planted in us at birth grow amid the thorns of our faults. Many of us look at ourselves and see only thorns, the defects.

We despair, thinking that nothing good can possibly come from us. We neglect to water the rose within us, and eventually it dies. We never realize our potential.

Some people do not see the rose within themselves;someone else must show it to them. One of the greatest gifts a person can possess it to be able to reach past the thorns of another and find the rose within them.

This is one of the characteristic of love:look at a person and, knowing his faults, recognize the nobility in his soul, and help him realize that he can overcome his faults. If we show him the rose within himself, he will conquer the thorns. Only then will he blossom times over.

心中的玫瑰

有个人种了一株玫瑰，一丝不苟地给它浇水。在玫瑰将要开花前，他仔细看了看。他看到花蕾马上就要绽放，但注意到花茎上的刺，心里想道："长了这么多尖刺的一棵植物怎么能开出美丽的花朵呢？"想到这个，他伤心起来，不再给花浇水了。就在准备开花时，这株玫瑰却死了。

许多人也是这样。每个人的心里都有一株玫瑰。我们出生时，植根在我们体内的那些高贵的品质生长在我们像尖刺的缺点中。我们许多人在审视自己时，只看到刺，只看到缺点。我们丧失信心，认为自己不可能做出什么好事。我们疏于浇灌内心的玫瑰，所以它最后死去。我们从未意识到自己的潜力。

有些人看不到自己内心的玫瑰，其他人必须告诉他。一个人所能具备的一个最伟大的天赋就是能忽略他人的尖刺，发现他内心的玫瑰。

这就是爱的其中一个特性：看一个人，知道他的缺点，同时认识到他灵魂中的高尚品质，帮助他认识到他可以克服自己的缺点。如果我们让他知道他内心的玫瑰，他就会克服那些尖刺。只有到那个时候，他的玫瑰才会再次绽放。

Your Mind is a Garden

Some time ago, Sophia and I were visiting some friends in the country. We were staying at a beautiful little cabin, surrounded by fruit trees, flowers and even a few goats. Painted above the doorway in brightly colored, flowing letters were the words:

Your mind is a garden.

Your thoughts are the seeds.

You can grow flowers or

You can grow weeds.

Little did we know it at the time, but this little poem was to have a profound affect both on our thought patterns as well as our artworks.

It started almost as a kind of game. We decided to make a real effort to watch our thoughts and see exactly what it was that we were planting in our own"Mind Gardens."

We gradually came to see how so many of the problems and difficulties we were encountering in our lives had their beginnings in the seeds of doubt, fear and anxiety we were continually planting in our minds.

As we become more and more aware of these negative thoughts we are able to say, "No, I won't plant this weed in the garden of my mind."

I will consciously choose to plant something better. The results are truly spectacular.

When you start to consciously cultivate your own mind garden, you will truly be amazed at the changes, which begin to happen in your life. Things that you once thought were either impossible or very far away will suddenly come into view.

Any garden is an ongoing process. It's not enough to just plant a single seed of happiness and forget about it. Weeds would soon choke your frail little seedling. It is necessary to continuously pull out and throw away those seeds of fear, doubt and anxiety as soon as they appear.

Love, happiness and tranquility are all contagious. People who keep planting these seeds in their own mind are also planting them in others'. Remember:

Your mind is a garden.

Your thoughts are the seeds.

You can grow flowers or

You can grow weeds.

So ask yourself, what are you going to grow in the florid garden of your mind?

Fill your life with love and happiness.

心 是 花 园

不久前，我和索菲娅去乡下拜访一些朋友，我们住在一座漂亮的小木屋里。小屋外果树和鲜花环绕，还有几只山羊。小屋屋门上方用颜色鲜艳、行云流水的字体写着：

心是花园，思想是种。可以种花，或种杂草。

尽管我们当时不大明白，但这首小诗会给我们的思维模式和艺术作品带来深远的影响。

开始时几乎就像一场游戏。我们决定真正努力观察自己的思想，要看一下我们自己的"思想花园"里种的到底是什么。

我们最终渐渐发现，我们在生活中遇到的许多问题和困难正是源于我们不断在心里种的怀疑、恐惧和忧虑的种子。

当我们越来越多地认识到这些消极思想时，我们就会说："不，我不会把这颗野草种在自己的心灵花园。"

我会有意识地选种一些更好的东西，结果确实激动人心。

当你开始有意识地耕种自己的心灵花园时，生活中发生的改变会让你大吃一惊。你曾认为不可能或遥远的东西会突然进入你的视野。

任何花园都处在不断变化中。只种下一粒幸福的种子，然后忘在脑后是不够的。杂草很快就会困死你的弱不禁风的幼苗。恐惧、怀疑和忧虑的杂草一出现，必须不断拔除、扔掉。

爱、幸福和宁静都会传染。那些不断在自己的心灵花园种下这些种子的人也正把爱、幸福和宁静种进别人的心田。记住：

心是花园，思想是种。可以种花，或种杂草。

所以，你问一下自己，你打算在自己绚丽的心灵花园种什么？

让你的生活充满爱和幸福。

The Praise That Changed the Life

When he was small, Hill was an acknowledged bad boy.

At the age of 9, his father married his stepmother. At that time they lived poor in the countryside while his stepmother was from a wealthy family.

His father introduced Hill to his stepmother as he said, "Dear, I hope you notice in the entire shire this is the worst boy, who has made me have no other way. Maybe before tomorrow morning he will throw a stone at you, or do a bad thing you will never imagine."

To Hill's surprise, his stepmother went up to him with a smile, held up his head and looked at him carefully. She then turned around to tell her husband, "You're wrong. He is not the worst boy in the entire shire, but the most intelligent and creative boy. Only he doesn't find a place to vent his passion."

His stepmother's words warmed his heart, his tears almost rolling down. With this, he started building friendship with his stepmother. And this became the drive of his life, making him create 28 successful golden rules, which helped tens of thousands of ordinary people set foot on the road to success and prosperity.

Before his stepmother came, no one praised him smart, and his father and neighbors identified him as a bad boy. However, his stepmother's words changed his life's destiny.

When Hill was 14 years old, his stepmother bought him a used typewriter and said to him, "I believe you will become a writer." Hill accepted his stepmother's gift and expectation, and started contributing to a local newspaper. He understood and enjoyed his stepmother's enthusiasm while he saw with his own eyes she had changed his family with her enthusiasm. Therefore, he would live up to her.

The strength from his stepmother aroused Hill's imagination, inspired his creativity, helped him link with a lot of wisdom and made him a rich man and famous writer in the United States and one of most influential figures in the 20th century.

Praise will never be superfluous, especially for children. A sincere praise may be better than 10,000 severe reproaches.

改变一生的赞美

拿破仑·希尔小时候是一个公认的坏男孩。

他9岁时，父亲把继母娶进了家门。当时，他们还是居住在乡下的贫苦人家，继母则来自富有的家庭。

父亲一边向继母介绍拿破仑·希尔，一边说："亲爱的，希望你注意这个全郡最坏的男孩，他已经让我无可奈何。说不定不到明天早上，他就会拿石头扔向你，或者做出你完全想不到的坏事。"

出乎拿破仑·希尔意料的是，继母微笑着走到他面前，托起他的头认真地看着他。接着，她回头对丈夫说："你错了，他不是全郡最坏的男孩，而是全郡最聪明、最有创造力的男孩。只不过他还没有找到发泄热情的地方。"

继母的话说得拿破仑·希尔心里热乎乎的，眼泪几乎滚落下来。就是凭着这一句话，他和继母开始建立友谊。也就是这一句话，成为激励他一生的动力，使他日后创造了成功的28项黄金法则，帮助千千万万的普通人走上成功和致富的道路。

在继母到来之前，没有一个人称赞过他聪明，他的父亲和邻居认定他就是坏男孩。但是，继母只说了一句话，便改变了他一生的命运。

拿破仑·希尔14岁时，继母给他买了一部二手打字机，并对他说："相信你会成为一名作家。"拿破仑·希尔接受了继母的礼物，理解了她的期望，并开始向当地的一家报纸投稿。他了解继母的热忱，也很欣赏她的那股热忱，他亲眼看到她用自己的热忱改变了他们的家庭。所以，他不愿意辜负她。

来自继母的这股力量，激发了拿破仑·希尔的想象力，激励了他的创造力，帮助他获得了很多智慧，使他成了美国的富豪和著名作家，成了20世纪最有影响的人物之一。

赞美永远都不多余，尤其是对孩子。一次真诚的赞美，可能胜过一万次严厉的责备。

The Power of the Violin

At noon that day, I drove back to the villa. Just as I entered the living room, I heard a slight sound coming from the bedroom upstairs-it was the sound of my favorite violin.

"Thief!"

I dashed upstairs. Sure enough, as expected, a boy of about 12 years old was petting my violin. The boy had disheveled hair and a thin face, his unfitting coat bulging, seemingly stuffed with something. At first glance, I found a new pair of shoes at the bed missing. It seemed he was surely a thief.

Then, I saw his eyes full of fear and despair. My anger was immediately replaced by a smile, I asked, "Are you Mr. Ram's nephew Rubens? I'm his butler. Two days ago I heard Mr. Ram say he has a nephew living in the countryside to come. It must be you. You're really like him!"

On hearing my words, the boy was first stunned, but then quickly said, "Has my uncle gone out? I think I'd better first go out for a walk and visit him again in a while."

I nodded and asked the boy who was preparing to put down the violin, "Do you like to play the violin so much?"

"Yes, but I'm so poor that I can't afford it," the boy replied.

"Then, I give this violin to you." The boy looked at me questioningly, but he picked up the violin. Going out of the living room, he suddenly saw on the wall my huge color photo I performed in the Grand Theater of Sydney. He involuntarily shivered for a moment and ran out without looking back.

I was sure that the boy had understood what happened because no master would decorate the living room with the butler's photo.

A few years later, at a music competition of senior high school students in Melbourne, I was invited to judge the final. Finally, a violin player called Merritt won the first prize with his solid strength!

After the award, Merritt ran to me holding a violin box, his face crimson, asked, "Mr. Brian, do you still know me? You have given me a violin, which I have been treasuring, until today! Today, I can give back this violin to you without regret…"

It turned out that he was"Mr. Ram's nephew Rubens"!

Tears welled up in my eyes.

小提琴的力量

那天中午，我驾车回到了别墅。刚进客厅门，我就听见了楼上的卧室里有轻微的响声，是我最喜欢的那把小提琴发出的声音。

"有小偷！"

我一个箭步冲上楼，果然不出所料，只见一个大约12岁的少年正在那里抚摸我的小提琴。那个少年头发蓬乱，脸庞瘦削，不合身的外套鼓鼓囊囊，里面好像塞了某些东西。我一眼瞥见自己放在床头的一双新皮鞋失踪了，看来他是个小偷无疑。

这时，我看见他的眼里充满了惶恐和绝望。我愤怒的表情顿时被微笑所代替，我问道："你是拉姆先生的外甥鲁本吗？我是他的管家。前两天，我听拉姆先生说他有一个住在乡下的外甥要来，一定是你了，你和他长得真像啊！"

听见了我的话，少年先是一愣，但很快说道："我舅舅出门了吗？我想我还是先出去转转，待会儿再来看他吧。"

我点了点头，然后问那位正准备将小提琴放下的少年："你很喜欢拉小提琴吗？"

"是的，但我很穷，买不起。"少年回答说。

"那我把小提琴送给你吧。"少年疑惑地看了我一眼，但还是拿起了小提琴。临出客厅时，他突然看见了墙上挂着一张我在悉尼大剧院演出的巨幅彩照，不由得颤栗了一下，然后头也不回地跑远了。

我确信那位少年已明白了是怎么回事，因为没有哪位主人会用管家的照片来装饰客厅。

几年后，在墨尔本市高中生的一次音乐比赛中，我应邀担任决赛评委。最后，一名叫梅里特的小提琴选手凭借雄厚的实力夺得了第一名！

颁奖大会结束后，梅里特拿着一只小提琴盒跑到我面前，脸色绯红地问："布赖恩先生，您还认识我吗？您曾送过我一把小提琴，我一直珍藏着，直到有了今天！今天，我可以无愧地将这把小提琴还给您了……"

原来，他就是"拉姆先生的外甥鲁本"！

我的眼里涌起了泪花。

The Miracle of the Spring

When spring came to the city of Cleveland, Ohio, it did not change Gates Avenue. The people who lived on the pretty streets near Gates Avenue were making gardens, painting their houses and getting their lawn mowers ready for the summer. But Gates Avenue continued to look dirty and ugly.

Gates Avenue was a short street. But it seemed long because it was so ugly, most of the families who lived there had very little money. They never expected to have much more.

Sometimes the men had jobs and sometimes they didn't. Their houses had not been painted in many years and did not even have running water. The Gates Avenue families carried their water from the hydrants on the street corners.

The street itself was ugly, too. It had no pavement and no streetlight. The railway at one end of Gates Avenue added noise and dirt.

Most of the little girls in the school near Gates Avenue wore pretty new clothes that spring. But the little girl from Gates Avenue wore the same dirty dress that she had worn all winter. It was probably the only dress she owned.

Her teacher sighed. The little girl was so nice! She always worked hard in school; she was always polite and friendly. But her face was dirty and her hair was untidy.

One day the teacher said, "Will you wash your face before you come to school tomorrow morning? Please do that for me." The teacher could see that girl was pretty under the dirt.

The next morning the child's pretty face had been washed. Her hair was clean and tidy, too. Before the little girl went home that afternoon, the teacher said, "Now, dear, please ask your mother to wash your dress."

But the little girl continued to wear the dirty dress. "Her mother is probably not interested in her," the teacher thought. So she bought a bright blue dress and gave it to the little girl. The child took the present and hurried home as fast as she could.

The next morning she came to school in the new blue dress, and she was clean and tidy. She told the teacher, "My mother was surprised when she saw me this morning in my new dress. My father wasn't at home; he had gone to work. But he will see me at supper this evening."

When her father saw her in the new blue dress, he was surprised to find that he had a pretty little girl. When the family sat down to eat supper, he was even more surprised to find a cloth on the table. The family had never used a tablecloth before. "What is the cloth for?" he asked.

"We're going to be more tidy here," his wife said. "It isn't nice to have a house that dirty and untidy when our daughter is so clean."

After supper the mother started to wash the floors. Her husband watched for a little while without saying anything. Then he went outside into the backyard and began to repair the fence. The next evening, with the family's help, he started digging for a garden.

During the next week, the man who lived in the next house watched what the little girl's family was doing. Then he started to paint his house for the first time in ten years.

A few days later the young minister of a church near Gates Avenue passed the two houses and saw the men working. He noticed that there was no pavement on Gates Avenue and no streetlight. He knew the houses had no running water. "People who are trying so hard to have clean homes and tidy yards on a street like this should be helped," the minister said to himself.

He went to see the men who were at the head of the city government. And he went to see important businessmen and the leaders of the churches and schools. He asked them to help the families living on Gates Avenue.

A few months later Gates Avenue looked like a different street. There was pavement now on the avenue. There was a street light on the corner. The houses had running water. Six months after the little girl got her new blue dress, Gates Avenue was a tidy street of friendly homes where respectable families lived.

People who knew about the changes called it the"Gates Avenue Cleanup." Everywhere the young minister went, he told the story of this miracle.

Other cities heard of the"cleanup," and began to organize their own"cleanup" campaign. Since 1997, thousands of U's. towns and cities have organized campaigns for painting and repairing homes. For the people who live in the homes, life has been made better.

Who knows what miracles may happen when a teacher gives a little girl a new blue dress?

春天的奇迹

春天来到俄亥俄州克利夫兰市时，发现盖茨大道没有改变。住在盖茨大道附近那些漂亮街道上的人们正在建花园、刷房子，而且为夏天准备好了草坪锄草机。但盖茨大道看上去还是那样肮脏丑陋。

盖茨大道是一条短街。但它显得很长，因为它很丑陋，住在那里的大多数家庭都没多少钱。他们压根就没想赚更多的钱。

男人们有时有活做，有时则没有。他们的房子已经好多年没有油漆过了，甚至连自来水都没有。住在盖茨大道的家庭是从街角的水龙头上接水。

　　街道本身也很丑陋。既没有人行道，也没有街灯。盖茨大道一端的铁路增加了噪音和灰尘。

　　盖茨大道附近学校的大多数小学女生那年春天都穿着漂亮的新衣服。但来自盖茨大道的那个小女孩还是穿着她已经穿了一冬天的那件脏衣服。大概她只有这一件衣服吧。

　　她的老师叹了口气。小女孩长得非常漂亮！她在学校总是非常用功；她总是礼貌友好。但她的脸很脏，头发也不整洁。一天，老师说："明天早上你上学前把脸洗一下好吗？请为我洗一下。"老师能看出那女孩洗去灰尘是非常漂亮的。

　　第二天早上，小女孩的漂亮脸蛋果然已经洗了。她的头发既干净又整洁。那天下午，小女孩回家前，老师说："听着，宝贝，让你妈妈洗一下你的衣服。"

　　但小女孩还是穿着那件脏衣服。"她的妈妈可能对她不感兴趣吧。"老师心里说。于是，她买了一件鲜蓝色连衣裙，送给了小女孩。小女孩接住礼物，飞快地跑回了家。

　　第二天早上，她穿着新买的蓝色连衣裙来到了学校，而且打扮得干净整洁。她告诉老师说："今天早上，妈妈看到我穿上新买的蓝色连衣裙时，吃了一惊。爸爸不在家；他上班去了。但今天吃晚饭时他会看到我的。"

　　她的父亲看到女儿穿着新买的蓝色连衣裙，吃惊地发现小女儿是那样漂亮。当一家人坐下来吃晚饭时，他甚至更加吃惊地发现桌子上铺了一块桌布。一家人以前从来没有使用过桌布。"垫布做什么用？"他问。

　　"我们这里要比以前更加整洁，"他的妻子说。"当我们的女儿这样干净时，让我们的房子这样脏乱不好。"

　　饭后，小女孩的妈妈开始擦洗地板。她的丈夫看了一会儿，没说一句话。随后，他走出门，来到后院，开始修整篱笆。第二天傍晚，在一家人的帮助下，他开始挖建花园。在接下来的一个星期里，住在隔壁的那个人看到了小女孩一家人的行动。随后，他开始油漆房子，这是10年以来的第一次。

　　几天后，盖茨大道附近一座教堂的一名年轻牧师从两家的房边经过，看到两个男人在那里忙活着。他注意到盖茨大道上既没有人行道，也没有街灯。他知道房子里没有自来水。"街上像这样竭尽全力想拥有干净住宅和整洁院子的人应该得到帮助。"牧师自言自语说。

　　他去见市政府的那些头头们，随后又去见商界要人和教堂与学校的领导。他要他们帮助住在盖茨大道上的那些家庭。

又过了几个月，盖茨大道看上去像换了一条街。现在已经有了人行道，街角安上了路灯，房子里有了自来水。小女孩穿上她新买的蓝色连衣裙后的6个月，盖茨大道成了一条整洁的街道，那里的住户都友好相处，那里住着受人尊敬的家庭。

知道这些变化的人们称之"盖茨大道大清扫"。年轻牧师每到一处，都讲述这个神奇的故事。其他城市听说了这个故事，随后也开始组织起自己的"大清扫"运动。自1997年以来，几千座美国乡镇和城市都组织起了粉饰和修补住宅的活动。对住在家里的人来说，生活已经变得更好了。

当一名老师送给一个小女孩一身新连衣裙时，谁知道会发生什么奇迹呢？

Bright Heart

Last year around Halloween, I was invited to participate in a carnival for Tuesday's Child, an organization that helps children with the AIDS virus. I was asked to attend because I'm on a television show; I went because I care. I don't think that most of the kids recognize me as a celebrity. They just thought of me as a big kid who came to play with them for the day. I think I like it better that day.

At the carnival they had all kinds of booths. I was drawn to one in particular because of all the children that had gathered there. At this booth, anyone who wanted to could paint a square. Later that square was going to be sewn together with the others, to make a quilt. The quilt would be presented to a man who had dedicated his life to this organization and would soon be retiring.

They gave everyone fabric paints in colors and asked the kids to paint something that would make the quilt beautiful. As I looked around at all the squares, I saw pink hearts and bright blue clouds, beautiful orange sunrises, green leaves and purple flowers. The pictures were all bright, positive and uplifting. All except for one.

The boy sitting next to me was painting a heart, but it was dark, lifeless. It lacked the bright, vibrant colors that his fellow artists had used.

At first I thought maybe he took the only paint that was left and it just happened to be dark. But when I asked him about it, he said his heart was that color. I asked him why and he told me that he was very sick. Not only was he very sick, but his mom was very sick as well. He looked straight into my eyes and said, "There's nothing anyone can do that will help."

I told him I was sorry that he was sick and I could certainly understand why he was so sad. I could even understand why he had made his heart a dark color. But…I told him, "It isn't true that there is nothing anyone can do to help. Other people may not be able to make him or his mom better, but we can do things like giving a hug, which in my experience can really help when you are feeling sad." I told him that if he would like, I would be happy to give him one so he could see what I meant. He instantly crawled into my lap and I thought my own heart would burst with the love I felt for this sweet little boy.

He sat there for a long time and when he had had enough, he jumped down to finish his coloring. I asked him if he felt any better and he said that he did, but he was still sick and nothing would change that. I told him I understood. I walked away feeling sad, but recommitted to this cause. I would do whatever I could to help.

As the day was coming to an end and I was getting ready to head home, I felt a tug on my jacket. I turned around and standing there with a smile on his face was the little boy. He said, "My heart is changing colors. It's getting brighter…I think those hugs really do work."

On my way home I felt my own heart and realized it, too, had changed to a brighter color.

明 亮 的 心

去年万圣节前夕，我应邀参加了"星期二孩子"的狂欢节。"星期二孩子"是一个帮助感染艾滋病的儿童的组织。我应邀参加，是因为我主持电视节目；我赴约，是因为我关心。我想，大多数孩子不会把我当作名人，只会把我当作一个过来陪他们玩的大孩子。我想我更喜欢这样。

在狂欢节上，他们有各种各样的棚子。所有孩子都聚在一个棚子下面，我被吸引了过去。在这个棚子里，大家都画了一个棉蕾。随后，棉蕾要和别的棉蕾缝在一起，做成一条被子。这被子将送给一个将其一生奉献给这个组织的人，因为他马上就要退休。

他们把各色颜料发给每个孩子，让孩子们把被子画得漂亮一些。我围绕着所有的棉蕾看着，只见有粉红色的心、鲜蓝色的云、美丽的橘黄色旭日、翠绿的叶子和紫色的花朵。所有的图案都是那样鲜亮、积极、向上。只有一幅例外。

坐在我旁边的那个男孩正在画一个心形图案，但这颗心黑乎乎的，毫无生气，缺乏伙伴们使用的那些明亮活泼的色彩。

起初，我还以为他只是随便画画，碰巧画成了黑色。但当我问他时，他说他的心就是这种颜色。我问他为什么，他告诉我说他病得很重。不仅他病得很重，他妈妈病得也很重。他望着我的眼睛说："谁也无能为力。"

我告诉他说，我对他生病感到难过，当然能明白他为什么那样伤心，甚至能明白他为什么把心画成黑色。可是……我告诉他："谁也无能为力是不对的。其他人也许无法使他们母子康复，但我们可以做一些事，比如给一个拥抱，根据我的经验，你感到伤心时，这确实能有帮助。"我告诉他，如果他愿意，我很高兴拥抱他一下，这样他就能明白我的用心了。他马上爬到我的膝间。我想我自己的心为这个可爱的男孩而一下子充满了爱。

他在我的膝间坐了好一阵子。当他感到满足时，才跳下去，继续涂起了画。我问他是不是感觉好了些。他说是的，但他仍然有病，什么也改变不了。我告诉他说我明白。我离开时感到伤心，但会为这件事再做努力，尽自己所能来帮助他。

当一天快要结束我准备回家时，我感到有人在拽我的夹克。我回头一看，只见面带微笑站在那里的是那个小男孩。他说："我的心正在改变颜色，它会变得越来越亮……我想那些拥抱确实有用。"

回家的路上，我摸了摸自己的心，感到它也变得越来越亮了。

The Reason of Einstein's Success

At the age of 16, Einstein failed in several courses because he mixed with a group of mischievous kids. One weekend morning, Einstein held a fishing rod and was about to fish with those kids, his father stopped him and said to him calmly, "Einstein, you're so fond of playing all the day that you failed in the examination. I'm so worried about your future with your mother."

"What are you worrying about? Jack and Robert also failed, but don't they go fishing as usual?"

"My boy, you can't think so." Looking at Einstein, his father said lovingly, "There goes a fable in our hometown. I hope you can listen to it carefully.

"There were two cats playing on the roof. Once off guard, a cat fell into the chimney holding another one. When the two cats climbed out of the chimney, a cat's face was stained with the soot while the other's face was clean. Seeing the soot-faced cat, the clean cat thought its face was dirty and ugly, so it quickly ran to the riverside and washed its face. The soot-faced cat saw the clean-faced cat, thinking its face was also clean, so it swaggered in the street.

"Einstein, no one can be your mirror. Only you are your own mirror. Taking other people to be your mirror, even a genius may become a fool."

Hearing this, Einstein was ashamed to lay down his fishing rod and returned to his small room.

Since then, Einstein often took himself as a mirror to examine and reflect, and kept hinting himself: I was unique, so I needn't be as mediocre as others. This was why Einstein succeeded.

1,000 people have 1,000 kinds of lifestyles with 1,000 kinds of wishes in life. Different ways and wishes will produce different attitudes towards life. You can consult the other people's attitude to determine your own, but you can never follow others to do so.

You must see yourself clearly, and know you're your pursue is. Your future doesn't depend on how others do, but on how you are going to do.

爱因斯坦成功的原因

16岁那年，爱因斯坦整天同一群调皮贪玩的孩子在一起，几门功课都不及格。一个周末的早晨，爱因斯坦正拿着钓鱼竿准备和那群孩子一起去钓鱼，父亲拦住了他，心平气和地对他说："爱因斯坦，你整日贪玩，功课不及格，我和你的母亲很为你的前途担忧。"

"有什么可担忧的？杰克和罗伯特他们也没及格，不照样去钓鱼吗？"

"孩子，你千万不能这样想。"父亲充满关爱地望着爱因斯坦说。"在我们故乡流传着这样一个寓言，我希望你能认真听一听。

"有两只猫在屋顶上玩耍。一不小心，一只猫抱着另一只猫掉到了烟囱里。当两只猫从烟囱里爬出来时，一只猫的脸上沾满了黑烟，另一只猫的脸上却干干净净。干净猫看见满脸黑灰的猫，以为自己的脸也又脏又丑，便快步跑到河边洗了脸。而黑脸猫看见干净猫，以为自己的脸也是干净的，就大摇大摆地上街闲逛去了。

"爱因斯坦，谁也不能成为你的镜子，只有自己才是自己的镜子。拿别人当自己的镜子，天才也会照成傻瓜的。"

听后，爱因斯坦羞愧地放下鱼竿，回到了自己的小屋里。

从此，爱因斯坦时常拿自己作为镜子来审视和映照自己，并不断地自我暗示：我是独一无二的，我没有必要像别人一样平庸。这就是爱因斯坦成功的原因。

一千个人有一千种生活方式，有一千种生活的愿望。不同的方式和愿望，就会产生不同的生活态度。你可以参照别人的态度确定自己的态度，但你永远不能照着别人那样做。

你必须看清自己，并清楚自己想追求什么。你的未来如何，不取决于别人怎样做，而是取决于你自己怎样做。

If You Can See It，You Can Be It

Arnold Schwarzenegger was not that famous in 1976 when he met with a newspaper reporter.

The reporter asked Schwarzenegger, "Now you've retired from bodybuilding, what do you plan to do next?"

Schwarzenegger answered very calmly and confidently, "I'm going to be the No. 1 movie star in Hollywood."

The reporter was shocked and amused at Schwarzenegger's plan. At that time, it was very hard to imagine how this muscle-bound bodybuilder, who was not a professional actor and who spoke poor English with a strong American Austrian accent, could ever hope to be Hollywood's No. 1 movie star.

So the reporter asked Schwarzenegger how he planned to make his dream come true, Schwarzenegger said, "I'll do it the same way I became the No. 1 bodybuilder in the world. What I do is to create a vision of whom I want to be, then I start living like that person in my mind as if it were already true." Sounds almost childishly simple, doesn't it? But it worked! Schwarzenegger did become the No. 1 highest-paid movie star in Hollywood!

Remember: "If you can see it, you can be it."

你能看到，就能做到

阿诺德·施瓦辛格在1976年还不是那样有名时遇到一位新闻记者。

记者问施瓦辛格："你现在从健美运动中退出，下一步打算做什么？"

施瓦辛格非常平静而自信地回答说："我打算成为好莱坞头号电影明星。"

记者听到施瓦辛格的打算，感到既震惊又可笑。当时，很难想象这位肌肉结实的健美运动员既不是职业演员，英语说得又差劲，还带有很重的奥地利口音，怎么可能有希望成为好莱坞头号电影明星呢？

当记者问施瓦辛格如何打算梦想成真时，施瓦辛格说："我会像当初成为世界头号健美运动员那样去做。我要做的就是创造一个自己想做的那个人的形象，然后像我心里想的那个人那样开始生活。"听起来是不是幼稚简单？但发挥了作用！施瓦辛格真的成了好莱坞收入最高的电影明星！

记住："你能看到，就能做到。"

Dig Three Feet Deeper

There's a story about the California gold rush that tells of two brothers who sold all they had and went prospecting for gold. They discovered a vein of the shining ore, staked a claim, and proceeded to get down to the serious business of getting the gold ore out of the mine. All went well at first, but then a strange thing happened. The vein of the gold ore disappeared! They had come to the end of the rainbow, and the pot of gold was no longer there. The brothers continued to pick away, but without success. Finally they gave up in disgust.

They sold their equipment and claim rights for a few hundred dollars, and took the train back home. Now the man who bought the claim hired an engineer to examine the rock strata of the mine. The engineer advised him to continue digging in the same spot where the former owners had left off. And three feet deeper, the new owner struck gold.

A little more persistence and the two brothers would have been millionaires themselves.

That's gold in you too. Do you need to dig three feet farther?

再挖三英尺

有个故事讲的是加州淘金潮时，有两个兄弟卖掉了他们所有的家产去加州淘金。他们发现了一个金光闪闪的矿脉，于是买下了这个矿藏的开采权，一定要把矿藏中的金子挖出来卖钱。开始进展得很顺利，但后来发生了一件奇怪的事情。金矿脉突然消失了！他们的幻想破灭了，金矿不在了！兄弟俩开始继续挖着，但仍然没有发现矿脉。最后，他们气急败坏地放弃了。

他们以几百美元的价格卖掉了自己的设备和开采权，然后坐着火车回到了家乡。现在，那个买了他们的金矿开采权的人雇了一个工程师去勘查了这个金矿的岩层结构。这个工程师建议他继续在那两个兄弟上次挖到的地方挖下去。于是又挖了三英尺后，这个人发现了金子。

如果那兄弟俩再多一点点坚持的话，也许现在已经是百万富翁了。

你本身也藏有金矿，你需要再多挖三英尺吗？

第六卷

予人玫瑰，手留余香

We All Can Become Angels

When I was a middle school student, a memorable thing occurred.

It was a Friday. On the way home from school I saw a classmate called Kyle, who carried a thick pile of books in his arms. I thought, "Why does he carry all the books home? He must be a bookworm."

Kyle was just transferred to our class. I shrugged and went on walking, when I suddenly saw a large group of children deliberately knocked down the books in his hands, and even some of them tripping Kyle, he immediately fell to the ground.

His glasses flying off, Kyle raised his head. I read the painful expression from his eyes and felt my heart tightened, so I ran to him. He was groping for his glasses on the ground. I handed his glasses to his hands. He thanked me with a smile on his face, which was the smile of gratitude from the bottom of his heart.

I learned where we lived was not far away from each other. So we returned home together. As I thought he was not bad and asked whether he took interest in playing soccer together on Saturday, he accepted.

Throughout the weekend we all mixed together and he made a very good impression on my friends and me.

It was Monday again. On the way to school, I once more saw Kyle carrying a pile of books in his arms.

Since then Kyle and I became best friends.

Years later, Kyle specially invited me to attend his graduation. In his speech, he said, "The graduation is the best moment to express his gratitude for those who have helped us. I would like to take this opportunity to thank my best friend."

Then, he began to talk about the story we had known each other. I was surprised to widen my eyes. Until the day I knew: that weekend many years ago, he had intended to commit suicide! He said he had carried all his books home, so that after his death his mother wouldn't have to specially go to the school to arranging his things left behind. Having said that, he looked at me sitting in the audience with a smile on his face and went on, "However, I was so lucky that my friend pulled me back from the brink of death."

At that moment, I truly understood what he said, "Never underestimate the power your behavior can produce, for your little action may change the fate of another person. Heaven makes each of us face and influence another life in some way."

Some people love to illuminate the lives of others with their own happiness and love. It is always worthwhile to do so. When we break our wings and can't fly, the friends around us are the angels who embrace us in their arms.

我们都能成为天使

我还是一名中学生时，发生了一件难忘的小事。

那是一个星期五，我在放学回家的路上看到了一个名叫凯尔的同学，他怀里抱着一摞厚厚的书。我想："为什么要把所有书都带回家呢？他一定是个书呆子。"

凯尔刚转到我们班上。我耸耸肩继续往前走。这时，我突然看到，一大帮孩子故意把他手中的书打翻在地，还有人在凯尔脚下使了个绊儿，他随即倒地。

凯尔的眼镜飞了出去，他抬起头看了看，我从他眼中读出了痛苦的神情，我的心随之一紧，然后朝他跑去。他趴在地上摸索着找眼镜。我把眼镜递到了他手上。他向我道谢，脸上浮现出了笑容，那是发自肺腑的感激的笑容。

我得知，原来我们住的地方相距不远。于是，我们结伴回了家。我觉得他这个人还不错，就问他是否有兴趣周六一起去踢球，他欣然同意了。

整个周末，我们都混在一起，他给我和我的朋友们留下了非常好的印象。

周一又到了，上学路上，我又看到了怀抱一摞书的凯尔。

此后，我和凯尔成了最好的朋友。

多年后，凯尔特别邀请我去参加他的大学毕业典礼。他在致辞中说："毕业典礼是对帮助过我们的人表达谢意的最好时刻。我要借这个机会，感谢我最好的朋友。"

接着，他开始讲我们认识的故事，我惊讶得睁大了眼睛。直到那天我才知道：多年前的那个周末，他原来是打算自杀的！他说自己把所有的书都抱回了家，这样，妈妈在他死后就不必特意去学校整理他的遗物。说到这里，他看着坐在台下的我，脸上展现出了笑容，他接着说："然而，我很幸运，是我的朋友把我从死亡的边缘拉了回来。"

那一刻，我才真正理解了他的话："永远不要低估你的行为能够产生的力量，你一个小小的举动就可能改变另一个人的命运。上天让我们每个人都要面对另一个生命，让我们以某种方式去影响另一个生命。"

有人乐于用自己的快乐和爱心去照亮他人的生活，这样做永远都是值得的。当我们的翅膀折断、无力飞翔时，身边的朋友就是把我们拥入怀中的天使。

The Boy and the Huge Rock

This story happened in a small village. One day there was an earthquake. Nothing was destroyed and no one was hurt. But a huge rock fell from a nearby mountain and stopped in the middle of the road.

When the earthquake stopped, many people came to the road and saw the huge rock. Some of the strongest men tried to lift the rock out of the road. But they couldn't move it. They tried to push in but failed. They tried to pull it with ropes but nothing worked.

"Well," they all agreed, "There's nothing we can do about it. We'll have to change the road."

At this time a boy about 12 years old said, "I think I can help you to move the rock."

"You?" they shouted. "What are you talking about?" The men all laughed at the boy.

The next morning some people came into the street. One of them shouted, "The rock is gone!" More people ran out to see. It was true. The rock wasn't in the road any more. It wasn't even near the road.

"This is impossible," they said. "Where did it go?"

The boy stood in the street, smiling, "I told you I could move it last night."

The boy walked over to where the rock had been and uncovered some dirt with shovel. "I buried it," he said.

The people looked surprised.

"You see," he said, "I dug a deep hole next to the rock and I dug a small incline up to the rock and the rock rolled down into the hole by itself. I covered it with dirt."

The crowds shouted, "Clever boy! Clever boy!"

And some of them said, "Why haven't we thought of this good method?"

男孩和巨石

这个故事发生在一个小村里。有一天发生了地震。什么东西也没有遭到破坏，也没有人员受到伤害。但一块巨石从附近的山上滚落下来，挡在了路中央。

当地震停止时，许多人来到路边，看到了这块巨石。有几个最身强力壮的人想设法把石头从路上搬开。但他们怎么也搬不动。他们设法向里推，无济于事。他们用绳子用力拉，也不起一点作用。

"唉，"他们都异口同声地说。"我们对此无能为力了。我们必须得改路了。"

这时，一个大约12岁的男孩说："我想我可以帮你们把石头移走。"

"你？"他们齐声喊道。"你在说什么呀？"他们都嘲笑起这个男孩。

第二天早上，有人来到街上。其中一个人大声叫道："巨石不见了！"越来越多的人跑出来看。石头果真不见了。路上也不见了石头，甚至也不在路边。

"这不可能，"他们说。"石头到哪里去了呢？"

那个男孩站在路中央，微微笑道："昨天晚上我就告诉你们我能移动石头。"

男孩走到巨石原来所在的地方，用铁铲掀起一些土。"我把它埋在了这里。"他说。

人们露出了惊讶的表情。

"你们明白，"他说。"我贴近巨石边挖了一个深坑，又在岩石上方挖了一道小斜坡，岩石自动就滚进了坑里。然后，我用土盖住了它。"

人们大声喊叫起来："聪明孩子！聪明孩子！"

随后，有些人说："为什么我们没有想到这个好方法呢？"

A Coin Can Also Make You Succeed

Two young men hunted for jobs together, one Englishman, the other Jew.

A coin lay on the ground. The English young man went on without looking but the Jewish young man picked it up excitedly.

The English young man scorned the Jewish young man, thinking: what a good-for-nothing, even picking up a coin!

Watching the English young man from behind, the Jewish young man sighed with emotion in his heart, what a good-for-nothing, letting the money slip away from him!

The two men walked into a company at the same time. The company was so small that any employee had to work hard at a low salary, but the English young man was pleased to stay.

Two years later, the two men met on the street, when the Jewish young man had become a boss but the British young man was still looking for a job. The English young man was puzzled and said, "You were so unpromising, how can you get rich so quickly?"

The Jewish young man said, "Because I didn't stride over one coin like a gentleman as you. You even didn't want a coin, so how will you make a fortune?"

The English young man did want money, but what he was staring at the pound instead of the penny, so his money was always in future. It was the answer to the question.

一枚硬币也能成功

两个年轻人一同寻找工作，一个是英国人，一个是犹太人。

一枚硬币躺在地上，英国青年看也不看就走了过去，犹太青年却激动地将它捡起。

英国青年对犹太青年的举动露出鄙夷之色：一枚硬币也捡，真没出息！

犹太青年望着远去的英国青年心生感慨：让钱白白从身边溜走，真没出息！

两个人同时走进一家公司。公司很小，工作很累，工资也低，英国青年不屑一顾地走了，犹太青年却高兴地留了下来。

两年后，两人在街上相遇，犹太青年已成了老板，英国青年还在寻找工作。英国青年对此不可理解，说："你这么没出息的人怎么能这么快地发了呢？"

犹太青年说："因为我没有像你那样绅士般从一枚硬币上迈过去。你连一枚硬币都不要，怎么会发大财呢？"

英国青年并非不要钱，可他眼睛盯着的是大钱而不是小钱，所以他的钱总在明天。这就是问题的答案。

A Real One Who Panned the Gold

Two Mexicans went along the Mississippi for panning. When they came to a mouth of the river, they parted because one thought he could pan more gold in the Arkansas and the other thought he would have a greater chance in the Ohio River.

Ten years later, the man who went to the Ohio River really made a fortune. There he not only found a lot of gold sand but also built the docks and roads while he made the place where he stayed a large market town. Now the business prosperity and industrial development of Pittsburgh along the Ohio River are thanks to all his pioneering and early development.

The man who went to the Arkansas seemed not to be so lucky, for there was no news about him since they parted. Some said he had gone to Davy Jones' locker and some said he had returned to Mexico. Until 50 years later a nugget of 2.7 kilograms caused a stir in Pittsburgh, so people had come to know about him. At that time, a reporter of Pittsburgh Newsweek wrote, "The largest nugget in U. S. A. came from Arkansas. A young man in the fish pound behind his house picked it up. From the diaries his grandfather left, this nugget was thrown into the pound by his grandfather.

Afterwards, the"Newsweek" published the grandfather's diaries, one of which wrote: Yesterday, I again found a piece of gold in the stream, greater than the piece of gold panned last year. Will I go into the city to sell it? Then there will be hundreds of people swarming here. The log shed my wife and I built with our own hands, the garden and the pond behind the house we opened up sweating all over, along with the campfire at nightfall, the loyal hound, the delicious stewed meat, the chickadees, the trees, the sky, the grassland as well as the precious peace and freedom will no longer exist. I would rather see the spray when it is thrown into the pound than just sit watching all these disappear from my eyes.

The 1760s were the age that the United States began to create millionaires, so everyone was in a frenzied pursuit of money. But this gold miner threw away the panned gold. A lot of people thought it an incredible story. Until now some people still doubt its authenticity. However, I always believe it is true because in my mind this gold miner was a real one who panned the gold.

真正的淘金人

两个墨西哥人沿密西西比河淘金，到了一个河汊分了手，因为一个人认为阿肯色河可以淘到更多的金子，一个人认为去俄亥俄河发财的机会更大。

10年后，进入俄亥俄河的人果然发了财，他在那里不仅找到了大量的金沙，而且建了码头，修了公路，还使他落脚的地方成了一个大集镇。现在，俄亥俄河岸边的匹兹堡市商业繁荣、工业发达，起因无不和他的拓荒与早期开发有关。

进入阿肯色河的人似乎没有那么幸运，自分手后就没了音信。有的说已经葬身鱼腹，有的说已经回了墨西哥。直到50年后，一个重2.7千克的自然金块在匹兹堡引起轰动，人们才知道他的一些情况。当时，匹兹堡《新闻周刊》的一位记者写道："这颗全美最大的金块来源于阿肯色，是一位年轻人在他屋后的鱼塘里捡到的，从他祖父留下的日记看，这块金子是他的祖父扔进去的。

随后，《新闻周刊》刊登了那位祖父的日记。其中一篇是这样的：昨天，我在溪水里又发现了一块金子，比去年淘到的那块更大，进城卖掉它吗？那就会有成百上千的人涌向这里，我和妻子亲手用一根根圆木搭建的棚屋，挥洒汗水开垦的菜园和屋后的池塘，还有傍晚的火堆、忠诚的猎狗、美味的炖肉、山雀、树木、天空、草原、大自然赠给我们的珍贵的静谧和自由都将不复存在。我宁愿看到它被扔进鱼塘时荡起的水花，也不愿眼睁睁地望着这一切从我眼前消失。

18世纪60年代正是美国开始创造百万富翁的年代，每个人都在疯狂地追求金钱。可是，这位淘金者把淘到的金子扔掉了。有很多人认为这是天方夜谭，直到现在还有人怀疑它的真实性。可是，我始终认为它是真的，因为在我的心中，这位淘金者是一位真正淘到金子的人。

The Seeds of Hope

One year, a newspaper of the United States published an announcement the horticultural institute offered a reward at a high price for the pure white marigold. The high reward attracted so many people, but in the kaleidoscopic nature, besides golden, the marigold is brown, but it is not easy to cultivate3 the white one. So after they were excited for a time, many people had forgotten the announcement.

20 years flew away. One normal day after 20 years, the horticultural institute that had published the announcement accidentally received a zealous letter and 100 seeds of pure white marigold. On that day the news spread like wildfire.

It turned out to be an old woman of over 70 years old. The institute had always been hesitating over the fact that the letter asserted with certainty that the seeds could bloom pure white marigold, and the need for verification became the focus of the debate. Whether they would make an experimental verification became the focus of controversy at one time.

Some said you would never live up to the old man's wish. Those seeds finally took root in the earth. The miracle appeared after one year: large patches of pure white marigold swayed in the breeze. Accordingly, the old woman who was always unknown to the public became a new focus.

Originally, the old woman was an out-and-out flower-lover. When she occasionally read the announcement 20 years ago, her heart kept thumping. But her eight children unanimously opposed her decision. After all, a woman who never knew the seed genetics couldn't complete what the experts could never accomplish, so her thought was only a lunatic raving!

Still, the old woman didn't change her mind and went on working without hesitation. She scattered some of the most common seeds and took good care of them. A year later, when the marigold bloomed, she chose one faintest from those golden and brown flowers and made it wither naturally in order to get the best seed. The next year, she again grew them and chose the faintest from these flowers to plant…day after day, year after year, through many cycles of spring sowing and autumn harvest, the old woman's husband died, her children flew far and high, a lot of things happened in her life, but only the desire to grow the pure white marigold took root in her heart.

Finally, after 20 years on the day we all know, in the garden she saw a marigold, which was not nearly white, but as white as silver or snow.

A problem even experts couldn't cope with was readily solved by an old woman who didn't understand genetics. Wasn't it a miracle? To take root in the heart, even the most common seed, can grow into a miracle!

希望的种子

当年，美国一家报纸曾刊登了一则园艺所重金悬赏征求纯白金盏花的启事。高额赏金让许多人趋之若鹜，但在千姿百态的自然界中，金盏花除了金色的，就是棕色的，能培植出白色的并非易事。所以，激动了一阵后，许多人就把那则启事抛到了九霄云外。

一晃20年过去了。20年后很平常的一天，当年那家曾刊登启事的园艺所意外地收到了一封热情的应征信和100粒"纯白金盏花"的种子。当天，这件事不胫而走。

寄种子的是一位年已古稀的老人。对信中言之凿凿能开出纯白金盏花的种子，园艺所一直举棋不定，该不该验证一时成了争论的焦点。

有人说：绝不应该辜负了一位老人的心意。那些种子终于落土生根。奇迹是在一年之后才出现的，大片大片纯白色的金盏花在微风中摇曳。一直默默无闻的老人因此成了新的焦点。

原来，老人是一个地地道道的爱花人。当她20年前偶然看到那则启事后，便怦然心动。她的决定却遭到了8个儿女的一致反对。毕竟，一个压根就不懂种子遗传学的人，一件让专家都不能完成的事，她的想法岂不是痴人说梦！

老人还是痴心不改，义无反顾地干了下去。她撒下了一些最普通的种子，精心侍弄。一年后，金盏花开了，她从那些金色的、棕色的花中挑选了一朵颜色最淡的，任其自然枯萎，以取得最好的种子。次年，她又把它们种下去，然后再从这些花中挑选出颜色最淡的花的种子栽种……日复一日，年复一年，春种秋收，周而复始，老人的丈夫去世了，儿女远走了，生活中发生了很多事情，唯有种出白色金盏花的愿望在她的心中生了根。

终于，在我们今天都知道的那个20年后的一天，她在那片花园中看到一朵金盏花，它不是近乎白色，而是如银如雪的白。

一个连专家都解决不了的问题，在一位不懂遗传学的老人手中迎刃而解，这不是奇迹吗？种在心里，即使一粒最普通的种子，也能长出奇迹！

The Secret of Success

A wise man was asked, "How can we succeed, please？"

The wise man smiled and handed him a peanut. "Pinch it forcibly."

The man pinched the peanut so hard that its shell broke, with only a kernel left.

"Rub it further," said the wise man.

The man did it as he was told. The red seed capsule was rubbed off, only leaving the white fruit.

"Pinch it again with your hands," said the wise man.

The man pinched it so hard, but he couldn't ruin it anyway.

"Rub it again with your hands," the wise man said.

Of course, nothing was rubbed off.

"Despite repeated setbacks, it has a strong and indomitable heart;it is the secret to success," said the wise man.

成功的秘密

有人问一位智者："请问，怎样才能成功呢？"

智者笑笑，递给他一颗花生。"用力捏捏它。"

那人用力一捏，花生壳碎了，只留下花生仁。

"再搓搓它。"智者说。

那人又照着做了，红色的种皮被搓掉了，只留下白白的果实。

"再用手捏它。"智者说。

那人用力捏着，却怎么也没法把它毁坏。

"再用手搓搓它。"智者说。

当然，什么也搓不下来了。

"虽然屡遭挫折，却有一颗坚强的百折不挠的心，这就是成功的秘密。"智者说。

Reaching the Summit

Whenever the sun dropped and the blue sky came up, my father and I used to climb the mountain near my house. Walking together, my father and I used to have a lot of conversations through which I learned lessons from his experiences. He always stressed to me, "You should have objectives and capacity like the mountain."

This has largely influenced my life. If we didn't enjoy mountain climbing, we couldn't have had enough time to spend together because my father was very busy. I believe mountaineering is really beneficial. It gave me time to talk with my father and to be in deep contemplation as well as develop my patience. I loved scaling mountains to get away from the noise and pollution of the city and breathe the fresh air.

One time we climbed a very high mountain. It was so challenging for me because I was only ten years old. During the first few hours of climbing, I enjoyed the fresh air, the birds' singing, and the beautiful dances of butterflies;but as time passed, I got a pain in both of my legs. At that moment, I wanted to quit climbing. Actually, I hated it at that moment, but my father said to me, "Spring is a season when everything comes to life again. The mountain and fields where we're standing are embroidered with flowers and trees. You can always see a beautiful sky at the top of the mountain, but you can't see it before you reach the top. You can always enjoy the scenes of many waterfalls and countless peaks and valleys at the top of the mountain, but you can't when you are halfway up. Only there at the top can you embrace all of those things, just like in life."

At that time, I was too young to understand his thoughts, but after that, I got new hope and confidence. Finally, I found myself standing at the top of the mountain. And there, I could see the whole of the sky, which was as clear as crystal.

攀 登 峰 顶

每当夕阳西下、天空湛蓝时，我和父亲常常去爬我家附近的那座山。我和父亲爬山时，总会有好多话题；通过交谈，我从父亲的经历中学到了很多东西。他总是对我强调："你应该像大山一样有目标和气量。"

这已经在很大程度上影响了我的人生。要不是我们俩都喜欢爬山，不可能有那么多时间在一起，因为父亲很忙。我相信登山确实有益。它给了我与父亲交谈的时间，并让我能够沉思和培养耐心。我爱登山，以便远离城市的噪音和污染，呼吸新鲜的空气。

有一次，我们去爬一座很高的山。对我来说，那真是一个挑战，因为那时我只有10岁。在爬山的最初几个小时，我享受到了清新的空气、小鸟的歌唱和蝴蝶的美丽舞姿。但随着时间过去，我的双腿开始酸痛。此刻，我想放弃爬山。实际上，我此刻讨厌爬山，但父亲对我说："春天是万物复苏的季节。我们脚下的山和田野都长满了花草树木。你在山顶总能看到美丽的天空，但到达山顶前，你无法看到。你在山顶总能欣赏到许多瀑布，看到无数的山峰和山谷，但你在半山腰无法看到。就像生活一样，只有到达峰顶，你才能拥抱所有那一切。"

那时，我还太小，无法理解他的想法，但那以后，我获得了新的希望和信心。最后，我登上了山顶。在那里，我可以看到像水晶般透明的整个天空。

A Bag of Seeds

Ford as Motor Magnate was not a closehanded man, but he rarely donated. He stubbornly believed that the value of money was not its amount but how to use. What worried him most was that the people who weren't good at using them often used the donations. Once, Schoolmaster Marsha Betty of Georgia came to ask Ford for donations, but he refused her.

She said, "So please donate me a bag of peanut seeds." Upon that, Ford bought her a bag of peanut seeds. Ford later forgot it. Unexpectedly, a year later, Ms. Betty visited him and handed him 600 dollars. It turned out that her students planted the bag of peanut seeds, and this was the harvest of one year. Ford said nothing, but took out six million dollars and handed it to Betty.

What Ford was worried about was not unnecessary because if the money is easy to get, the people who get it are hard to feel the hardship and wisdom hidden behind the money. I more appreciate Betty's highest respect for a little bit favor. What she led the children to sow was virtually enough to prove that they had the qualification to receive the benefaction from others.

一 袋 种 子

汽车大王福特不是一个吝啬的人，但他很少捐款。他顽固地认为，金钱的价值并不在于多寡，而在于使用方法。他最担心的就是捐款经常会落到不善于运用它们的人手里。有一次，佐治亚州的玛莎·贝蒂校长为了扩建学校来请求福特捐款，福特拒绝了她。

她说："那么就请捐给我一袋花生种子吧。"于是，福特买了一袋花生种子送给了她。福特后来就忘了这件事。没想到一年后，贝蒂女士又是上门了，交给了他600美元。原来，学生们播种了当初的那袋花生种子，这就是一年的收获。福特什么都没说，立即拿出了600万美元交给了贝蒂。

福特的担心绝不是多余的，太轻易得来的金钱往往很难让受施者感受到金钱后面潜藏着的苦与智。我更赞赏贝蒂对点滴施与的至高尊重，她带领孩子们撒播下的其实足以证明他们有领受他人恩惠的资格。

The Sound of Waterfalls

A young man who reveled in painting and calligraphy wanted to acknowledge a great artist as teacher, so with the painting he completed with one whole year he went to see the artist. The artist looked at it and gently shook his head. "Not bad. But you couldn't have drawn the sound of waterfalls!"

A year later, the young man again begged for an audience offering the better waterfall painting who flattered himself to the artist. The artist shook his head again. "What a pity. You did the same!"

Another year later, so confidently, the young man again requested an interview holding the smugly perfect waterfall painting to the artist. The artist shook his head again. "Young man, you did just the same!"

The young man felt perplexed and said, "Master, as your pupil I don't see light. Please point me out a pathway!"

The artist picked up a paintbrush, drew on the young man's painting, on which standing across the shores of the pool under the waterfalls were two people, one of whom was shouting with his hands cupping his mouth while the other one was all ears. The young man came to get over how to paint the sound of the waterfalls.

瀑布的声音

一位酷爱书画的年轻人想拜在书画大师门下。于是，他带着自己花费了整整一年时间才画成的一幅画去求见大师。大师看了看，轻轻地摇了摇头，说："还好，只是没能画出瀑布的声音！"

一年后，年轻人再次求见大师，将一幅自以为更好的瀑布画捧给大师。大师看了看，又摇了摇头说："遗憾，还是没能画出瀑布的声音！"

又过了一年，年轻人颇有信心地再次求见大师，将一幅自以为完美无缺的瀑布捧给大师。大师再次摇了摇头说："年轻人，你还是没能画出瀑布的声音！"

年轻人感到困惑，说："大师，晚辈确实不能悟出其中道理，求您明示！"

大师提起画笔，在年轻人的画上作起了画。他在瀑布下水潭的岸上画上两个相对而站的人，其中一个正双手拢在嘴边大声喊，另一个正伸着耳朵仔细听。年轻人终于明白怎样才能画出瀑布的声音了。

Christmas Morning

A light drizzle was falling as my sister Jill and I ran out of the Methodist Church, eager to get home and play with the presents that Santa had left for us and our baby sister, Sharon. Across the street from the church was a Pan-American gas station where the Greyhound bus stopped. It was closed for Christmas, but I noticed a family standing outside the locked door, huddled under the narrow overhang in an attempt to keep dry. I wondered briefly why they were there but then forgot about them as I raced to keep up with Jill.

Once we got home, there was barely time to enjoy our presents. We had to go off to our grandparents' house for our annual Christmas dinner. As we drove down the highway through town, I noticed that the family was still there, standing outside the closed gas station.

My father was driving very slowly down the highway. The closer we got to the turnoff for my grandparents' house, the slower the car went. Suddenly, my father U-turned in the middle of the road and said, "I can't stand it!"

"What?" asked my mother.

"It's those people back there at the Pan-Am, standing in the rain. They've got children. It's Christmas. I can't stand it."

When my father pulled into the service station, I saw that there were five of them: the parents and three children—two girls and a small boy.

My father rolled down his window. "Merry Christmas," he said.

"Howdy," the man replied. He was very tall and had to stoop slightly to peer into the car.

Jill, Sharon, and I stared at the children, and they stared back at us.

"You waiting on the bus?" my father asked.

The man said that they were. They were going to Birmingham, where he had a brother and prospects of a job.

"Well, that bus isn't going to come along for several hours, and you're getting wet standing here. Winborn's just a couple miles up the road. They've got a shed with a cover there, and some benches," my father said. "Why don't y'all get in the car and I'll run you up there."

The man thought about it for a moment, and then he beckoned to his family. They climbed into the car. They had no luggage, only the clothes they were wearing.

Once they settled in, my father looked back over his shoulder and asked the children if Santa had found them yet. Three glum faces mutely gave him his answer.

"Well, I didn't think so," my father said, winking at my mother, "because when I saw Santa this morning, he told me that he was having trouble finding all, and he asked me if he could leave your toys at my house. We'll just go get them before I take you to the bus stop."

All at once, the three children's faces lit up, and they began to bounce around in the back seat, laughing and chattering.

When we got out of the car at our house, the three children ran through the front door and straight to the toys that were spread out under our Christmas tree. One of the girls spied Jill's doll and immediately hugged it to her breast. I remember that the little boy grabbed Sharon's ball. And the other girl picked up something of mine. All this happened a long time ago, but the memory of it remains clear. That was the Christmas when my sisters and I learned the joy of making others happy.

My mother noticed that the middle child was wearing a short-sleeved dress, so she gave the girl Jill's only sweater to wear. My father invited them to join us at our grandparents' for Christmas dinner, but the parents refused. Even when we all tried to talk them into coming, they were firm in their decision. Back in the car, on the way to Winborn, my father asked the man if he had money for bus fare. His brother had sent tickets, the man said.

My father reached into his pocket and pulled out two dollars, which was all he had left until his next payday. He pressed the money into the man's hand. The man tried to give it back, but my father insisted. "It'll be late when you get to Birmingham, and these children will be hungry before then. Take it. I've been broke before, and I know what it's like when you can't feed your family."

We left them there at the bus stop in Winborn. As we drove away, I watched out the window as long as I could, looking back at the little girl hugging her new doll.

圣诞节的早晨

细雨霏霏，我和姐姐吉尔跑出了卫理公会教堂，渴望回家玩圣诞老人留给我们和小妹妹莎伦的礼物玩具。教堂对面是一家泛美加油站，灰狗长途汽车会在那里中途停站。因为是圣诞节，加油站没开，但我注意到一家人站在那扇紧锁的门外，他们挤在狭小的挑檐下，想尽量不让雨淋湿。我一时间不知道他们为什么站在那里，但当我飞奔着去赶吉尔时，就把他们忘到了脑后。

我们一回到家，几乎没有时间去享受礼物了。我们必须得去爷爷奶奶家吃一年一度的圣诞大餐。我们驱车经过刚才那条公路时，我注意到那家人仍站在加油站紧闭的门外。

爸爸的车在公路上开得很慢。越接近去爷爷奶奶家的岔道，车子就越慢。突然，爸爸在途中来了个反向转弯，说："我真不忍心！"

"什么？"妈妈问道。

"就是那些雨中站在泛美加油站那里的人。他们带着小孩。都圣诞节了。我真不忍心啊。"

爸爸把车开到油站，我看见那一家有五个人：父母亲和三个孩子——两个女孩和一个小男孩。

爸爸摇下车窗，说："圣诞快乐！"

"你好。"那人答道。他长得很高，必须得稍微弯下腰，才能朝我们车里看。

我和吉尔、莎伦盯着那几个孩子，他们也盯着我们。"你们在等汽车吗？"爸爸问道。男人回答说是，他们准备去伯明翰，他有个哥哥在那里，而且期望能找到一份工作。

"噢，汽车好几个小时都来不了，站在这里你们会淋湿的。向前两三英里就是温邦站，那里有个棚屋，还有一些长凳，"爸爸说，"你们何不都上车，我送你们到那里。"

男人想了一会儿，然后向他的家人招手。他们钻进车里。他们没有任何行李，只有身上穿着的衣服。他们一坐好，爸爸就转过头问那几个孩子，圣诞老人是否找到了他们。三张闷闷不乐的脸给了他无声的回答。

"噢，我想不是这样，"爸爸向妈妈眨了眨眼说，"因为早上我看到圣诞老人时，他对我说他很难找到所有的人，然后他问我是否能把给你们的玩具放到我的房里。我们这就就去拿礼物，然后我再送你们去车站。"

三个孩子顿时神采奕奕，开始在后排座位又蹦又跳、有说有笑。

到了我们家，我们钻出车子，那三个孩子跑过前门，直奔摆在圣诞树下的那些玩具。其中一个女孩发现了吉尔的洋娃娃，马上把它抱在了胸前。我记得那个小男孩飞快地抓起莎伦的球，另一个女孩拿起了一件我的东西。这些都是很久以前的事了，回忆起来却仍是如此清晰。我和姐妹们正是在那个圣诞节领会到让别人快乐而得到的喜悦。

妈妈注意到他们家的老二穿着短袖裙，就把吉尔仅有的毛线衣送给了她穿。爸爸邀请他们跟我们一起去爷爷奶奶家吃圣诞大餐，但他们夫妇谢绝了。回到车里，在去温邦的路上，爸爸问那男人是否有钱买车票。那人说他的哥哥已经寄来了车票。

爸爸将手伸进口袋，掏出仅剩下的两美元，那本来是我们要熬到下次发工资那天的。他把钱塞进了那人手里。那人想尽力把钱推回来，但爸爸坚持让他收下。"你们到伯明翰时间会很晚，这些孩子不到那时就会饿的。收下吧。我以前也曾身无分文，我知道让家人吃不饱是什么滋味。"

我们把他们送到了温邦公共汽车站。我们驱车离开时，我从车窗回望了很久，回望着那个抱着新洋娃娃的小女孩。

The Boy and a Drop of Dew

One morning, a small boy was squatting motionless on the grass in the garden for a long time.

His mother felt so odd that she walked close to see what had happened. The boy, in earnest, squatted in front of a blade of grass, on which a round dew in the sun gave a colorful light, exceedingly beautiful. As he enjoyed the dew, the small boy put his hands under the grass in silence.

Seeing his mother walk over to him, the boy said sadly, "Mother, the dew's dying."

The mother said to her son with a smile, "Even if you put your hands under the grass, you cannot stop the dew disappear from this world."

The boy said, "Mother, I'm only thinking not to throw it in pain when it falls."

男孩与露珠

一天早上，一个小男孩蹲在花园的草地上，久久不动。

母亲觉得蹊跷，便凑上前看个究竟。只见男孩非常认真地蹲在一片草叶面前。草叶上，在太阳的照射下，一颗圆圆的露珠正幻出七彩的光芒，格外美丽。小男孩一边欣赏着这滴露珠，一边把双手摊开，静候在草叶下。

看到妈妈走过来，男孩忧伤地说："妈妈，露珠快要死了。"

母亲微笑着对儿子说："你就是把双手放在草叶下面，还是阻止不了露珠在这个世界上消失的命运啊。"

男孩说："妈妈，我只是想，它落下来时，别摔疼了它。"

The Mystery of Success

At 50, Socrates had been bald and wrinkled on his forehead, coupled with the deep eye sockets.

However, an 18-year-old beautiful girl madly fell in love with him and eventually became his wife.

Someone couldn't help making a secret inquiry of Socrates about the secret of success, "Sir, what method did you use to get the young girl?"

Socrates said, "I don't really have time to study this question, just focusing on doing my own things."

The man didn't believe and went on asking, "What a beautiful girl! If you didn't pursue her, how would she love you?"

Looking up at the sky, Socrates said, "Please look at the moon in the sky. The more you try to follow her, the more she doesn't allow you to catch up;but when you hurry on with your journey wholeheartedly, she will follow you closely."

成功的奥秘

苏格拉底50岁时，头顶已经秃顶，额头上布满皱纹，眼窝深陷。

然而，一个18岁的漂亮姑娘疯狂地爱上了他，并且最终成了他的妻子。

有个人忍不住向苏格拉底刺探成功的奥妙："先生，你是用什么方法把小姑娘追到手的？"

苏格拉底说："我实在没有时间研究这个问题，我只是专心致志地做自己的事。"

那人不相信，继续穷追不舍："这么漂亮的姑娘，你不追她，她怎么会爱上你呢？"

苏格拉底抬头望着天空，说："请看看天上的月亮吧。你越是拼命地追她，她越是不让你追上；而当你一心一意地赶自己的路时，她却会紧紧地跟着你。"

The Mountain Doesn't Come and I'll Go to It

A master led several disciples to meditate.

The disciples said, "Master, we have heard many magic arts. Can you show us?"

The master said, "Alright. I will show you a great art of moving the mountain here." Then, the master began to sit in meditation.

An hour later, the mountain was still across them.

The disciples said, "Master, why does the mountain come here?"

The master said unhurriedly, "Now that the mountain doesn't come here, I'll go to it." Then, he stood up and went over to the opposite mountain.

When we do something, we might as well change the way of thinking from a new angle if a method can't work.

The journey of life is like sailing on the ocean. Maybe we can't change the direction of the wind, but we can change the direction of the sails.

山不过来，我就过去

一位大师带领几位徒弟参禅悟道。

徒弟说："师父，我们听说您会很多法术，能不能让我们见识一下？"

师父说："好吧，我就给你们露一手'移山大法'，把对面那座山移过来。"说着，师父开始打坐。

一个小时过去了，对面的山仍在对面。

徒弟们说："师父，山怎么不过来呢？"

师父不慌不忙地说："既然山不过来，那我就过去。"说着，他站起来，走到了对面的山上。

当我们做一件事情用一种方法难以奏效时，不妨换一种思维方式，换一种角度。

人生的旅程正如在大海上行船一样，也许我们无法改变风的方向，但我们可以改变帆的方向。

Open Your Mind

A few decades ago in New York, there was a girl named Emily, whose ideal was like each young girl's: to find a handsome ideal lover to marry and live to old age. But the girls around her had married successively and she was still alone. She was always full of remorse all day, firmly believing that her dream would never come true.

After her family's persuasion, Emily went to see a famous psychologist. When they shook hands, her cold fingers made the psychologist quiver, and her sad eyes and pale gaunt face were telling him, "I'm hopeless, and what way will you have?"

After pondering for a long while, the psychologists said, "Emily, I want to ask you to help me. I really need your help, can you?" Emily nodded doubtfully.

"My family will have an evening party on Tuesday, but my wife has more work than she can cope with alone. You come to help me entertain the guests. Tomorrow morning, you first go to buy a new set of clothes, and then do your hair. You will help me entertain the guests, saying that you welcome them on behalf of me and help them, particularly the lonely people." Emily looked uneasy, so the psychologist encouraged her, "It doesn't matter. In fact, it is very simple. For example, when you find someone doesn't carry a cup of coffee, hand it to him or her; if it is too sultry, open the window or something." Emily finally agreed to try it.

On Tuesday, Emily came to the party with decent hairstyle and dress. According to the psychologist's requirement, she fulfilled her duty, doing nothing but to help others. Her eyes lively and smiling, she completely forgotten her worry and became the most popular one at the evening party. After the party, three young men offered to escort her home.

Week by week, the three young men were pursuing Emily ardently. She eventually agreed with the proposal of one of them. The psychologist was invited as a guest to attend their wedding. Looking at the happy bride, the people said that the psychologist created a miracle.

If you don't go into the other people's mind, they won't enter your world because you keep the door closed.

Against this, the psychologist's prescription is: try opening the closed door of mind, look at whether the light you project on others will be reflected on your own body a hundred times.

敞 开 心 扉

几十年前，纽约有一位名叫埃米丽的姑娘，她的理想跟每一位妙龄姑娘一样：找一位潇洒的白马王子结婚，白头偕老。可周围的姑娘们都先后成家了，她还是独身一人。她整天自怨自艾，认定自己梦想永远不可能实现了。

埃米丽在家人的劝说下去找一位著名的心理学家。握手时，她那冰凉的手指让人心颤，还有那伤感的眼神、苍白憔悴的面孔，都在向心理学家说："我没指望了，你会有什么办法呢？"

心理学家沉思良久，说道："埃米丽，我想请你帮我一个忙，我真的很需要你的帮忙，可以吗？"埃米丽将信将疑地点了点头。

"我家星期二要开个晚会，但我妻子一个人忙不过来，你来帮我招呼客人。明天一早，你先去买一套新衣服，然后去做个发型。你要帮我去招呼客人，说是代表我欢迎他们，要注意帮助他们，特别是显得孤单的人。"埃米丽一脸不安，心理学家鼓励她说，"没关系，其实很简单。比如说，看谁没咖啡就端一杯，要是太闷热了，就开开窗户什么的。"埃米丽终于同意试一试。

星期二这天，埃米丽发式得体、衣衫合身，来到晚会上。按照心理学家的要求，她尽职尽力，只想着帮助别人。她眼神活泼，笑容可掬，完全忘掉了自己的心事，成了晚会上最受欢迎的人。晚会结束后，有三个青年都提出要送她回家。

一周又一周，三个青年热烈地追求着埃米丽，她最终答应了其中一位的求婚。心理学家作为被邀请的贵宾，参加了他们的婚礼。望着幸福的新娘，人们说心理学家创造了一个奇迹。

你走不进别人的心里，别人也走不进你的世界，那是因为你自己把门关上了。

对此，心理学家开出的处方是：试着把封闭的心扉敞开，看看你投射在别人身上的光芒，会不会一百倍地射回你自己的身上。

Play It Again，Dad

From second grade on, there was one event I dreaded every year: the piano recital. A recital meant I had to practice a boring piece of music and perform in front of strangers who, I was sure, knew the notes much better than I. It also meant wearing a crinkly crinoline dress and enduring the bright lights of a movie camera as I swished across the church stage. Each year I would ask my father if I could skip the recital"just this once". And each year he'd say no, muttering something about building self-confidence and working toward a goal.

So it was with great satisfaction that I stood in church one recent Sunday, video camera in hand, and watched my father sweat in his shirt and tie before rising to play the piano in his very first recital.

Eight-year-old Patrick Gumery led off the event, followed by Susannah Thomson, nine. Then came my 68-year-old dad, Robert Sessions, who sat down at the Kawai grand piano and taught me more about courage and persistence than all the words he used those 30-plus years ago.

From the time he was small, my father had longed to play music. His mother, a factory worker, couldn't afford lessons, so a kindly couple in the small Arkansas town where he lived offered to pay. But he soon stopped after being teased by other boys his age. "I quit and always regretted it." He recalled.

He could have gone on regretting it, as too many of us do. But though he was rooted in his past, he wasn't stuck there. Three years ago, when he retired from the faculty at the University of Richmond, he asked his church music director, Charles Staples, to take him as a student. Staples had the good grace not to laugh. Just before the recital, he told me my dad was playing"the best I've ever seen him. I keep waiting for him to reach his peak, but he hasn't yet."

For a moment after my father sat down at the keyboard to play, he simply stared down at his fingers, and I wondered whether he would even begin. He had tried to keep the event quiet, telling my stepmother she didn't need to come. But she had every intention of coming, and also invited my sisters and me as well as my dad's three golfing partners who, much to his dismay, showed up.

As we waited those few seconds, I knew he was worrying that his music would sound juvenile—that we'd expect more from a 68-year-old than an eight-year-old, even someone who had been playing for so short a time. His sense of dignity was on the line. He's forgotten the notes, I worried, remembering those split seconds decades ago when my mind would go blank and my fingers would freeze.

But then the sure, poignant strains of Aram Khachaturian's "Melody" emerged, from the same large fingers that once baited my fishing lines, and I realized he had been doing what music teachers always tell their novitiates to do: focus on the music and pretend the rest of us aren't there.

Also in the audience was my 11-year-old son Jeff. My father has taught his grandson how to play hearts, pitch a tent, cast a fishing rod, swing a golf club and compose music on the computer. He encouraged Jeff to start the piano even when the boy insisted he would never play in a recital, two years ago, Dad was there when Jeff did what he said he would never do. So somehow it was fitting to hear Jeff offer my father some advice about performing. "Just remember, if you make a mistake, it's not the end of the world," my son told him, "Probably no one won't notice it anyway."

My dad made it through"Melody" and sailed through Burgmuller's"Arabesque". What he lacked in precision, he more than made up for in feeling. He then rose, turned to his audience and curtsied.

"So what did you think about your granddad?" I asked Jeff later.

"He was great," Jeff replied, "I'm glad he did it.And I bet he is too."

"I'm proud of him for starting something new at his age," I said.

"Yeah, and doing it so well," Jeff added, "It would be like Dr. Spock taking up baseball at 90. I guess he could do it, but it would be hard."

T. Berry Brazelton, the pediatrician and author, said grandparents show grandchildren the mountaintops, while parents teach the drudgery of how to get there. My father may not have reached his peak musically, but as far as his grandson is concerned, he's at the top of the mountain.

再弹一次，爸爸

从二年级起，有一件事我每年都非常害怕，那就是钢琴独奏会。独奏会意味着我必须得练习一首无聊的乐曲，并在许多陌生人面前演奏，我敢肯定，这些人远比我熟悉那些音符；同时意味着我要穿上飒飒作响、四周鼓出的裙子，忍受电影摄像机耀眼的灯光，飕飕走过教堂的舞台。我每年都求父亲能不能略过独奏会，"就这一次"。他每年都说不行，同时咕哝着说要树立自信、向目标努力这样的话。

所以，最近的一个周期日，我站在教堂里，手持摄像机，望着衬衣和领结都汗津津的父亲准备第一次钢琴独奏时，感到非常高兴。

8岁的帕特里克·加梅里首先独奏，接着是9岁的苏珊娜·汤姆森，随后就是我68岁的爸爸罗伯特·塞森斯。他在佳威牌平台钢琴前坐下，他的勇气和恒心比他30多年来教给我的要多。

我父亲从小就渴望弹奏乐曲。他的母亲是一名工人，拿不起学费，于是他所住的阿肯色州一个小镇的一对好心夫妇自愿掏钱。但被其他同龄的男孩们取笑后，他不久就停了下来。"我放弃学琴，总是感到遗憾。"他回忆说。

他本可能继续遗憾，像我们这样的人太多了。但尽管他对过去念念不忘，却没有沉湎其中。3年前从里士满大学的教职上退休后，他请教堂的音乐指挥查尔斯·斯坦普尔斯收他做学生。斯坦普尔斯温文尔雅，没有发笑。就在独奏会前，他告诉我说，我爸爸弹得"从来没有这样好过。我一直在等着他达到演奏的顶点，但他还在进步"。

我父亲在钢琴键盘前坐下准备演奏后，他一时间只是低头看着自己的手指，我不知道他会不会开始弹。他一直隐瞒这件事，吩咐继母不必来听。但她一心想来，不仅请了我和姐妹们，还请了我爸爸的3个高尔夫球友。那3个球友到场时，爸爸大为惊慌。

我们等了几秒钟，我知道他在担心他弹的琴声会非常幼稚，担心我们会期望68岁的人比8岁的人弹得好，即便是他学了这么短的一段时间。他的尊严感正经受着考验。我担心他已经忘了那些音符，同时想起了几十年前我好多次一时间脑海里一片空白、手指僵硬的情景。

但艾拉姆·哈恰图良的坚定、生动的《旋律》的音符从那些曾给我的钓鱼线装诱饵的粗大手指上流了出来，我意识到他正在按照音乐老师对初学者的吩咐去做：对乐曲聚精会神，装作我们其他人都不在场。

听众当中还有我11岁的儿子杰夫。我父亲教过外孙怎样玩红心牌、搭帐篷、投钓竿、挥高尔夫球棒和在电脑上作曲。他鼓励杰夫弹钢琴，即使当时那男孩坚持说绝不在独奏会演奏。两年前，杰夫做了他曾坚持说绝对不做的事，爸爸也去听了。所以，不管怎样，听杰夫给我父亲提一些有关演奏的忠告是合适的。"请记住，就是你弹错了，也不是世界末日。"我儿子对他说。"也许根本没人会注意到这一点。"

爸爸弹完了《旋律》，又弹起了伯格穆勒的《阿拉伯风格曲》。尽管他的演奏缺乏精确，但他能用情感去弥补。随后，他站起身，转向听众，屈膝行礼。

"那你认为外公怎么样？"我后来问杰夫。"他当时真棒，"杰夫回答说，"我很高兴他那样做。我敢说他也很高兴。""他这样的年龄开始新的东西，我为他感到自豪。"我说。"是的，而且做得是那样好，"杰夫补充说，"这就像斯波克医生90岁才打棒球。我想他能行，但会不容易。"

儿科医生兼作家T.贝利·布里兹顿说，祖父母把山顶指给孙子孙女，父母教子女怎样克服困难到达那里。我父亲也许还没有登上音乐的顶峰，但对他的外孙来说，他已经站在了山顶上。

The Spring Will Come

I remember one winter my dad needed firewood, and he found a dead tree and sawed it down.

In the spring, to his dismay, new shoots sprouted around the trunk.

He said, "I thought sure it was dead. The leaves had all dropped in the wintertime. It was so cold that twigs snapped as if there were no life left in the old tree. But now I see that there was still life at the taproot." He looked at me and said, "Bob, don't forget this important lesson. Never cut a tree down in the wintertime. Never make a negative decision in the low time. Never make your most important decisions when you are in your worst mood. Wait. Be patient. The storm will pass. The spring will come."

春天一定会来

我记得有一年冬天，爸爸需要柴火。随后，他就找到了一棵枯树，将它锯下来。

第二年春天，让他吃惊的是，树干周围发出了新芽。

他说："我还以为它肯定死了呢。冬天，树叶都掉光了。天这样冷，小树枝一折就断，好像老树没有了生命，但现在我看到主根还有生命。"他看着我说，"鲍勃，别忘了这个重要教训。千万别在冬天把一棵树砍倒，千万别在运气低谷时作出消极决定，千万别在情绪最糟时作出最重要的决定。要等待，要耐心。风暴会过去，春天一定会来。"

The Discovery at the Bend

A young man travelled by train. As the train was rumbling across a wilderness, the passengers looked out of the windows idly and aimlessly.

When it approached a bend, the train slowed down and then an unadorned house came into view. It was so conspicuous against the desolate landscape that everybody on the train turned to admire it with eyes wide open. Some passengers even began a discussion about it.

The young man was also impressed by the scene. On his return he got off the train at the nearest station and found his way to the house. Its owner told him that troubled by the noise of the train he wanted to sell the house but nobody would buy it.

Soon after the young man spent thirty thousand dollars for the house, regarding it as a favorable site for advertisement. It was facing the railway bend where the train had to slow down and the weary passengers would cast their eyes at the house to refresh themselves.

He managed to get access to big companies and tried his best to convince them of the advantage of the place for advertisement. Finally, the Coca Cola Company took a lease on it to put up promotion signs. The young man was paid 180 thousand for a three-year rent.

The story is absolutely true. It proves that any discovered potential may lead to success.

拐弯处的发现

有一位年轻人乘火车旅行。当火车隆隆驶过一片荒野时，乘客们都百无聊赖、毫无目的地望着车窗外。

接近一个拐弯处时，火车放慢了速度。随后，一座没有装饰的房子进入了视野。它和荒凉的地貌形成了鲜明对照，车上的人都睁大眼睛欣赏起来。有的乘客甚至开始对这座房子讨论了起来。

那个年轻人也对这座房子留下了深刻的印象。回程时，他在离那座房子最近的站点下了车，找到了通向那座房子的路。房子的主人告诉他说，由于火车噪音困扰，他想卖掉房子，但没人愿意买。

年轻人把这座房子看作是广告的有利场所，不久以后便花3万美元买了下来。房子面对着铁路拐弯处，火车在那里不得不减速，疲惫的乘客常常会把目光投向这座房子上，来消除疲劳。

他设法和一些大公司取得了联系，尽力使他们相信用那个地方登广告的优势。最后，可口可乐公司租用那里，竖起了促销的招牌，付给了年轻人18万美元租金，租期3年。

这个故事绝对真实。它证明，只要发现有可能，就会走向成功。

Acres of Diamonds

There was a farmer in Africa who was happy and content. One day a wise man came to him and said, "If you had a diamond the size of your thumb, you could have your own city; if you had a diamond the size of your fist you could probably own your own country." And then he went away. That night the farmer couldn't sleep. He was unhappy because he was discontent, and he was discontent because he was unhappy.

The next morning he made arrangements to sell off his farm, took care of his family and went in search of diamonds. He looked all over Africa and couldn't find any. He looked all through Europe and couldn't find any. When he got to Spain, he was emotionally, physically and financially broke. He got so disheartened that he threw himself into the Barcelona River.

Back home, the man who had bought his farm was watering the camels at a stream that ran through the farm. Across the stream, the rays of the morning sun hit a stone and made it sparkle like a rainbow. He thought it would look good on the mantelpiece. He picked up the stone and put it in the living room. That afternoon the wise man came and saw the stone sparkling. He asked, "Is Hafiz back?" The new owner replied, "No, why do you ask?" The wise man said, "Because that is a diamond. I recognize one when I see one." The man said, "No, that's just a stone I picked up from the stream. Come, I'll show you. There are many more." They went and picked some samples and sent them for analysis. Sure enough, the stones were diamonds. They found that the farm was indeed covered with acres and acres of diamonds.

What is the moral of this story?

When our attitude is right, we realize that we are all walking on acres and acres of diamonds. Opportunity is always under our feet. We don't have to go anywhere else. All we need to do is recognize it.

钻 石 宝 地

非洲有一位快乐而满足的农夫。有一天，一位智者走到他身边，说："如果你拥有一块拇指大的钻石，你就能拥有一座自己的城市；如果你拥有拳头大的一块钻石，你就可能拥有一个自己的国家。"说完，他就离开了。那天夜里，农夫难以入眠。他因不满足而闷闷不乐，也因为闷闷不乐而不满足。

第二天早上，他卖掉了自己的农场，安顿好了家人，就去寻找钻石了。

他找遍了非洲，一无所获。他找遍了欧洲，也一无所获。他到达西班牙时，已经身心疲惫、一文不名了。他心灰意冷，纵身跳进了巴塞罗那河。

此时在他的家乡，买下他农场的那个人正在潺潺流过农场的小溪边给骆驼饮水。小溪对面，晨阳照射在了一块石头上，使那块石头像一道彩虹那样闪耀。他想：这块石头摆在壁炉架上一定非常好看。他捡起了石头，把它放到了客厅里。当天下午，那个智者又来了，看到那块石头在闪闪发光，便问道："哈菲兹回来了吗？"新主人回答说："没有，你为什么这样问？"智者说："因为那是一块钻石。我一眼就能认出来。"那人说："不，那只是我从小溪边捡起的一块石头。过来，我领你去看。那里还有更多呢。"他们走到了小溪边，挑了一些样品，将它们送去分析。那些石头果然是钻石。他们发现这整个农场确实蕴藏着大量的钻石。

这个故事的寓意是什么呢？

当我们态度端正时，就会意识到我们都走在广阔的钻石地上。机会总在我们脚下。我们不必到其他地方去寻找，需要做的就是加以识别。

The Golden Window

A small boy lived on a farm that seemed so far away from everywhere. He needed to get up before sunrise every morning to start his chores and out again later to do the evening ones.

During sunrise he would take a break and climb up on the fence so in the distance he could see the house with golden windows. He thought how great it would be to live there and his mind would wander to imagine the modern equipment and appliances that might exist in the house. "If they could afford golden windows, then there must have other nice things." He then promised himself, "Someday I will go there and see this wonderful place."

Then one morning his father told him to stay at home and his father would do the chores. Knowing that this was his chance, he packed a sandwich and headed across the field towards the house with the golden windows.

As the afternoon went on, he began to realize how he misjudged the distance and something else was very wrong. As he approached the house, he saw no golden windows but instead a place with in bad need of a painting surrounded by a broken down fence. He went to the tattered screen door and knocked. A small boy very close to his age opened the door.

He asked him if he had seen the house with the golden windows. The boy said, "Sure, I know," and invited him to sit on the porch. As he sat there, he looked back from where he just came where the sunset turned the windows on his home to gold.

金色窗户

有一个小男孩住在一个农场，这个农场好像离所有的地方都很远。每天早上太阳出来以前，他需要起床做杂务，晚些时候再出来做一次晚上的杂务。

太阳升起时，他会休息一下，爬上篱笆。这样，他就可以看到远处那座有金色窗户的房子。他认为住在那里是非常了不起的事儿，他常常想象着房子里的现代化设备和电器。"要是他们能装得起金色窗户，那肯定还有其他好东西。"随后，他向自己许诺说，"总有一天，我要到那里去看这个了不起的地方。"

后来有一天早上，他父亲让他待在家里，自己要去做这些杂务。他知道这是一个机会，就带上一块三明治，穿过田野，朝那座有金色窗户的房子走去。

下午来临时，他开始意识到自己错估了到那座房子的距离，其他事情也大相径庭。当走近那座房子时，他没有看到金色窗户，而是看到了一个急需粉刷、四周篱笆坏掉的地方。他走到那扇破门前，敲了敲。一个和他年龄非常接近的男孩打开了门。

他问那男孩是否见过那个有金色窗户的房子。那男孩说："我当然知道。"并请他坐在门廊上。他坐在那里，回头向自己刚才来的方向望去，只见落日把他的家染成了金色。

Two Acorns

If you want to understand adversity, take two identical acorns from the same oak tree and plant them in two different locations. Plant the first in the middle of a dense forest, and the other on a hill by itself.

Here's what will happen. The oak standing on a hillside is exposed to every storm and gale. As a result its roots plunge deep into the earth and spread in every direction, even wrapping themselves around giant boulders. At times it may seem the tree isn't growing fast enough-but the growth is happening underground. It's as if the roots know they must protect the tree from the threatening elements.

What about the acorn planted in the forest? It becomes a weak, frail sapling. And since it is protected by its neighbors, the little oak doesn't sense the need to spread its roots for support.

Don't be afraid of adversity! Welcome it! That's your surefire route to ultimate success.

两 个 橡 果

如果你想理解什么是逆境，就去拿两个从同一棵树上摘下来的相同的橡果，并把他们种到不同的地方。第一颗种在浓密的树林当中，另外一颗则单独种在一座山上。

事情的结果便是这样。那棵长在山上的橡树经历了大风大雨，结果它的根深深地扎进了泥土中，并不断向四周扩张，甚至把自己置身于巨大的石块中。有时，它可能看起来长得不是很快，却在地下悄悄生长着，好像它的根知道自己必须快速生长，以免树木受自然危害的影响。

而种在树丛中的橡果是什么样子的呢？它变成了一棵虚弱的小树苗。因为有周围树丛的保护，所以这棵小树苗便不知道要把自己的根扎得更深。

不要害怕困难！要欢迎它！那是你最终成功的必经之路。

Pinkie Victory Over Big Iron Hammer

The world No. 1 salesman was asked to share his secret of success upon his retirement. 2, 500 salesmen came to listen to his speech. He set a very big iron ball and a big hammer on the stage.

Then he asked, "Who can move this iron ball?" One man in the audience said, "I want to try." He went on the stage and knocked at the big iron ball once with the hammer.

It didn't budge.

Then came more men. The iron ball still didn't move. At this time the speaker said, "Now I will teach you the secret." He then poked the iron ball every 5 seconds with his pinkie. The iron ball began to move a little after 40 minutes. But the iron ball swung fiercely after 50 minutes.

He then asked, "Who can stop the iron ball on the stage?"

The people down the stage all said it couldn't be done.

The world No. 1 salesman said, "This is my secret of success. I visit customers every day until they give in. You see, they just can't block me when I succeed."

以小搏大的成功之道

世界头号推销员退休时接受邀请，分享他的成功秘诀。2500名推销员来听他演讲。他在台上放了一只很大的铁球和一把大铁锤。

随后，他问道："谁能移动这只铁球？"台下有个人说："我想试一下。"那人上台，用铁锤敲了一下大铁球。

铁球没有动。

随后，又上来几个人。铁球还是没有动。这时，演讲者说："现在我来教给你们其中的秘诀。"接着，他就每过5秒钟用小手指捅一下大铁球。40分钟后，铁球微微移动。但50分钟后，铁球剧烈晃动起来。

他接着问："谁能上台停住铁球？"

台下的人都说这做不到。

世界头号推销员说："这就是我成功的秘诀。我每天都拜访顾客，直到他们让步。你看到了吧，我成功时，谁都挡不住。"

Move Back Is Also a Success

When he just went to hold the post in the new parish, a pastor encountered a hot potato: there was a garden in front of the pastor gate and a number of children would cross the garden to school, so the flowers were picked from time to time.

That spring, the flowers of the garden were in full bloom. One early morning, the pastor stood in the garden waiting for the children going to school. Soon, some of them came along; a little boy asked the pastor, "Can I snap a flower?"

"Which one do you want?" the pastor asked genially. The boy chose a tulip.

The pastor said, "Very good. It belongs to you now. However, if you leave the flower here, it can still bloom for several days; if you pick it now, you can only play for a little while. You are a smart kid, so you choose by yourself."

The little boy thought for a while and said, "Then I leave it here. I will come back to see it until class is over."

On that day, more than 20 children agreed to leave the flowers in the garden until they wilt.

That spring, the pastor left the whole garden to the people, but he had never lost one.

退一步也是成功

一位牧师刚到新教区任职，便碰到了一个棘手的问题：教区门前有一个花园，每天不少孩子上学都要横穿花园，因此鲜花被摘的现象时有发生。

那年春天，花园的鲜花开得格外茂盛。这天，牧师一大早就站在了花园中，等待着上学的孩子们。不一会儿，有几个孩子走过来，其中有一个小男孩开口问牧师："我能折枝花吗？"

"你想要哪一枝？"牧师和蔼地问道。小男孩选了一枝郁金香。

牧师说："好啊，这花归你了。不过，如果你把花儿留在这里，它还能开好几天；如果你现在折了它，那就只能玩一会儿了。你是个聪明的孩子，你自己作个选择吧。"小男孩想了想，说："那我就把它留在这里，等我放学回来再看。"

那天，有20多个孩子都同意把花留在花园里，直到它们枯萎。

那年春天，牧师把整个花园的花全给了人，却没有丢一枝。

The Strength of Success

After the rain, a spider crawled hard to the frayed web. Because the wall was so damp, it slipped down as it crawled at a certain height. It still crawled up again and again when it dropped down…

The first person saw it, saying to himself with a sign, "Isn't my life is like this spider's? I'm always busy but get nothing." Then he was downhearted day by day.

The second person saw it, saying, "What a stupid spider! Why not move around and crawl from the dry wall nearby? I shouldn't be as foolish as it in future." Then he became more intelligent.

When the third person saw it, the spirit of the spider who suffered repeated defeats but continued to struggle moved him right away. Then he became stronger.

Spirits of success can always detect the strength of success.

成功的力量

雨后，一只蜘蛛艰难地向墙上已经支离破碎的网爬去。由于墙壁潮湿，它爬到一定的高度，就会掉下来。它一次次地向上爬，又一次次地掉下来……

第一个人看到了，他叹了口气，自言自语说："我的一生不正如这只蜘蛛吗？忙忙碌碌而无所得。"于是，他日渐消沉。

第二个人看到了，说："这只蜘蛛真愚蠢，为什么不从旁边干燥的地方绕一下爬上去？我以后可不能像它那样愚蠢。"于是，他变得聪明起来。

第三个人看到了，他立刻被蜘蛛屡败屡战的精神感动了。于是，他变得坚强起来。

成功的心态总能发掘成功的力量。

Confidence Is the Key of Success

Confidence is the key of success. When you're truly and justifiably confident, it radiates from you like sunlight, and attracts success to you like magnet.

It's so important to believe in yourself. Believe that you can do it under any circumstances. Because if you believe you can, you really will. That belief just keeps you searching for the answers, and you can get it pretty soon.

Confidence is more than an attitude. It comes from knowing exactly where you are going, exactly how you are going to get there. It comes from acting with integrity and a strong sense of purpose. It comes from a strong commitment to take responsibility, rather than just let life happen.

One way to develop self-confidence is to do the thing you fear and get the successful experiences from it.

Confidence is compassionate and understanding. It is not arrogant. Arrogance is born out of fear and insecurity. Confidence comes from strength and integrity.

Confidence is not just believing you can do it. Confidence is knowing you can do it. Knowing that you are capable of accomplishing anything you want, and live your life with confidence.

Anything can be achieved through focused, determined effort, commitment and self-confidence. If your life is not what you want it to be, you have the power to change it. But you must change it step by step. Live each moment with your goals and your plan of action. Live each moment with your priorities in your heart. Act with your own purpose and you will have the life you want.

自信是成功的钥匙

自信是成功的钥匙。当你真正有足够的理由自信时，自信会像阳光一样从你身上散发出来，并像磁铁一样把成功吸引到你身边。

相信自己非常重要。在任何情况下都要相信自己能行。因为如果你相信自己能行，你就会真正做到。那种信念正好使你不断寻找答案，然后很快你就能得到答案。

自信不仅仅是一种态度。自信来自你准确知道自己去哪里，准确知道你如何到达那里。自信来自正直诚实的行动和坚定的目标感。自信来承担责任的坚定承诺，而不是仅仅随波逐流。

发扬自信的一个方法就是去做你害怕做的事情，从中获取成功的体验。

自信富于同情和理解。自信不是傲慢自大。傲慢自大来自害怕和缺乏安全感。自信来自力量和诚实。

　　自信不仅仅是相信你能行，自信是知道自己能行，知道你有能力完成自己想做的一切，从而充满自信地生活。

　　通过明确坚定的努力、承诺和自信，任何事情都能做到。如果你的生活不如意，你有力量去改变它。但你必须一步步地改变。每时每刻都带着目标和行动计划去生活。每时每刻心里都要带着轻重缓急去生活。有的放矢地行动，你就会得到自己想要的生活。

第七卷

从梦想之火到最后胜利

Dream to Fly

Larry Walters is among the relatively few who have actually turned their dreams into reality. His story is true, even though you may find it hard to believe.

Larry was a truck driver, but his lifelong dream was to fly. When he graduated from high school, he joined the Air Force in hopes of becoming a pilot. Unfortunately, poor eyesight disqualified him. So, when he finally left the service, he had to satisfy himself with watching others fly the fighter jets that crossed the skies over his backyard. As he sat there in his lawn chair, he dreamed about the magic of flying.

Then one day, Larry Walters got an idea. He went down to the local Army-Navy surplus store and bought a tank of helium and forty-five weather balloons. These were not your brightly colored party balloons; these were heavy-duty spheres measuring more than four feet across when fully inflated. Back in his yard, Larry used straps to attach the balloons to his lawn chair, the kind you might have in your own backyard.

He anchored the chair to the bumper of his jeep and inflated the balloons with helium. Then he packed some sandwiches and drinks and loaded a BB gun, figuring he could pop a few of those balloons when it was time to return to earth.

His preparation complete, Larry Walters sat in his chair and cut the anchoring cord. His plan was to lazily float up, and then lazily back down to terra firma. But, things didn't quite work out that way.

When Larry cut the cord, he didn't float lazily up—he shot up as if fired from a cannon! Nor did he go up a couple hundred feet. He climbed and climbed, until he finally leveled off at eleven THOUSAND feet! At that height, he could hardly risk deflating any of the balloons, lest he should unbalance the load and really experience flying! So, he stayed up there, sailing around for fourteen hours, totally at a loss as to how to get down. At least, Larry drifted into the corridor for Los Angeles International Airport. A Pan-Am pilot radioed the tower about passing a guy in a lawn chair at eleven thousand feet…with a gun in his lap.

The airport is right on the ocean, and you may know that at nightfall, the winds on the coast begin to change. So, as dusk fell, Larry began drifting out to sea.

At that point, the Navy dispatched a helicopter to rescue him. But, the rescue team had a hard time getting to him, because the draft from their propeller kept pushing this home-made contraption farther and farther away. Eventually they were able to hover over him and drop a rescue line with which they gradually hauled him back to earth.

As soon as Larry hit the ground, he was arrested.

But as he was being led away by the police, a television reporter called out to ask, "Mr. Walters, why did you do it?"

Larry stopped, eyed the man for a moment and replied nonchalantly, "A man can't just sit around."

飞 翔 之 梦

拉里·沃尔特斯是人类史上少数真正梦想成真的人之一。这是一个真实的故事，即使你们可能很难相信。

拉里是一名卡车司机，但他毕生的梦想是飞翔。高中毕业后，他便加入了空军，希望能成为一名飞行员。不幸的是，弱视让他失去了资格。因此退役后，他不得不满足于在自己的后院观望其他人开着战斗机翱翔于天空。他坐在草坪的躺椅上时，情不自禁地联想到飞翔的魔力。

后来有一天，拉里想到个主意。他去了当地一家陆海军用剩余物资商店，买回一罐氦气和45个气象气球。这些气球可不是你在派对上见到的那种五颜六色的气球，而是膨胀后可长达1.2米的那种重型球体。拉里回到自己家后院，用粗绳将气球固定在自己的躺椅上，说不定你自家还会有呢。

他将躺椅固定在吉普车的保险杠上，用氦气充满了气球，然后打包了一些三明治和饮料，将一支BB型气枪上了膛，心中盘算着等该降落时直接一枪打爆气球。

准备妥当，拉里·沃尔特斯坐在躺椅上，一刀割断绑绳。他的计划是慢悠悠升空，再慢悠悠回归大地。然而，结果并不如愿。

拉里割断绳子时，并没有慢慢升天——而是迅速上升，就像出膛的炮弹一般猛烈！而且他并不是仅仅上升了数百米。飞啊飞，最后他居然飞到了距离地面3000多米的高空！飞到这种高度，他很难冒险打爆任何气球，唯恐失去平衡，快速坠落！因此，他不得不停留在半空中，漫无目的地翱翔了14小时之久，对于如何安全降落地面完全不知。他飘到了洛杉矶国际机场的跑道。一名泛美航空的飞行员立刻无线电通知塔台，报告说他看见在3000多米的高空中有个家伙坐在躺椅上飞翔……膝盖上放着一支气枪。

机场就建在海边，夜幕降临时，海风就会开始变化。所以，拉里借着风势飘到了海面上。

此刻，海军派遣了一架直升机来营救他。可是，救援队很难接近他，因为推进器的拉引力不停地让这种本土造的直升机越飞越远。最终，他们飞到了拉里的正上方，降下一条软梯，终于将他顺利地接回了地面。

拉里脚刚一着地，就被捕了。

可是，正当他要被警方带走时，一名新闻记者大声问道："沃尔特斯先生，你为什么要那样做？"

拉里停下脚步，凝视了对方一会儿，最后若无其事地答道："一个人不能只是坐着。"

Become What You Wants to Be

A little girl was born into a very poor family in a shack in the Backwoods of Tennessee. She was the 20th of 22 children, prematurely born and weak. When she was four years old, she had double pneumonia and scarlet fever—a deadly combination that left her with a paralyzed and useless feet leg. She had to wear an iron leg brace. Yet she was fortunate in having a mother who encouraged her.

Well, this mother told her little girl who was very bright, that despite the brace and leg, she could do whatever she wanted to do in her life. She told her that all she needed to do was to have faith, persistence, courage and indomitable spirit.

So at nine years of age, the little girl removed the leg brace, and she took the step the doctors told her she would never take normally. In four years, she developed a rhythmic stride, which was a medical wonder. Then this girl got the incredible notion that she would like to be the world's greatest woman runner.

At age 13, she entered a race. She came in last. She entered every race in high school, and in every race she came in last. Everyone begged her to quit! However, one day, she came in next to last. And then there came a day when she won a race. From then on, Wilma Rudolph won every race that she entered.

Wilma went to Tennessee State University, where she met a coach named Ed Temple. Coach Temple saw the indomitable spirit of the girl, that she was a believer and that she had great natural talent. He trained her so well that she went to the Olympic Games.

There she was pitted against the greatest woman runner of the day, a German girl named Jutta Heine. Nobody had ever beaten Jutta. But in the 100-meter dash, Wilma Rudolph won. She beat Jutta again in the 200-meters. Now Wilma had two Olympic gold medals.

Finally came the 400-meter relay. It would be Wilma against Jutta once again. The first two runners on Wilma's team made perfect handoffs with the baton. But when the third runner handed the baton to Wilma, she was so excited that she dropped it, and Wilma saw Jutta taking off down the track. It was impossible that anybody could catch this fleet and nimble girl. But Wilma did just that! Altogether

Wilma Rudolph earned three Olympic gold medals.

实现自己的梦想

一个小女孩出生于田纳西州蛮荒之地一户穷人家的窝棚里。这户人家有22个子女，她排行20，还是个早产儿，身体虚弱。她4岁那年得了肺炎和猩红热——这对她是致命一击，导致她后来一条腿瘫痪。她不得不装了铁制假腿。幸好，她有一位经常在身边鼓励她的母亲。

母亲告诉她，她很聪明，虽然腿有残疾，但日后定能成大器。母亲还告诉她说她现在最需要的是要有信念、毅力、勇气和坚韧不拔的精神。

9岁那年，小女孩撤掉了假腿，采纳了医生的治疗方案。此前，医生也告诉过她这种疗法绝不是她所能承受的。4年时间里，她终于迈出了奇迹般的步伐，这也成了医学界的一大奇迹。后来，小女孩产生了一个惊人的念头——她要成为全世界女子赛跑冠军。

13岁那年，她入围一场赛跑比赛，最终以倒数第一的败绩告终。高中时期，每逢赛跑她必参加，而每场比赛均以最后一名的败绩告终。所有人都祈求她放弃！然而有一天，她得了个倒数第二的成绩。之后终于有一天，她赢得了一场比赛。从那以后，威尔玛·鲁道夫逢赛必赢！

威尔玛后来进了田纳西州立大学。在那里，她遇到了一位名叫埃德·坦普尔的教练。坦普尔渐渐发现了这个女孩坚韧不拔的精神，她是一个永远坚信成功的人，而且她身上有很大的潜力。他对她进行严格训练，所以后来她才能入围奥林匹克运动会。

那天，她遇到了前所未有的劲敌——一个名叫尤塔·海涅的德国女孩，全世界最有名气的女子赛跑选手。之前从来没有人能击败尤塔，但在100米比赛中，威尔玛一举夺魁。在后来的200米比赛中，威尔玛再次击败了尤塔。此时，威尔玛已赢得了两枚奥运会金牌。

最后进入了400米接力赛，这轮比赛中，威尔玛将再次挑战尤塔。威尔玛所在队的前两名选手战绩不错，顺利地交接了接力棒，但当第三名选手给威尔玛传递时，她太激动了，竟然不慎将接力棒丢到地上，而此刻威尔玛看到尤塔已经拿到接力棒遥遥领先了。对一般人来说，已经根本不可能追上这个敏捷的女子赛手尤塔了，更何况是在敌手已然占尽先机的情况下，显然胜负已定。可是，威尔玛却做到了！这次比赛，威尔玛总计获得3枚奥运会金牌。

Deal with Obstacles Now

An old farmer had plowed around a large rock in one of his fields for years. He had broken several plowshares and a cultivator on it and had grown rather morbid about the rock.

After breaking another plowshare one day, and remembering all the trouble the rock had caused him through the years, he finally decided to do something about it.

When he put the crowbar under the rock, he was surprised to discover that it was only about six inches thick and that he could break it up easily with a sledgehammer. As he was carting the pieces away he had to smile, remembering all the trouble that the rock had caused him over the years and how easy it would have been to get rid of it sooner.

现在就克服障碍

一位老农在自己的一块地里围着一块巨岩耕耘多年。迄今为止，他已耕坏了数把犁和一部耕耘机，而巨岩周围的庄稼收获仍很差。

一天，他又用坏了一把犁。想想多年来这块巨岩带给他的诸多麻烦，最终，他决定要干一件事。

在岩石下面插入一根撬棍后，他突然发现只有大约6英寸（1英寸＝2.54厘米）厚，他只要找个长柄大锤就能轻易将其敲碎。在搬运岩石碎片时，他无奈地苦笑了一下，想想多年来这块巨岩带给他的诸多麻烦，若早日铲除这个障碍该有多好啊！

A Music Lesson

One day while walking through the forest, a bear saw a sign "Forest Band Tryouts Next Weeks."

"Wow, a band, I would love to be in a band," he thought. He had never played an instrument before but he was willing to try. He had seen concerts in the forest before and really admired the animals that could sing and play instruments.

He hurried home to tell his parents of the tryouts. His Mom was cooking dinner. Dad was sitting in his favorite chair reading the newspaper when he rushed in with the news.

"Mom, Dad, guess what, I am going to be in a band." Well, his parents were stunned since they knew the little cub did not know the first thing about a musical instrument. His

Mom just hesitated for a second and then said, "Well, that is great dear, uh, what will you play?" She didn't want to disappoint the cub, so she tried to be encouraging.

"I am going to play the harmonica," he replied. "I just know I can do that. I know I can." He then ran to his room to practice, and he practiced every day for the next week until the tryouts. He woke up bright eyed and bushy tailed on the day of the tryouts and ran to the forest only to see all of his friends there. Sammy the squirrel was there with his guitar, Robby the rabbit with his drum set and everyone was practicing until their name was called.

Finally, they got to the Bear and he was nervous but he went in and did his very best. When he was finished, he was told that he was good but no good enough for band, the judges were sorry but he just could not be in the band.

The Bear was heart-broken, especially since all the other animals were chosen for the band and he wasn't. With his head down he headed home, trying not to cry. He was almost home when he heard his name being called, "Wait, wait, I have to talk to you," said one of the judges running to him. The Bear couldn't imagine what was going on since he was already told he could not join his friends in the band.

"We need a manager for the band, can you do that?" The Bear stood for a second and then replied, "I don't know how to be a band manager, what if I mess up?"

"Well, you won't know until you try, and anyway, all of your friends want you to be a part of the band, so will you do it?" Just at that time all the other animals joined the Bear. "Please do it," they all shouted. "Come on, you can do it," said Sammy the squirrel.

"OK, I will do it, thanks guys." Everyone won that day, the other animals would be in the band and the Bear would be their manager.

It just goes to show that if you don't find success in one area, have patience and you will find it in another!

一堂音乐课

一天，一头熊在树林中散步时，突然看到一个标语牌"接下来几周会举行森林乐队大比拼的预赛"。

"哇，乐队，我真的好想加入某个乐队喔。"他心里想。他以前从未玩过乐器，但他跃跃欲试。他以前看过森林里举办的音乐会，并且非常钦佩那些会唱歌会演奏乐器的动物。

他匆匆赶回家，告知父母关于预赛的事情。当他高兴地带着这个好消息冲进家门时，发现他的母亲正在准备晚餐，而父亲正坐在他那把最喜爱的长椅上看报纸。

"老爸老妈，猜猜看什么事，我就要加入乐队了。"一听到这个消息，父母都感到很惊讶，因为他们知道小家伙根本不懂任何乐器。他老妈踌躇了一下，然后说道："呃，这是件好事，宝贝，那你想演奏什么乐器呢？"她并不想伤害小家伙的自尊心，因此尽力鼓励他。

"我要吹口琴，"他回复道，"我知道我肯定行的，我很确定！"然后，他飞速奔向自己的房间开始演练起来，直到预赛开始之前，他每天都有在练。预赛那天，他早早起身，双目炯炯有神，全身毛发抖擞，一鼓作气跑到森林里来看看他的伙计们的状况。小松鼠萨米已经到场，身上背着吉他，小兔子罗比已经备好了大鼓，每个人都在不停地练习，直到主持人喊出他们的名字让他们上场演出。

最后终于轮到了小熊。他有点紧张，但还是镇静上场并尽最大的努力演好自己的节目。下场后，他被告知他的演奏很不错，但如果想加入乐队，还远远不够，评委们对此很抱歉，他落选了。

小熊的心都碎了，尤其是其他动物都被选入乐队，只有他一人落选。他垂头丧气地朝家的方向走去，忍住没有大哭出来。就在他快到家的那一刹那，突然听到有人叫他的名字。"等等，等一下，我要和你谈谈。"一位评委边喊边朝他跑来。自从自己被落选，不能和朋友们一起加入乐队以来，小熊无法想象接下来会发生什么事。

"我们需要一位乐队经理，你能胜任吗？"

小熊愣了一下，回道："我不知道如何做好一名乐队经理，万一搞砸了呢？"

"啊，你不去试，永远也不会知道结果。不管怎么说，你所有的朋友都想让你成为乐队的一分子，那你到底愿不愿做呢？"就在那一刻，所有其他动物都已聚在小熊身边。"求你了，答应吧，"他们异口同声喊道，"来吧，我相信你能行的！"松鼠萨米说。

"好吧，让我试试。多谢了，伙计们！"那天全都赢了：其他动物是乐队的成员，小熊是他们的经理。

这个故事告诉我们：如果你在某个领域受挫，要有耐心，你一定会在另一个领域成功！

A Car Accident Brought Success

Have you ever wondered how some of the worst things that happen in your life turn out to be some of the best experiences you've ever had? Well, a fellow member of my church once told a story about such an experience that changed his life.

For years, he had difficulty saving to buy a house because something would always occur and consume more money than he had expected to spend. Despite his efforts he simply could not go long before spending the extra cash that he had saved.

Then one day a car accident badly damaged the car his wife was driving. Their mechanic estimated the cost of repairs at five thousand dollars. Unfortunately, they were presently in a financial bind and so the car would have to wait. After contemplating the situation he realized they needed a solution to their financial problems. To remedy the situation he worked long and hard for weeks, saving and managing his money in a way he had never done before. In a few months he had saved enough funds to have his wife's car repaired.

Once the car was repaired, he discussed with his wife how quickly they had put aside the money they needed. During their discussion his wife encouraged him to open a second bank account so they could continue to put away the same amount of money that we were saving every week for the car repair. This money would go towards the house they had always wanted to purchase.

He was convinced that if he could save thousand of dollars in a few months he could eventually save enough to buy a house. For many years they had both wanted to buy their dream house but could not seem to come up with the down payment.

However, in a little over a year he had saved more than twenty thousand dollars and was able to make the down payment. He had done something in a short while that he had failed to accomplish in his previous attempts to properly handle his finances.

Consequently, this man's experiences gave him a different feeling about money. He and his wife have continued to maintain their second account. This time they have decided to start saving for their retirement, putting away just a little less every week than they did for their house.

The experience of a single misfortune taught him a valuable lesson and challenged him to reprogram his saving, and spending habits. In the process he also changed his family's life. He now enjoys the material benefits along with a sense of accomplishment and pride.

The value of making the most of our experiences is that they teach us lessons about life—about failures, successes, and everything in between.

In the midst of our challenges always remember success often comes in disguise.

车祸带来的成功

你有没有想过，你一生中发生的一些最糟糕的事情竟能最后变成你最幸福的体验？啊，我的一位教友就告诉过我这样一个改变他人生的体验。

多年来，他都攒不够钱买栋房子，因为生活琐碎，经常不是这里花一点，就是那里花一点，总是超出他的预算。尽管他很努力，但攒的钱仍不够额外花。

后来有一天，他们外出，不幸出了车祸，严重损毁了他太太驾驶的车。维修师预计修理费至少要5000美元。不幸的是，最近他们手头较紧，因此只好暂时放弃维修。经过一番周密考虑后，他意识到他们需要尽快解决财政危机。为了达到这一目的，他加倍努力工作，比以往任何时候都省吃俭用。没过几个月，他就攒够了修理太太爱车的钱。

车修好后，他和太太一同商议如何能够尽快攒够他们需要的钱。商议时，太太劝他再开一个户头，这样他们就能继续往里存入修车时每周积攒的相同金额，而这笔钱正是用来购买他们早就梦寐以求的那栋房子的。

他坚信，如果能在短短几个月内攒够几千美元，最后一定能买下那套房产。多年来，他们俩一直想买下那栋房子，可连分期付款的钱都筹不出来。

然而，不到一年，他居然攒了2万多美元，已经足够预付首期款了。他在如此短的时间里，就完成了多年来一直未能完成的事情，妥善解决了自己的财政收入。

结果，这段经历给了他对钱的一种不同感受。他和太太决定继续保留他们的第二个户头，甚至这次他们决定开始筹措自己的养老金，还是每周存一次钱，只是比以前买房阶段稍少一点。

一次不幸的遭遇带来的经验给他上了宝贵的一课，使他重新制订了攒钱计划，并养成了节省的好习惯。在此过程中，不光他一人，他也改变了自己家庭的命运。现在，他正享受着无限的物质财富及其带来的自豪和成就感。

吸取经验的价值给我们上了一堂宝贵的人生课——失败或成功，往往就在一念之间。

在我们遇到挫折时，请永远记住：成功经常乔装而来。

A Simple Idea from a Billionaire

It's simple and powerful. The philosophy of successful people is often easy to understand. The more I look at how successful people got that way, the more I realize how straightforward they think.

For example, consider these comments from Mark Cuban, billionaire, mercurial owner of the Dallas Mavericks, and star of the reality TV series "The Benefactor."

When asked the key to recognizing opportunity, he sites doing one's homework as the most important factor. "The hard part is doing the homework to know if the idea could work in an industry," he says. "Then doing the preparation to be able to execute on the idea."

He admits that he does not have original ideas. He combines existing ideas in unique ways that no one else is doing. Of course, he knows no one else is doing it because he has thoroughly studied his industry.

He says that the characteristics of an entrepreneur are willingness to learn, focus, ability to absorb information, and no illusions about competitors' desire to overtake you.

Cuban says that when he set the goal to retire at 35, he studied everything he could find about business and the industries that interested him. He actually considered any job as a paid opportunity to learn more about a business.

He advises entrepreneurs to learn as much about their businesses as possible and never take shortcuts. Over and over again, he emphasizes homework, superior knowledge, the drive to learn, and the need to get to work.

Nothing complicated in this philosophy, is there?

Anyone could adopt his ideas and do well at anything. Regardless of your dream, if you do your homework, you greatly enhance your odds of success.

Do yourself a favor. Do your homework. It's simple and insures success. And you can be your own benefactor.

亿万富翁的简单想法

成功人士的哲理往往容易理解、简单有效。我认识的成功人士越多，慢慢发现他们的想法越简单直接。

我来举个例子吧，想想看公众舆论对马克·库班的评论——一个亿万富翁，达拉斯小牛队的大东家，真人秀节目《恩人》明星。

当问到他发掘机遇的关键时，他说做好自己的准备工作是至关重要的因素。"最难的部分是要做好准备工作，要知道自己的想法能否在企业中付诸实践，"他说。"然后就要按着原定思路往下进行。"

他承认自己并无原定想法，只是把已经存在、前人未曾做过的想法融会贯通，自创了一套独一无二的思路。他理所当然地知道没有人做过，因为此前他全面调查了他的企业市场。

他说要当一名企业家，就必须不断求知、不耻下问，要一心一意有始有终，要有掌握信息的能力和手段，还有就是不能疑神疑鬼，老担心你的竞争对手哪天会把你吃掉。

库班说，当他给自己定了个目标，就是要在35岁退休时，研读所有他能找到的关于生意、企业的让他很感兴趣的资料和书籍。事实上，他认为任何工作都是花钱都买不到的探索求知商机的宝贵机遇。

他建议所有的企业家都应该尽可能多了解、学习自己的生意，千万不要偷懒图省事走捷径。在谈话中，他一再强调成功的关键是准备工作、渊博的学识、强烈的求知欲，以及亲身体验工作的必要性。

这种哲理根本都不复杂，不是吗？

其实，任何人都可以采用他的方法，都会把事情做好。无论你有什么梦想，只要做好准备工作，就会极大提高成功的概率。

帮自己一个忙：为自己作好充分准备！这很简单，并确保成功，你可以成为自己的恩人！

The Greatest Hitter

A little boy was overheard talking to himself as he strutted through the backyard, wearing his baseball cap and toting a ball and bat. "I'm the greatest hitter in the world," he announced. Then, he tossed the ball into the air, swung at it, but missed.

"Strike One!" he yelled. Undaunted, he picked up the ball and said again, "I'm the greatest hitter in the world!"

He tossed the ball into the air. When it came down he swung again and missed. "Strike Two!" he cried out.

The boy then paused a moment to examine his bat and ball carefully. He spit on his hands and rubbed them together. He straightened his cap and said once more, "I'm the greatest hitter in the world!" Again he tossed the ball up in the air and swung at it. He missed. "Strike Three!"

"Wow!" he exclaimed. "I'm the greatest pitcher in the world!"

Your attitude determines how circumstances impact your life. The little boy's circumstances hadn't changed, but his optimistic attitude prompted him to give an encouraging meaning to what had happened.

What difficult time are you going through right now? Can you do something to change it? If you can, don't wait another day. Make the needed changes. If you can't change the circumstance, however, change your attitude. You'll discover circumstances won't have the last word.

The world is so constructed that if you wish to enjoy its pleasures, you must also endure its pains. Like it or not, you can't have one without the other.

Success is not measured by what you accomplish. It's measured by the opposition you encounter and the courage with which you maintain your struggle against the odds.

You'll find all things are difficult before they are easy. The greater your obstacles, the more glory in overcoming them.

最伟大的击球手

一个戴着棒球帽、拿着球和球棒的小男孩趾高气扬地穿越后院时，有人无意中听到他在自言自语。"我是全世界最伟大的击球手，"他宣称道，然后将球抛到空中，挥棒而击，但没有击中。

"第一击！"他喊道，然后不服气地捡起球，又说，"我是全世界最伟大的击球手！"

他再次将球抛向空中。在它快要降到地面时，他又挥棒一击，然而又没击中。"第二击！"他喊道。

小男孩停下来，仔细检查了球和球棒，朝自己掌心猛啐一口，使劲搓了搓，然后正了正球帽又说："我是全世界最伟大的击球手！"再次将球抛向空中奋力一击，然而又没击中。"第三击！"

"哇唔！"他惊呼道。"我是全世界最伟大的投手！"

你的处事态度决定了周围环境对你人生的影响。对小男孩来说，他身边的环境并没有改变，但他积极乐观的态度不断在鼓励他不要轻言放弃。

你现在最艰难的时刻是什么？你会不会想办法被动转主动？如果你能，就不要继续往下拖，现在就立刻转变逆境！如果你不能，那也不要紧，转变你看待事物的态度。最终你会发现环境因素的障碍并不能持久到最后一刻！

这个大千世界的结构如此复杂，如果你真想享乐其中，就必须同时承受它付给你的痛苦。无论你喜不喜欢，这都是一个必经的过程。

成功的标准并不限于你的辉煌战绩，而是取决于挫败时，你是否能鼓起勇气面对它，不断抗争，最终会克服障碍！

你会发现万事开头难。你遭遇的障碍越大，攻破它们时，你的荣誉感就越高。

A Ten-cent Idea

When young F. W. Woolworth was a store clerk, he tried to convince his boss to have a ten-cent sale to reduce inventory.

The boss agreed, and the idea was a resounding success. This inspired Woolworth to open his own store and price items at a nickel and a dime. He needed capital for such a venture, so he asked his boss to supply the capital for part interest in the store.

His boss turned him down flat. "The idea is too risky," he told Woolworth. "There are not enough items to sell for five and ten cents." Woolworth went ahead without his boss's backing, and he not only was successful in his first store, but eventually he owned a chain of F. W. Woolworth stores across the nation.

Later, his former boss was heard to remark, "As far as I can figure out, every word I used to turn Woolworth down cost me about a million dollars."

10美分的主意

年轻的F. W. 伍尔沃斯还是个店员时，曾尽力说服老板开一家10美分的小杂货店来减少库存积压。

老板表示同意，这个明智的想法的确带来了不断的成功。这就刺激了伍尔沃斯自己也要开这样一家10美分店的想法，将商品的价格定位在5美分或10美分。想将这个大胆主意付诸实践，他需要启动资金。于是，他找到老板，想让他为自己的小店赞助启动资金，作为本店的部分股息。

老板一口拒绝了他。"这个想法太冒险了，"他告诉伍尔沃斯，"咱们店没有太多的5美分或10美分的廉价货。"于是，伍尔沃斯在没有老板赞助的情况下自己着手筹措，后来他不仅成功地开起了第一家小店，最终还拥有了全国连锁的F. W. 伍尔沃斯超市。

后来，他的前任老板听说此事后发表评论："据我目前估计，当年我拒绝伍尔沃斯的每个词都价值100万美元。"

Serious Business

Let me take you back a couple years. Come with me as we relearn a lesson, one that has truck with me, in my present memory, and inspires me yet.

We walk into Elida Road Hardware, an old-fashioned hardware store. No automatic door, no computer in the building. Nothing unusual about the day, or the fact that we go to that store. It is one that I go to fairly often. As we enter the door, two sounds greet us. The sleigh bells of last year, the ones that make that sweet, peaceful tinkle as we open the door. The other sound is the beeper that alerts Andy of our presence.

"Good afternoon, Ryan," comes the cheerful acknowledgment Andy Bianco is a very friendly sort of proprietor. He is of medium build and height, and the smile on his face welcomes us.

We walk across the old wood floor—destitute of stain, and worm smooth—with its squeaky spots, and uneven joints. Andy asks us what he can help us with. I tell him we are looking for a spring. He patiently replies, "I carry lots of springs. You're going to need to be more specific."

"Beats me what they're called. Just a spring for an old-fashioned screen door."

"That's it. A screen door spring. Right down there." We turn to where he is pointing, and sure enough, there they are. Andy knows his store, and his produces. That's why I come here. The service can't be beat. The price, Yes. But service and satisfaction? No.

I pick up one and follow him to the counter. A keg of peanuts sits beside the counter, and beside it, another for the hulls. Covering the counter is a piece of Plexiglas, and under it, all manners of business cards.

"Hey, got a card? Put one under here. Free advertising space."

"Thanks, Andy, but I already have one. See, over here."

He figures up the price, doing the math in his head. "$1.88, with Uncle Sam's share comes to $1.99."

"Put it on Pop's account."

He nods and smiles, remembering that this is the third item this week that has received that. "Good old Pop's account." He chuckles. "I don't know what you boys would do without Pop's account!"

He hands me the ticket and as I sign it, I ask, "You really trust my signature?" His reply startles, yet gladdens me. "When I can't trust Jerry Hoover's boys, I can't trust anybody!"

We leave, and the brain immediately starts to forget things, in order of importance. But what Andy Bianco said that day, rang in my ears. And it rings in my ears today. That's a tall order to live up to. It's a high standard of integrity. My father made a reputation for that name, and I get to enjoy the benefits thereof. But by the same token, I must maintain that reputation. And that's serious business.

真正的生意

让我们时空穿梭回到几年前，和我一起来重上一堂课，使我毕生难忘的一课，即使到今天仍存在我的脑海中激励着我。

我们一起进入埃利达路的那家五金器具店——一家出售早已过时的五金

器具的小店，整个大楼内没有一扇自动门，没有一台电脑。那天没什么不寻常的，反正我们就是进了这家店。这是一家我还算经常光顾的小店。进门后，只有两种声音欢迎我们的到来：一种是去年装的雪铃发出的声音，就是那种我们一开门就能听到会发出温柔祥和的叮当声；另一种是能马上惊动安迪的警报器的声音。

"下午好，瑞恩。"此刻传来了安迪·比安科的欢快的欢迎声。他是一位非常友好的业主。他的体型和身高中等，每次欢迎我们时，脸上都挂着微笑。

我们穿过旧木地板——没有斑点没有虫咬——就是吱嘎作响，衔接处凹凸不平。安迪问我们有什么需要他帮助的，我告诉他我们要买根弹簧。他耐心地告诉我们："我这里有很多种弹簧，你得说具体点要哪种。"

"我才不管它们的种类或名字，就给我拿一个能用在过时的纱门上的那种。"

"明白！纱门专用弹簧是吧，就在那里头。"我们顺着他手指的方向望去，没错，就是那种弹簧。安迪非常熟悉他的小店及他出售的产品，这就是我喜欢来这里光顾的原因，服务态度没得说，价格也很便宜，但要说到满意程度，我不是太中意。

我随便挑了一个，便跟他一起来到柜台前，一小桶花生放在柜台旁，它旁边还有一小桶带皮的花生，一块胶质玻璃覆盖了整个台面，下面叠放了各种各样的业务名片。

"喂，有名片吗？拿一张放进这里，免费的广告空间。"

"多谢了，安迪，但我已经放过一张了。瞧见没有，就在这里。"

他心算了一下价格。"1.88美元，含税的话是1.99美元。"

"把它算到老波普的账户上。"

他点点头笑了一下，算起来这是本周第三件类似的物品。"老好人老波普啊，"他咯咯笑道，"我真无法想象，如果没有老波普的户头，你们这些年轻人该怎么办！"

他将小票递给我，我签名时问道："你真相信我的签名？"他的回答让我很吃惊，也很高兴，"如果连自己的同胞都信不过，我还能相信谁呢？"

我们离开时，因为轻重缓急的关系，大脑已迅速开始忘掉刚才的事情。但是，安迪·比安科那天说的话至今仍在我耳中回荡。这种话一般人说不出来，即便能说出来也很难执行，这是诚实的最高境界！我老爹曾因他的名字获得了极高荣誉，我也因此跟着沾了不少光。虽然是借了他的光，但我仍必须维护这种殊荣，这才是真正的生意。

Keep Your Goals away from the Trolls

There is a type of crab that cannot be caught—it is agile and clever enough to get out of any crab trap. And yet, these crabs are caught by the thousands every day, thanks to a particular human trait they possess.

The trap is a wire cage with a hole at the top. Bait is placed in the cage, and the cage is lowered into the water. One crab comes along, enters the cage, and begins munching on the bait. A second crab joins him. A third. Crab Thanksgiving. Eventually, however, all the bait is gone.

The crabs could easily climb up the side of the cage and through the hole, but they do not. They stay in the cage. Other crabs come along and join them—long after the bait is gone. And more.

Should one of the crabs realize there is no further reason to stay in the trap and attempts to leave, the other crabs will gang up on him and stop him. They will repeatedly pull him off the side of the cage. If he is persistent, the others will tear off his claws to keep him from climbing. If he persists still, they will kill him.

The crabs—by force of the majority—stay together in the cage. The cage is hauled up, and it's dinner time on the pier.

The chief difference between these crabs and humans is that these crabs live in water and humans on land.

Anyone who has a dream—one that might get them out of what they see to be a trap—had better be aware of the fellow-inhabitants of the trap.

The human crabs (we call them trolls) do not usually use physical force—although they are certainly not above it. They generally don't need it, however. They have more effective methods at hand, and in mouth—doubt, ridicule, innuendo, mockery, sarcasm, scorn, humiliation, jeering, taunting, teasing, lying, and dozen others not listed in our dictionary.

Our suggestion: keep the trolls away from your goals.

让钓饵远离你的目标

世上有一种螃蟹永远都不会被逮住——这种螃蟹足够灵活、聪明，任何捉螃蟹的陷阱都逮不到它。然而，近年来，这些螃蟹每日都被数以万计的陷阱活捉，这要归功于设计这种精巧机关的人的智商。

这种陷阱是一种顶部带有小洞的钢丝笼。诱饵事先被放入笼内，然后将笼子降到水里。一只螃蟹游过来，钻进笼内，然后开始咀嚼钓饵。第二只螃蟹加入了它的行列，然后是第三只……真是螃蟹感恩节！实在是太棒了！然而，到最后，所有的钓饵都被吃光了。

螃蟹们吃完后完全可以轻易地爬到笼子顶端，从小洞里钻出去，但它们没有这样做，而是选择留在笼内。其他的螃蟹见状，也都凑过来加入了它们的队伍——而此时已经根本没有钓饵了，但越来越多的螃蟹继续往陷阱里钻。

此刻，只要有一只螃蟹意识到根本没有必要留在笼内试图离开，其他所有的螃蟹就会联合起来一同阻止它。它们会不间断地把每次快要爬到出口的螃蟹给拽回来。如果这只螃蟹仍然固执己见，其他螃蟹会把它的钳子扯下来，阻止它往上爬。如果它还是坚持，其他螃蟹最终会杀了它。

螃蟹的团队意识很强，天生都是少数服从多数——要么一起留在笼子里，要么一起逃出去。等笼子被人拉上去时，它们就都成了码头餐馆的开胃菜。

这些螃蟹和人类最大的区别在于，螃蟹住在水里，人类居住在陆地上。

任何有梦想的人——一个类似那只想逃出去的螃蟹的想法的人——要时刻警惕陷阱里的同胞们！

人蟹（我们称之为钓饵）通常不会使用肉体的力量——再说它们也没有这种力量，而且它们一般不需要。它们有更有效的办法，那就是嘴——怀疑、荒谬、含沙射影、嘲笑、讽刺挖苦、藐视、羞辱、嘲弄揶揄、辱骂、戏弄挑逗、撒谎，还有我们的字典上根本无法查到的数不尽的手段。

我们的建议是：让钓饵远离你的目标。

The Four-Dollar Servant

A rich man, whose name was Mr. Seidman, employed many servants. He treated them all kindly, and they were fond of him and often told him their troubles and asked for his advice. Among these servants were two men, named John and Joseph. John was paid four dollars a week as wages, and Joseph ten dollars a week.

The two men often saw each other at their tasks. John's work was nearly always hard. He had to move heavy furniture about, and carry large boxes and packages up and down stairs. Joseph's work was much easier. He ran errands for his master, worked for him among his books, and wrote letters for him.

John often wondered why Joseph received so large a wage for light work, while he himself worked much harder for less money. He determined to ask Mr. Seidman the reason. He knew that his master was his friend and would be willing to answer his question.

"There is something that puzzles me," he said to Mr. Seidman one day. "I wish you would explain it to me." And he told him his trouble.

Mr. Seidman listened, and then answered, "Yes, I will explain to you the reason for the difference between your wages and Joseph's. But first, do you see the loaded wagon that has stopped in the street? Ask the driver, please, what he has in his load."

John went out to the street and returned at once, saying that the wagon was loaded with wheat. "Where is the wheat going?" asked Mr. Seidman. Again John went out to the wagon.

"The wheat is to be delivered in Brod," he reported. "And from where does it come?" Mr. Seidman asked. Once more John was obliged to go out to the street and speak to the driver of the wagon. Then Mr. Seidman wished to know how much grain there was in the load. As soon as John had learned this, his master asked what the price was per bushel. Again John ran out to the wagon.

Altogether he made five trips in order to answer his master's questions.

Then Mr. Seidman sent for Joseph, who was busy at his work in another room. "Joseph," he said, "run out to that driver and ask him what he has in his wagon. I want to know."

Joseph quickly ran out to the street; and it was not very long—in fact only as long as it took John to ask his first question—before he came back.

"Well?" asked the master. "The driver comes from the town of Sinyava," answered Joseph, "but his load of wheat comes from Svod, and he says he is taking it to Brod. Since early morning he has been on the road, but expects to get to Bond before night. He has more than one hundred and twenty bushels of wheat in the load, and it is worth seventy-five cents a bushel. He tells me the wheat crop has been large this year, and that we may expect a fall in the price before long. Is that all, Mr. Seidman?"

"Yes, that is all, Joseph. Now, John," said Mr. Seidman, "do you understand why Joseph is worth a larger wage than you are?"

John nodded. "Yes," he replied, "He THINKS while he works."

The future is full of promise for those who think and show initiatives.

身价4美元的仆人

从前有个名叫赛德曼的富翁，家里雇了很多仆人，富翁对他们都很好，他们也很爱戴他，他们有什么困惑或想不开时，总是前来寻求富翁的建议。这些仆人中有两个叫约翰和约瑟夫的家伙，约翰周薪4美元，而约瑟夫是10美元。

工作时，二人经常能碰头。约翰的工作繁重辛苦，经常得搬动一些沉重的家具、楼上楼下地搬大箱子和包裹；约瑟夫相对活儿较轻，主要负责主人的一些日常事务安排，替他清理规划书籍与代笔写写信什么的。

约翰一直不理解为何约瑟夫活儿那么轻，但能获得如此高的报酬；而他自己活儿这么重，薪酬却很低。他决定找赛德曼先生问个究竟。他知道主人心地善良，又是他的好友，他一定会回答他的所有疑问。

"有件事我一直很困惑，"有一天，他开门见山道，"我希望你能给我一个合理的解释。"于是，他将自己的疑虑告诉了主人。

赛德曼先生洗耳恭听之后答道："噢，是的，我会告诉你为何你和约瑟夫的薪酬差异这么大。但首先，我想问一下，你看到街上停滞的那辆载满货物的四轮马车了吗？我想请你去问一下车夫，他车上都装了些什么货。"

约翰走到街上，不一会儿就回来了，回复说车上装满了小麦。"这些小麦要运到哪里？"赛德曼又问道。约翰只好再次上街问个究竟。

"小麦是要运到布罗德的，"他回复道，"那它们又是从哪里运来的呢？"赛德曼又问道。约翰不得不再次上街询问车夫，回来复命后，赛德曼又想知道货物中有多少谷粒。约翰刚问清楚并复命后，主人又想知道每蒲式耳（美制1蒲式耳＝35.24升）的价格，约翰只好再次去一问究竟。

为了回答主人的所有问题，约翰总计跑了5趟。

然后，赛德曼先生找来此刻正在另一间房内忙活的乔瑟夫。"约瑟夫，"他说，"出去问问那个马车夫，他车里都有什么货。我想知道。"

约瑟夫迅速跑到街上，不一会儿就跑回来了——事实上和约翰每次跑个来回的时间差不多。

"情况怎么样？"主人问道。"车夫来自辛亚瓦镇，"乔瑟夫回道。"但他车上的小麦运自斯佛德，他说准备运往布罗德。他今天一早启程上路，预计傍晚前行至邦德。他车上共计120多蒲式耳小麦，每蒲式耳价值75美分。他告诉我说今年的小麦产量很高，过不了多久可能得降价，我们或许能廉价收购。还有什么问题吗，赛德曼先生？"

"好了，没问题了，约瑟夫。约翰，"赛德曼说，"现在你明白为何约瑟夫拿的薪酬比你多了吗？"

约翰点点头。"是的，"他答道，"他在工作时总是不断思考。"

成功的未来永远是为那些会思考并有首创精神的人准备的。

Success or Failure

A troubled man made an appointment with a rabbi. He was a wise and gentle rabbi. "Rabbi," said the man, wringing his hands, "I'm a failure. More than half the time I do not succeed in doing what I know I must."

"Oh," murmured the rabbi.

"Please say something wise, rabbi," pleaded the man. After much pondering, the rabbi replied, "Ah, my son, I give you this bit of wisdom: Go and look on page 930 of *The New York Times Almanac* for year 1970, and maybe you will find peace of mind."

Confused by such strange advice, the trouble man went to the library to look up the source. And this is what he found—lifetime batting averages for the world's greatest baseball players. Ty Cobb, the greatest slugger of them all, had a lifetime average of . 367. Even the King of Swat, Babe Ruth, didn't do that well.

So the man returned to the rabbi and questioned, "Ty Cobb,. 367. That's it?"

"Correct," countered the rabbi. "Ty Cobb,. 367. He got a hit once out of every three times at bat. He didn't even hit . 500. So what do you expect already?"

"Aha," said the man, who thought he was a wretched failure because he succeeded only half the time at what he must do.

成功或失败

一个困惑的人约见了一名拉比。他是一名睿智文雅的拉比。"拉比，"这人搓着双手说，"我是个失败者！我虚度了大半生，还没有在我认为自己必须做的事情上成功过。"

"噢。"拉比咕哝道。

"请告诉我该怎么办，拉比。"男人恳求道。深思熟虑后，拉比回复道："啊，我的孩子，我来给你出个聪明的点子：去看一下1970年《纽约时报历书》第930页，或许你会有所觉悟。"

困惑者虽然被这个奇怪建议搞得困惑不解，但他还是去图书馆查阅了一下相关资料，然后发现了这样一条信息——全世界最知名棒球手的终生击球率。泰·柯布，全球最知名的棒球强击手，一生的击球率为0.367，即便是全垒打王贝比·鲁斯也没有他的战绩高。

然后，困惑者回到拉比身边问道："泰·柯布，击球率0.367，就这么多吗？"

"没错，"拉比反驳道，"泰·柯布，击球率0.367。他以前的命中率是1/3，甚至没有过0.500的战绩。那你还指望什么呢？"

"啊哈。"困惑者说，之所以他是个可怜的失败者，是因为他只用了半生时间做他想取得成功之事。

A True Champion

When our second child was born, Jim and I thought she was perfect, but the doctor pointed out that her feet were turned inward. "Left uncorrected, it would be a problem," he told us.

We vowed to do anything we could to help our baby. When only two weeks old, I brought her back to the doctor, just as he had directed, and the doctor put her tiny feet into casts, her precious baby toes just barely visible. Because she was growing, I had to take her back to the doctor every two weeks to have each foot recast.

Eventually the casting was finished and it was time for corrective shoes and bars. Jim and I watched with hope and concern as she struggled to walk. Those first, awkward steps made us so proud. By the time she entered preschool, her steps appeared quite normal. Encouraged by her progress, we looked for something else to help strengthen her lower body.

As it turned out, she loved the ice!

When she turned six, we enrolled her in skating lessons and soon she was gliding like a swan. We watched in amazement as she skimmed the ice. She wasn't the fastest or the most coordinated skater. She had to work hard at every new movement, but she loved the ice and her dedication paid off. At fifteen, she competed in both pairs-skating and the ladies' singles at the 1988 World Junior Championships in Australia, winning both events! At the senior World Championships in 1991, she won the ladies' singles. Then we found ourselves filled with love and admiration in France, at the 1992 Winter Olympics, as our daughter, Kristi Yamaguchi won the gold medal.

I thought back to the early years of challenge for Kristi—the years of fear for us as her parents, and the same years of frustration for her as a child who simply wanted to walk; the endless doctor visits; the arduous first baby steps with bars and corrective shoes. During those years, we didn't expect gold medals and a stunning professional career ahead of her. We stood in awe of Kristi herself, respecting her strength and dedication, and how far she had come on two tiny feet that had once been bound in heavy casts. In our eyes, Kristi had always walked with the grace of a true champion.

真正的冠军

当我们第二个孩子出世时，我和吉姆都认为她很健康，但医生指出她的双脚偏内侧。"如不矫正，会成问题。"他告诉我们说。

我们发誓要尽最大努力帮助我们的孩子。她两周大时，我带她又去拜访了那位医生。诚如医生所说，当把她细弱的双脚并在一起时，她那细嫩的小脚趾头几乎都看不到了。因为她正在成长阶段，所以我只得每两周带她来看医生，以便重新匹配双脚。

最终，矫正手术成功，该是买合脚的鞋和扶手的时候了。我和吉姆满怀希望地注视她蹒跚行走，心里却如五味瓶。最初拙笨的步履让我们好生喜悦，到上幼儿园时，她的步履看上去仍很正常。受她恢复进展的鼓舞，我们决定找出帮她增长身高的方法。

结果证明，她非常喜爱溜冰。

她6岁时，我们给她报了学溜冰的小班。不久，她就能像天鹅一般在冰上滑翔。看着她在冰上如履平地，我们叹为观止。但她并不是那种速度最快动作最协调的溜冰者，因此每学一个新动作后，她都要加倍苦练，但她特别喜欢冰，还有那一腔学习溜冰的热血和壮志。15岁那年，她在澳大利亚举办的1988年度世界青少年锦标赛中分别参加了双人自由滑和女子单人滑项目，并一举夺冠！1991年度世界青少年晋级锦标赛中又获得了女子单人滑冠军！此刻，我们发现自己在全法国境内极受欢迎和崇拜；在1992年度冬季奥林匹克运动会上，我们的宝贝女儿克丽斯蒂·山口又获得了一枚金牌。

我不禁回想起克丽斯蒂早些年经受的磨砺和挑战——那些年，我们作为家长，一直很为她担忧，她仅仅还是个学走路的孩子时经受的不断挫败；我们带她看过无数医生；我们的第一个孩子费力穿上合脚的鞋的情景。那些年里，我们绝没有想过她将来有一天会得到如此多的金牌，为自己赢得了令人惊叹的职业生涯。我们对克丽斯蒂无比敬畏，一直惊叹她的能力与热忱奉献事业的精神，同时想想她如何是从一个两只脚曾被深度绑定矫正的小孩子成长为今天举世瞩目的世界冠军走过来的这一路。在我们眼里，克丽斯蒂总是以一名真正冠军的优雅漫步人生路。

A Mirror in the Coffin

One day all the employees reached the office and they saw a big advice on the door on which it was written: "Yesterday, the person who has been hindering your growth in this company passed away. We invite you to join the funeral in the room that has been prepared—the gym."

In the beginning, they all got sad for the death of one of their colleagues, but after a while they started getting curious to know who had hindered the growth of his colleagues and the company itself.

The excitement in the gym was such that security agents were ordered to control the crowd within the room. The more people reached the coffin, the more excitement heated up. Everyone thought, "Who is this guy who was hindering my progress? Well, at least he died!"

One by one the thrilled employees got closer to the coffin, and when they looked inside it they suddenly became speechless. They stood nearby the coffin, shocked and in silence, as if someone had touched the deepest part of their soul.

There was a mirror inside the coffin. Everyone who looked inside it could see himself. There was also a sign next to the mirror that said, "There is only one person who is capable to set limits to your growth: It is YOU."

Yes, the sign is right. You are the only person who can revolutionize your life. You are the only person who can influence your happiness, your realization and your success. You are the only person who can help yourself. Your life does not change when your boss changes, when your friends change, when your parent change, when your partner changes, when your company changes. Your life changes when YOU change, when you go beyond your limiting beliefs, when you realize that you are the only one responsible for your life. "The most important relationship you can have is the one you have with yourself."

Examine yourself, watch yourself. Don't be afraid of difficulties, impossibilities and losses. Be a winner, build yourself, and build your reality.

The world is like a mirror. It gives back to anyone reflection of the thoughts in which one has strongly believed.

The world and your reality are like mirrors lying in a coffin, which show to any individual the death of his divine capability to imagine and create his happiness and his success. It's the way you face life that makes the difference.

棺材里的一面镜子

有一天，所有的员工进办公室时，看见门上有个大标语：公司里一直阻挠你们成长的人昨天已死。我们邀请你们一起到指定房间参加葬礼——就在体育馆。

起初，所有人都为他们过世的同僚感到难过，但过了一会儿，他们不禁觉得奇怪：公司里哪位阻挠了同事们的成长公司的发展呢？

体育馆内人群骚动，大批保安奉命监控室内的人群。靠近棺材的人越多，室内的骚动越强烈。每个人此刻都在想："究竟是谁阻挠我的发展？不过，至少他死了！"

恐惧的员工们一个接一个靠近棺材，可当他们看清里面的东西后顿时缄默无声。他们静静地站在棺木旁，全身不住颤抖，好似某人触摸到了他们灵魂最深处的部分。

棺材里是一面镜子，每个人通过镜子都能清晰地看到自己，镜子旁边还有一条标语：世上唯独有一人可以阻挠你的成长——那就是你自己！

是的，这句话说得一点也不错，只有你自己才能改变你的人生，只有你自己才能操控你的幸福、意识和成功，只有你自己能帮助你！你的人生不会因老板、朋友、父母、伙伴或公司的改变而改变，而只因你自己的改变。当你能冲破自己传统局限的信仰，并意识到自己才是唯一对自己人生要负责的人时而改变。"你人生中最重要的人际关系就是你一定要和自己搞好关系。"

反省自己，观察自己。永远不要怕困难、麻烦、损失，如果要成为一名大赢家，那就树立自己的形象，实现自己的梦想。

世界就像一面镜子，任何时候都能反映你坚信的真实想法。

世界和你的现实就像同时躺在棺材里的两面镜子，将任何人的纯洁想象及创造自己幸福与成功的能力扼杀于此。这就是你面对截然不同人生的策略。

Visualize Your Goal

The Catalina Island is twenty-one miles away from the coast of California, and many people have taken the challenge to swim across it.

On July 4th 1952, Florence Chadwick stepped into the water off Catalina Island to swim across to the California coast. She started well and on course, but later fatigue set in, and the weather became cold.

She persisted, but fifteen hours later, numb and cold, she asked to be taken out of the water. After she recovered, she was told that she had been pulled out only half a mile away from the coast. She commented that she could have made it, if the fog had not affected her vision and she would have just seen the land. She promised that this would be the only time that she would ever quit.

She went back to her rigorous training. And two months later she swam that same channel. The same thing happened. The fatigue set in, and the fog obscured her view, but this time she swam with faith and vision of the land in her mind. She knew that somewhere behind the fog was land.

She succeeded and became the first woman to swim the Catalina Channel. She even broke the men's record by two hours.

Success Principle: When you set your goal, keep pressing one even when you are tired, physically and mentally, and even though there are many challenges ahead. Keep the vision of your goal crystal clear before you and never, never, never give up! See the reaching, commit to it, and you will surely see your goal realized.

想象你的目标

圣卡塔利娜岛离加利福尼亚州的海滨相距34千米远，有不少人尝试过从一端游到另一端的挑战。

1952年7月4日，弗罗伦斯·查德维克从圣卡塔利娜岛上踏入水中，准备游到对岸的加州海滨。开始，她按照原定路线游得很好，但过了一会儿感到全身疲劳，而且天气变冷了。

她坚持不懈，可15小时后，她既麻木又冰冷，因此马上要求救援人员将她打捞出水面。等她恢复后，别人告诉她当时她已游到离目的地只有半英里远的海域而被人打捞了出来。她评论道，如果不是大雾影响她的视觉，她一定能看到陆地取得成功，并发誓这是她一生中第一次也是最后一次半途而废。

她又回到了严格训练中。两个月后，她再次挑战同样的比赛，这次又发生了相同的事情：全身疲惫不堪，浓雾遮挡了她的视线。但这次她心存信念，脑海中充满了陆地的景象，她知道大雾后边某处就是陆地。

这次，她获得了成功，成为第一个游过圣卡塔利娜水道的女人，甚至以2小时的最快战绩打破了男人的纪录。

成功的定律就是：你定好目标时，就要坚持实现这一目标，即便你身心疲惫，即便前面有许多挑战。永远看清自己的目标，绝对绝对绝对不要放弃！看到目的地时，努力赶上它，你肯定会实现自己的目标。

Kind Act Repaid in Full

One stormy night many years ago, an elderly man and his wife entered the lobby of a small hotel in Philadelphia. Trying to get out of the rain, the couple approached the front desk hoping to get some shelter for the night.

"Could you possibly give us a room here?" the husband asked. The clerk, a friendly man with a winning smile, looked at the couple and explained that there were three conventions in town.

"All of our rooms are taken," the clerk said. "But I can't send a nice couple like you out in the rain at one o'clock in the morning. Would you perhaps be willing to sleep in my room? It's not exactly a suite, but it will be good enough to make you comfortable for the night."

When the couple declined, the young man pressed on. "Don't worry about me. I'll make out just fine," the clerk told them. So the couple agreed.

As he paid his bill the next morning, the elderly man said to the clerk, "You are the kind of manager who should be the boss of the best hotel in the United States. Maybe someday I'll build one for you."

The clerk looked at the couple and smiled. The three of them had a good laugh. As they drove away, the elderly couple agreed that the helpful clerk was indeed exceptional, as finding people who are both friendly and helpful isn't easy.

Two years passed. The clerk had almost forgotten the incident when he received a letter from the old man. It recalled that stormy night and enclosed a round-trip ticket to New York, asking the young man to pay them a visit.

The old man met him in New York, and led him to the corner of Fifth Avenue and 34th street. He then pointed to a great new building there, a palace of reddish stone, with turrets and watchtowers thrusting up to the sky.

"That," said the older man, "is the hotel I have just built for you to manage."

"You must be joking," the young man said.

"I can assure you that I am not," said the older man, a sly smile playing around his mouth.

The old man's name was William Waldorf Astor, and the magnificent structure was the original Waldorf-Astoria Hotel. The young clerk who became its first manager was George C. Boldt. This young clerk never foresaw the turn of events that would lead him to become the manager of one of the world's most glamorous hotels. The Bible says that we are not to turn our backs on those who are in need— for we might be entertaining angels.

善 行 全 还

多年前的一个暴雨之夜，一位老人和他的妻子进了费城一家小旅馆的大厅。为躲避外面的暴雨，夫妇俩走向前台，希望今晚能在那里借宿。

"你能给我们开间房吗？"丈夫问道。店员是个友善的人，脸上挂着胜利的微笑。他看了看夫妇俩，解释说镇里最近刚开了三个集会。

"我们所有的房间都满了，"店员说，"但我也不能眼睁睁地看着像你们这样一对善良夫妇在凌晨一点被大雨淋坏。你们愿意睡我的房间吗？虽然它不是什么标准套间，但至少你们今晚能好好睡一觉。"

当夫妇俩婉言谢绝时，年轻人又督促道："别担心我，我自有安排。"夫妇俩经不住他一再的好意，最后终于同意了。

翌日清晨付账时，老人告诉店员说："我觉得你应该是那种适合在全美国境内拥有最棒饭店的大老板。也许有一天，我会为你建一座饭店。"

店员看了看夫妇俩，笑了笑，他们三人不约而同大笑起来。当夫妇俩开车上路后，他们都认同这个乐于助人的店员的确与众不同，要知道世上能找到一位乐善好施的人的确不容易。

两年后，店员几乎淡忘了当年的这件事。不过，有一天，他收到了那位老人的一封信，信中提到了那个暴雨之夜，还附了一张往返纽约的双程票，老人邀请他去看看他们。

老人在纽约见到了这位年轻人，并带他到第5大道和第34街的交口处，然后指着面前一栋新落成的宏伟大厦——一座用红色石料筑成、附带有许多直冲云霄的塔楼和瞭望塔的"皇宫"。

"那就是，"老人说，"我专门为你建造的饭店。"

"你一定是在开玩笑。"年轻人说。

"我可以向你保证不是。"老人说，嘴上挂起了一丝会意的微笑。

这位老人就是威廉·沃尔道夫·阿斯特，而眼前的这栋宏伟壮观的建筑物就是世上第一家沃尔道夫酒店，这位名叫乔治·C.博尔特的年轻店员成了第一任经理。年轻人做梦也没有想到自己将来有一天能成为全世界顶尖星级酒店之一的总经理。圣经说：我们不要对那些需要帮助的人视若无睹——因为也许我们正款待的是天使。

Success Breeds Success

There was a farmer who grew superior quality and award-winning corn. Each year he entered his corn in the state fair where it won honor and prizes.

One year a newspaper reporter interviewed him and learnt something interesting about how he grew it. The reporter discovered that the farmer shared his seed corn with his neighbors.

"How can you afford to share your best seed corn with your neighbors when they are entering corn in competition with yours each year?" the reporter asked.

"Why sir," said the farmer, "didn't you know? The wind picks up pollen from the ripening corn and swirls it from field to field. If my neighbors grow inferior, substandard and poor quality corn, cross-pollination will steadily degrade the quality of my corn. If I am to grow good corn, I must help my neighbors grow good corn."

The farmer gave a superb insight into the connectedness of life. His corn cannot improve unless his neighbor's corn also improves. So it is in other dimensions! Those who choose to be at harmony must help their neighbors and colleagues to be at peace; those who choose to live well must help others to live well, for the value of a life is measured by the lives it touches; those who choose to be happy must help others to find happiness, for the welfare of each is bound up with the welfare of all.

If we are to grow good quality corn, we must help our neighbors grow good quality corn too.

成功孕育成功

曾经有个农场主种植了大量获奖的优质庄稼。每年，他都会带着自己的谷物参加国家博览会，那里是他荣获荣誉和奖金的地方。

有一年，一名新闻记者采访了他，并学到一些他种植庄稼的有趣方法。记者发现农场主经常和自己的邻居共享谷种。

"你为何会与邻居们分享自己最优质的谷种呢？要知道他，们每年都在和你竞争。"记者问道。

"是啊，先生，"农场主答道，"难道你不知道？大风经常从成熟的庄稼地里挑出许多花粉并在各个田里撒播。若我的邻居们种出劣等的庄稼，异花传粉效应也会让我的庄稼质量大打折扣。如果想种出上好的庄稼，我必须帮助邻居们也种出优等的庄稼。"

农场主对人生的连通性洞察幽微。如果邻居们的庄稼质量上不去，他的也无法提高。所以，其他领域也一样！那些想要获得和谐的人，必须帮助他们的邻居和同事也获取和谐；想要生活舒坦的人，也要帮助其他人活得舒坦，因为生命的价值是靠它给予的其他生命评价的；想要活得幸福的人必先帮助其他人找到幸福，因为每个人的幸福永远都和整体的幸福紧紧相连。

如果想要种出上等庄稼，我们也必须帮助邻居们种出上等庄稼。

Obstacles Don't Have to Stop You

I can remember a period in my life when I was unemployed and money was running short. I needed a job very badly and it seemed as if nobody was hiring.

A very good friend of mine approached me one day with an offer. "I'm going to have to let this job go and I was wondering if you would like to take it over?"

"That would be great," I replied.

I went to speak with the manager and he said he could use me, but never gave me a start date. Really needing the job, I decided to go and check in with him every day. I knew he would eventually get tired of me and give me a starting period. Finally one day he said, "You can start Monday morning."

The next Monday morning, I showed up for work extra early. I was ready to do my best. When I went inside I was informed that I would be buffing the floors. My friend was there to show me how to operate the buffer.

"It's real easy," he said, running the machine very smoothly. He handed it over to me and said, "Here, you give it a try."

I grabbed the handles with a "no problem" attitude and gave it some gas. To my surprise, the buffer whipped around in a big circle, running over my friend's brand new pair of boots, and sending him jumping up on a check-out counter.

Several times, I tried to run it again and failed. I really had to fight that thing to make it go.

"What am I going to do?" I thought to myself. "I finally found a job and I can't do it. Am I going to have to tell them I have to quit?"

After several rough days of buffering, I finally made up my mind that I was going to do this. For about a week, I struggled with the buffer, putting all my weight and strength into it. Eventually, I learned the trick was not to struggle with it at all, just go with the flow of it, and by the second week, I was showing off and running it with one hand.

A few months later, I thought back and wondered what would have happened if I had given up that first week. I certainly would not have had the newfound confidence or a paycheck. Sometime after that experience, I started a new job that required the use of a buffer. I even had to train others to use it, and I always got a kick out of seeing them run it for the first time. I knew, though, if they stuck with it, they would do just fine; they just needed a little encouragement and a lot of practice.

Michael Jordan said, "Obstacles don't have to stop you. If you run into a wall, don't turn around and give up. Figure out how to climb it, go through it, or work around it."

没有过不去的坎儿

我记得在我生命里曾有过那样一段时光——那时候，我正好失业，手头越来越紧。我急需一份工作，可当时好像没人雇我。

有一天，我的一位密友登门拜访，并给我带来了一个工作机遇："我正打算辞职，不知道你想不想接我的班？"

"那太好了。"我答道。

我去见了经理，他说他可以录用我，但并没说什么时候开始上班。迫于对工作的急需，我决定每天都去拜访经理详细了解。我知道他最终肯定会被我折腾得很烦并给我一个确切的回复。终于有一天，他告诉我："你周一早上可以来上班。"

周一早上，我来得特别早，打算好好干一场。我进去后，被告知是来擦地板的，我的朋友也在那里，要给我示范如何使用擦拭器。

"真的很简单，"他一边说，一边熟练操作机器，然后递给我，"拿着试试！"

我非常自信地握住手柄准备放气，但让我惊讶的是，擦拭器只是不停地原地转大圈，一下子窜到朋友的新皮靴上，使他被迫跳到结账柜台上。

又试了几次，但还是没有成功，我真要好好斗斗这部机器，让它听话了。

"我该怎么办？"我暗自想道，"我好不容易找到一个工作，却不能胜任！难道我去告诉他们我要辞职吗？"

经受了艰难操练的数天后，最终我决定要做好这份工作。大约一周时间里，我努力操练机器，全身心地投入工作中。最后，我终于掌握了小窍门，就是不要试图控制机器，要随着机器的运转而操控。到了第二周，我就显摆地单手操作它了。

几个月后，我回想起当初刚进公司的情景，心想如果当时我在第一周就辞掉这份工的话自己会怎么样，我一定不会拥有今日重新树立的自信和薪水。那段经历之后又过了一段时间，我找到一份新工作，仍是要求会使用擦拭器的人。现在，我已能训练其他员工了，看到新手第一次使用擦拭器的情景，我联想到自己的第一次总是忍不住偷笑。他们现在虽不能很好地驾驭它，但我相信终有一天他们可以胜任，他们所需的就是一点点鼓励和大量练习。

迈克尔·乔丹说过："没有过不去的坎儿。如果你不慎钻进了一条死胡同，不要回头也不要轻言放弃，你要冷静想想如何翻越它、穿越它，或者尽快适应它。"

The Three Masters

When one Guru was dying, one of his disciples asked him, "Master, who was your master?"

He said, "I had thousands of masters. If I just relate their names it will take months, years and it is too late. But three masters I will certainly tell you about.

"One was a thief. Once I got lost in the desert, and when I reached a village it was very late. Everything was closed. But at last I found one man who was trying to make a hole in the wall of a house. I asked him where I could stay and he said, 'At this time of night it will be difficult, but you can stay with me—if you can stay with a thief.' I stayed for one month! And each night he would say to me, 'Now I am going to my work. You rest, you pray.' When he came back I would ask, 'Did you get anything?' He would say, 'Not tonight. But tomorrow I will try again.' He was never in a state of hopelessness; he was always happy.

"When I was meditating and meditating for years on end and nothing was happening, many times the moment came when I was so desperate and hopeless that I wanted to stop all this. And suddenly I would remember the thief who would say every night, 'tomorrow it is going to happen.'

"My second master was a dog. I was going to the river, thirsty and a dog came. He was also thirsty. He looked into the river and saw another dog—his own image—and became afraid. He would bark and run away, but his thirst was so much that he would come back. Finally, despite his fear, he just jumped into the water, and the image disappeared. And I knew that a message had come to me from God: one has to jump in spite of all fears.

"And the third master was a small child. I entered a town and a child was carrying a lit candle. He was going to the mosque to put the candle there. 'Just joking,' I asked the boy, 'have you lit the candle yourself?' He said, 'Yes sir.' And I asked, 'There was a moment when the candle was unlit, then there was a moment when the candle was lit. Can you show me the source from which the light came?' And the boy laughed, blew out the candle, and said, 'Now you have seen the light going. Where has it gone? You tell me!'

"My ego was shattered, my whole knowledge was shattered. And that moment I felt my own stupidity. Since then I dropped all my knowledgeability. It is true that I had no master. That does not mean I was not a disciple—I accepted the whole existence as my master. My disciplehood was a greater involvement than yours. I trusted the clouds, the trees. I trusted existence as such. I had no master because I had millions of masters. I learned from every possible source. To be a disciple is a must on the path. What does it mean to be a disciple? It means to be able to learn, to be available to learn, and to be vulnerable to existence. With a master you start learning to learn. The master is a swimming pool where you can learn how to swim. Once you have learned, all the oceans are yours."

三 位 大 师

一位宗师弥留之际，他的一名弟子问道："师父，我想知道谁是你的师父？"

他回道："我有很多位师父，如果要我说出他们的名字可能要花上好几个月或好几年，但恐怕为师撑不了那么久了。但有三位大师，我一定要告诉你。

"第一位是个贼。有一次，我在沙漠中迷了路，到达某个村庄时，天色已晚，所有人家都关门了。但我发现有个人正在一户人家的墙上凿洞。我问他在哪里可以借宿一宿，他便告诉我说：'已经这么晚了，恐怕很难，但你晚上可以和我一起睡——如果你不介意我是个贼的话。'我和他一起住了一个月！每晚他都会告诉我说：'现在我要开工了。你就在家静养为我祈祷吧！'等他回来后，我就会问他：'今晚有收获吗？'他便会说：'什么也没捞着，但明天我会继续努力！'他永远都没有绝望过，总是很开心。

"多年来，我一直不停地思考、思考再思考，到头来什么也没发生，很多时候我都会绝望无助，我想努力克服它，突然我就想到当年那个贼每晚对我说的同样的话：'明天我一定会成功！'

"我的第二位大师是一条狗。我来到河边，当时口渴难耐，这时看到一条狗走过来，看上去它也很渴。它向河中望去，看到另一条狗——实际上是它的倒影——便心生恐惧。它吠了两声，便跑开了，但又实在抵挡不住干渴，就又跑了回来。最终，虽然充满了恐惧，但它还是跳进水里，那倒影也随之消失了。于是，我从上帝那里得到了一条信息：即便充满了恐惧，也要迎头而上。

"第三位大师是个小孩。我进入一座小镇，看到一个小孩端着一支点燃的蜡烛。他准备去清真寺并把蜡烛放在那里。'问句玩笑话，'我问那个男孩，'是你自己点的蜡烛吗？'他说：'是的，先生！'然后我又问道：'蜡烛有时不亮，有时亮，你能告诉我它的光源来自哪里吗？'男孩大笑起来，将蜡烛吹灭，然后反问道：'现在它不亮了。你能告诉我光去哪里了吗？'

"我的自尊受到了打击，我的全部学问也都随之烟灭。那一刻，我感受到了自己的愚蠢之至。从那以后，我放弃了自己所有的学问。说真的，我并没有师父，但这并不意味着我以前不是一位弟子——我将以前所有的经验总结出来，这就成了我的大师。我的弟子生涯远比你的复杂得多，我相信天上的云、地上的树，还有自己以往的经验教训。我之所以没有师父，是因为我有太多的师父，任何潜在的知识我都会虚心学习、不耻下问。当弟子是人生路上的必要阶段！要不然，你说说当弟子是什么意思？其实就是要勤奋学习、有效学习，并折服于现实。身边有大师指点，你才算开始学习如何学习。当你学游泳时，大师就是一个现成的游泳池。一旦你学会，所有大洋就都是你的了。"

A Speech by the CEO of Apple

When I was 17, I read a quote that went something like, "If you live each day as if it was your last, someday you'll most certainly be right." It made an impression on me, and since then, for the past 33 years, I have looked in the mirror every morning and asked myself, "If today were the last day of my life, would I want to do what I am about to do today?" And whenever the answer has been "No" for too many days in a row, I know I need to change something.

Remembering that I'll be dead soon is the most important tool I've ever encountered to help me make the big choices in life. Because almost everything—all external expectations, all pride, all fear of embarrassment or failure—these things just fall away in the face of death, leaving only what is truly important. Remembering that you are going to die is the best way I know to avoid the trap of thinking you have something to lose. There is no reason not to follow your heart.

About a year ago I was diagnosed with cancer. I had a scan at 7 : 30 in the morning, and it clearly showed a tumor on my pancreas. I didn't even know what a pancreas was. The doctors told me this was almost certainly a type of cancer that is incurable, and that I should expect to live no longer than three to six months. My doctor advised me to go home and get my affairs in order, which is doctor's code for preparing to die. It means to try to tell your kids everything you thought you'd have the next 10 years to tell them in just a few months. It means to make sure everything is buttoned up so that it would be as easy as possible for your family. It means to say your goodbyes.

I lived with that diagnosis all day. Later that evening I had a biopsy, where they stuck an endoscope down my throat, through my stomach and into my intestine, put a needle into my pancreas and got a few cells from the tumor. I was sedated, but my wife, who was there, told me that when they viewed the cells under a microscope the doctors started crying because it turned out to be a very rare form of pancreatic cancer that is curable with surgery. I had the surgery and I'm fine now.

This was the closest I've been to facing death, and I hope it's the closest I get for a few more decades. Having lived through it, I can now say this to you with a bit more certainty then when death was a useful but purely intellectual concept.

No one wants to die. Even people who want to go to heaven don't want to die to get there. And yet death is the destination we all share. No one has ever escaped it. And that is as it should be, because death is very likely the single best invention of life. It is life's change agent. It clears out the old to make way for the new. Right now the new is you, but someday not too long from now, you will gradually become the old and be cleared away. Sorry to be so dramatic, but it is quite true.

Your time is limited, so don't waste it living someone else's life. Don't be trapped by dogma—which is living with the results of other people's thinking. Don't let the noise of others' opinions drown out your own inner voice. And most importantly, have the courage to follow your heart and intuition. They somehow already know what you truly want to become. Everything else is secondary.

苹果公司总裁的一次演讲

17岁那年，我读了一份这样的引文："如果每天都像过生命中的最后一天那样，总有一天你肯定会顺风顺水！"这篇引文让我印象深刻，从那以后，过去33年来，我每天早晨都会面对镜子问自己："如果今天是我生命中的最后一天，我是不是要干出点什么呢？"可是，一连许多天，我仍碌碌无为，我明白我必须有所改变。

一生中，我遇到重大选择时，都在心里默默告诉自己今天是我在尘世中的最后一天，这样让我更加发奋努力。因为几乎世间万物——所有外在的期望、骄傲、对尴尬或失败的恐惧——这些其实在死亡面前都已不再重要，而真正重要的因素不多。永远记得你终有一死，这样你才能避免陷入总是顾虑怕会损失什么的漩涡中。你没有理由不相信自己的直觉。

大约一年前，我被诊断出患了癌症。我早上7点30分作了扫描，清晰显示出我的胰腺内有个肿瘤。我当时甚至不知道什么叫胰腺。医生告诉我说这种癌症根本无可救药，我活不过3至6个月。医生建议我回去准备料理后事，看来医生是已经对我开了死亡通行证了。这意味着你以前安慰自己的孩子说你还能再活10年，事实上却没几个月可活了，也意味着一切都已成定局，回去后你也不必再隐瞒什么，对你的家人说实话，还意味着对你自己诀别。

整整一天，我都在医院诊疗，晚上晚些时候，我又作了个活组织检查，医生们将内诊镜插入我的喉部，直穿胃部透入肠子里，在胰腺内插了根小针，从肿瘤上取了一些组织细胞。我当时很镇静，但太太事后告诉我说医生们用显微镜检查了那些组织细胞发出惊叹，因为他们发现我的病实际上是一种非常罕见的胰腺癌，但可以用手术治疗。后来，我便做了手术，现在已经康复了。

这是我平生直面死神最玄乎的一次，我希望这次的炼狱经历能让我多活几年。遭此经历后，我现在可以直言不讳地告诉你们大家：死亡并不可怕，可怕的是我们没有勇气面对它。

没有人想死。即使那些死后想上天堂的人现在也不愿死。而死亡确是我们共同的目的地，没有人能逃脱死神的魔爪。而且应该是这样，因为死亡十有八九也是生命的最好产物，它就像是生命的促变者——清除腐朽的事物并创造出新鲜的产物！此刻，你们就是那新的产物，但过不了多久，你们终有一天也会变成腐朽的东西而被清理掉。很抱歉我说得这么刻薄，但它却是不争的事实。

人生短暂，因此不要浪费自己的生命去过他人的生活。不要受传统教条或规则的束缚——这样你会和大多人一样一辈子平庸。不要让他人的评论和闲言碎语淹没自己的想法。还有最重要的一点，那就是鼓起勇气跟着自己的想法和直觉走。终有一天，世人会理解你。其他的一切都是次要的。

Be Patient

This is a true story which happened in the United States. A man came out of his home to admire his new truck. To his puzzlement, his three-year-old son was happily hammering dents into the shiny paint.

The man ran to his son, knocked him away, and hammered the little boy's hands into pulp as punishment.

When the father calmed down, he rushed his son to the hospital. Although the doctor tried desperately to save the crushed bones, he finally had to amputate the fingers from both the boy's hands.

When the boy woke up from the surgery and saw his bandaged stubs, he innocently said, "Daddy, I'm sorry about your truck." Then he asked, "But when are my fingers going to grow back?"

The father went home and committed suicide.

Think about the story the next time you see someone spill milk at a dinner table or hear a baby crying. Think first before you lose your patience with someone you love. Trucks can be repaired. Broken bones and hurt feelings often can't.

Too often we fail to recognize the difference between the person and the performance. People make mistake. We are allowed to make mistakes. But the actions we take while in a rage will haunt us forever. Pause and ponder. Think before you act. Be patient. Understand and love.

凡事要忍耐

这是发生在美国的一个真实故事。一个男人走出家门去欣赏他的新卡车。令他费解的是，他3岁大的儿子正开心地在闪亮的车漆上砸小洞。

男人跑过去把他赶到一边。作为惩罚，他使劲地捶打起儿子的双手，打得血肉模糊。

等父亲冷静下来后，立刻带着儿子去了医院。尽管医生试尽了各种办法来矫正被打折的骨头，但最后还是要切除小男孩双手的所有手指。

小男孩从手术中醒来后，看到自己缠满绷带的双手，无辜地说道："爸爸，我不是故意损坏你的卡车。"然后想了一下，他又问道，"但我的手指什么时候能长回来呢？"

这位父亲，回家就自杀了。

如果下次你看到某人在饭桌上弄洒了牛奶或听到婴儿的啼哭声，就想一下这个故事。在你失去耐性和理智即将要伤害到自己所爱的人时，先冷静地思考。损毁的卡车可以修理，但被打折的骨头和被伤害的感情再也无法修复。

我们很多时候都意识不到人和行为的差异。人会犯错误，我们每个人都被允许犯错误。但是，在狂怒时采取的行动可能会让我们悔恨终生。遇事要学会冷静思考，在你作出任何举动之前，要好好想想。凡事要忍耐、理解和爱。

Performance Check

A little boy went into a drug store and asked for a phone call.

The boy asked, "Lady, can you give me the job of cutting your lawn?"

The woman replied, "I already have someone cut my lawn."

"Lady, I will cut your lawn for half the price of the person who cuts your lawn now," replied the boy.

The woman responded that she was very satisfied with the person who was presently cutting her lawn.

The little boy found more perseverance and offered, "Lady, I'll even sweep your curb and your sidewalk, so on Sunday you will have the prettiest lawn in all of North-Palm beach, Florida." Again the woman answered in the negative.

With a smile on his face, the little boy replaced the receiver.

The store-owner who was listening all the time walked over to the boy and said, "Son, I like your attitude. I like that positive spirit and would like to offer you a job."

The little boy replied, "No thanks, I was just checking my performance with the job I already have. I am now working for that lady I was talking to!"

自 我 检 测

一个小男孩走进一家杂货店，要求打电话。

男孩问："夫人，你能给我一份剪你们家草坪的工作吗？"

妇人回答说："我的草坪已经有人剪了。"

"夫人，我只收那个给你剪草坪的人的费用的一半。"男孩回答说。

妇人回答说："我对现在给我剪草坪的人非常满意。"

小男孩似乎更加坚定不移地要求道："夫人，我甚至可以为你打扫路边石和人行道。这样，星期日，你就可以拥有佛罗里达北棕榈海岸最漂亮的草坪了。"夫人再次表示拒绝。

小男孩脸上露出了微笑，放下话筒。

那个听了谈话全过程的店主，此时走向小男孩说："孩子，我喜欢你的态度，欣赏你这种积极的精神，我很乐意给你提供这份工作。"

小男孩回答说："不，谢谢，刚才我只是检测我干的这份工作的表现，我要去给刚才和我通话的夫人工作了。"

第八卷

让生活充满阳光

Live in "Day-tight Compartments"

In the spring of 1871, a young man picked up a book and read twenty-one words that had a profound effect on his future. A medical student at the Montreal General Hospital, he was worried about passing the final examination, worried about what to do, where to go, how to build up a practice, how to make a living.

The twenty-one words that this young medical student read in 1871 helped him to become the most famous physician of his generation. He organised the world-famous Johns Hopkins School of Medicine. He became Regius Professor of Medicine at Oxford—the highest honour that can be bestowed upon any medical man in the British Empire. He was knighted by the King of England. When he died, two huge volumes containing 1, 466 pages were required to tell the story of his life.

His name was Sir William Osler. Here are the twenty-one words that he read in the spring of 1871—twenty-one words from Thomas Carlyle that helped him lead a life free from worry: "Our main business is not to see what lies dimly at a distance, but to do what lies clearly at hand."

Forty-two years later, on a soft spring night when the tulips were blooming on the campus, this man, Sir William Osler, addressed the students of Yale University. He told those Yale students that a man like himself who had been a professor in four universities and had written a popular book was supposed to have"brains of a special quality". He declared that that was untrue. He said that his intimate friends knew that his brains were"of the most mediocre character."

What, then, was the secret of his success? He stated that it was owing to what he called living in"daytight compartments". What did he mean by that? A few months before he spoke at Yale, Sir William Osler had crossed the Atlantic on a great ocean liner where the captain standing on the bridge, could press a button and—presto! — there was a clanging of machinery and various parts of the ship were immediately shut off from one another—shut off into watertight compartments. "Now each one of you," Dr. Osler said to those Yale students, "is a much more marvellous organization than the great liner, and bound on a longer voyage. What I urge is that you so learn to control the machinery as to live with'day-tight compartments'as the most certain way to ensure safety on the voyage. Get on the bridge, and see that at least the great bulkheads are in working order. Touch a button and hear, at every level of your life, the iron doors shutting out the Past—the dead yesterdays. Touch another and shut off, with a metal curtain, the Future—the unborn tomorrows. Then you are safe—safe for today!…Shut off the past! Let the dead past bury its dead…Shut out the yesterdays which have lighted fools the way to dusty death…The load of tomorrow, added to that of yesterday, carried today, makes the strongest falter. Shut off the future as tightly as the past…The future is today…There is no tomorrow. The day of man's salvation is now. Waste of energy, mental distress, nervous worries dog the steps of a man who is anxious about the future…Shut close, then the great fore and aft bulkheads, and prepare to cultivate the habit of life of'day-tight compartments'."

Did Dr. Osler mean to say that we should not make any effort to prepare for tomorrow? No. Not at all. But he did go on in that address to say that the best possible way to prepare for tomorrow is to concentrate with all your intelligence, all your enthusiasm, on doing today's work superbly today. That is the only possible way you can prepare for the future. By all means take thought for the tomorrow, yes, careful thought and planning and preparation. But have no anxiety.

活在"完全独立的今天"

1871年春天，一个年轻人看到一本书，读到了对他的前途产生莫大影响的21个字。作为蒙特利尔综合医院的一名医科学生，他正担心怎样通过期末考试、将来怎么办、毕业以后去哪里、怎样才能开业、如何谋生？

这位年轻的医科学生在1871年看到的那21个字，使他成为他那一代最著名的医学家。他创建了世界著名的约翰·霍普金斯医学院，并且成为牛津大学医学院的钦定教授——这是英国医学人员所获得的最高荣誉。他还被英国国王封为爵士。他去世时，需要厚达1466页的两大本书来记述他的一生。

他的名字叫威廉·奥斯勒。下面就是他在1871年春天看到的那21个字。它们出自托马斯·卡莱尔之手，使他免除了忧虑的困扰，这21个字就是：我们的主旨非观远处模糊之事，乃做手边清晰之事。

42年后，在郁金香开满校园的一个温和的春夜，威廉·奥斯勒爵士给耶鲁大学的学生作了一次演讲。他对那些耶鲁大学的学生们说，像他这样一位在四所大学当过教授又写过一本很受欢迎的书的人，似乎应该有一颗"特殊的大脑"，但其实并不是这样。他说，他的一些好朋友都知道，他的大脑"最普通不过了"。

那么，他成功的秘诀究竟是什么呢？他认为这完全是因为他生活在"一个完全独立的今天"。这究竟是什么意思呢？就在去耶鲁大学演讲的几个月之前，奥斯勒爵士搭乘一艘大型轮船横渡大西洋，有一次看见船长站在船舵室中，按下一个按钮，立即听到一阵机械运转的声音，轮船的各个部分立刻彼此隔绝开来，成了几个完全防水的隔离舱。"你们每一个人，"奥斯勒博士对那些耶鲁大学的学生说，"头脑都要比那艘大轮船精密得多，要走的路程也更远。我要求的是你们也必须学习控制一切，活在一个'完全独立的今天'，这才是在航程中确保安全的最好方法。如果到船舱室去，你将会发现那些大的隔离舱至少都可以使用。按下按钮，用铁门隔断过去——已经过去的昨天。再按下另一个按钮，用铁门隔断未来——尚未到来的明天。然后，你就保险了——今天安全了…切断过去，埋葬已逝的过去……切断那些会把傻瓜引到死亡之路的昨天……明天的重担加上昨天的重担，就会成为今天最大的障碍。要把未来像过去一样紧紧地关在门外……未来就在于今天……没有明天。人类得到救赎的日子就是现在。精力的浪费、精神的郁闷、神经的忧虑，都会紧紧跟随着一个担忧未来的人……那么，把船前船后的隔离舱都关掉吧，准备养成活在'完全独立的今天'的习惯。"

奥斯勒博士是不是说我们不必为明天做准备呢？不是，绝对不是。在那次演讲中，他继续说："为明天做准备的最好方法，就是集中你所有的智慧和热忱，把今天的工作做得尽善尽美，这就是你能应对未来的唯一可行的方法。"

一定要为明天着想——不错，一定要仔细考虑、计划和准备，但不要焦虑。

One Grain of Sand at a Time

In April, 1945, I had worried until I had developed what doctors call a"spasmodic transverse colon" —a condition that produced intense pain. If the war hadn't ended when it did, I am sure I would have had a complete physical breakdown.

I was utterly exhausted. I was a Graves Registration, noncommissioned Officer for the 94th Infantry Division. My work was to help set up and maintain records of all men killed in action, missing in action, and hospitalised. I also had to help disinter the bodies of both Allied and enemy soldiers who had been killed and hastily buried in shallow graves during the pitch of battle. I had to gather up the personal effects of these men and see that they were sent back to parents or closest relatives who would prize these personal effects so much. I was constantly worried for fear we might be making embarrassing and serious mistakes. I was worried about whether or not I would come through all this. I was worried about whether I would live to hold my only child in my arms—a son of sixteen months, whom I had never seen. I was so worried and exhausted that I lost thirty-four pounds. I was so frantic that I was almost out of my mind. I looked at my hands. They were hardly more than skin and bones. I was terrified at the thought of going home a physical wreck. I broke down and sobbed like a child. I was so shaken that tears welled up every time I was alone. There was one period soon after the Battle of the Bulge started that I wept so often that I almost gave up hope of ever being a normal human being again.

　　I ended up in an Army dispensary. An Army doctor gave me some advice which has completely changed my life. After giving me a thorough physical examination, he informed me that my troubles were mental. "Ted", he said,"I want you to think of your life as an hourglass. You know there are thousands of grains of sand in the top of the hourglass; and they all pass slowly and evenly through the narrow neck in the middle. Nothing you or I could do would make more than one grain of sand pass through this narrow neck without impairing the hourglass. You and I and everyone else are like this hourglass. When we start in the morning, there are hundreds of tasks which we feel that we must accomplish that day, but if we do not take them one at a time and let them pass through the day slowly and evenly, as do the grains of sand passing through the narrow neck of the hourglass, then we are bound to break our own physical or mental structure."

　　I have practised that philosophy ever since that memorable day that an Army doctor gave it to me. "One grain of sand at a time…One task at a time." That advice saved me physically and mentally during the war; and it has also helped me in my present position of public Relations and Advertising Director for the Adcrafters Printing & Off-set Co. Inc. I found the same problems arising in business that had arisen during the war: a score of things had to be done at once—and there was little time to do them. We were low in stocks. We had new forms to handle, new stock arrangements, changes of address, opening and closing offices, and so on. Instead of getting taut and nervous, I remembered what the doctor had told me. "One grain of sand at a time. One task at a time." By repeating those words to myself over and over, I accomplished my tasks in a more efficient manner and I did my work without the confused and jumbled feeling that had almost wrecked me on the battlefield.

一次只流过一粒沙子

　　1945年4月，我因为忧虑而患上了一种被医生称为"结肠痉挛"的病，这种病很痛苦。如果战争不在那时结束的话，我想我整个人都会垮掉。

　　当时，我筋疲力尽。我在第94步兵师担任士官，负责建立和保管在作战中死伤和失踪士兵的名录，还要帮助发掘那些在战争期间被打死而草草掩埋的敌我双方的士兵尸体。我必须收集那些人的私人物品，把这些东西准确地送回重视这些私人物品的父母或近亲手中。我一直担心自己会造成一些让人难堪的或严重的错误，还担心我是否撑得过去，担心自己还能不能活着回去搂抱我的独生子——我从来没有见过的儿子已经16个月大了。我既担心又疲劳，整整瘦了34磅，而且几乎要发疯了。我眼看着自己的两只手瘦得只剩下皮包骨。一想到自己瘦弱不堪地回家，我就害怕。我崩溃了，像个孩子一样哭了，每当独自一人时，我就眼泪汪汪。有一段时间，也就是在大反攻开始不久，我常常哭泣，几乎放弃了做一个正常人的希望。

最后，我住进了部队医院。一位军医给了我一些忠告，彻底改变了我的生活。在给我做完一次全面检查之后，他告诉我说我的问题纯粹是精神上的。"泰德，"他说，"我希望你把自己的生活想象成一个沙漏。你知道，在沙漏的上半部分有成千上万粒的沙子，它们都缓慢而均匀地流过中间那条细缝。除非把沙漏弄坏，你和我都不能让两粒以上的沙子同时穿过那条窄缝。你和我，以及每一个人，都像这个沙漏。每天早上，我们都有许许多多的工作要在这一天之内完成。但如果我们不是每次只做一件，让它们缓慢而均匀地通过这一天，就像沙粒通过沙漏的窄缝一样，那我们就会损害自己的身体或精神。"

从这个值得纪念的日子开始，这位军医告诉我这些之后，我就一直奉行这种哲学。"一次只流过一粒沙子……一次只做一件事。"这个忠告在战时挽救了我的身心；现在，它对我在工艺印刷公司的公关广告部中的工作也极有帮助。我发现商场上有时也有和战场上一样的问题：一次要做好几件事情，但没有时间。例如我们的材料不够用了，有新的表格等待处理，要安排新的资料，要变更地址，新开设或关闭分公司，等等。我不再紧张不安，因为我记住了那个军医告诉我的："一次只流过一粒沙子，一次只做一件事情。"我一再重复这两句话，工作比以前更有效率了，工作时再也不会有那种在战场上几乎使我崩溃的迷惑而混乱的感觉了。

Every Day Is a New Life

In 1937, I lost my husband, I was very depressed—and almost penniless. I wrote my former employer, Mr. Leon Roach, of the Roach-Fowler Company of Kansas City, and got my old job back. I had formerly made my living selling *World Book* to rural and town school boards. I had sold my car two years previously when my husband became ill; but I managed to scrape together enough money to put a down payment on a used car and started out to sell books again.

I had thought that getting back on the road would help relieve my depression; but driving alone and eating alone was almost more than I could take. Some of the territory was not very productive, and I found it hard to make those car payments, small as they were.

In the spring of 1938, I was working out of Versailles, Missouri. The schools were poor, the roads bad; I was so lonely and discouraged that at one time I even considered suicide. It seemed that success was impossible. I had nothing to live for. I dreaded getting up each morning and facing life. I was afraid of everything: afraid I could not meet the car payments; afraid I could not pay my room rent; afraid I would not have enough to eat. I was afraid my health was failing and I had no money for a doctor. All that kept me from suicide were the thoughts that my sister would be deeply grieved, and that I did not have enough money to pay my funeral expenses.

Then one day I read an article that lifted me out of my despondence and gave me the courage to go on living. I shall never cease to be grateful for one inspiring sentence in that article. It said: "Every day is a new life to a wise man." I typed that sentence out and pasted it on the windshield of my car, where I saw it every minute I was driving. I found it wasn't so hard to live only one day at a time. I learned to forget the yesterdays and to not-think of the tomorrows. Each morning I said to myself: "Today is a new life."

I have succeeded in overcoming my fear of loneliness, my fear of want. I am happy and fairly successful now and have a lot of enthusiasm and love for life. I know now that I shall never again be afraid, regardless of what life hands me. I know now that I don't have to fear the future. I know now that I can live one day at a time—and that"Every day is a new life to a wise man."

每天都是一个新生命

我在1937年失去丈夫，非常颓丧——而且几乎身无分文。我给我以前的东家、堪萨斯市罗奇－弗勒公司的老板利奥·罗奇先生写信，回去干我以前的工作。我以前给学校推销《世界百科全书》为生。两年前，丈夫生病时，我卖掉了汽车；现在，我又勉强凑足了钱，分期付款买了一辆旧车，重新开始出去卖书。

我原想再回去工作或许可以帮助我摆脱颓丧；可是，一个人驾车，一个人吃饭，让我几乎无法忍受。有些地方，我干得很差，虽然分期付款买车的数额不大，却很难付清。

1938年春天，我在密苏里州维萨里市推销。那里的学校都很穷，公路也差，我一个人孤独沮丧，有一次甚至想自杀。我觉得成功很难，而活着又没有什么希望。每天早上，我都很怕起床面对生活。我什么都担心：付不起分期付款的车钱，付不出房租，没有足够的东西吃，担心我的健康恶化却没有钱看病。但是，我没有自杀，唯一的理由是我担心姐姐会因此难过，而我又没有足够的钱支付丧葬费用。

然后有一天，我读到一篇文章，它使我从消沉中振作起来，有了继续活下去的勇气。我对那篇文章中一句令人振奋的话永远心存感激："对一个聪明人来说，每天都是一个新生命。"我用打字机打出这句话，贴在我汽车前面的挡风玻璃上。这样，我开车的时候，每分钟都能看得见。我发现，每次只活一天并不难。我学会了忘记过去，不再担心未来。每天早上，我都会对自己说："今天又是一个新生命。"

我成功地克服了孤寂的恐惧感。我现在过得很快乐，还算比较成功，而且对生命充满了热诚和爱。现在，我也知道，不论在生活上碰到什么事情，我都不会再害怕了；我还知道，我不必害怕未来；我还知道，每次只要活一天——而"对一个聪明人来说，每天都是一个新生命"。

Life Is in the Living

The late Edward S. Evans of Detroit almost killed himself with worry before he learned that life"is in the living, in the tissue of every day and hour." Brought up in poverty, Edward Evans made his first money by selling newspapers, then worked as a grocer's clerk. Later, with seven people dependent upon him for bread and butter, he got a job as an assistant librarian. Small as the pay was, he was afraid to quit. Eight years passed before he could summon up the courage to start out on his own. But once he started, he built up an original investment of fifty-five borrowed dollars into a business of his own that made him twenty thousand dollars a year. Then came a frost, a killing frost. He endorsed a big note for a friend—and the friend went bankrupt. Quickly on top of that disaster came another: the bank in which he had all his money collapsed. He not only lost every cent he had, but was plunged into debt for sixteen thousand dollars. His nerves couldn't take it.

"I couldn't sleep or eat," he told me. "I became strangely ill. Worry and nothing but worry," he said, "brought on this illness. One day as I was walking down the street, I fainted and fell on the sidewalk. I was no longer able to walk. I was put to bed and my body broke out in boils. These boils turned inward until just lying in bed was agony. I grew weaker every day. Finally my doctor told me that I had only two more weeks to live. I was shocked. I drew up my will, and then lay back in bed to await my end. No use now to struggle or worry. I gave up, relaxed, and went to sleep. I hadn't slept two hours in succession for weeks; but now with my earthly problems drawing to an end, I slept like a baby. My exhausting weariness began to disappear. My appetite returned. I gained weight.

"A few weeks later, I was able to walk with crutches. Six weeks later, I was able to go back to work. I had been making twenty thousand dollars a year; but I was glad now to get a job for thirty dollars a week. I got a job selling blocks to put behind the wheels of automobiles when they are shipped by freight. I had learned my lesson now. No more worry for me—no more regret about what had happened in the past—no more dread of the future. I concentrated all my time, energy, and enthusiasm into selling those blocks."

Edward S. Evans shot up fast now. In a few years, he was president of the company—the Evans Product Company. It has been listed on the New York Stock Exchange for years. When Edward S. Evans died in 1945, he was one of the most progressive businessmen in the United States. If you ever fly over Greenland, you may land on Evans Field—a flying-field named in his honour.

Here is the point of the story: Edward S. Evans would never have had the thrill of achieving these victories in business and in living if he hadn't seen the folly of worrying—if he hadn't learned to live in day-tight compartments.

生命就在生活里

底特律已故的爱德华·伊文斯在学会"生命就在生活里，就在每一天每一刻"这个道理之前，几乎因忧虑而自杀。爱德华·伊文斯出生在一个贫苦的家庭，起先是靠卖报为生，然后在一家杂货店打工。后来，由于家里七口人要靠他吃饭，他找到了一个助理图书管理员的工作，虽然薪水很少，但他不敢辞职。直到8年后，他才鼓足勇气开始自己的事业。他用借来的55美元干出了一番事业，一年赚进两万美元。随后，厄运降临：他替一个朋友背负（票据权利转移方式）了一张大额支票，那位朋友却破产了。这次灾祸之后，接着又来了另一次灾祸——他存进所有财产的那家银行倒闭了。他不但损失了所有的钱财，还负债16000美元。他精神上承受不住了。

"我吃不下，睡不着，"他告诉我说，"我得了奇怪的病。没有别的原因，只是因为忧虑。有一天，我正走在街上，突然昏倒在路边上，以后就再也不能走路了。我躺在床上，全身都烂了。伤口逐渐往里面烂，连躺在床上都受不了。我日渐虚弱。最后，医生告诉我，我只能活两个星期。我大吃一惊，写好遗嘱，就躺在床上等死。挣扎或忧虑都没有用了，我只好放弃，开始放松下来，闭目休息。连续好几个星期，我都睡不到两个小时；但现在一切困难都快要结束了，我反而睡得像个婴儿。那些令人疲倦的忧虑渐渐消失了，胃口变好了，体重也开始增加。

"几个星期之后，我就能撑着拐杖走路了。六个星期之后，我又能回去工作了。以前，我一年赚过两万美元，但现在我很高兴找到一星期30美元的工作。我的工作是推销运送汽车的轮船上用在轮子后面的挡板。这时，我已经学会不再忧虑，不再为过去发生的事情后悔，也不再害怕将来。我把所有的时间、精力和热忱都放在推销挡板上。"

爱德华·伊文斯进步非常快。没几年，他就成了伊文斯工业公司的董事长。多年以来，这家公司一直是纽约股票交易所的一家公司。1945年伊文斯去世时，他已成为美国最进步的企业家。如果你乘飞机去格陵兰，很可能降落在伊文斯机场——这个机场是为了纪念他而命名的。

这个故事的启示在于：如果爱德华·伊文斯没有学会"生活在完全独立的今天"的话，他绝不可能获得这样惊人的成就。

A Magic Formula for Solving Worry Situations

Would you like a quick, sure-fire recipe for handling worry situations—a technique you can start using right away, before you go any further in reading this book?

Then let me tell you about the method worked out by Willis H. Carrier, the brilliant engineer who launched the air-conditioning industry, and who is now head of the world-famous Carrier Corporation in Syracuse, New York. it is one of the best techniques I ever heard of for solving worry problems, and I got it from Mr. Carrier personally when we were having lunch together one day at the Engineers' Club in New York.

"When I was a young man," Mr. Carrier said, "I worked for the Buffalo Forge Company in Buffalo, New York. I was handed the assignment of installing a gas-cleaning device in a plant of the Pittsburgh Plate Glass Company at Crystal City, Missouri—a plant costing millions of dollars. The purpose of this installation was to remove the impurities from the gas so it could be burned without injuring the engines This method of cleaning gas was new. It had been tried only once before—and under different conditions. In my work at Crystal City, Missouri, unforeseen difficulties arose. It worked after a fashion—but not well enough to meet the guarantee we had made.

"I was stunned by my failure. It was almost as if someone had struck me a blow on the head. My stomach, my insides, began to twist and turn. For a while I was so worried I couldn't sleep.

"Finally, common sense reminded me that worry wasn't getting me anywhere; so I figured out a way to handle my problem without worrying. It worked superbly. I have been using this same anti-worry technique for more than thirty years. It is simple. Anyone can use it. It consists of three steps:

"Step I. I analysed the situation fearlessly and honestly and figured out what was the worst that could possibly happen as a result of this failure. No one was going to jail me or shoot me. That was certain. True, there was also a chance that I would lose my position; and there was also a chance that my employers would have to remove the machinery and lose the twenty thousand dollars we had invested.

"Step II. After figuring out what was the worst that could possibly happen, I reconciled myself to accepting it, if necessary. I said to myself: This failure will be a blow to my record, and it might possibly mean the loss of my job; but if it does, I can always get another position. Conditions could be much worse; and as far as my employers are concerned—well, they realise that we are experimenting with a new method of cleaning gas, and if this experience costs them twenty thousand dollars, they can stand it. They can charge it up to research, for it is an experiment.

"After discovering the worst that could possibly happen and reconciling myself to accepting it, if necessary, an extremely important thing happened: I immediately relaxed and felt a sense of peace that I hadn't experienced in days.

"Step III. From that time on, I calmly devoted my time and energy to trying to improve upon the worst which I had already accented mentally.

"I now tried to figure out ways and means by which I might reduce the loss of twenty thousand dollars that we faced. I made several tests and finally figured out that if we spent another five thousand for additional equipment, our problem would be solved. We did this, and instead of the firm losing twenty thousand, we made fifteen thousand.

"I probably would never have been able to do this if I had kept on worrying, because one of the worst features about worrying is that it destroys our ability to concentrate. When we worry, our minds jump here and there and everywhere, and we lose all power of decision. However, when we force ourselves to face the worst and accept it mentally, we then eliminate all these vague imaginings and put ourselves in a position in which we are able to concentrate on our problem.

"This incident that I have related occurred many years ago. It worked so superbly that I have been using it ever since; and, as a result, my life has been almost completely free from worry."

Now, why is Willis H. Carrier's magic formula so valuable and so practical, psychologically speaking? Because it yanks us down out of the great grey clouds in which we fumble around when we are blinded by worry. It plants our feet good and solid on the earth. We know where we stand. And if we haven't solid ground under us, how in creation can we ever hope to think anything through?

Professor William James, the father of applied psychology, has been dead in 1910. But if he were alive today, and could hear this formula for facing the worst, he would heartily approve it. How do I know that? Because he told his own students: "Be willing to have it so…Be willing to have it so," he said, "because…acceptance of what has happened is the first step in overcoming the consequences of any misfortune."

The same idea was expressed by Lin Yutang in his widely read book, *The Importance of Living*. "True peace of mind," said this Chinese philosopher, "comes from accepting the worst. Psychologically, I think, it means a release of energy."

That's it, exactly! Psychologically, it means a new release of energy! When we have accepted the worst, we have nothing more to lose. And that automatically means—we have everything to gain! "After facing the worst," Willis H. Carrier reported, "I immediately relaxed and felt a sense of peace that I hadn't experienced in days. From that time on, I was able to think."

消除忧虑的魔法公式

你是否想找到一种快速有效消除忧虑的药方——也就是那种你不必再往下多看之前，就能立即应用的方法？

那么，让我告诉你威利斯·H. 卡瑞尔发明的这个方法。卡瑞尔是一位聪明的工程师，他创建了空调制造公司，现在是世界闻名的纽约州塞瑞卡斯市卡瑞尔公司的负责人。这是我听过的消除忧虑的最好办法之一，我和卡瑞尔先生在纽约工程师俱乐部吃午饭的时候，亲自从他那里得知的这个方法。

"我年轻时，"卡瑞尔先生说，"我在纽约州水牛城的水牛锻造公司工作。有一次，我被派到密苏里州水晶城的匹兹堡玻璃公司——一座花好几百万美元建造的工厂，去安装一台瓦斯清洁机，以便清除瓦斯中的杂质，使瓦斯燃烧时不至于烧坏引擎。这是一种新的清洁瓦斯的方法，以前只试过一次，而且当时的情况很不相同。当我去密苏里州水晶城工作的时候，没有预料到的困难发生了。经过一番调整，机器总算可以用了，但并没有达到我们保证的程度。

"我对自己的失败非常吃惊，觉得好像有人在我头顶猛击了一下，胃部和整个腹部开始疼痛起来。有好一阵于，我担心得难以入睡。

"最后，常识告诉我，忧虑并不能解决问题；于是，我想出了一个无须忧虑就可以解决问题的办法，非常有效。我使用这个办法已经30多年。这个办法很简单，任何人都可以用。它有三个步骤：

"第一步：毫不害怕而且诚恳地分析整个情况，然后找出万一失败将会出现什么最坏的情况。没有人会把我关起来，或者枪毙我，这一点可以肯定。不错，我很可能会丢掉工作，我的老板也可能会拆掉整个机器，使投入的两万美元泡汤。

"第二步：找出可能发生的最坏情况之后，我就让自己在必要时接受它。我对自己说：这次失败对我的人生纪录是一个打击，我可能会丢掉工作。但即使是这样，我还是可以找到另外的工作，而且事情可能更糟。至于我的老板，他们也知道我们现在正在试验一种新的清洁煤气的方法，如果这个试验要花两万美元，他们还付得起。他们可以把这笔账记在研究费用上，因为这只是一种试验。

"当分析到可能发生的最坏情况，并让自己必要时接受它之后，一件非常重要的事情发生了：我马上轻松下来，感受到了几天以来未曾经历过的平静。

"第三步：从那以后，我就平静地把时间和精力用于改善我在心理上已经接受的最坏情况。

"我努力寻找各种办法，以减少我们目前面临的两万美元的损失。我做了几次实验，最后发现，如果我们再多花5000美元加装一些设备，我们的问题就可以解决了。我们按照这个办法去做，公司不但没有损失两万美元，反而赚了15000美元。

"如果我一直担心，恐怕再也不可能做到这一点。因为忧虑的最大害处，就是毁掉我集中精神的能力。我们忧虑时，思想会到处乱转，从而丧失所有的决策能力。然而，当我们强迫自己面对最坏的情况，并从精神上接受它时，就能权衡所有可能的情形，使我们可以集中精力解决问题。

"刚才我所说的这件事发生在很多年以前，因为这种方法非常好，所以我一直使用它。结果，我的生活几乎不再有烦恼了。"

那么，为什么威利斯·H.卡瑞尔的魔法公式从心理的角度来讲有这么大的价值，如此实用呢？因为它能够把我们从那巨大的灰暗色云层中拉出来，使我们不再因为忧虑而盲目地摸索；它可以使我们脚踏实地，而我们也都知道自己身处何处。如果我们脚下没有这块结实的土地，又怎么能想通事情呢？

应用心理学之父威廉·詹姆斯教授在1910年去世，但如果他今天还在世，听到这个解除忧虑的公式的话，一定也会大加赞同的。我怎么会知道呢？因为他曾经对他的学生说："你们要愿意承担这种情况……因为接受既成事实，是克服随之而来的任何不幸的第一步。"

林语堂在他那本广被阅读的《生活的艺术》中也表达了同样的观点："思想上的真正平和，"这位中国哲学家说，"来自接受最坏的情况。从心理而言，我认为这就意味着能量的释放。"

这就对了，一点不错。在心理上，你就能发挥出新的能力。我们接受最坏的情况时，就不会再损失什么，也就是说一切都可以重新获得。"在面对最坏的情况之后，"威科斯·H.卡瑞尔说，"我马上轻松下来，感受到了好几天以来没有经历过的平静。然后，我就能思考了。"

Face the Facts! Quit Worrying

Do you love life? Do you want to live long and enjoy good health? Here is how you can do it. I am quoting Dr. Alexis Carrel again. He said: "Those who keep the peace of their inner selves in the midst of the tumult of the modern city are immune from nervous diseases."

Can you keep the peace of your inner self in the midst of the tumult of a modem city? If you are a normal person, the answer is"yes." "Emphatically yes." Most of us are stronger than we realize. We have inner resources that we have probably never tapped. As Thoreau said in his immortal book, *Walden*:

"I know of no more encouraging fact than the unquestionable ability of man to elevate his life by a conscious endeavour…If one advances confidently in the direction of his dreams, and endeavours to live the life he has imagined, he will meet with a success unexpected in common hours."

Surely, many of the readers of this book have as much will power and as many inner resources as Olga K. Jarvey has. Her address is Box 892, Coeur d'Alene, Idaho. She discovered that under the most tragic circumstances she could banish worry. I firmly believe that you and I can also—if we apply the old, old truths discussed in this volume. Here is Olga K. Jarvey's story as she wrote it for me: "Eight and a half years ago, I was condemned to die—a slow, agonising death—of cancer. The best medical brains of the country, the Mayo brothers, confirmed the sentence. I was at a dead-end street, the ultimate gaped at me! I was young. I did not want to die! In my desperation, I phoned to my doctor at Kellogg and cried out to him the despair in my heart. Rather impatiently he upbraided me: 'What's the matter, Olga, haven't you any fight in you? Sure, you will die if you keep on crying. Yes, the worst has overtaken you. O. K. —face the facts! Quit worrying! And then do something about it! 'right then and there I took an oath, an oath so solemn that the nails sank deep into my flesh and cold chills ran down my spine: 'I am not going to worry! I am not going to cry! And if there is anything to mind over matter, I am going to win! I am going to LIVE! '

"The usual amount of X-ray in such advanced cases, where they cannot apply radium, is $10^{1/2}$ minutes a day for 30 days. They gave me X-ray for $14^{1/2}$ minutes a day for 49 days; and although my bones stuck out of my emaciated body like rocks on a barren hillside, and although my feet were like lead, I did not worry! Not once did I cry! I smiled! Yes, I actually forced myself to smile.

"I am not so idiotic as to imagine that merely smiling can cure cancer. But I do believe that a cheerful mental attitude helps the body fight disease. At any rate, I experienced one of the miracle cures of cancer. I have never been healthier than in the last few years, thanks to those challenging, fighting words of Dr. McCaffery: 'Face the facts: Quite worrying; then do something about it! '"

面对现实，不要忧虑

你热爱生活吗？你想健康长寿吗？下面就是你能做到的。我正在引用亚利西斯·卡雷尔医生的话："在现代城市的喧嚣中，只有维持内心平静的人才不会变成神经病。"

你能在现代城市的喧嚣中保持内心的平静吗？如果你是一个正常人，答案是"可以"，"绝对可以"。我们大多数人比我们所认为的都要坚强。我们拥有许多也许从未发现的内在力量，就像梭罗在他的不朽名著《瓦尔登湖》里所写的：

"我不知道还有什么比一个人决心改善生活更令人振奋的……要是一个人自信地朝理想的方向努力，决心过他想过的生活，一定会得到意外的成功。"

我相信，本书的许多读者都具有欧嘉·詹维那种意志和内在力量。她住在爱达荷州科尔·达勒的布克斯892号。即使在最悲惨的情况下，她发现自己也能克服忧虑。我坚信，只要我们应用这本书介绍的古老真理，你和我也都能做到。下面就是欧嘉·詹维写给我的故事："八年半前，医生宣称我将会缓慢而痛苦地死于癌症。国内最有名的医生梅育兄弟也证实了这个诊断。我无药可救了，死亡降临到了我头上。可是我还年轻，还不想死。在绝望之余，我打电话给我住在克洛格的麦卡费雷医生，将我内心的绝望告诉他。他不耐烦地拦住我说：'怎么了，欧嘉？难道你一点斗志都没有了？你要是一直这样哭下去，你必死无疑。不错，你是碰上了最坏的情况。好吧！面对现实，不要忧虑，然后想想办法。'就在那时，我立下重誓，指甲都深深地掐进了肉里，而且背上一阵阵发冷：'我不会再忧虑，不会再哭泣！如果还有什么要想的，就是我一定要赢！一定要活下去！'

"在不能用镭照射的情况下，通常是照10.5分钟的X射线，但我连续49天每天照14.5分钟的X射线。虽然我瘦得皮包骨头，双腿重如铅块，但我并不忧虑，也没有哭过一次！我面带笑容！不错，我的确是在勉强自己笑。

"我当然不会傻到相信只要笑就能治好癌症。但我的确相信，愉快的精神状态有助于身体抵抗疾病。总之，我亲身经历了一次癌症治愈的奇迹。在过去几年里，我再也没有像现在这么健康过，多亏了麦卡费雷医生'面对现实，不要忧虑，然后想想办法'这句富于挑战和战斗性的话。"

Analyzing Worry and Meeting It head-on

Galen Litchfield was the Far Eastern Director for Starr, Park and Freeman, Inc. , III John Street, New York, representing large insurance and financial interests.

In fact, Galen Litchfield was one of the most important American businessmen in Asia; and he confessesd that he owes a large part of his success to this method of analyzing worry and meeting it head-on.

"Shortly after the Japanese bombed Pearl Harbour," Galen Litchfield began, "they came swarming into Shanghai. I was the manager of the Asia Life Insurance Company in Shanghai. They sent us an'army liquidator'—he was really an admiral—and gave me orders to assist this man in liquidating our assets. I didn't have any choice in the matter. I could cooperate—or else. And the'or else'was certain death.

"I went through the motions of doing what I was told, because I had no alternative. But there was one block of securities, worth $750,000, which I left off the list I gave to the admiral. I left that block of securities off the list because they belonged to our Hong Kong organisation and had nothing to do with the Shanghai assets. All the same, I feared I might be in hot water if the Japanese found out what I had done. And they soon found out.

"I wasn't in the office when the discovery was made, but my head accountant was there. He told me that the Japanese admiral flew into a rage, and stamped and swore, and called me a thief and a traitor! I had defied the Japanese Army! I knew what that meant. I would be thrown into the Bridge house!

"The Bridge house! The torture chamber of the Japanese Gestapo! I had had personal friends who had killed themselves rather than be taken to that prison. I had had other friends who had died in that place after ten days of questioning and torture. Now I was slated for the Bridge house myself!

"What did I do? I heard the news on Sunday afternoon. I suppose I should have been terrified. And I would have been terrified if I hadn't had a definite technique for solving my problems. For years, whenever I was worried I had always gone to my typewriter and written down two questions—and the answers to these questions:

"1. What am I worrying about?

"2. What can I do about it?

"I used to try to answer those questions without writing them down. But I stopped that years ago. I found that writing down both the questions and the answers clarifies my thinking.

"So, that Sunday afternoon, I went directly to my room at the Shanghai YMCA, and got out my typewriter. I wrote:

"1. What am I worrying about?

" I am afraid I will be thrown into the Bridge house tomorrowmorning.

"Then I typed out the second question:

"2. What can I do about it?

"I spent hours thinking out and writing down the four courses of action I could take—and what the probable consequence of each action would be.

1. I can try to explain to the Japanese admiral. But he"no speak English". If I try to explain to him through an interpreter, I may stir him up again. That might mean death, for he is cruel, would rather dump me in the Bridge house than bother talking about it.

2. I can try to escape. Impossible. They keep track of me all the time. I have to check in and out of my room at the YMCA. If I try to escape, I'll probably be captured and shot.

3. I can stay here in my room and not go near the office again. If I do, the Japanese admiral will be suspicious, will probably send soldiers to get me and throw me into the Bridge house without giving me a chance to say a word.

4. I can go down to the office as usual on Monday morning. If I do, there is a chance that the Japanese admiral may be so busy that he will not think of what I did. Even if he does think of it, he may have cooled off and may not bother me. If this happens, I am all right. Even if he does bother me, I'll still have a chance to try to explain to him. So, going down to the office as usual on Monday morning, and acting as if nothing had gone wrong gives me two chances to escape the Bridge house.

"As soon as I thought it all out and decided to accept the fourth plan—to go down to the office as usual on Monday morning—I felt immensely relieved.

"When I entered the office the next morning, the Japanese admiral sat there with a cigarette dangling from his mouth. He glared at me as he always did; and said nothing. Six weeks later—thank God—he went back to Tokyo and my worries were ended.

"As I have already said, I probably saved my life by sitting down that Sunday afternoon and writing out all the various steps I could take and then writing down the probable consequences of each step and calmly coming to a decision. If I hadn't done that, I might have floundered and hesitated and done the wrong thing on the spur of the moment. If I hadn't thought out my problem and come to a decision, I would have been frantic with worry all Sunday afternoon. I wouldn't have slept that night. I would have gone down to the office Monday morning with a harassed and worried look; and that alone might have aroused the suspicion of the Japanese admiral and spurred him to act.

"Experience has proved to me, time after time, the enormous value of arriving at a decision. It is the failure to arrive at a fixed purpose, the inability to stop going round and round in maddening circles, that drives men to nervous breakdowns and living hells. I find that fifty per cent of my worries vanishes once I arrive at a clear, definite decision; and another forty per cent usually vanishes once I start to carry out that decision.

"So I banish about ninety per cent of my worries by taking these four steps:

"1. Writing down precisely what I am worrying about.

"2. Writing down what I can do about it.

"3. Deciding what to do.

"4. Starting immediately to carry out that decision."

Why is his method so superb? Because it is efficient, concrete, and goes directly to the heart of the problem. On top of all that, it is climaxed by the third and indispensable rule: Do something about it.

Unless we carry out our action, all our fact-finding and analysis is whistling upwind—it's a sheer waste of energy.

William James said this, "When once a decision is reached and execution is the order of the day, dismiss absolutely all responsibility and care about the outcome." （In this case, William James undoubtedly used the word "care" as a synonym for "anxiety". ） He meant—once you have made a careful decision based on facts, go into action. Don't stop to reconsider. Don't begin to hesitate, worry and retrace your steps. Don't lose yourself in self-doubting which begets other doubts. Don't keep looking back over your shoulder.

I once asked Waite Phillips, one of Oklahoma's most prominent oil men, how he carried out decisions.

He replied, "I find that to keep thinking about our problems beyond a certain point is bound to create confusion and worry. There comes a time when any more investigation and thinking are harmful. There comes a time when we must decide and act and never look back."

Why don't you employ Galen Litchfield's technique to one of your worries right now?

Here is:

Question No. 1—What am I worrying about? (Please pencil the answer to that question in the space below.)

Question No. 2—What can I do about it? (Please write your answer to that question in the space below.)

Question No. 3—Here is what I am going to do about it.

Question No. 4—When am I going to start doing it?

分析并敢于正视忧虑

格伦·利奇菲尔德是纽约市第三约翰大街斯塔尔-帕克-弗里曼公司的亚洲区总经理，代表大保险集团和大金融集团的利益。事实上，他是亚洲重要的几位美国商人之一，他诚恳地说：他的成功应归功于分析并敢于正视忧虑的方法。

"日军轰炸珍珠港之后不久，"格伦·利奇菲尔德说，"他们攻占了上海（公共租界）。当时，我是亚洲人寿保险公司的经理。他们派来了一个'军方清算员'（他实际上是一位海军大将），命令我协助他清算我们的财产。这种事，我毫无办法，要么合作，要么算了——而所谓算了，当然是死。

"我只好遵命行事，因为我无路可走。不过，我没有将一笔大约75万美元的保险费填写在清单上。我之所以不填进去，是因为这笔钱属于我们香港的分公司，和上海分公司的资产无关。但我还是担心万一日本人发现了这件事可能会对我不利。他们很快就发现了。

"他们发现时，我恰巧不在办公室，但会计部主任在场。他告诉我，日本海军大将大发脾气，还拍桌子直骂人，说我是强盗和叛徒，我侮辱了日本皇军。我知道这是什么意思，我可能会被关进宪兵队。

"宪兵队是日本秘密警察的行刑室。我有几个朋友，他们情愿自杀也不愿被送到那个地方。我还有一些朋友在那里被审讯折磨了10天后，死在那里。而我现在也要被关进宪兵队了。

"我该怎么办？我星期天下午得知这个消息，我想我当时应该吓得要命。如果我找不到解决问题的方法，我一定会被吓死的。多年来，每当我担心的时候，总会坐在打字机前打出下面两个问题，以及问题的答案：

"第一，我担心什么？

"第二，我能做什么？

"以往，我都不把答案写下来，只是在心里回答问题。不过几年前，我就不再那样做了。我发现把问题和答案都写下来，会使我的思路变得清晰。所以，在那个星期天的下午，我直接回到我在上海基督教青年会的房间，取出打字机写道：

"第一，我担心什么？

"我担心明天早上会被关进宪兵队。

"第二，我能做什么？

"我思考了几个小时，写下了我能采取的四种行动，以及每一种行动可能带来的后果。

"第一，我可以试着向日本海军大将解释。可是，他不会说英文，若是我找翻译对他解释，可能会让他再次生气，那可能是死路一条，因为他是个凶残的人，我宁愿被关进宪兵队，也不愿和他谈话。

"第二，我可以逃走。但这不可能，因为他们一直都在监视我。我从基督教青年会进进出出都要登记，如果我想逃走，可能被抓住枪毙。

"第三，我也可以留在房间不再上班。如果这样做，那位日本海军大将就会怀疑，也许会派人来抓我，根本不给我任何说话的机会，直接把我关进宪兵队。

"第四，我可以星期一早上照常上班。如果我这样做，那位日本海军大将很可能正在忙着，忘掉了我的事情。而且即使他想到了，也可能已经冷静下来，不再找我的麻烦。如果是这样，我就万事大吉了。就是他还来找我，我仍有机会向他解释。所以我应该和平常一样在星期一早上去办公室，就像什么事也没有发生过，可以给我个逃避被关进宪兵队的机会。

"通盘考虑后，我决定采取第四个计划——像往常一样，在星期一早上去上班——我大大松了口气。

"我第二天早上走进办公室时，那位日本海军大将坐在那里，嘴里叼着香烟，像平常一样看了我一眼，但什么话也没说。六个星期之后——谢天谢地——他调回东京去了，我的忧虑也就此告终！

"如前所说，我之所以能捡回这条命，大概就因为我在那个星期天下午写出了可以采取各种不同步骤，以及每个步骤可能产生的后果，然后镇定地作出了决定。如果不那样做，我可能会思想混乱或犹豫不决，在紧要关头就会出错。如果我没有分析问题并作出决定，那我整个星期天下午就会心急如焚，那天晚上也睡不着觉，星期一早上上班时可能满面惊慌、面带愁容——仅此一点，就会使那位日本海军大将起疑心，而使他采取行动。

"以后一次又一次的经验证明，逐渐作出决定的确大有价值。人们正是因为不能实现既定的目的，而且不能控制自己，总是局限在一个令人难以忍受的小圈子里，才会精神崩溃和生活窘迫。我发现，一旦作出清晰明确的决定，50%的忧虑会立即消失，而另外的40%通常会在我按照决定去做之后消失。

"采取以下四个步骤，通常就能消除90%的忧虑：

"第一，清楚写下我们担心的是什么。

"第二，写下我们可以怎么办。

"第三，决定该怎么办。

"第四，马上就照决定去做。"

为什么这种方法如此管用？因为它有效可行，直抵问题的核心。最重要的是，它遵循了第三项且是不可或缺的原则：决定该怎么办。

除非我们作出决定该怎么办，否则我们寻找并分析事实的做法都将化为泡影——那真是在白费精力。

威廉·詹姆斯说："一旦作出决定，当天就要付诸实践，同时不要理会责任问题，也不要关心后果。"意思是说，一旦你以事实为基础作出了谨慎的决定，就要付诸实行，而不是停下来再重新考虑，要毫不迟疑、毫不担忧、毫不犹豫，不要怀疑自己。

我曾问俄克拉何马州成功的石油商人之一怀特·菲利浦，他是如何把决心付诸行动的，他回答说："我发现，如果在超过某种限度后还一直思考问题，一定会导致混乱和忧虑。当调查和思考过度对我们有害时，也就是我们必须下定决心、付诸行动、不再犹豫的时候。"

何不马上运用格伦·利奇菲尔德的方法来解决你的忧虑？下面就是：

第一个问题——我担忧什么？（请在下面空白处写下你的答案）

第二个问题——我能做什么？（请在下面空白处写下你的答案）

第三个问题——我决定怎么做？

第四个问题——我什么时候开始做？

Analyze the Problem and Overcome Anxiety

Frank Bettger was one of the best-known life-insurance salesmen in America. He is with Fidelity Mutual of Philadelphia, and writes a million dollars worth of policies a year. But he was on the point of giving up. He was on the point of admitting failure—until analyzing the problem gave him a boost on the road to success.

"Years ago," said Frank Bettger, "when I first started to sell insurance, I was filled with a boundless enthusiasm and love for my work. Then something happened. I became so discouraged that I despised my work and thought of giving it up. I think I would have quit—if I hadn't got the idea, one Saturday morning, of sitting down and trying to get at the root of my worries.

"1. I asked myself first: 'Just what is the problem?'the problem was: that I was not getting high enough returns for the staggering amount of calls I was making. I seemed to do pretty well at selling a prospect, until the moment came for closing a sale. Then the customer would say: 'Well, I'll think it over, Mr. Bettger. Come and see me again.'It was the time I wasted on these follow-up calls that was causing my depression. "2. I asked myself: 'What are the possible solutions?'But to get the answer to that one, I had to study the facts. I got out my record book for the last twelve months and studied the figures.

"I made an astounding discovery! Right there in black and white, I discovered that seventy per cent of my sales had been closed on the very first interview! Twenty-three per cent of my sales had been closed on the second interview! And only seven per cent of my sales had been closed on those third, fourth, fifth, etc. , interviews, which were running me ragged and taking up my time. In other words, I was wasting fully one half of my working day on a part of my business which was responsible for only seven per cent of my sales!

"3. 'What is the answer?'the answer was obvious. I immediately cut out all visits beyond the second interview, and spent the extra time building up new prospects. The results were unbelievable. In a very short time, I had almost doubled the cash value of every visit I made from a call!"

分析问题，克服忧虑

弗兰克·贝特格是美国最著名的人寿保险推销员之一，每年推销的保险都在100万美元以上。可是，他曾经想要放弃，几乎就要承认自己的失败——分析问题使他走上了成功之路。

"很多年以前，"弗兰克·贝特格说，"我刚开始推销保险，对自己的工作充满了热情和喜爱。而后来发生了一件事使我变得非常沮丧，让我看不起我的工作，甚至想到过放弃。我几乎都要辞职了，但我突然想起了一件事。一个星期六的早晨，我坐下来，想找出忧虑的根源。

"第一，我问自己：'问题到底出在哪里？'我的问题是：我拜访过那么多人，可是业绩并不理想。直到成交之前，我跟那些希望很大的顾客谈得很好。然后，顾客会说：'啊！我想再考虑考虑，贝特格先生。什么时候决定再说吧。'于是，我又得再次拜访，这样就浪费掉不少时间，这使我觉得很沮丧。

"第二，我问自己：'有什么解决办法？'可是要找出问题的答案，就得研究事实。我拿出过去12个月的记录本，研究上面的数据。

"结果，我有了一个惊人的发现！我卖出的保险有70%是在第一次拜访时成交的，23%是在第二次拜访时成交的！只有7%是在第三、第四甚至第五次才成交的。这让我觉得难过，因为它很浪费时间。换句话说，我的工作时间几乎有一半浪费在实际上只有7%的业务上。

"第三，'问题的答案是什么？'答案很明显，我立刻停止了第二次以后的所有拜访，多出来的时间用来寻找新的客户。结果令人难以置信：在很短的时间内，我的业绩提高了近一倍。"

How to Crowd Worry out of Your Mind

I shall never forget the night, a few years ago, when Marion J. Douglas was a student in one of my classes. (I have not used his real name. He requested me, for personal reasons, not to reveal his identity.) But here is his real story as he told it before one of our adult-education classes. He told us how tragedy had struck at his home, not once, but twice. The first time he had lost his five-year-old daughter, a child he adored. He and his wife thought they couldn't endure that first loss; but, as he said, "Ten months later, God gave us another little girl—and she died in five days."

This double bereavement was almost too much to bear. "I couldn't take it," this father told us. "I couldn't sleep, I couldn't eat, I couldn't rest or relax. My nerves were utterly shaken and my confidence gone." At last he went to doctors; one recommended sleeping pills and another recommended a trip.

He tried both, but neither remedy helped. He said, "My body felt as if it were encased in a vice, and the jaws of the vice were being drawn tighter and tighter." The tension of grief—if you have ever been paralysed by sorrow, you know what he meant.

"But thank God, I had one child left—a four-year-old son. He gave me the solution to my problem. One afternoon as I sat around feeling sorry for myself, he asked: 'Daddy, will you build a boat for me?' I was in no mood to build a boat; in fact, I was in no mood to do anything. But my son is a persistent little fellow! I had to give in.

"Building that toy boat took about three hours. By the time it was finished, I realised that those three hours spent building that boat were the first hours of mental relaxation and peace that I had had in months!

"That discovery jarred me out of my lethargy and caused me to do a bit of thinking—the first real thinking I had done in months. I realised that it is difficult to worry while you are busy doing something that requires planning and thinking. In my case, building the boat had knocked worry out of the ring. So I resolved to keep busy.

"The following night, I went from room to room in the house, compiling a list of jobs that ought to be done. Scores of items needed to be repaired: bookcases, stair steps, storm windows, window shades, knobs, locks, leaky taps. Astonishing as it seems, in the course of two weeks I had made a list of 242 items that needed attention.

"During the last two years I have completed most of them. Besides, I have filled my life with stimulating activities. Two nights per week I attend adult-education classes in New York. I have gone in for civic activities in my home town and I am now chairman of the school board. I attend scores of meetings. I help collect money for the Red Cross and other activities. I am so busy now that I have no time for worry."

No time for worry! That is exactly what Winston Churchill said when he was working eighteen hours a day at the height of the war. When he was asked if he worried about his tremendous responsibilities, he said, "I'm too busy. I have no time for worry."

Charles Kettering was in that same fix when he started out to invent a self-starter for automobiles. Mr. Kettering was, until his recent retirement, vice-president of General Motors in charge of the world-famous General Motors Research Corporation. But in those days, he was so poor that he had to use the hayloft of a barn as a laboratory. To buy groceries, he had to use fifteen hundred dollars that his wife had made by giving piano lessons; later, he had to borrow five hundred dollars on his life insurance. I asked his wife if she wasn't worried at a time like that. "Yes," she replied, "I was so worried I couldn't sleep; but Mr. Kettering wasn't. He was too absorbed in his work to worry."

The great scientist, Pasteur, spoke of "the peace that is found in libraries and laboratories." Why is peace found there?Because the men in libraries and laboratories are usually too absorbed in their tasks to worry about themselves. Research men rarely have nervous breakdowns. They haven't time for such luxuries.

Why does such a simple thing as keeping busy help to drive out anxiety?Because of a law—one of the most fundamental laws ever revealed by psychology. And that law is: that it is utterly impossible for any human mind, no matter how brilliant, to think of more than one thing at any given time.

消除思想上的忧虑

我永远都忘不了几年前的一个晚上。当时，马利安昂·J. 道格拉斯是我班上的一个学员（我没用他的真名。出于个人原因，他要求我不要说出他的身份）。但这是他的真实故事，他在我一个成人教育班上讲过。他告诉我们他家里遭受的不幸——不止一次，而是两次。第一次，他失去了五岁的女儿，这是他非常喜爱的孩子。他和他的妻子都以为他们无法承受这个打击；可是，正如他所说的："十个月后，上帝又赐给我们另一个小女儿——她只活了五天。"

接连而来的打击几乎使人无法承受。"我受不了，"这个父亲告诉我们，"我睡不着吃不下，也无法休息或放松。我精神上受到了致命的打击，信心全没了。"最后，他去看了医生。有一位医生建议他吃安眠药，而另一位医生建议他去旅行。

他试了这两个方法，可都没有用。他说："我的身体犹如夹在一把铁钳里，铁钳愈夹愈紧。"那种悲哀——如果你曾因悲哀而感觉麻木的话，就知道是什么感受了。

"不过，感谢上帝，我们还有一个孩子——一个四岁大的儿子。他使我找到了解决问题的方法。一天下午，我悲伤地呆坐着，他问我：'爸爸，你肯不肯给我做一条船？'我实在没有心情；事实上，我没有心情做任何事。可是，我的儿子是个很会缠人的小家伙，我不得不屈服。

"做那条玩具船花了三个小时。等做好后，我发现这三个小时竟成了我这几个月以来第一次心情放松的时间。

"这个发现使我从恍惚中惊醒过来，也使我想了许多——这是我几个月来第一次认真思考。我发现，如果你忙着做一些需要计划和思考的事情时，就很难去忧虑了。对我来说，做那条船时忧虑全都消失了，所以我决定让自己忙起来。

"第二天晚上，我看了看每一个房间，把要做的事情列成一张单子。有许多东西如书架、楼梯、屋顶窗、窗帘、门把、门锁、漏水的龙头都需要修理。让人震惊的是，我在两个星期里竟然列出了242件需要做的事情。

"在过去的两年里，这些事情大部分都已经做完了。此外，我还给生活增加了富有启发的活动：每个星期到纽约市参加两个晚上的成人教育课，并参加了小镇上的一些活动；现在，我是校董事会主席，参加过很多会议，并协助红十字会和其他活动进行募捐。现在，我忙得没有时间忧虑。"

没有时间忧虑！这也正是丘吉尔说过的，当时战事紧张，他每天工作18个小时。当别人问他是不是担心无法承担这一巨大责任时，他说："我太忙了，没有时间忧虑。"

查尔斯·吉特林着手发明汽车自动点火器时，也碰到过类似的情形。吉特林先生一直担任通用汽车公司的副总裁，主管世界知名的通用汽车研究公司，不久前才退休。可是当年他穷得只能租堆稻草的谷仓当实验室；全家的开销靠他太太教钢琴赚来的1500美元支撑。后来，他不得不用他的人寿保险当抵押借来500美元。我问他太太，她在那段时期是不是很忧虑。"当然，"她回答说，"我担心得睡不着，可我丈夫一点都不担心。他沉浸在工作中，没有时间忧虑。"

伟大的科学家巴斯特也谈过"在图书馆和实验室找到的平静"。为什么会在那儿找到平静呢？因为在图书馆和实验室工作的人，通常都埋头于工作，没时间为自己担忧。研究人员也很少精神崩溃，因为他们没有时间享受这种奢侈。

为什么"让自己忙着"这么简单的一件事情，就能把忧虑赶走呢？因为有这么一个定理——这是心理学所发现的基本定理之一。这条定理就是：一个人不论多么聪明，都不可能在同一时间想一件以上的事情。

Don't Let the Beetles Get You Down

Here is a dramatic story that I'll probably remember as long as I live. It was told to me by Robert Moore, of 14 Highland Avenue, Maplewood, New Jersey.

"I learned the biggest lesson of my life in March, 1945," he said, "I learned it under 276 feet of water off the coast of Indo-China. I was one of eighty-eight men aboard the submarine Baya S. S. 318. We had discovered by radar that a small Japanese convoy was coming our way. As daybreak approached, we submerged to attack. I saw through the periscope a Jap destroyer escort, a tanker, and a mine layer.

"We fired three torpedoes at the destroyer escort, but missed. Something went haywire in the mechanics of each torpedo. The destroyer, not knowing that she had been attacked, continued on. We were getting ready to attack the last ship, the mine layer, when suddenly she turned and came directly at us. (A Japanese plane had spotted us under sixty feet of water and had radioed our position to the Japanese mine layer.) We went down to 150 feet, to avoid detection, and rigged for a depth charge. We put extra bolts on the hatches; and, in order to make our sub absolutely silent, we turned off the fans, the cooling system, and all electrical gear.

"Three minutes later, all hell broke loose. Six depth charges exploded all around us and pushed us down to the ocean floor—a depth of 276 feet. We were terrified. To be attacked in less than a thousand feet of water is dangerous—less than five hundred feet is almost always fatal. And we were being attacked in a trifle more than half of five hundred feet of water—just about knee-deep, as far as safety was concerned. For fifteen hours, that Japanese mine layer kept dropping depth charges.

"If a depth charge explodes within seventeen feet of a sub, the concussion will blow a hole in it. Scores of these depth charges exploded within fifty feet of us. We were ordered 'to secure'—to lie quietly in our bunks and remain calm. I was so terrified I could hardly breathe. 'this is death,'I kept saying to myself over and over. 'This is death!…This is death!'With the fans and cooling system turned off, the air inside the sub was over a hundred degrees; but I was so chilled with fear that I put on a sweater and a fur-lined jacket; and still I trembled with cold. My teeth chattered. I broke out in a cold, clammy sweat. The attack continued for fifteen hours. Then ceased suddenly. Apparently the Japanese mine layer had exhausted its supply of depth charges, and steamed away. Those fifteen hours of attack seemed like fifteen million years. All my life passed before me in review.

"I remembered all the bad things I had done, all the little absurd things I had worried about. I had been a bank clerk before I joined the Navy. I had worried about the long hours, the poor pay, the poor prospects of advancement. I had worried because I couldn't own my own home, couldn't buy a new car, couldn't buy my wife nice clothes. How I had hated my old boss, who was always nagging and scolding! I remembered how I would come home at night sore and grouchy and quarrel with my wife over trifles. I had worried about a scar on my forehead—a nasty cut from an auto accident.

"How big all these worries seemed years ago! But how absurd they seemed when depth charges were threatening to blow me to kingdom come. I promised myself then and there that if I ever saw the sun and the stars again, I would never, never worry again. Never! Never!! Never!!! I learned more about the art of living in those fifteen terrible hours in that submarine than I had learned by studying books for four years in Syracuse University."

不要为小事而垂头丧气

下面这个富有戏剧性的故事我也许终生难忘。讲述这个故事的人叫罗伯特·摩尔，他住在新泽西州枫林市第十四大道。

"1945年3月，我学到了我人生当中最重要的一课。"他说，"我是在中南半岛附近276英尺深的海底学到的。当时，我和另外87个人一起在'贝雅'S.S.号318潜水艇上。我们从雷达上发现正有一小支日本舰队朝我们这边驶来。天将亮的时候，我们浮出水面发动攻击。我从潜望镜里发现了一艘日本驱逐舰、一艘油轮和一艘布雷舰。

"我们向那艘驱逐舰发射了3枚鱼雷，但未击中目标。那艘驱逐舰并不知道正遭受攻击，继续向前驶去。我们又打算攻击最后那艘布雷舰。突然，它转过头径直朝我们驶来（有一架日本飞机从上空看见我们在深水下，把我们的位置用无线电通知了日本布雷舰）。我们潜到150英尺深处，以免被它探测到，同时作好准备应付深水炸弹：我们在所有的舱盖上都多加了几层铁栓，为了让我们的潜艇保持绝对稳定，我们关掉了所有的电扇和冷却系统及发电设备。

"3分钟后，突然天崩地裂：6枚深水炸弹在我们四周爆炸，把我们推到海底276英尺深处。我们吓呆了！在不到1000英尺深的海水里遭受攻击是很危险的——如果不到500英尺就就几乎难逃厄运。而我们当时在不到500英尺一半深的水下受到攻击，从安全角度来说，水深等于只到膝盖处。那艘日本布雷舰不停地投掷深水炸弹，连续攻击15个小时。

"如果深水炸弹距潜水艇不到17英尺，炸弹就会在潜艇上炸出一个大洞来。大约有十几颗深水炸弹就在离我们50英尺的地方爆炸，我们奉命'固守'——静躺在床上，保持镇定。我吓得几乎无法呼吸。'这下死定了。'我一直不停地对自己说着，'这下死定了……这下死定了。'电扇和冷却系统全都关闭之后，潜水艇内的温度高达40多摄氏度，我却害怕得全身发冷，虽然穿了一件毛衣，如一件皮领夹克，可还是冷得发抖。我的牙齿不停地打战，全身冒出阵阵冷汗。攻击持续了15个小时，然后突然停止。显然，那艘日本布雷舰用光了所有的深水炸弹，这才离开。这15个小时的攻击，就像是1500万年。过去的生活一一呈现在我眼前。

"我记起了以前做过的所有坏事，以及我曾担心的所有小事。加入海军之前，我是一个银行职员，曾为工作时间太长、薪水太少、没有多少升迁机会而发愁。我曾经因为没有办法买自己的房子、没有钱买新车、没有钱给我太太买好衣服而忧虑。我非常讨厌我以前的老板，他总是给我找麻烦。我还记得，每天晚上回到家里时，我总是又累又困，常常因为芝麻大的小事跟我太太吵架。我甚至还为额头上一次车祸留下的伤痕发愁。

"多年以前，那些令人发愁的事看起来很大！可是在深水炸弹就要夺走我生命的那一刻，这些事情又是多么荒谬和微不足道。就在那时，我答应自己，如果我还有机会活下去，永远也不会再忧虑了。永远！永远！！永远都不！！！在潜艇里那15个可怕的小时中，我学到的生活道理比我在大学4年所学的东西要多得多。"

Cast away Foolish Worry

One summer, I met Mr. and Mrs. Herbert H. Salinger, of 2298 Pacific Avenue, of San Francisco. Mrs. Salinger, a poised, serene woman, gave me the impression that she had never worried. One evening in front of the roaring fireplace, I asked her if she had ever been troubled by worry. "Troubled by it?" she said. "My life was almost ruined by it. Before I learned to conquer worry, I lived through eleven years of self-made hell. I was irritable and hot-tempered. I lived under terrific tension. I would take the bus every week from my home in San Mateo to shop in San Francisco. But even while shopping, I worried myself into a dither: maybe I had left the electric iron connected on the ironing board. Maybe the house had caught fire. Maybe the maid had run off and left the children. Maybe they had been out on their bicycles and been killed by a car. In the midst of my shopping, I would often worry myself into a cold perspiration and rush out and take the bus home to see if everything was all right. No wonder my first marriage ended in disaster.

"My second husband is a lawyer—a quiet, analytical man who never worries about anything. When I became tense and anxious, he would say to me,'relax. Let's think this out…What are you really worrying about?Let's examine the law of averages and see whether or not it is likely to happen.'

"For example, I remember the time we were driving from Albuquerque, New Mexico, to the Carlsbad Caverns—driving on a dirt road—when we were caught in a terrible rainstorm.

"The car was slithering and sliding. We couldn't control it. I was positive we would slide off into one of the ditches that flanked the road; but my husband kept repeating to me: 'I am driving very slowly. Nothing serious is likely to happen. Even if the car does slide into the ditch, by the law of averages, we won't be hurt.'His calmness and confidence quieted me.

"One summer we were on a camping trip in the Touquin Valley of the Canadian Rockies. One night, we were camping seven thousand feet above sea level, when a storm threatened to tear our tents to shreds. The tents were tied with guy ropes to a wooden platform. The outer tent shook and trembled and screamed and shrieked in the wind. I expected every minute to see our tent torn loose and hurled through the sky. I was terrified! But my husband kept saying: 'Look, my dear, we are travelling with Brewster's guides. Brewster's know what they are doing. They have been pitching tents in these mountains for sixty years. This tent has been here for many seasons. It hasn't blown down yet and, by the law of averages, it won't blow away tonight; and even if it does, we can take shelter in another tent. So relax…'I did; and I slept soundly the balance of the night.

"A few years ago an infantile-paralysis epidemic swept over our part of California. In the old days, I would have been hysterical. But my husband persuaded me to act calmly. We took all the precautions we could: we kept our children away from crowds, away from school and the movies. By consulting the Board of Health, we found out that even during the worst infantile-paralysis epidemic that California had ever known up to that time, only 1, 835 children had been stricken in the entire state of California. And that the usual number was around two hundred or three hundred. Tragic as those figures are, we nevertheless felt that, according to the law of averages, the chances of any one child being stricken were remote.

"'By the law of averages, it won't happen.'that phrase has destroyed ninety per cent of my worries; and it has made the past twenty years of my life beautiful and peaceful beyond my highest expectations."

摒弃愚蠢的忧虑

一年夏天，我遇到了旧金山市的赫伯特·H.赛林格夫妇。赛林格太太是一个平静沉着的女人，她给我的印象是她从来没有忧虑。一天晚上，我们坐在熊熊燃烧的炉火前，我问她是不是曾因忧虑而烦恼过。"烦恼？"她说，"我以前的生活几乎被忧虑毁了。学会征服忧虑之前，我在自找的苦难中生活了11年。那时，我脾气很坏，又很急躁，终日生活在紧张的情绪中。我每个星期都要从家里搭乘公共汽车去旧金山买东西，可是即使在买东西时，我也会担心得要命：也许我又把电熨斗放在熨衣板上了；也许房子着火了；也许女用人丢下孩子跑了；也许孩子们骑自行车出去被汽车撞死了。我买东西时，常常会因忧虑而冷汗直冒，会冲出店去，搭乘公共汽车回家，看看一切是否如常。所以，我的第一次婚姻没有好结果。

"我第二个丈夫是律师。他是一个平静安分、善于分析的人，从不为任何事情忧虑。每当我神情紧张或焦虑时，他就会对我说：'放松，让我们好好想想……你真正担心的是什么？让我们来算算平均概率，看看这种事情究竟会不会发生。'

"例如，我记得有一次我们从新墨西哥州的阿尔伯克基开车去卡斯白洞窟，走在一条土路上，遇到了一场可怕的暴风雨。

"汽车一路打滑，没法控制。我想我们会滑到路边的水沟里，可是我丈夫一直不停地对我说：'我现在开得很慢，不会出事的。即使车子滑到沟里，根据平均概率，我们也不会受伤。'他的镇定和信心使我平静下来。

"有一年夏天，我们去加拿大的落基山区托昆谷露营。一天晚上，我们的帐篷扎在海拔很高的地方，突然下起了暴风雨，我们的帐篷都快被撕成碎片了。帐篷用绳子绑在一个木制平台上，头顶的帐篷在风中摇晃着，发出尖啸声。我每一分钟都在想：我们的帐篷要被吹垮，吹到天上去了。我真的吓坏了，可是我丈夫不停地说：'亲爱的，我们有好几个布鲁斯特向导，他们对这些了如指掌。他们在这些山地里扎营60年了，这个帐篷在这里也过了很长时间，可是至今还没有被吹倒。根据平均概率，今天晚上也不会被吹倒。而且即使被吹倒，我们还可以去另外的帐篷，所以请放松……'我放松心情，后半夜睡得很香。

"几年前，小儿麻痹在加利福尼亚州我们住的那一带肆虐。要是在以前，我一定会不知所措，可是我丈夫让我镇定，我们尽可能地采取了各种预防方法，不让孩子们出入公共场所，暂时不去上学和去电影院。与卫生署联系之后，我们得知，到目前为止，即使加利福尼亚州发生过的最严重的一次小儿麻痹症流行期，整个州也只有1835名儿童患病，而平常只在二三百人之间。虽然这些数字听起来让人害怕，但我们觉得，根据平均概率，某一个孩子感染的可能性实在是很小。

"'根据平均概率，这种事不会发生。'这一句话就消除了我90%的忧虑，使我过去20年的生活过得美好而平静，超出了我的最高期望。"

Cooperate with the Inevitable

A few years ago, I met a man who was running a freight elevator in one of the downtown office buildings in New York. I noticed that his left hand had been cut off at the wrist. I asked him if the loss of that hand bothered him. He said, "Oh, no, I hardly ever think about it. I am not married; and the only time I ever think about it is when I try to thread a needle." It is astonishing how quickly we can accept almost any situation—if we have to—and adjust ourselves to it and forget about it.

I often think of an inscription on the ruins of a fifteenth-century cathedral in Amsterdam, Holland. This inscription says in Flemish: "It is so. It cannot be otherwise."

As you and I march across the decades of time, we are going to meet a lot of unpleasant situations that are so. They cannot be otherwise. We have our choice. We can either accept them as inevitable and adjust ourselves to them, or we can ruin our lives with rebellion and maybe end up with a nervous breakdown.

Here is a bit of sage advice from one of my favourite philosophers, William James. "Be willing to have it so," he said. "Acceptance of what has happened is the first step to overcoming the consequence of any misfortune." Elizabeth Connley, of 2840 NE 49th Avenue, Portland, Oregon, had to find that out the hard way. Here is a letter that she wrote me recently: "On the very day that America was celebrating the victory of our armed forces in North Africa," the letter says, "I received a telegram from the War Department: my nephew—the person I loved most—was missing in action. A short time later, another telegram arrived saying he was dead.

"I was prostrate with grief. Up to that time, I had felt that life had been very good to me. I had a job I loved. I had helped to raise this nephew. He represented to me all that was fine and good in young manhood. I had felt that all the bread I had cast upon the waters was coming back to me as cake!…

"Then came this telegram. My whole world collapsed. I felt there was nothing left to live for. I neglected my work; neglected my friends. I let everything go. I was bitter and resentful. Why did my loving nephew have to be taken? Why did this good boy—with life all before him—why did he have to be killed?I couldn't accept it. My grief was so overwhelming that I decided to give up my work, and go away and hide myself in my tears and bitterness.

"I was clearing out my desk, getting ready to quit, when I came across a letter that I had forgotten—a letter from this nephew who had been killed, a letter he had written to me when my mother had died a few years ago.

"'Of course, we will miss her,'the letter said, 'and especially you. But I know you'll carry on. Your own personal philosophy will make you do that. I shall never forget the beautiful truths you taught me. Wherever I am, or how far apart we may be, I shall always remember that you taught me to smile, and to take whatever comes, like a man.'

"I read and reread that letter. It seemed as if he were there beside me, speaking to me. He seemed to be saying to me: 'Why don't you do what you taught me to do?Carry on, no matter what happens. Hide your private sorrows under a smile and carry on.'

"So, I went back to my work. I stopped being bitter and rebellious. I kept saying to myself, 'It is done. I can't change it. But I can and will carry on as he wished me to do.'I threw all my mind and strength into my work. I wrote letters to soldiers—to other people's boys. I joined an adult-education class at night—seeking out new interests and making new friends. I can hardly believe the change that has come over me. I have ceased mourning over the past that is forever gone. I am living each day now with joy—just as my nephew would have wanted me to do. I have made peace with life. I have accepted my fate. I am now living a fuller and more complete life than I had ever known."

Elizabeth Connley, out in Portland, Oregon, learned what all of us will have to learn sooner or later: namely, that we must accept and cooperate with the inevitable. "It is so. It cannot be otherwise." That is not an easy lesson to learn. Even kings on their thrones have to keep reminding themselves of it. The late George V had these framed words hanging on the wall of his library in Buckingham Palace:

"Teach me neither to cry for the moon nor over spilt milk." The same thought is expressed by Schopenhauer in this way: "A good supply of resignation is of the first importance in providing for the journey of life."

Obviously, circumstances alone do not make us happy or unhappy. It is the way we react to circumstances that determines our feelings. Jesus said that the kingdom of heaven is within you. That is where the kingdom of hell is, too.

We can all endure disaster and tragedy and triumph over them—if we have to. We may not think we can, but we have surprisingly strong inner resources that will see us through if we will only make use of them. We are stronger than we think.

接受不可避免的事实

几年前，我碰到一个人，他在纽约市中心一家办公大楼开货运电梯。我注意到他的左手被齐腕割断了。我问他缺了那只手是否觉得难过。他说："噢，不会，我根本就不会想到它。我没结婚，只有在穿针时才会想起此事。"如果有必要，我们几乎可以很快接受任何情况，使自己适应它，然后完全忘了它。这多么令人吃惊啊！

我经常想到一行字，它刻在荷兰阿姆斯特丹一座15世纪老教堂的废墟上："事实就是这样，而不是别的样子。"

在漫长的岁月里，你和我一定会遇到一些令人不快的事情，既然它们是这样，就不可能是别的样子。我们也可以有所选择：或者把它们当做不可避免的事实而加以接受并适应它们；或者用忧虑来摧毁我们的生活，最后精神崩溃。

下面是我最喜欢的哲学家之一威廉·詹姆斯的忠告："乐于承认事实如此，"他说，"接受已经发生的事实，是克服随之而来的任何不幸的第一步。"住在俄勒冈州波特兰市东北第四十九大道2840号伊丽莎白·康莉，经过很多困难才学到这一道理。下面是她最近写给我的一封信："在美国庆祝我们陆军在北非获胜的那一天，"信中说，"我接到一封国防部送来的电报：我的侄儿——我最爱的人——在战场上失踪了。没过多久，又一封电报说他死了。

"我悲伤至极。在那之前，我一直觉得命运对我很好。我有自己喜欢的工作，抚养侄儿成人。在我看来，他代表了年轻人一切美好的东西。我觉得自己以前所有的努力现在都得到了回报……

"然后，来了这封电报，我的整个世界碎了，觉得再活下去毫无意义。我开始忽视工作、朋友。我开始抛弃一切，既冷淡又怨恨。为什么我最亲爱的侄儿会死？为什么这么好的孩子，还没有开始生活却要死在战场上？我无法接受这个事实。我悲伤过度，决定放弃工作，远离家乡，把自己埋在泪水和痛苦之中。

"就在我清理桌子准备辞职时，突然看到一封我早已忘了的信。这是我已故侄儿的信。几年前，我母亲去世的时候，他给我写了这封信。

"'当然，我们都会想念她，'信上说，'尤其是你。但是，我知道你一定能挺过去。以你个人的人生哲学，你能挺过去。我永远都不会忘记你教给

我的美好真理：不论在哪里，也不论我们离得多远，我永远都会记得你教我要微笑，要像一个男子汉，勇于承受既成事实。'

"我把那封信读了一遍又一遍，觉得他好像就在我身边，正在对我说话。他好像对我说：'为什么不照你教我的办法去做呢？挺住！不论发生什么事情，把你个人的悲伤掩藏在微笑之下，继续过下去。'

"于是，我又回去工作，不再对人冷淡无礼。我一再告诫自己：'事情既已发生，我不能改变它，但是我能够像他所希望的那样去做。'我将所有的思想和精力都投入工作中，我给士兵们写信——他们是别人的儿子；晚上，我又参加了成人教育班——寻找新的兴趣点，结识新朋友。我几乎不敢相信发生在我身上的变化。我不再为永远过去的事情悲伤。现在，我每天都充满了快乐——就像我的侄儿要我做的那样。我的生活已找到宁静的港湾。我接受了命运。我现在过着更加充实而有意义的生活。"

伊丽莎白·康莉学到了我们所有人迟早都要学到的道理，那就是我们必须接受和适应不可避免的事实。这一课可不容易学会，就连那些在位的皇帝也必须经常提醒自己这样做。已故的乔治五世在白金汉宫的图书馆墙上写着下面的名言：

"我不要为月亮哭泣，也不要因事而后悔。"

叔本华也表达了同样的想法，他说："顺应势事，是踏上人生旅途的最重要的一件事。"

显然，环境本身并不能使我们快乐或不快乐，只有我们对环境的反应才决定了我们的感受。耶稣说天国就在你的心中，而那也是地狱之所在。

在必要的时候，我们都可以忍受灾难和悲剧，甚至战胜它们。我们会认为自己办不到，但我们有令人惊叹的潜能，只要我们愿意利用，它就能帮助我们克服一切困难。我们要比自己想象的更强大。

Put A "Stop-Loss" Order on Your Worries

Would you like to know how to make money on the Stock Exchange?Well, so would a million other people—and if I knew the answer, this book would sell for a fabulous price. However, there's one good idea that some successful operators use. This story was told to me by Charles Roberts, an investment counselor with offices at 17 East 42nd Street, New York.

"I originally came up to New York from Texas with twenty thousand dollars which my friends had given me to invest in the stock market," Charles Roberts told me. "I thought," he continued, "that I knew the ropes in the stock market; but I lost every cent. True, I made a lot of profit on some deals; but I ended up by losing everything.

"I did not mind so much losing my own money," Mr. Roberts explained, "but I felt terrible about having lost my friends' money, even though they could well afford it. I dreaded facing them again after our venture had turned out so unfortunately, but, to my astonishment, they not only were good sports about it, but proved to be incurable optimists.

"I knew I had been trading on a hit-or-miss basis and depending largely on luck and other people's opinions. As H. I. Phillips said, I had been 'playing the stock market by ear'.

"I began to think over my mistakes and I determined that before I went back into the market again, I would try to find out what it was all about. So I sought out and became acquainted with one of the most successful speculators who ever lived: Burton S. Castles. I believed I could learn a great deal from him because he had long enjoyed the reputation of being successful year after year and I knew that such a career was not the result of mere chance or luck.

"He asked me a few questions about how I had traded before and then told me what I believe is the most important principle in trading. He said: 'I put a stop-loss order on every market commitment I make. If I buy a stock at, say, fifty dollars a share, I immediately place a stop-loss order on it at forty-five.' that means that when and if the stock should decline as much as five points below its cost, it would be sold automatically, thereby, limiting the loss to five points.

"'If your commitments are intelligently made in the first place,' the old master continued, 'your profits will average ten, twenty-five, or even fifty points. Consequently, by limiting your losses to five points, you can be wrong more than half of the time and still make plenty of money?'

"I adopted that principle immediately and have used it ever since. It has saved my clients and me many thousands of dollars.

"After a while I realised that the stop-loss principle could be used in other ways besides in the stock market. I began to place a stop-loss order on any and every kind of annoyance and resentment that came to me. It has worked like magic.

"For example, I often have a luncheon date with a friend who is rarely on time. In the old days, he used to keep me stewing around for half my lunch hour before he showed up. Finally, I told him about my stop-loss orders on my worries. I said: 'Bill, my stop-loss order on waiting for you is exactly ten minutes. If you arrive more than ten minutes late, our luncheon engagement will be sold down the river—and I'll be gone.'"

Man alive! How I wish I had had the sense, years ago, to put stop-loss orders on my impatience, on my temper, on my desire for self-justification, on my regrets, and on all my mental and emotional strains. Why didn't I have the horse sense to size up each situation that threatened to destroy my peace of mind and say to myself: "See here, Dale Carnegie, this situation is worth just so much fussing about—and no more" ?…Why didn't I?

However, I must give myself credit for a little sense on one occasion, at least. And it was a serious occasion, too—a crisis in my life—a crisis when I stood watching my dreams and my plans for the future and the work of years vanish into thin air. It happened like this. In my early thirties, I had decided to spend my life writing novels. I was going to be a second Frank Norris or Jack London or Thomas Hardy. I was so in earnest that I spent two years in Europe—where I would live cheaply with dollars during the period of wild, printing-press money that followed the First World War. I spent two years there, writing my magnum opus. I called it *The Blizzard*. The title was a natural, for the reception it got among publishers was as cold as any blizzard that ever howled across the plains of the Dakotas. When my literary agent told me it was worthless, that I had no gift, no talent, for fiction, my heart almost stopped. I left his office in a daze. I couldn't have been more stunned if he had hit me across the head with a club. I was stupefied. I realised that I was standing at the crossroads of life, and had to make a tremendous decision. What should I do?Which way should I turn?Weeks passed before I came out of the daze. At that time, I had never heard of the phrase"put a stop-loss order on your worries". But as I look back now, I can see that I did just that. I wrote off my two years of sweating over that novel for just what they were worth—a noble experiment—and went forward from there. I returned to my work of organising and teaching adult-education classes, and wrote biographies in my spare time—biographies and nonfiction books such as the one you are reading now.

Am I glad now that I made that decision?Glad?Every time I think about it now I feel like dancing in the street for sheer joy! I can honestly say that I have never spent a day or an hour since, lamenting the fact that I am not another Thomas Hardy.

One night a century ago, when a screech owl was screeching in the woods along the shore of Walden Pond, Henry Thoreau dipped his goose quill into his homemade ink and wrote in his diary: "The cost of a thing is the amount of what I call life, which is required to be exchanged for it immediately or in the long run."

To put it another way: we are fools when we overpay for a thing in terms of what it takes out of our very existence.

让忧虑 "到此为止"

你想不想知道如何在股票交易中赚钱？当然，有数百万、数千万的人都想知道。如果我知道这个问题的答案，那我这本书就要卖个高价了。不过，有一个很好的理念，很多成功炒股者都应用过它。下面这个故事是查尔斯·罗伯兹告诉我的，他是一个投资顾问，在纽约东42大街17号办公。

"我刚从得克萨斯州来纽约的时候带了两万美元，是我朋友给我用来炒股的。"查尔斯·罗伯兹告诉我，"我原以为，我对股票市场很在行，可是我赔得分文不剩。不错！我在某些交易上赚了几笔，可是最后全都赔光了。

"我并不在乎把自己的钱都赔光了。可我认为把我朋友的钱赔光了不是件好事，虽然他们都很有钱。在我们的投资出现这种不幸的结局之后，我很害怕再见到他们。但我没有想到的是，他们对这件事情不仅看得很开，而且还非常乐观。

"我知道我的交易是漫无目标的，大部分靠运气和别人的股评。就像菲利普说的，我'是靠小道消息炒股'。

"我开始仔细研究我的错误，决定在再度进入股票市场之前，一定要先弄明白股票市场到底是何物。于是，我找到一位最成功的预测专家波顿·卡斯特，和他交上了朋友。我相信我能从他那里学到很多东西，因为他多年来一直非常成功，我知道能做出这番事业的人，不可能全靠机遇和运气。

"他先问了我几个问题，并问我以前是如何操作的，然后又告诉我股票交易中最重要的一条原则。他说：'我在股票市场上购买的每一只股票，都设定了一条止损线。例如，我买了一只50美元的股票，我设定的止损线是45美元。'也就是说，万一这只股票跌价达到5美元时，就立刻卖出去，这样损失就可以限定在5美元。

"'如果你当初买得聪明的话，'这位大师继续说，'你可能平均赚10～25美元，甚至50美元。因此，在把你的损失限定在5美元以后，即使你有一半以上的判断出现错误，还能赚很多钱。'

"我很快就采用了这个法则，从此一直使用它。这个办法替我的顾客和我挽回了许多钱。

"过了一段时间，我发现这一'到此为止'原则也可以用于炒股以外的地方。我开始在每种烦恼和不快的事情上都加上一个'到此为止'的限制，结果太妙了。

"例如，我经常和一个很不守时的朋友共进午餐。他以前总是在我的午餐时间过去大半后才赶来。而现在，我会告诉他我的底线原则，对他说：'以后我只等你10分钟，要是你在10分钟以后才赶到，那我们的午餐就算告吹——我会先走。'"

啊！我真希望在很多年以前就学会将这种"到此为止"的原则，用在我的每个方面：缺乏耐心、发脾气、自我适应的欲望、悔恨及所有精神与情感的压力上。为什么我以前没有想到用它来克服我的忧虑呢？为什么我不会对自己说"这件事情不值得这么担心——不能再去多管"呢？为什么我没有呢？

不过，我觉得自己至少在一件事上做得还不错。那是一次很严重的情况——是我生命中的一次危机。当时，我几乎眼看着我的梦想、我未来的计划以及多年来的工作全都付诸东流。事情是这样的：刚30岁时，我决定一辈子以写小说为职业，梦想当弗兰克·诺瑞斯、杰克·伦敦或哈代第二。我充满了热情，在欧洲住了两年。第一次世界大战结束后的那段时期，用美元在欧洲生活还是很合算的。我在那儿待了两年，完成了我的"杰作"。我给它取名为《暴风雪》。这书名取得太好了，因为所有出版商对它的态度都像呼啸着刮过达科他平原的暴风雪一样冷酷。当经纪人告诉我说这部作品一文不值，我没有写小说的天才时，我的心跳几乎停止了。我茫然失措地离开了他的办公室。当时，即使他用棒子敲打我的脑袋，我也不会吃惊——我惊呆了。我发现自己正站在生命的十字路口，必须作一个非常重大的决定。我该怎么办？该往哪个方向走？几周后，我才从茫然中醒悟过来。当时，我从来没有听过"让你的忧虑'到此为止'"的说法。可是现在回想起来，我当时正好做了这件事。我把自己费尽心血写那本小说看作一次宝贵的教训，然后从那里出发。我重新回去从事成人教育，有时间则写一些传记和非小说类的书，例如你现在正看的这本书。

我是不是很高兴做了这样的决定呢？何止高兴！现在只要是想起它我就会得意地想在大街上跳舞。我可以很坦诚地说，从那以后我从来没有后悔没有成为哈代第二。

100年前的一个夜晚，当一只鸟在瓦尔登湖畔的树林里鸣叫时，梭罗用鹅毛笔蘸着自制墨水，在他的日记里写道："一件事物的代价，即我称之为生活的总值，需要当场交换，或在最后付出。"

用另一种方式来说：如果我们以生活的一部分来付出代价，而且付得太多的话，那我们就是傻子。

Eight Words That Can Transform Your Life

A few years ago, I was asked to answer this question on a radio programme: "What is the biggest lesson you have ever learned?"

That was easy: by far the most vital lesson I have ever learned is the importance of what we think. If I knew what you think, I would know what you are. Our thoughts make us what we are. Our mental attitude is the X factor that determines our fate. Emerson said, "A man is what he thinks about all day long."…How could he possibly be anything else?

I now know with a conviction beyond all doubt that the biggest problem you and I have to deal with—in fact, almost the only problem we have to deal with—is choosing the right thoughts. If we can do that, we will be on the highroad to solving all our problems. The great philosopher who ruled the Roman Empire, Marcus Aurelius, summed it up in eight words—eight words that can determine your destiny: "Our life is what our thoughts make it."

Yes, if we think happy thoughts, we will be happy. If we think miserable thoughts, we will be miserable. If we think fear thoughts, we will be fearful. If we think sickly thoughts, we will probably be ill. If we think failure, we will certainly fail. If we wallow in self-pity, everyone will want to shun us and avoid us. "You are not," said Norman Vincent Peale, "you are not what you think you are; but what you think, you are."

As a result of thirty-five years spent in teaching adults, I know men and women can banish worry, fear, and various kinds of illness, and can transform their lives by changing their thoughts. I know! I know!! I know!!! I have seen such incredible transformations performed hundreds of times. I have seen them so often that I no longer wonder at them.

For example, one of these transformations happened to one of my students. Frank J. Whaley, of 1469 West Idaho Street, Saint Paul, Minnesota. He had a nervous breakdown. What brought it on? Worry. Frank Whaley tells me, "I worried about everything: I worried because I was too thin; because I thought I was losing my hair; because I feared I would never make enough money to get married; because I felt I would never make a good father; because I feared I was losing the girl I wanted to marry; because I felt I was not living a good life. I worried about the impression I was making on other people. I worried because I thought I had stomach ulcers. I could no longer work; I gave up my job. I built up tension inside me until I was like a boiler without a safety valve. The pressure got so unbearable that something had to give—and it did. If you have ever had a nervous breakdown, pray God that you never do, for no pain of the body can exceed the excruciating pain of an agonised mind.

"My breakdown was so severe that I couldn't talk even to my own family. I had no control over my thoughts. I was filled with fear. I would jump at the slightest noise. I avoided everybody. I would break out crying for no apparent reason at all.

"Every day was one of agony. I felt that I was deserted by everybody—even God. I was tempted to jump into the river and end it all.

"I decided instead to take a trip to Florida, hoping that a change of scene would help me. As I stepped on the train, my father handed me a letter and told me not to open it until I reached Florida. I landed in Florida during the height of the tourist season. Since I couldn't get in a hotel, I rented a sleeping room in a garage. I tried to get a job on a tramp freighter out of Miami, but had no luck. So I spent my time at the beach. I was more wretched in Florida than I had been at home; so I opened the envelope to see what Dad had written. His note said,'son, you are 1, 500 miles from home, and you don't feel any different, do you? I knew you wouldn't, because you took with you the one thing that is the cause of all your trouble, that is, yourself. There is nothing wrong with either your body or your mind. It is not the situations you have met that have thrown you; it is what you think of these situations. "As a man thinketh in his heart, so is he." When you realise that, son, come home, for you will be cured.'

"all this swept the accumulated litter out of my brain. I was able to think clearly and sensibly for the first time in my life. I realised what a fool I had been. I was shocked to see myself in my true light: here I was, wanting to change the whole world and everyone in it—when the only thing that needed changing was the focus of the lens of the camera which was my mind.

"The next morning I packed and started home. A week later I was back on the job. Four months later I married the girl I had been afraid of losing. We now have a happy family of five children. At the time of the breakdown I was a night foreman of a small department handling eighteen people. I am now superintendent of carton manufacture in charge of over four hundred and fifty people. Life is much fuller and friendlier. I believe I appreciate the true values of life now. When moments of uneasiness try to creep in（as they will in everyone's life）I tell myself to get that camera back in focus, and everything is OK.

"I can honestly say that I am glad I had the breakdown, because I found out the hard way what power our thoughts can have over our mind and our body. Now I can make my thoughts work for me instead of against me. I can see now that Dad was right when he said it wasn't outward situations that had caused all my suffering, but what I thought of those situations. And as soon as I realised that, I was cured—and stayed cured." Such was the experience of Frank J. Whaley.

I am deeply convinced that our peace of mind and the joy we get out of living depends not on where we are, or what we have, or who we are, but solely upon our mental attitude. Outward conditions have very little to do with it.

If half a century of living has taught me anything at all, it has taught me that"Nothing can bring you peace but yourself."

I am merely trying to repeat what Emerson said so well in the closing words of his essay on "Self-Reliance" : "A political victory, a rise in rents, the recovery of your sick, or the return of your absent friend, or some other quite external event, raises your spirits, and you think good days are preparing for you. Do not believe it. It can never be so. Nothing can bring you peace but yourself."

8个字可以改变你的生活

几年前，我在一个电台的广播节目中被主持人问道："你所学到的最重要的一课是什么？"

这个问题回答起来很简单：我所学到的最重要的一课，就是"思想的重要性"。只要知道你在想什么，我就可以知道你是什么人。因为我们的思想造就了我们，我们的命运也取决于我们的心理状态。爱默生曾说："一个人就是他成天所想象的那种样子。"……他怎么可能成为另一种样子呢？

我现在可以肯定地说，你和我必须面对的最大问题就是如何选择正确的思想——事实上，这几乎是我们必须应对的唯一问题。如果我们能够做到这一点，就可以解决一切问题。马库斯·奥勒留——这位曾经统治罗马帝国的伟大哲学家，把这些总结成八个字——决定你命运的八个字："生活乃由思想形成。"

不错，如果我们想的都是快乐的东西，我们就会快乐；如果我们想的都是悲伤之事，我们就会悲伤；如果我们想的是恐怖的事情，我们就会恐惧；如果我们想的是不好的念头，我们恐怕就不得安宁了；如果我们想的是失败，我们就会失败；如果我们沉浸在自我哀怜之中，别人都会有意躲开我们。"你并不是，"诺曼·文森特·皮尔说，"你并不是你想象中的那种样子；但你心里想什么，就会成为什么样的人。"

从事成人教育35年，我知道人们只要改变他们的想法，就能够消除忧虑、恐惧和各种疾病，就能改变他们的生活。我知道！我知道！我知道！这种不可思议的变化，我目睹过好几百次，因为我见到如此之多，以至于见怪不怪了。

例如，这种转变就曾发生在我的一个学生身上。他是明尼苏达州圣保罗市西伊达荷街1469号的弗兰克·J.威利。他曾经历了精神崩溃，原因是什么呢？是忧虑。他对我说："我对什么事情都忧虑。我之所以忧虑，是因为我太瘦了，我发现我正在掉头发，担心我永远都赚不到足够的钱娶老婆，担心我永远做不了一个好父亲，担心会失去我想娶的那个女孩子，担心我现在的生活不够好，担心我给别人的印象不好。我还担心我得了胃溃疡，于是无法再工作，只好辞职。我内心越来越紧张，就像一个没有安全阀的锅炉，终于达到了令人难以忍受的地步，必须有一个退路——结果真的出事了。如果你经历过精神崩溃，祈祷上帝！永远也不要有这种体验吧！因为任何一种肉体上的痛苦都比不上这种精神上的极度痛苦。

"我精神崩溃到不能和我的家人沟通。我无法控制自己的思想，充满了恐惧。只要稍有一点点声响，我就会跳起来。我躲开每一个人，常常无缘无故地哭。

"每天都是一种煎熬。我觉得被所有的人抛弃了——甚至上帝也抛弃了我。我真想跳进河里，一死了之。

"但是，我后来决定去佛罗里达旅行，希望换个环境对我有所帮助。我登上火车之后，父亲交给我一封信，并告诉我到佛罗里达后再拆开。我到佛罗里达时正值旅游旺季，因为在旅馆订不到房间，就租了一家汽车旅馆的房子住了下来。我想在迈阿密一艘不定期的货船上找一份差事，但没有找到，于是就在海滩上消磨时间。我在佛罗里达比在家更难受。这时，我拆开那封信，看看父亲写了些什么。他写道：'儿子，你现在离家750千米，但你并没有觉得有何不同，对不对？我知道你不会觉得有何不同，因为你还带着你所有麻烦的根源——也就是你自己。其实，你的身体和你的精神都没有问题。并不是你所遇到的环境给了你挫折，而是由你的各种想象造成的。"一个人心里想什么，他就会成为什么样子。"当你理解这点之后，儿子，回家来吧，因为那时你就能恢复了。'

"这一切将我脑子里积聚的不快一扫而光。于是，我能清晰理智地思考了，并发现自己确实是一个大傻瓜。看清楚了自己，这一点实在使我非常震惊，本来我还想改变这个世界及全世界所有的人呢——但事实上唯一需要改变的，是我大脑中那架思想相机镜头的焦点。

"第二天一大早，我收拾好行李回了家。一周后，我又回去工作了。4个月后，我娶了我一直害怕失去的那个女孩子，现在我们有了一个快乐的家庭，还有5个子女。在我精神崩溃的时候，我只是一个小部门的晚班工头，下面有18个工人；现在我成了一家纸箱厂的厂长，管理着450名员工。和以前相比，生活变得更充实、更美好了。我认为我现在已经了解了生命的真正价值。每当消极思想进入我的大脑（就像每个人遇到的那样）的时候，我就会告诉自己，只要把相机的焦距调好，一切都好办了。

"坦诚地说，我很高兴我曾经历过那次精神崩溃，因为它使我发现思想对身心两方面所具有的控制力。现在我能使我的思想为我所用，而不会对我造成损伤。我现在才知道我父亲是对的——使我痛苦的不是外在因素，而是我对各种事情的看法。一旦了解这点之后，我完全好了——而且不再生病了。"这就是弗兰克·J. 威利的体验。

我深信，我们内心的平静和我们从生活中所得到的快乐，并不取决于我们在哪里、我们有什么或我们是谁，而只取决于我们的心境。外在条件并没有多大的影响。

如果说半个世纪的生活教会了我什么的话，那就是"除了你自己，没有任何东西可以给你带来平静"。

我想再重复一次爱默生在他的散文《自力更生》中所写的那句结束语："不要认为一次政治上的获胜、收入的提高、病体的康复、分别许久的好友归来或其他纯粹外在的事物能提高你的兴致，使你觉得前程美好。不要相信，事情绝不会如此简单。除了你自己，没有任何东西能给你带来平静。"

Just for Today

Just for today I will be happy. This assumes that what Abraham Lincoln said is true, that "most folks are about as happy as they make up their minds to be." Happiness is from within; it is not a matter of externals.

Just for today I will try to adjust myself to what is, and not try to adjust everything to my own desires. I will take my family, my business, and my luck as they come and fit myself to them.

Just for today I will take care of my body. I will exercise it, care for it, nourish it, not abuse it nor neglect it, so that it will be a perfect machine for my bidding.

Just for today I will try to strengthen my mind. I will learn something useful. I will not be a mental loafer. I will read something that requires effort, thought and concentration.

Just for today I will exercise my soul in three ways: I will do somebody a good turn and not get found out. I will do at least two things I don't want to do, as William James suggests, just for exercise.

Just for today I will be agreeable. I will look as well as I can, dress as becomingly as possible, talk low, act courteously, be liberal with praise, criticise not at all, nor find fault with anything and not try to regulate nor improve anyone.

Just for today I will try to live through this day only, not to tackle my whole life problem at once. I can do things for twelve hours that would appall me if I had to keep them up for a lifetime.

Just for today I will have a programme. I will write down what I expect to do every hour. I may not follow it exactly, but I will have it. It will eliminate two pests, hurrying and indecision.

Just for today I will have a quiet half-hour all by myself and relax. In this half-hour sometimes I will think of God, so as to get a little more perspective into my life.

Just for today I will be unafraid, especially I will not be afraid to be happy, to enjoy what is beautiful, to love, and to believe that those I love, love me.

只 为 今 天

只为今天，我要很快乐。如果林肯所说的"大部分人只要下定决心，都能很快乐"这句话是对的，那么快乐是来自人的内心，而不是来自外界。

只为今天，我要使自己适应一切，而不是让一切来适应我的欲望。我要以这种态度来接受我的家庭、我的事业和我的运气。

只为今天，我要爱惜我的身体。我要多运动，照顾好自己，珍惜自己，不损伤身体，不忽视身体，使它成为我心灵的殿堂。

只为今天，我要强化我的思想。我要学一些有用的知识，不做胡思乱想的人。我要看一些需要精力思考、使我专注的书。

只为今天，我要从三个方面来锻炼我的灵魂：我要为别人做一件好事，但不要让人家知道；我还要做两件我并不想做的事，就像威廉·詹姆斯建议那样，只是为了锻炼自己。

只为今天，我要做个受人欢迎的人。我要尽量修饰外表，尽量穿着得体，说话要低声，行动要优雅，不在乎别人的毁誉。对任何事都不挑毛病，也不干涉或教训别人。

只为今天，我要努力思考如何过好今天，而不是一次解决我一生的问题。虽然我可以持续12个小时地工作，但我若一辈子这样做下去的话，就会毁了我。

只为今天，我要制订一个计划。我要写下每小时该做些什么，也许我不会完全照着它去做，但还是要订下这个计划。这样至少可以消除两大缺点——匆忙和犹豫。

只为今天，我要为自己留下半小时的安静，放松下来。在这半小时里，我要感激神，使我的生命更充满希望。

只为今天，我要毫不惧怕，尤其不能害怕快乐，要去欣赏一切美，去爱一切，相信我爱的那些人也会爱我。

Count Your Blessings, not Your Troubles

You and I may have the services of"Doctor Merryman" free every hour of the day by keeping our attention fixed on all the incredible riches we possess—riches exceeding by far the fabled treasures of Ali Baba. Would you sell both your eyes for a billion dollars? What would you take for your two legs? Your hands? Your hearing? Your children? Your family? Add up your assets, and you will find that you won't sell what you have for all the gold ever amassed by the Rockefellers, the Fords and the Morgans combined.

But do we appreciate all this? Ah, no. As Schopenhauer said: "We seldom think of what we have but always of what we lack." Yes, the tendency to"seldom think of what we have but always of what we lack" is the greatest tragedy on earth. It has probably caused more misery than all the wars and diseases in history.

Would you like to know how to make even dishwashing at the kitchen sink a thrilling experience? If so, read an inspiring book of incredible courage by Borghild Dahl. It is called I Wanted to See.

This book was written by a woman who was practically blind for half a century. "I had only one eye," she writes, "and it was so covered with dense scars that I had to do all my seeing through one small opening in the left of the eye. I could see a book only by holding it up close to my face and by straining my one eye as hard as I could to the left."

But she refused to be pitied, refused to be considered"different". As a child, she wanted to play hopscotch with other children, but she couldn't see the markings. So after the other children had gone home, she got down on the ground and crawled along with her eyes near to the marks. She memorised every bit of the ground where she and her friends played and soon became an expert at running games. She did her reading at home, holding a book of large print so close to her eyes that her eyelashes brushed the pages. She earned two college degrees: an A. B. from the University of Minnesota and a Master of Arts from Columbia University.

She started teaching in the tiny village of Twin Valley, Minnesota, and rose until she became professor of journalism and literature at Augustana College in Sioux Falls, South Dakota. She taught there for thirteen years, lecturing before women's clubs and giving radio talks about books and authors. "In the back of my mind," she writes, "there had always lurked a fear of total blindness. In order to overcome this, I had adopted a cheerful, almost hilarious, attitude towards life."

Then in 1943, when she was fifty-two years old, a miracle happened: an operation at the famous Mayo Clinic. She could now see forty times as well as she had ever been able to see before.

A new and exciting world of loveliness opened before her. She now found it thrilling even to wash dishes in the kitchen sink. "I begin to play with the white fluffy suds in the dish-pan," she writes. "I dip my hands into them and I pick up a ball of tiny soap bubbles. I hold them up against the light, and in each of them I can see the brilliant colours of a miniature rainbow."

As she looked through the window above the kitchen sink, she saw "the flapping grey-black wings of the sparrows flying through the thick, falling snow."

She found such ecstasy looking at the soap bubbles and sparrows that she closed her book with these words: "'Dear Lord,'I whisper, 'Our Father in Heaven, I thank Thee. I thank Thee.'"

Imagine thanking God because you can wash dishes and see rainbows in bubbles and sparrows flying through the snow!

You and I ought to be ashamed of ourselves. All the days of our years we have been living in a fairyland of beauty, but we have been too blind to see, too satiated to enjoy.

If we want to stop worrying and start living, Rule 4 is:

Count your blessings—not your troubles!

想想你得到的恩惠，不要理会你的烦恼

每一天的每个小时，你和我都能得到"快乐医生"的免费服务，只要我们把精力集中在我们拥有的那么多令人难以置信的财富上——这些财富远远超过了阿里巴巴的珍宝。你愿意以10亿美元出卖你的双眼吗？你愿意把你的双腿卖多少钱？还有你的双手、听觉、孩子、家庭？把你所有的资产加在一起，你就会发现你绝不会卖掉现在拥有的一切，即使把洛克菲勒、福特和摩根拥有的黄金都加在一起也不卖。

可是，我们欣赏了这些吗？啊，很难做到。正如叔本华所说："我们很少想到我们拥有的，而总是想到我们没有的。"这正是世界上最大的悲剧，它造成的痛苦可能比历史上所有的战争和疾病都要多。

你想不想知道如何将在厨房的水槽中洗碗变成一次宝贵的体验呢？如果想知道，可以去看鲍吉尔德·达尔的书，它主要谈论令人难以置信的勇气，颇具启发性。该书名叫《我希望能看见》。

这本书的作者是一位女性，她失明达50年之久。"我只有一只眼睛，"她写道，"而眼睛上还满是疤痕，只能透过眼睛左边的一个小洞来看外界。看书的时候必须将书移到离脸很近的地方，而且不得不把另一只眼睛往左边斜过去。"

可是她拒绝别人的怜悯，更不愿被认为"与众不同"。小时候，她想和其他小孩一起玩跳房子的游戏，可是她看不见画在地上的线。于是，等其他孩子都回家以后，她趴在地上，把眼睛贴在地上察看。她把那块地方的每一处都牢记在心，不久就成为这个游戏的好手了。她在家中看书时，把印有大字的书紧贴眼睛，几乎连眼睫毛都碰到书页上。她获得了两个学位：明尼苏达州立大学学士学位和哥伦比亚大学硕士学位。

她开始是在明尼苏达州双谷镇一个小村子里教书，然后逐渐晋升为南达科他州奥格塔那学院的新闻学和文学教授。她在那里工作了13年，还在许多妇女俱乐部发表演说，在电台点评图书和作者。"在我的脑海深处，"她写道，"常常怀着一种担心完全失明的恐惧。为了克服这种恐惧，我对生活采取了一种快乐而近乎戏谑的态度。"

然后，1943年，她52岁时，奇迹发生了：她去著名的梅育医院做了一次手术，视力比以前好了40倍。

一个令人兴奋、可爱全新的世界展现在她眼前。现在她发现，即使是在厨房的水槽里洗碟子，也会让她开心。"我开始玩洗碗槽中的肥皂泡，"她写道，"我把手伸进去，抓起一大把小小的肥皂泡，把它们迎着光举起来，看到了一道小小彩虹般的明亮色彩。"

从水槽上方的厨房的窗口望出去，她看到了"振动黑色翅膀飞过厚厚积雪"的麻雀。

能有幸看见肥皂泡和麻雀，因此书中以下面的话作为结尾："'亲爱的主，'我低语，'我的父亲啊，我感谢你，我感谢你。'"

想想，因为你能看见洗碗时泡沫中的彩虹和飞过雪地的麻雀，要感谢上帝吧！

你和我都应该感到惭愧。这么多年来，我们每天都生活在一个美丽的童话王国里，可是我们视而不见，不懂得珍惜和享受。

因此，要想得到快乐，请记住这项规则：

想想你得到的恩惠，不要理会你的烦恼。

Find Yourself and Be Yourself

If you can't be a pine on the top of the hill.
Be a scrub in the valley—but be
The best little scrub by the side of the rill;

Be a bush, if you can't be a tree.
If you can't be a bush, be a bit of the grass.
And some highway happier make;
If you can't be a muskie, then just be a bass—
But the liveliest bass in the lake!
We can't all be captains, we've got to be crew.
There's something for all of us here.
There's big work to do and there's lesser to do
And the task we must do is the near.
If you can't be a highway, then just be a trail,
If you can't be the sun, be a star;
It isn't by the size that you win or you fail—
Be the best of whatever you are!

保持自我本色

如果你不能成为山顶的青松，

就做一丛小树，生长在山谷中，

但必须是溪边最好的一丛小树。

如果你不能成为一棵大树，

就做一丛灌木。

如果你不能成为一丛灌木，

就做一片绿草，

给大路增添几分景致。

如果你不能成为一条北美狗鱼，

就做一条鲈鱼，

但必须是湖里最好的一条鱼。

我们不能都当船长，我们得当海员；

世上的事情多得做不完，

工作有大有小，

我们该做的工作，就在手边。

如果你不能当一条公路，就当一条小径；

如果你不能当太阳，就当一颗星星。

不能凭大小来判断你的输赢，

不论做什么，都要做你自己。

Do A Good Deed Every Day

If you want to banish worry and cultivate peace and happiness, here is the nlle:

Forget yourself by becoming interested in others. Do every day a good deed that will put a smile of joy on someone's face.

the story of C. R. Burton was an excellent example.

"I lost my mother when I was nine years old, and my father when I was twelve," Mr. Burton wrote me. "My father was killed, but my mother simply walked out of the house one day nineteen years ago; and I have never seen her since. Neither have I ever seen my two little sisters that she took with her. She never even wrote me a letter until after she had been gone seven years. My father was killed in an accident three years after Mother left. He and a partner bought a café in a small Missouri town; and while Father was away on a business trip, his partner sold the café for cash and skipped out. A friend wired Father to hurry back home; and in his hurry, Father was killed in a car accident at Salinas, Kansas. Two of my father's sisters, who were poor and old and sick took three of the children into their homes. Nobody wanted me and my little brother. We were left at the mercy of the town. We were haunted by the fear of being called orphans and treated as orphans. Our fears soon materialised, too. I lived for a little while with a poor family in town. But times were hard and the head of the family lost his job, so they couldn't afford to feed me any longer. Then Mr. and Mrs. Loftin took me to live with them on their farm eleven miles from town. Mr. Loftin was seventy years old, and sick in bed with shingles. He told me I could stay there'as long as I didn't lie, didn't steal, and did as I was told.' Those three orders became my Bible. I lived by them strictly. I started to school, but the first week found me at home, bawling like a baby. The other children picked on me and poked fun at my big nose and said I was dumb and called me an'orphan brat'. I was hurt so badly that I wanted to fight them; but Mr. Loftin, the farmer who had taken me in, said to me: 'Always remember that it takes a bigger man to walk away from a fight than it does to stay and fight.'I didn't fight until one day a kid picked up some chicken manure from the schoolhouse yard and threw it in my face. I beat the hell out of him; and made a couple of friends. They said he had it coming to him.

"I was proud of a new cap that Mrs. Loftin had bought me. One day one of the big girls jerked it off my head and riffled it with water and ruined it. She said she filled it with water so that'the water would wet my thick skull and keep my popcorn brains from popping'.

"I never cried at school, but I used to bawl it out at home. Then one day Mrs. Loftin gave me some advice that did away with all troubles and worries and turned my enemies into friends. She said: 'ralph, they won't tease you and call you an "orphan brat" any more if you will get interested in them and see how much you can do for them.' I took her advice. I studied hard; and I soon headed the class. I was never envied because I went out of my way to help them.

"I helped several of the boys write their themes and essays. I wrote complete debates for some of the boys. One lad was ashamed to let his folks know that I was helping him. So he used to tell his mother he was going possum hunting. Then he would come to Mr. Loftin's farm and tie his dogs up in the barn while I helped him with his lessons. I wrote book reviews for one lad and spent several evenings helping one of the girls on her math.

"Death struck our neighbourhood. Two elderly farmers died and one woman was deserted by her husband. I was the only male in four families. I helped these widows for two years. On my way to and from school, I stopped at their farms, cut wood for them, milked their cows, and fed and watered their stock. I was now blessed instead of cursed. I was accepted as a friend by everyone. They showed their real feelings when I returned home from the Navy. More than two hundred farmers came to see me the first day I was home. Some of them drove as far as eighty miles, and their concern for me was really sincere. Because I have been busy and happy trying to help other people, I have few worries; and I haven't been called an 'orphan brat' now for thirteen years."

Hooray for C. R. Burton! He knows how to win friends! And he also knows how to conquer worry and enjoy life.

每天做一件好事

如果你想消除忧虑，获得平安与幸福，请记住这项规则：

要对别人感兴趣，忘掉你自己；每天做一件让别人高兴的事。

波顿先生的故事就是一个极好的例子。

"我9岁时没了母亲，12岁时又没了父亲，"波顿先生写道，"父亲死于意外，母亲在19年前的某一天离家出走，从此以后我就再也没有见过她，也没有见过被她带走的两个小妹妹。直到离家7年之后，她才给我写了封信。父亲在母亲离家3年之后死于一次意外。他和一个合伙人在密苏里州一个小镇买下了一家咖啡店，这个合伙人趁父亲出差时，把咖啡店卖了并卷款潜逃。一个朋友给我父亲发电报，叫他赶快回家。父亲匆忙之下，在堪萨斯州萨莱纳城的一次车祸中丧生。我有两个姑姑，她们又穷又老，病魔缠身。她们把我们5个孩子中的3个带到她们家里去。没有人要我和我最小的弟弟，我们只好依靠镇上的人救济度日。我们怕被人家叫孤儿，或被当孤儿来看待，但我们担心的事情很快就发生了。我在镇上一个贫民家庭里住了一段时间，但日子很艰难，男主人不久后失业，他们没办法再供养我。后来，洛夫汀先生和夫人收留了我，住在他们一个离镇子约20千米远的农庄里。当时，洛夫汀先生70岁，得了带状疱疹躺在床上。他告诉我说，只要我不说谎，不偷窃，能听话做事，我就可以留在他家里。这三项要求成了我的圣令，我严格遵守。我开始上学了，可是第一周我就像婴儿似的躲在家里号啕大哭。其他孩子都来捉弄我，取笑我的大鼻子，说我是个笨蛋，还说我是个'小臭孤儿'。我伤心得想揍他们一顿，可是收养我的洛夫汀先生对我说：'要永远记住，能走开而不打架的人要比打架的人伟大得多。'所以，我一直没有和人打过架。直到有一天，有个小孩在学校的院子里抓起一把鸡屎朝我脸上扔来。我狠狠地揍了他一顿，结果交上了好几个朋友，他们都说他是自找苦吃。

"我非常喜欢洛夫汀夫人给我买的一顶新帽子。一天，有个大女孩把我的帽子扯了下来，在里面装满了水，弄坏了帽子。她说她之所以往里面装水，是想让那些水弄湿我的大脑瓜，好让我那玉米花似的脑筋不要乱爆。

"我在学校从来没有哭过，但我常常在家里号啕大哭。然后，有一天，洛夫汀夫人给了我一些忠告，消除了我所有的烦恼和忧虑，并使我的敌人变成了朋友。她说：'拉尔夫，只要你对他们感兴趣，而且注意你能够为他们做些什么，他们就不会再捉弄你，或叫你"小臭孤儿"了。'我接受了她的忠告。我努力学习，不久就得了第一名。但从来没有人妒忌我，因为我总是尽力帮助别人。

"我帮过好多男孩子写作文，还为好几个男孩子写过完整的报告。有一个孩子不愿让他父母知道我在帮他，所以他常常告诉他母亲，说他要去抓田鼠，然后跑到洛夫汀先生的农场来，把他的狗关在谷仓中，让我教他功课。我还替一个孩子写过读书报告，还花了好几个晚上教另一个女孩子数学。

"死神来到了我们附近：两个年老的农夫死了，另一位妇女被丈夫抛弃了。我是这四户人家中唯一的男人。我帮了这些寡妇们两年。我上学放学的路上都会去她们的农场，帮她们砍柴、挤牛奶，给她们的家畜喂饲料喂水。现在，大家都很喜欢我，不再骂我，每个人都把我当朋友。当我从海军退役回来时，他们向我表达了他们的感情。我到家的第一天，两百多个农夫赶来看我，其中还有许多人从100千米以外开车过来。他们对我的关怀非常真诚，因为我一直很高兴帮助其他人，所以我没有什么忧虑。而且，13年来再也没有人叫我'小臭孤儿'了。"

让我们为波顿喝彩吧！他知道如何赢得朋友！他也知道如何克服忧虑、享受生活。

No One Ever Kicks a Dead Dog

An event occurred in 1929 that created a national sensation in educational circles. Learned men from all over America rushed to Chicago to witness the affair. A few years earlier, a young man by the name of Robert Hutchins had worked his way through Yale, acting as a waiter, a lumberjack, a tutor, and a clothes-line salesman. Now, only eight years later, he was being inaugurated as president of the fourth richest university in America, the University of Chicago. His age? Thirty. Incredible! The older educators shook their heads. Criticism came roaring down upon the "boy wonder" like a rockslide. He was this and he was that—too young, inexperienced— his educational ideas were cockeyed. Even the newspapers joined in the attack.

The day he was inaugurated, a friend said to the father of Robert Maynard Hutchins: "I was shocked this morning to read that newspaper editorial denouncing your son."

"Yes," the elder Hutchins replied, "it was severe, but remember that no one ever kicks a dead dog."

Yes, and the more important a dog is, the more satisfaction people get in kicking him. The Prince of Wales who later became Edward VIII（now Duke of Windsor） had that forcibly brought home to him.

He was attending Dartmouth College in Devonshire at the time—a college that corresponds to the Naval Academy at Annapolis. The Prince was about fourteen. One day one of the naval officers found him crying, and asked him what was wrong. He refused to tell at first, but finally admitted the truth: he was being kicked by the naval cadets. The commodore of the college summoned the boys and explained to them that the Prince had not complained, but he wanted to find out why the Prince had been singled out for this rough treatment.

After much hemming and hawing and toe scraping, the cadets finally confessed that when they themselves became commanders and captains in the King's Navy, they wanted to be able to say that they had kicked the King!

So when you are kicked and criticised, remember that it is often done because it gives the kicker a feeling of importance. It often means that you are accomplishing something and are worthy of attention.

没有人会踢一只死狗

1929年，美国发生了一件震惊教育界的大事，美国各地的学者都赶往芝加哥恭迎盛会。几年前，一个名叫罗伯特·哈金斯的年轻人，半工半读从耶鲁大学毕业，他当过服务生、伐木工人、家庭教师和成衣推销员。现在，仅仅8年之后，他就被任命为美国第四富有的大学——芝加哥大学的校长。他多大了？30岁！难以置信！老一辈教育人士都大加反对，批评就像山崩石落一样打在这位"神童"头上，说他这样或那样：太年轻了，经验不足。甚至说他的教育观念荒谬，连各大报纸也参与了对他的攻击。

就任那天，一个朋友对哈金斯的父亲说："我今天早上看见报纸社论攻击你的儿子，真把我吓坏了。"

"不错，"老哈金斯回答说，"攻击得很厉害。可是请记住，从来没有人会踢一只死狗。"

是的，这只狗越贵重，踢它的人就越可以获得满足。后来成为英王爱德华八世的威尔士亲王，他也有过这种遭遇。他曾就读于德文郡的达特茅斯学院——这个学院相当于美国安纳波利斯的海军学院。王子那时只有14岁。一天，一位海军军官发现他在哭，就问他出了什么事。他开始不肯说，但最后终于说了真话：他被一位海军幼校生踢了一脚。指挥官把所有的学生都召集起来，向他们解释王子并没有告状，但他想弄清楚为什么有人如此粗暴地对待王子。

大家相互推诿了半天，踢人者终于承认说：如果他自己将来成了皇家海军的指挥官或舰长，他希望能够告诉别人，他曾踢过国王。

所以，如果你被别人踢了，或者遭到了批评，请记住，因为这样做可以给踢人者一种虚荣心上的满足，这通常意味着你已经有所成就，并且值得人们关注。

Spend Your Days

All of us have read thrilling stories in which the hero had only a limited and specified time to live. Sometimes it was as long as a year; sometimes as short as twenty-four hours. But always we were interested in discovering just how the doomed man chose to spend his last days or his last hours. I speak, of course, of free men who have a choice, not condemned criminals whose sphere of activities is strictly delimited.

Such stories set us thinking, wondering what we should do under similar circumstances. What events, what experiences, what associations should we crowd into those last hours as mortal beings? What happiness should we find in reviewing the past, what regrets?

Sometimes I have thought it would be an excellent rule to live each day as if we should die tomorrow. Such an attitude would emphasize sharply the values of life.

We should live each day with a gentleness, a vigor, and a keenness of appreciation which are often lost when time stretches before us in the constant panorama of more days and months and years to come. There are those, of course, who would adopt the Epicurean motto of "Eat, drink, and be merry", but most people would be chastened by the certainty of impending death.

In stories the doomed hero is usually saved at the last minute by some stroke of fortune, but almost always his sense of values is changed. He becomes more appreciative of the meaning of life and its permanent spiritual values. It was often been noted that those who live, or have lived, in the shadow of death bring a mellow sweetness to everything they do.

Most of us, however, take life for granted. We know that one day we must die, but usually we picture that day as far in the future. When we are in buoyant health, death is all but unimaginable. We seldom think of it. The days stretch out in an endless vista. So we go about our petty tasks, hardly aware of our listless attitude toward life.

The same lethargy, I am afraid, characterizes the use of all our faculties and senses. Only the deaf appreciate hearing, only the blind realize the manifold blessings that lie in sight. Particularly does this observation apply to those who have lost sight and hearing in adult life. But those who have never suffered impairment of sight or hearing seldom make the fullest use of these blessed faculties. Their eyes and ears take in all sights and sounds hazily, without concentration and with little appreciation. It is the same old story of not being grateful for what we have until we lose it, of not being conscious of health until we are ill.

I have often thought it would be a blessing if each human being were stricken blind and deaf for a few days at some time during his early adult life. Darkness would make him more appreciative of sight; silence would tech him the joys of sound.

Now and then I have tested my seeing friends to discover what they see. Recently I was visited by a very good friends who had just returned from a long walk in the woods, and I asked her what she had observed. "Nothing in particular," she replied. I might have been incredulous had I not been accustomed to such reposes, for long ago I became convinced that the seeing see little.

How was it possible, I asked myself, to walk for an hour through the woods and see nothing worthy of note? I who cannot see find hundreds of things to interest me through mere touch. I feel the delicate symmetry of a leaf. I pass my hands lovingly about the smooth skin of a silver birch, or the rough, shaggy bark of a pine. In the spring I touch the branches of trees hopefully in search of a bud the first sign of awakening Nature after her winter's sleep. I feel the delightful, velvety texture of a flower, and discover its remarkable convolutions; and something of the miracle of Nature is revealed to me. Occasionally, if I am very fortunate, I place my hand gently on a small tree and feel the happy quiver of a bird in full song. I am delighted to have the cool waters of a brook rush thought my open finger. To me a lush carpet of pine needles or spongy grass is more welcome than the most luxurious Persian rug. To me the pageant of seasons is a thrilling and unending drama, the action of which streams through my finger tips.

At times my heart cries out with longing to see all these things. If I can get so much pleasure from mere touch, how much more beauty must be revealed by sight. Yet, those who have eyes apparently see little. The panorama of color and action which fills the world is taken for granted. It is human, perhaps, to appreciate little that which we have and to long for that which we have not, but it is a great pity that in the world of light the gift of sight is used only as a mere conveniences rather than as a means of adding fullness to life.

If I were the president of a university I should establish a compulsory course in "How to Use Your Eyes". The professor would try to show his pupils how they could add joy to their lives by really seeing what passes unnoticed before them. He would try to awake their dormant and sluggish faculties.

Perhaps I can best illustrate by imagining what I should most like to see if I were given the use of my eyes, say, for just three days. And while I am imagining, suppose you, too, set your mind to work on the problem of how you would use your own eyes if you had only three more days to see. If with the on-coming darkness of the third night you knew that the sun would never rise for you again, how would you spend those three precious intervening days? What would you most want to let your gaze rest upon?

I, naturally, should want most to see the things which have become dear to me through my years of darkness. You, too, would want to let your eyes rest on the things that have become dear to you so that you could take the memory of them with you into the night that loomed before you.

If, by some miracle, I were granted three seeing days, to be followed by a relapse into darkness, I should divide the period into three parts.

珍惜每一天

我们大家都读过一些激动人心的故事，这些故事的主人公只有有限而且特定的时间可活，有时长达一年，有时短到只剩下24小时。但我们总是有兴趣去发现那注定要死的人是如何度过他生命的最后几天或几小时的。当然，我说的是那些有选择自由的人，而不是那些活动范围受到严格限定的判刑的犯人。

这样的故事让我们思考，我们处在相似的情况下应该怎么办。作为终有一死的生命，在这最后的几个小时内，我们会有什么遭遇、什么经历、什么感受？回顾往事，我们将会发现什么快乐、什么悔恨呢？

有时，我会想到，过好每一天或许是一个非常好的习惯，就好像我们明天就会死去一样。这种态度非常尖锐地强调了生命的价值。我们每天都应该和蔼友善、精力充沛、充满向往地生活。随着岁月流逝，这些品质常常也会一点点丧失。当然，也有人愿意按照伊壁鸠鲁"吃喝玩乐"的信条去生活，但绝大多数人还是受到了必将来临的死亡的折磨。

在这些故事中，注定要死亡的主人公往往在最后的时刻由于某种命运的突变而得救，他的价值观也几乎从此被改变了。他对生活的意义和生命永恒的精神意义有了更深的领悟。我们常常可以看到，那些受到或曾经受到死亡威胁的人，都会从他们所做的每件事中发现芳醇甜美。

但是，我们大多数人都认为人生是理所当然的。我们知道，某一天我们一定会死去，而我们通常会把那天想得非常遥远。当我们身体强健时，死亡几乎是不可想象的，我们很少会想到它。日子无穷无尽地延续下去，于是我们每天干一些琐碎的事情，几乎没有意识到我们对生活的倦怠态度。

我以为，同样的懒散也会作用于我们所有的本能和感觉，并形成固有的特点。只有聋子才会珍惜听力，只有瞎子才能体会到看见事物的巨大幸福，这种结论特别适合于那些在成年阶段失去了视力和听力的人。然而，那些从没有体会过失去视力或听力痛苦的人，却很少充分利用这些天赐的官能。他们的眼睛和耳朵漫无目的地看着或听着四周的景色和声音，毫无重点，不知道珍惜这一切。还是那句相同的老话：直到有一天失去了，才知道珍惜我们所有的感官；直到有一天生病了，才知道健康的可贵。

我常常想，如果每个人在他早期的成年时期曾经致瞎致聋，那将是一种幸事。黑暗会使他更珍惜视力，聋哑会教导他喜爱声音。

我经常询问我那些能看得见东西的朋友，问他们看到了什么。最近，一位好友来看我，她刚从森林里散了很长时间的步回来，我问她看到了什么，她回答道："没什么特别的东西。"如果我不是对这种回答习以为常，我都可能不相信，因为很久以前我就已经确信，能看得见的人却看不到什么。

我问自己，这怎么可能呢？一个人在森林里散步一小时，却没有看到任何值得注意的东西！而我自己，一个看不见东西的人，仅仅通过触觉，就发现了许多令我感兴趣的东西。我可以感触到一片树叶的完美对称。我充满欢喜地用手抚摸白桦树光滑的树皮或松树粗糙的树皮。春天，我摸着树枝，满怀希望地摸索着嫩芽，这是大自然在严冬的沉睡之后苏醒的第一个征兆。我抚摸到了鲜花那令人愉快的天鹅绒般的花瓣，感觉到了它那奇妙的卷曲。大自然就这样向我展现了它的奇迹。有时，如果幸运的话，我把手轻轻地放在一棵小树上，还能感受到小鸟高声歌唱时的欢悦喜跳。我很高兴让小溪的凉水流过我张开的手指。在我看来，一片茂密的松针叶或松软而富有弹性的草地铺成的地毯，比最豪华的波斯地毯更受欢迎。对我来说，四季的兴衰更迭是一部令人激动、无穷无尽、壮观华丽的戏剧，它从我的指尖流淌而过。

有时，我的内心在哭泣，因为我渴望能看到这一切。如果仅通过我的触觉就能感受到这么多的愉快，那么通过视觉将会有多少美丽的东西展现出来啊！然而，那些看得见的人显然看得很少。在他们看来，充满世界的万花筒般的景象都是理所当然的。或许这就是人类共有的特性：对我们所拥有的看不上眼，对于我们没有的却渴望得到。然而，在光明的世界里，将视力的天赋仅仅看作是一种方便，而没有作为增添生活美满的手段，这是极其令人遗憾的。

如果我是一所大学的校长，我将开设一门强制性的必修课"如何应用你的眼睛"。上课的教授应该试图给学生展示如何观察那些在他们面前一闪而过的东西来增添他们生活的乐趣，尽量唤醒他们沉睡和懒散的天赋。

如果让我来用我的眼睛，哪怕只有三天时间，或许我能以我想象得到的最喜欢看见的东西来很好地说清楚这个问题。而且在我这么想时，也请你思考这个问题。假如你也只有三天的时间来看世界，你该如何用你自己的眼睛？如果面对即将到来的第三个夜晚的黑暗，对你来说太阳将永远不再升起了，那么你将如何度过这宝贵的三天呢？你最想让你的目光注视什么东西呢？

当然，我最希望看到的是多年来在黑暗中对我最亲切的东西，你也一定希望让你的目光停留在那些让你感到最亲切的东西上。这样，你就能把它们带进那正在逼近你的长夜之中。

如果出现某种奇迹，使我能有三天光明，随后又陷入一片黑暗之中，我将把这段时间分成三个部分。

The First Day

On the first day, I should want to see the people whose kindness and gentleness and companionship have made my life worth living. First I should like to gaze long upon the face of my dear teacher, Mrs. Anne Sullivan Macy, who came to me when I was a child and opened the outer world to me. I should want not merely to see the outline of her face, so that I could cherish it in my memory, but to study that face and find in it the living evidence of the sympathetic tenderness and patience with which she accomplished the difficult task of my education. I should like to see in her eyes that strength of character which has enabled her to stand firm in the face of difficulties, and that compassion for all humanity which she has revealed to me so often.

I do not know what it is to see into the heart of a friend through that "Window of the soul", the eye. I can only "see" through my finger tips the outline of a face. I can detect laughter, sorrow, and many other obvious emotions. I know my friends from the feel of their faces. But I cannot really picture their personalities by touch. I know their personalities, of course, through other means, through the thoughts they express to me, through whatever of their actions are revealed to me. But I am denied that deeper understanding of them which I am sure would come through sight of them, through watching their reactions to various expressed thoughts and circumstances, through noting the immediate and fleeting reactions of their eyes and countenance.

Friends who are near to me I know well, because through the months and years they reveal themselves to me in all their phases; but of casual friends I have only an incomplete impression, an impression gained from a handclasp, from spoken words which I take from their lips with my finger tips, or which they tap into the palm of my hand.

How much easier, how much more satisfying it is for you who can see to grasp quickly the essential qualities of another person by watching the subtleties of expression, the quiver of a muscle, the flutter of a hand. But does it ever occur to you to use your sight to see into the inner nature of a friends or acquaintance? Do not most of you seeing people grasp casually the outward features of a face and let it go at that?

For instance can you describe accurately the faces of five good friends? some of you can, but many cannot. As an experiment, I have questioned husbands of long standing about the color of their wives' eyes, and often they express embarrassed confusion and admit that they do not know. And, incidentally, it is a chronic complaint of wives that their husbands do not notice new dresses, new hats, and changes in household arrangements.

The eyes of seeing persons soon become accustomed to the routine of their surroundings, and they actually see only the startling and spectacular. But even in viewing the most spectacular sights the eyes are lazy. Court records reveal every day how inaccurately "eyewitnesses" see. A given event will be "seen" in several different ways by as many witnesses. Some see more than others, but few see everything that is within the range of their vision.

Oh, the things that I should see if I had the power of sight for just three days!

The first day would be a busy one. I should call to me all my dear friends and look long into their faces, imprinting upon my mind the outward evidences of the beauty that is within them. I should let my eyes rest, too, on the face of a baby, so that I could catch a vision of the eager, innocent beauty which precedes the individual's consciousness of the conflicts which life develops.

And I should like to look into the loyal, trusting eyes of my dogs - the grave, canny little Scottie, Darkie, and the stalwart, understanding Great Dane, Helga, whose warm, tender, and playful friendships are so comforting to me.

On that busy first day I should also view the small simple things of my home. I want to see the warm colors in the rugs under my feet, the pictures on the walls, the intimate trifles that transform a house into home. My eyes would rest respectfully on the books in raised type which I have read, but they would be more eagerly interested in the printed books which seeing people can read, for during the long night of my life the books I have read and those which have been read to me have built themselves into a great shining lighthouse, revealing to me the deepest channels of human life and the human spirit.

In the afternoon of that first seeing day. I should take a long walk in the woods and intoxicate my eyes on the beauties of the world of Nature trying desperately to absorb in a few hours the vast splendor which is constantly unfolding itself to those who can see. On the way home from my woodland jaunt my path would lie near a farm so that I might see the patient horses ploughing in the field （perhaps I should see only a tractor!） and the serene content of men living close to the soil. And I should pray for the glory of a colorful sunset.

When dusk had fallen, I should experience the double delight of being able to see by artificial light which the genius of man has created to extend the power of his sight when Nature decrees darkness.

In the night of that first day of sight, I should not be able to sleep, so full would be my mind of the memories of the day.

第 一 天

第一天，我想看到这些人，他们的善良和友情使我的生活值得过下去。首先，我想长久地凝视我亲爱的老师安妮·莎莉文·梅西夫人的面容，当我还是一个孩子时，她就来到了我面前，为我打开了外面的世界。我不仅想看清她的脸部轮廓，这样我就能把它珍藏在我的记忆之中，我还要研究这张脸庞，从中找到富有同情心、温柔和耐心的生动证据，她就是以这种温柔和耐心完成了教育我的艰巨任务。我希望看到她眼睛里的坚强性格，它使得她在困难面前那么坚定。我要看她对所有人的同情心，她也经常如此对我显露出来。

我不知道通过"心灵之窗",即从眼睛来看透一个朋友的内心意味着什么。我只能通过我的指尖来"看"一张脸庞的轮廓。我能够察觉到欢笑、悲伤和其他许多明显的情感。我是从面部的感触来认识我的朋友的,但我不能正确地凭触摸来描绘他们的个性特征。当然,我还要通过其他方式来了解他们的品格,例如通过他们对我表达的思想,通过他们对我表现的任何行为。而我无法对他们有更深刻的了解。而要获得更深刻的了解,我相信通过看到他们,观察他们对别人表达出来的思想和情况的反应、通过注意他们眼睛和相貌的直接和迅即反应可以做到。

我对身边的朋友都很了解,因为通过长年累月的时间,他们在各方面对我展现了他们自己。而对于那些偶然接触的朋友,我只有一个不完整的印象,这个印象还是我从一次握手、从我的指尖感触他们的双唇所说的话,或者是他们在我的手掌上轻轻地拍抚而得到的。

但是对于你们能看见的人来说,要很快了解另一个人的本质是多么容易又多么令人满足的事情啊!你可以通过观察一些微妙的表情———一条肌肉的颤抖、一只手的摆动,很快抓住他的本质。但是,你曾经用你的双眼去看透一个朋友或熟人的内在吗?你们这些能看见的人,是不是偶然地抓住一张脸孔的外部特征就不再去想了呢?

例如,你们能精确地描述五个好朋友的面容吗?你们有些人能做到,但许多人不能。作为一个实验,我曾问过那些相处多年的丈夫们,他们太太的眼睛是什么颜色的。结果,他们常常显得非常窘迫,承认他们不清楚。而且,顺便说一句,妻子们还总是埋怨她们的丈夫不注意新衣服、新帽子和家中摆设的变化。

眼睛能看见的人,他们的眼睛很快就习惯了周围的环境。他们实际上只看到了那些惊人的和壮观的景象,然而,即使是那些最壮观的景象,他们的眼睛也是懒散的。法庭记录每天都表明"见证人"是看得多么不准确。例如,同一个事件要求"目击者"从尽可能多的方面去"看",有些人看得比另一些人要多,但很少有人看到了他们的视线范围内所有的事情。

啊,假如给我三天光明,我能看多少东西啊!

第一天将会是非常忙碌的一天,我要把我所有亲爱的朋友都叫来,长久地凝视他们的面容,把他们内在美的外部迹象深深地铭记在我的脑海中。我还要让我的目光停留在一个婴儿的脸上,以便我能捕获一种热切期望的纯美的视觉,这是个人在意识到生活带来的冲突之前天真无邪的美的视觉。

我还要看看我那忠诚的、令人信赖的狗的眼睛——沉着机警的小斯科蒂·达基和高大健壮、善解人意的大戴恩·赫尔加，它们的热情温柔和顽皮的友谊对我是如此巨大的安慰。

在这繁忙的第一天，我还要看看我家里那些简单的小东西。我要看我脚下地毯温暖的颜色、墙上挂的画，看看使这间屋子变成一个家的所有亲切而琐碎的东西。我的目光还要虔诚地注视那些我读过的凸字书，但我会更加热切地看那些视力正常的人看的出版物，因为在我生命的漫长黑夜里，我读过的书和别人为我读过的书已经筑成了一座伟大而明亮的灯塔，向我揭示了人类生活和人类精神的最深的航道。

在光明的第一天下午，我要在树林中远足，让我的眼睛陶醉在大自然的美景之中。在几个小时中，努力吸收那经常展现在视力正常的人面前的壮丽景观。在从森林回家的路上，我要走在农庄附近的小路上，这样，我就能看到在田间耕作的温驯的马儿（或许我只能看见一台拖拉机），看看紧贴着泥土生活的人们安详的满足。而且，我将要为辉煌的落日景观而祈祷。

当夜幕降临时，我应该感受到双倍的愉快，因为能看到人造的光明，这是人类的天才创造出来的，以便在大自然进入黑夜时扩大他的视力。

在能看见的第一个晚上，我将无法入睡，脑海中充满了白天的记忆。

The Second Day

The next day—the second day of sight—I should arise with the dawn and see the thrilling miracle by which night is transformed into day. I should behold with awe the magnificent panorama of light with which the sun awakens the sleeping earth.

This day I should devote to a hasty glimpse of the world, past and present. I should want to see the pageant of man's progress, the kaleidoscope of the ages. How can so much be compressed into one day? Through the museums, of course. Often I have visited the New York Museum of Natural History to touch with my hands many of the objects there exhibited, but I have longed to see with my eyes the condensed history of the earth and its inhabitants displayed there - animals and the races of men pictured in their native environment; gigantic carcasses of dinosaurs and mastodons which roamed the earth long before man appeared, with his tiny stature and powerful brain, to conquer the animal kingdom; realistic presentations of the processes of development in animals, in man, and in the implements which man has used to fashion for himself a secure home on this planet; and a thousand and one other aspects of natural history.

I wonder how many readers of this article have viewed this panorama of the face of living things as pictured in that inspiring museum. Many, of course, have not had the opportunity, but I am sure that many who have had the opportunity have not made use of it. there, indeed, is a place to use your eyes. You who see can spend many fruitful days there, but I with my imaginary three days of sight, could only take a hasty glimpse, and pass on.

My next stop would be the Metropolitan Museum of Art, for just as the Museum of Natural History reveals the material aspects of the world, so does the Metropolitan show the myriad facets of the human spirit. Throughout the history of humanity the urge to artistic expression has been almost as powerful as the urge for food, shelter, and procreation. And here , in the vast chambers of the Metropolitan Museum, is unfolded before me the spirit of Egypt, Greece, and Rome, as expressed in their art. I know well through my hands the sculptured gods and goddesses of the ancient Nile-land. I have felt copies of Parthenon friezes, and I have sensed the rhythmic beauty of charging Athenian warriors. Apollos and Venuses and the Winged Victory of Samothrace are friends of my finger tips. The gnarled, bearded features of Homer are dear to me, for he, too, knew blindness.

My hands have lingered upon the living marble of roman sculpture as well as that of later generations. I have passed my hands over a plaster cast of Michelangelo's inspiring and heroic Moses; I have sensed the power of Rodin; I have been awed by the devoted spirit of Gothic wood carving. These arts which can be touched have meaning for me, but even they were meant to be seen rather than felt, and I can only guess at the beauty which remains hidden from me. I can admire the simple lines of a Greek vase, but its figured decorations are lost to me.

So on this, my second day of sight, I should try to probe into the soul of man through this art. The things I knew through touch I should now see. More splendid still, the whole magnificent world of painting would be opened to me, from the Italian Primitives, with their serene religious devotion, to the Moderns, with their feverish visions. I should look deep into the canvases of Raphael, Leonardo da Vinci, Titian, Rembrandt. I should want to feast my eyes upon the warm colors of Veronese, study the mysteries of El Greco, catch a new vision of Nature from Corot. Oh, there is so much rich meaning and beauty in the art of the ages for you who have eyes to see!

Upon my short visit to this temple of art I should not be able to review a fraction of that great world of art which is open to you. I should be able to get only a superficial impression. Artists tell me that for deep and true appreciation of art one must educated the eye. One must learn through experience to weigh the merits of line, of composition, of form and color. If I had eyes, how happily would I embark upon so fascinating a study! Yet I am told that, to many of you who have eyes to see, the world of art is a dark night, unexplored and unilluminated.

It would be with extreme reluctance that I should leave the Metropolitan Museum, which contains the key to beauty- a beauty so neglected. Seeing persons, however, do not need a metropolitan to find this key to beauty. The same key lies waiting in smaller museums, and in books on the shelves of even small libraries. But naturally, in my limited time of imaginary sight, I should choose the place where the key unlocks the greatest treasures in the shortest time.

The evening of my second day of sight I should spend at a theatre or at the movies. Even now I often attend theatrical performances of all sorts, but the action of the play must be spelled into my hand by a companion. But how I should like to see with my own eyes the fascinating figure of Hamlet, or the gusty Falstaff amid colorful Elizabethan trappings! How I should like to follow each movement of the graceful Hamlet, each strut of the hearty Falstaff! And since I could see only one play, I should be confronted by a many-horned dilemma, for there are scores of plays I should want to see. You who have eyes can see any you like. How many of you, I wonder, when you gaze at a play, a movie, or any spectacle, realize and give thanks for the miracle of sight which enables you to enjoy its color , grace, and movement?

I cannot enjoy the beauty of rhythmic movement except in a sphere restricted to the touch of my hands. I can vision only dimly the grace of a Pavlowa, although I know something of the delight of rhythm, for often I can sense the beat of music as it vibrates through the floor. I can well imagine that cadenced motion must be one of the most pleasing sights in the world. I have been able to gather something of this by tracing with my fingers the lines in sculptured marble; if this static grace can be so lovely, how much more acute must be the thrill of seeing grace in motion.

One of my dearest memories is of the time when Joseph Jefferson allowed me to touch his face and hands as he went through some of the gestures and speeches of his beloved Rip Van Winkle. I was able to catch thus a meager glimpse of the world of drama, and I shall never forget the delight of that moment. But, oh, how much I must miss, and how much pleasure you seeing ones can derive from watching and hearing the interplay of speech and movement in the unfolding of a dramatic performance! If I could see only one play, I should know how to picture in my mind the action of a hundred plays which I have read or had transferred to me through the medium of the manual alphabet.

So, through the evening of my second imaginary day of sight, the great fingers of dramatic literature would crowd sleep from my eyes.

第 二 天

第二天——也就是光明的第二天——我会和黎明一道起床，目睹黑夜转成白昼的激动人心的奇迹。我要怀着敬畏的心情，仰望太阳唤醒沉睡的大地时壮丽的景观。

我要将这一天用来对整个世界的过去和现在作匆匆的扫视。我想看人类发展的进程，看时代变化的万花筒。这么多东西怎么能压缩在一天之内呢？当然是通过博物馆了。我已经参观过纽约自然历史博物馆许多次，用我的手触摸那里陈列的许多物品。但我渴望亲眼看到地球的简史，以及那里陈列的地球居民——在自然环境中展示出来的动物和人类，巨大的恐龙和剑齿虎化石。在人类出现之前，这些动物就在地球上漫游，后来，人类以小巧的身材和强有力的大脑征服了动物王国。还要观看动物和人类及人类工具的进化过程，人类曾用这些工具在这个星球上为他们建造舒适安全的住所，还有自然历史的其他许多方面。

我不知道这篇文章的读者中，有多少人看过这个生动的博物馆所展示的千姿百态的事物的壮观景象。当然，许多人没有这种机会，但我相信许多人的确有这种机会而没有利用。在那里，的确是使用你的眼睛的好去处，你们看得见的人将在那里度过许多颇有收获的日子。可是我呢，只能有想象中的三天光明的日子，只能匆匆忙忙地一瞥而过。

我的下一站将是大都会艺术博物馆。正像自然历史博物馆展示了世界的物质方面那样，大都会艺术博物馆将展示人类精神的诸多方面。贯穿人类历史全过程的那种对艺术表现形式的冲动，几乎就像人类对于食物、住所和生育的迫切需求同样强烈。在这里，在大都会博物馆宽敞的展示大厅里，展现在我们面前的是古埃及、古希腊和古罗马的精神世界，它们是以艺术形式表现出来的。我通过我的手，清楚地了解了雕刻而成的古代尼罗河土地上的诸神，抚摸了帕提农神庙中文物的复制品，我体会到了向前冲锋的雅典武士的韵律之美。阿波罗、维纳斯和长有翅膀的萨莱色雷斯的胜利女神令我爱不释手。对于我来说，荷马那长满了胡须、布满了节瘤的面部雕像无比亲切，因为他也知道什么是失明。

我的手曾停留在栩栩如生的罗马大理石雕像和后世的雕刻上。我曾抚摸过米开朗琪罗雕刻的鼓舞人心的英雄摩西石膏像；我感受到了法国雕塑家罗丹的力量，对哥特木刻的虔诚精神感到敬畏。这些能用手触摸到的艺术作品，对我来说具有真实的意义，但这些艺术品即使是既可观看又可抚摸，我也只能是猜测那躲避着我的美妙。我能欣赏一只古希腊花瓶简单的线条，但我对它带有装饰的图案一无所知。

所以，光明的第二天，我将努力通过人类的艺术来探究人类的灵魂。我将看到我通过触摸已经知道的东西。更加奇妙的是，所有的神奇世界将展现在我面前——从拥有平静宗教色彩的意大利文艺复兴前期作品到充满狂热梦幻的现代派作品。我将仔细欣赏拉斐尔、莱奥纳多·达·芬奇、提香和伦勃朗的油画。我要让我的眼睛饱享维勒内兹油画炽烈的色彩，研究艾尔·格列柯绘画的神秘，从柯罗的绘画中领略大自然的新视觉。啊！对你们能用眼睛去看的人来说，在那个时代的艺术中有多么丰富的意义和美丽啊！

在对这座艺术殿堂的短暂访问中，我没有资格评论那呈现在你眼前的伟大艺术世界的任何部分。我只能获得一个表面的印象。艺术家们告诉我，一个人要想真正而深刻地鉴赏艺术，就必须训练他的眼睛。他必须通过经验学会品评线条、构图、形态和色彩。如果能看见，我将会多么愉快地去做令人如此着迷的研究工作！但是，有人告诉我，对你们视力正常的许多人来说，艺术的世界是一个深沉的黑夜，未曾开发，也未曾照亮。

要离开大都会博物馆，我是多么不情愿啊！那里有美的钥匙，而这种美又被忽视了。看得见的人不必去大都会博物馆寻找这开启美的钥匙，这相同的钥匙正在较小的博物馆，甚至小图书馆的书架上的书中等着。但是，在我想象的有限光明中，我当然要选择在最短的时间内打开最伟大宝库的钥匙的地方。

在能看见的第二天晚上，我要在戏院或电影院中度过。即使现在我还经常去看各种戏剧表演，但需要由一个同伴将剧情写在我的手上。我是多么想亲眼看到莎士比亚戏剧中哈姆雷特的迷人形象，或者穿着伊丽莎白时代艳丽多彩服饰的生气勃勃的福斯塔夫！我多想模仿优雅的哈姆雷特的每个动作，模仿热忱的福斯塔夫的每个昂首阔步的举动！我只能看一场戏，这将使我面临进退两难的困境，因为我想看的戏剧有几十部。你们视力正常的人，可以看你们喜欢的任何一部戏剧。不过我怀疑，当你们全神贯注地观看一部戏剧、一场电影或任何奇观时，你们中间有多少人会意识到，并感激那使你们享受到色彩、优雅和动作的视力奇迹呢？

除了我的手能触摸到的东西，我不能享受富有节奏的动作蕴含的美感。尽管我懂得一些节奏的愉快，因为当音乐通过地板振动时我经常能感觉到它的节拍，但我也只能是隐隐约约地想象一下芭蕾舞演员巴甫洛娃的优美。我能想象到，富有节奏韵律的动作一定是世界上最令人愉快的景象。我已经通过手指摸索到的大理石雕刻的线条轮廓来获得这样的感受；如果这种静态的雅致都是如此可爱，那么，看见动态的美将会更加令人震惊！

我最珍贵的回忆之一，是约瑟夫·杰斐逊排练他心爱的角色瑞普·凡·温克尔时，在做动作和对白时让我摸他的脸和手。这样，对戏剧我只有这么一点点接触，我将永远忘不了那个时刻的愉快。但是，啊，我可能失去了许多，你们能看见的人从戏剧表演中看动作，倾听角色对白，将会得到多少快乐啊！假如能看到哪怕是一部戏剧，我就会知道如何在我的脑海中描绘我曾经读过或通过盲文书向我转述的上百部戏剧的动作。

这样，在我想象中能看见的第二天晚上，戏剧文学中的许多人物会因我用眼睛看了之后，又都在我的睡梦中涌现出来。

The Third Day

The following morning, I should again greet the dawn, anxious to discover new delights, for I am sure that, for those who have eyes which really see, the dawn of each day must be a perpetually new revelation of beauty.

This, according to the terms of my imagined miracle, is to be my third and last day of sight. I shall have no time to waste in regrets or longings; there is too much to see. The first day I devoted to my friends, animate and inanimate. The second revealed to me the history of man and Nature. Today I shall spend in the workaday world of the present, amid the haunts of men going about the business of life. And where can one find so many activities and conditions of men as in New York? So the city becomes my destination.

I start from my home in the quiet little suburb of Forest Hills, Long Island. Here, surrounded by green lawns, trees, and flowers, are neat little houses, happy with the voices and movements of wives and children, havens of peaceful rest for men who toil in the city. I drive across the lacy structure of steel which spans the East River, and I get a new and startling vision of the power and ingenuity of the mind of man. Busy boasts chug and scurry about the river-racy speed boat, stolid, snorting tugs. If I had long days of sight ahead, I should spend many of them watching the delightful activity upon the river.

I look ahead, and before me rise the fantastic towers of New York, a city that seems to have stepped from the pages of a fairy story. What an awe-inspiring sight, these glittering spires, these vast banks of stone and steel-structures such as the gods might build for themselves! This animated picture is a part of the lives of millions of people every day. How many, I wonder, give it so much as a seconds glance? Very few, I fear. Their eyes are blind to this magnificent sight because it is so familiar to them.

I hurry to the top of one of those gigantic structures, the Empire State Building, for there, a short time ago, I "saw" the city below through the eyes of my secretary. I am anxious to compare my fancy with reality. I am sure I should not be disappointed in the panorama spread out before me, for to me it would be a vision of another world.

Now I begin my rounds of the city. First, I stand at a busy corner, merely looking at people, trying by sight of them to understand something of their live. I see smiles, and I am happy. I see serious determination, and I am proud. I see suffering, and I am compassionate.

I stroll down Fifth Avenue. I throw my eyes out of focus, so that I see no particular object but only a seething kaleidoscope of colors. I am certain that the colors of women's dresses moving in a throng must be a gorgeous spectacle of which I should never tire. But perhaps if I had sight I should be like most other women-too interested in styles and the cut of individual dresses to give much attention to the splendor of color in the mass. And I am convinced, too, that I should become an inveterate window shopper, for it must be a delight to the eye to view the myriad articles of beauty on display.

From Fifth Avenue I make a tour of the city-to Park Avenue, to the slums, to factories, to parks where children play. I take a stay-at-home trip abroad by visiting the foreign quarters. Always my eyes are open wide to all the sights of both happiness and misery so that I may probe deep and add to my understanding of how people work and live. My heart is full of the images of people and things. My eye passes lightly over no single trifle; it strives to touch and hold closely each thing its gaze rests upon. Some sights are pleasant, filling the heart with happiness; but some are miserably pathetic. To these latter I do not shut my eyes, for they, too, are part of life. To close the eye on them is to close the heart and mind.

My third day of sight is drawing to an end. Perhaps there are many serious pursuits to which I should devote the few remaining hours, but I am afraid that on the evening of that last day I should again run away to the theater, to a hilariously funny play, so that I might appreciate the overtones of comedy in the human spirit.

At midnight my temporary respite from blindness would cease, and permanent night would close in on me again. Naturally in those three short days I should not have seen all I wanted to see. Only when darkness had again descended upon me should I realize how much I had left unseen. But my mind would be so crowded with glorious memories that I should have little time for regrets. Thereafter the touch of every object would bring a glowing memory of how that object looked.

Perhaps this short outline of how I should spend three days of sight does not agree with the program you would set for yourself if you knew that you were about to be stricken blind. I am, however, sure that if you actually faced that fate your eyes would open to things you had never seen before, storing up memories for the long night ahead. You would use your eyes as never before. Everything you saw would become dear to you. Your eyes would touch and embrace every object that came within your range of vision. Then, at last, you would really see, and a new world of beauty would open itself before you.

I who am blind can give one hint to those who see-one admonition to those who would make full use of the gift of sight: Use your eyes as if tomorrow you would be stricken blind. And the same method can be applied to the other senses. Hear the music of voices, the song of a bird, the mighty strains of an orchestra, as if you would be stricken deaf tomorrow. Touch each object you want to touch as if tomorrow your tactile sense would fail. Smell the perfume of flowers, taste with relish each morsel, as if tomorrow you could never smell and taste again. Make the most of every sense: glory in all the facets of pleasure and beauty which the world reveals to you through the several means of contact which Nature provides. But of all the senses, I am sure that sight must be the most delightful.

第 三 天

接下来的早上，我再次欢呼黎明，渴望发现新的惊喜，因为我确信，对那些眼睛真的能看见的人来说，每天的黎明一定是一个永远重复的新的美景。

根据我想象中的奇迹的时限，这将是我能看见的第三天，也是最后一天。我没有时间浪费在后悔或渴望之中，要看的东西太多了。第一天我献给了我的朋友们——有生命的和无生命的朋友。第二天向我展示了人类和自然的历史。今天，我将在当今的平凡世界度过，去那些为了生活工作而忙碌的人经常去的地方。在哪里能找到像纽约这样多的活动和条件呢？所以，纽约便成了我的目的地。

我从我在长岛森林山寂静的乡间小屋出发。这里，绿草、树木和鲜花环绕着整洁的小房，妇女和孩子们欢声笑语，实在是城里辛劳的男人们安宁的避风港。我驾车驶过那跨越东河的条带状钢铁桥梁，对人类智慧的创造力获得了一个新的令人震惊的视觉印象。繁忙的船只在河上往来航行——高速飞驰的快艇和笨重喘气的驳船。如果我能看见的日子再长一些，我要花更多的时间看看这河上生机勃勃的景象。

我向前眺望，纽约的高楼大厦在我前面升起，似乎是从童话故事中出现的一座城市。多么令人敬畏的景象啊！这些辉煌的尖塔，这些巨大的石头与钢铁的建筑群，就像诸神为他们自己修建的！这幅生动的图景是千百万人每天生活的一部分。我不知道到底有多少人会对它多看一眼？我以为恐怕会很少，他们的眼睛对这辉煌的景象只会熟视无睹，因为他们对此太熟悉了。

我匆匆爬上这些宏伟建筑之一——帝国大厦的顶端，因为在那里，不久以前，我曾通过秘书的眼睛"看"过下面的城市。我渴望把我的想象同现实作一番比较。我确信，我不会对展现在我面前的景色失望，因为对我来说它是另一个世界的景象。

现在，我开始周游这座城市。首先，我站在一个繁华的街角，仅仅是看着人们，希望通过审视他们来理解他们生活的某些东西。看到笑容，我就会高兴；看到严肃的决心，我就会骄傲；看到苦难，我就会同情。

我漫步在第五大道上，把目光从聚精会神的注视中解放出来，不去留意特别的目标，仅仅看那川流不息的彩色万花筒。我相信那成群的女人的服装色彩一定是一种百看不厌的灿烂奇观。或许，如果我能看见的话，我也会像其他大多数女人一样，也对式样和剪裁时髦的服装感兴趣，而忽视了集聚的色彩斑斓。我也相信，我会成为一个习惯浏览橱窗的顾客，因为看那陈列的无数美好的商品一定是一种享受。

从第五大道开始，我将环游这座城市——到派克大道去，到贫民窟去，到工厂去，到儿童游乐园去。我还将参观外国居民区，作一次不出门的国外旅行。我始终睁大眼睛，注视着所有幸福的和悲哀的景象，以便深入探究和进一步理解人们是如何工作和生活的。我心中充满了人和事物的形象，我的目光不会轻易放过任何一件细小的东西，力求触及并紧紧抓住看见的每件东西。有些景象是令人愉快的，它让你心里充满喜悦；有些则是悲惨的，对此，我并不闭上我的眼睛，因为这也是生活的一部分，闭起双眼不看它们，就是关闭心灵与大脑。

我拥有光明的第三天行将结束了。也许还有许多强烈的愿望，我应花最后的几个小时去实现它们。但是，我怕在这最后一天的晚上又会跑到戏院，去欣赏一部欢快有趣的戏剧。这样，我就可以欣赏到人类精神上的美妙韵律。

到了午夜，我摆脱失明的短暂时刻就要结束了，永恒的黑夜重又包围了我。当然，在这短短的三天时间里，我不能看到我想看的所有事情，只有在黑暗重又向我袭来时，我才意识到还留下多少东西没有看到。不过，我的脑海里充满了这么多美好的记忆，以致我没有什么时间来后悔的。此后，每摸到一件物品，都将带给我一个强烈的记忆，那东西看起来是怎样的。

也许，我这篇关于怎样度过这三天光明的简短概述和你们自己如有一天遭受失明之后所设想的不一致。然而，我确信，如果你真的面临那样的不幸，你的双眼一定会对过去从未看过的事情而睁大，为你今后的漫长黑夜储存记忆。你将会以过去从未有过的方式来利用你的眼睛。你所看到的每件事物对你都会变得珍贵起来，你的眼睛将会仔细端详每件进入你视线范围之内的事物。

然后，你将发现一个前所未有的美丽新世界在你面前展开。

我——一个盲人——可以给那些能看见的人一个提示——给那些想充分利用视觉天赋的人一个忠告：善用你的双眼，就像你明天就会失明一样。同样的方法也可以用于其他的感官：聆听悦耳的乐曲，鸟儿的歌唱，乐队强劲的旋律，就像你明天就要失聪一样；触摸你想摸的每个物体，就像你的触觉明天就要失灵一样；闻闻花朵的芳香，品尝一口美味佳肴，就像你明天再也不能闻到，再也不能尝到一样。

尽量利用你所有的感官吧！从各个方面尽情体会这个世界的快乐和美丽吧！这些感觉都是大自然恩赐给你的。但是，我相信，在所有的感官中，视觉一定是最令人欣喜的。

第九卷

克服忧虑的快乐生活

Six Major Troubles Hit Me All at Once

In the summer of 1943, it seemed to me that half the worries of the world had come to rest on my shoulders.

For more than forty years, I had lived a normal, carefree life with only the usual troubles which come to a husband, father, and business man. I could usually meet these troubles easily, but suddenly—wham!wham!!wham!!!wham!!!!WHAM!!!!!WHAM!!!!!!Six major troubles hit me all at once. I pitched and tossed and turned in bed all night long, half dreading to see the day come, because I faced these six major worries:

1. My business college was trembling on the verge of financial disaster because all the boys were going to war; and most of the girls were making more money working in war plants without training than my graduates could make in business offices with training.

2. My older son was in service, and I had the heart-numbing worry common to all parents whose sons were away at war.

3. Oklahoma City had already started proceedings to appropriate a large tract of land for an airport, and my home—formerly my father's home—was located in the centre of this tract. I knew that I would be paid only one tenth of its value, and, what was even worse, I would lose my home; and because of the housing shortage, I worried about whether I could possibly find another home to shelter my family of six. I feared we might have to live in a tent. I even worried about whether we would be able to buy a tent.

4. The water well on my property went dry because a drainage canal had been dug near my home. To dig a new well would be throwing five hundred dollars away because the land was probably being appropriated. I had to carry water to my livestock in buckets every morning for two months, and I feared I would have to continue it during the rest of the war.

5. I lived ten miles away from my business school and I had a class B petrol card: that meant I couldn't buy any new tyres, so I worried about how I could ever get to work when the superannuated tyres on my old Ford gave up the ghost.

6. My oldest daughter had graduated from high school a year ahead of schedule. She had her heart set on going to college, and I just didn't have the money to send her. I knew her heart would be broken.

One afternoon while sitting in my office, worrying about my worries, I decided to write them all down, for it seemed no one ever had more to worry about than I had. I didn't mind wrestling with worries that gave me a fighting chance to solve them, but these worries all seemed to be utterly beyond my control. I could do nothing to solve them. So I filed away this typewritten list of my troubles, and, as the months passed, I forgot that I had ever written it. Eighteen months later, while transferring my files, I happened to come across this list of my six major problems that had once threatened to wreck my health. I read them with a great deal of interest—and profit. I now saw that not one of them had come to pass. Here is what had happened to them:

1. I saw that all my worries about having to close my business college had been useless because the government had started paying business schools for training veterans and my school was soon filled to capacity.

2. I saw that all my worries about my son in service had been useless: he was coming through the war without a scratch.

3. I saw that all my worries about my land being appropriated for use as an airport had been useless because oil had been struck within a mile of my farm and the cost for procuring the land for an airport had become prohibitive.

4. I saw that all my worries about having no well to water my stock had been useless because, as soon as I knew my land would not be appropriated, I spent the money necessary to dig a new well to a deeper level and found an unfailing supply of water.

5. I saw that all my worries about my tyres giving out had been useless, because by recapping and careful driving, the tyres had managed somehow to survive.

6. I saw that all my worries about my daughter's education had been useless, because just sixty days before the opening of college, I was offered—almost like a miracle—an auditing job which I could do outside of school hours, and this job made it possible for me to send her to college on schedule.

I had often heard people say that ninety-nine per cent of the things we worry and stew and fret about never happen, but this old saying didn't mean much to me until I ran across that list of worries I had typed out that dreary afternoon eighteen months previously.

I am thankful now that I had to wrestle in vain with those six terrible worries. That experience has taught me a lesson I'll never forget. It has shown me the folly and tragedy of stewing about events that haven't happened—events that are beyond our control and may never happen.

Remember, today is the tomorrow you worried about yesterday. Ask yourself: How do I KNOW this thing I am worrying about will really come to pass?

困扰我的6大烦恼

1943年夏天，似乎这个世界的一半烦恼都降临到了我身上。

四十多年来，我一直过着正常而无忧无虑的生活，平时遇到的是作为一个丈夫、父亲、商人遇到的小问题。我通常都可以轻易处理好这些，但突然间，我的天啊！竟然有六项主要烦恼突然同时打击着我。我整夜在床上辗转反侧，害怕白天的到来。因为我面临的是下面六大忧虑：

第一，我的商学院濒临破产边缘，因为所有的男孩子都参军了，而大部分女孩子即使没有接受商业训练，她们在军火厂所赚的钱也比在我的商学院毕业后去公司赚的钱多。

第二，我的大儿子正在服役，跟所有父母一样，我十分担心。

第三，俄克拉何马市政府已开始计划征收一大片土地建造机场，我家的房子——以前是我父亲的房子——正好位于这片土地的中央。我知道我只能得到1/10的补偿；更糟糕的是，我将失去我的房子；加上当时房源缺乏，我担心能不能找到另一栋房子让一家六口度日。我担心我们也许必须住在帐篷里；我甚至担心我们是否有能力购置帐篷。

第四，由于我家附近刚刚挖了一条大排水沟，使得我土地上的水井干了。若是再挖一口新井，等于浪费500美元，因为这块土地也许会被征收。我已经接连两个月每天早上提水喂牲口，我担心战争结束前必须每天都这么做。

第五，我的住处离学校有10英里远，而我领的是"B级汽油卡"，这表明我不能购买任何新轮胎。因此，我担心一旦我那辆过时的福特车的轮胎爆了，我就无法上班了。

第六，我大女儿提前一年高中毕业，她想上大学，但我没钱供她上大学。我知道她一定很伤心。

一天下午，我正在办公室担心这些烦恼，于是将它们全部记下来，因为似乎没有人比我的烦恼更多了。只要有机会，我并不在乎花时间和精力去解决它们，但现在这一切困难似乎超出了我的能力。我根本无法解决。所以我就用打字机把这些困难全部写出来。几个月后，我忘了这件事。18个月后，我整理文件时，碰巧又看到了这张列有一度令我几乎崩溃的六大困难的单子。我极感兴趣地看了一遍，获益不少。现在，我发现所有的困难都不复存在了。这是它们后来的变化：

第一，我发现担心商学院会被迫关门是瞎操心。因为政府开始拨款补助商学院，代为培训退伍军人，我的学校很快又恢复了活力。

第二，我发现担心儿子也没有用。他安然无恙地接受了战争的洗礼。

第三，我发现担心土地被征收也是多余的，因为在我农场附近找到了石油，建造机场的计划停了下来。

第四，我发现担心没有水井打水喂牲口也是不必要的，因为当我得知土地不再被征收之后，就立刻花钱打了一口新井，水源不绝。

第五，我发现担心我的轮胎破裂也是不必要的，因为我将那个旧轮胎补了之后，只要小心驾驶，它绝对没问题。

第六，我发现担心我女儿上大学的事也是不必要的，因为在开学前六天，我获得了一个查账的工作机会——这简直是个奇迹——这使我能够即时送她上大学。

我常听人说，我们所担心的事99%都不会发生，但我对这种说法一直不以为然，直到看见18个月前那个可怕的下午打的那张单子之后，我才明白这一道理。

虽然我白白为这些烦恼而忧虑，但我现在十分感激。因为这段经历给了我永难磨灭的教训，它使我明白，成天担心永远不会发生的事情是多么悲哀啊！

记住，今天就是你昨天担心的明天。一定要问自己：我怎样才能"知道"我现在担心的事真的会发生呢？

I Can Turn Myself into a Shouting

Optimist within an HourWhen I find myself depressed over present conditions, I can, within one hour, banish worry and turn myself into a shouting optimist.

Here is how I do it. I enter my library, close my eyes, and walk to certain shelves containing only books on history. With my eyes still shut, I reach for a book, not knowing whether I am picking up Prescott's *Conquest of Mexico* or Suetonius' *Lives of the Twelve Caesars*. With my eyes still closed, I open the book at random. I then open my eyes and read for an hour; and the more I read, the more sharply I realize that the world has always been in the throes of agony, that civilisation has always been tottering on the brink. The pages of history fairly shriek with tragic tales of war, famine, poverty, pestilence, and man's inhumanity to man. After reading history for an hour, I realise that bad as conditions are now, they are infinitely better than they used to be. This enables me to see and face my present troubles in their proper perspective as well as to realize that the world as a whole is constantly growing better.

Here is a method that deserves a whole chapter. Read history! Try to get the viewpoint of ten thousand years—and see how trivial your troubles are, in terms of eternity.

做一个乐观的人

每当发现自己对眼前的景况感到沮丧时，我可以在一小时内抛弃所有的烦恼，使自己成为一个高高兴兴的乐观者。

下面就是我的办法：

我走进书房，闭上眼睛，走向专放历史书的书架前。我仍旧闭着眼睛，随手取出一本书——根本不知道是普里斯科特写的《墨西哥征服史》，还是史东尼所著的《凯撒传》。我仍然把眼睛闭上，随便翻到一页。然后，我睁开眼睛，读上一个小时。我越往下读，就越能体会到这个世界总是痛苦不断，人类文明总是濒临毁灭的边缘。历史上充满了悲剧故事：战争、饥荒、穷困、瘟疫、惨无人道。

读了一小时的历史之后，我就会明白，即使是目前处境恶劣，实际上也比以前好许多。这使我能够朝好的方面看我现在遇到的困难，明白这个世界正在不断朝着更好的方向发展。

上述方法值得用一整章来介绍。读读历史吧！试着将你的眼光扩展到1万年——从永恒的角度来看，"你的"烦恼真是微不足道。

How I Got Rid of an Inferiority Complex

When I was fifteen I was constantly tormented by worries and fears and self-consciousness. I was extremely tall for my age and as thin as a fence rail. I stood six feet two inches and weighed only 118 pounds. In spite of my height, I was weak and could never compete with the other boys in baseball or running games. They poked fun at me and called me"hatchet-face". I was so worried and self-conscious that I dreaded to meet anyone, and I seldom did, for our farmhouse was off the public road and surrounded by thick virgin timber that had never been cut since the beginning of time. We lived half a mile from the highway; and a week would often go by without my seeing anyone except my mother, father, and brothers and sisters.

I would have been a failure in life if I had let those worries and fears whip me. Every day and every hour of the day, I brooded over my tall, gaunt, weak body. I could hardly think of anything else. My embarrassment, my fear, was so intense that it is almost impossible to describe it. My mother knew how I felt. She had been a school-teacher, so she said to me: "Son, you ought to get an education, you ought to make your living with your mind because your body will always be a handicap."

Since my parents were unable to send me to college, I knew I would have to make my own way; so I hunted and trapped opossum, skunk, mink, and raccoon one winter; sold my hides for four dollars in the spring, and then bought two little pigs with my four dollars. I fed the pigs slop and later corn and sold them for forty dollars the next fall. With the proceeds from the sale of the two hogs I went away to the Central Normal College—located at Danville, Indiana. I paid a dollar and forty cents a week for my board and fifty cents a week for my room. I wore a brown shirt my mother had made me. (Obviously, she had used brown cloth because it wouldn't show the dirt.) I wore a suit of clothes that had once belonged to my father. Dad's clothes didn't fit me and neither did his old congress gaiter shoes that I wore—shoes that had elastic bands in the sides that stretched when you put them on. But the stretch had long since gone out of the bands, and the tops were so loose that the shoes almost dropped off my feet as I walked. I was so embarrassed to associate with the other students, so I sat in my room alone and studied. The deepest desire of my life was to be able to buy some store clothes that fit me, clothes that I was not ashamed of.

Shortly after that, four events happened that helped me to overcome my worries and my feeling of inferiority. One of these events gave me courage and hope and confidence and completely changed all the rest of my life. I'll describe these events briefly:

First: After attending this normal school for only eight weeks, I took an examination and was given a third-grade certificate to teach in the country public schools. To be sure, this certificate was good for only six months, but it was fleeting evidence that somebody had faith in me—the first evidence of faith that I ever had from anyone except my mother.

Second: A country school board at a place called Happy Hollow hired me to teach at a salary of two dollars per day, or forty dollars per month. Here was even more evidence of somebody's faith in me.

Third: As soon as I got my first cheque I bought some store clothes—clothes that I wasn't ashamed to wear. If someone gave me a million dollars now, it wouldn't thrill me half as much as that first suit of store clothes for which I paid only a few dollars.

Fourth: The real turning point in my life, the first great victory in my struggle against embarrassment and inferiority occurred at the Putnam County Fair held annually in Bain-bridge, Indiana. My mother had urged me to enter a public-speaking contest that was to be held at the fair. To me, the very idea seemed fantastic. I didn't have the courage to talk even to one person—let alone a crowd. But my mother's faith in me was almost pathetic. She dreamed great dreams for my future. She was living her own life over in her son. Her faith inspired me to enter the contest.

I chose for my subject about the last thing in the world that I was qualified to talk on: "The Fine and Liberal Arts of America". Frankly, when I began to prepare a speech I didn't know what the liberal arts were, but it didn't matter much because my audience didn't know, either. I memorised my flowery talk and rehearsed it to the trees and cows a hundred times. I was so eager to make a good showing for my mother's sake that I must have spoken with emotion. At any rate, I was awarded the first prize.

I was astounded at what happened. A cheer went up from the crowd. The very boys who had once ridiculed me and poked fun at me and called me hatchet-faced now slapped me on the back and said: "I knew you could do it, Elmer." My mother put her arms around me and sobbed.

As I look back in retrospect, I can see that winning that speaking contest was the turning point of my life. The local newspapers ran an article about me on the front page and prophesied great things for my future. Winning that contest put me on the map locally and gave me prestige, and, what is far more important, it multiplied my confidence a hundredfold. I now realize that if I had not won that contest, I probably would never have become a member of the Linked States Senate, for it lifted my sights, widened my horizons, and made me realize that I had latent abilities that I never dreamed I possessed. Most important, however, was the fact that the first prize in the oratorical contest was a year's scholarship in the Central Normal College.

I hungered now for more education. So, during the next few years—from 1896 to 1900—I divided my time between teaching and studying. In order to pay my expenses at De Pauw University, I waited on tables, looked after furnaces, mowed lawns, kept books, worked in the wheat and cornfields during the summer, and hauled gravel on a public road-construction job.

In 1896, when I was only nineteen, I made twenty-eight speeches, urging people to vote for William Jennings Bryan for President. The excitement of speaking for Bryan aroused a desire in me to enter politics myself. So when I entered De Pauw University, I studied law and public speaking. In 1899 I represented the university in a debate with Butler College, held in Indianapolis, on the subject "Resolved that United States Senators should be elected by popular vote." I won other speaking contests and became editor-in-chief of the class of 1900 College Annual, The Mirage, and the university paper, The Palladium.

After receiving my A. B. degree at De Pauw, I took Horace Greeley's advice— only I didn't go west, I went southwest. I went down to a new country: Oklahoma. When the Kiowa, Comanche, and Apache Indian reservation was opened, I home-steaded a claim and opened a law office in Lawton, Oklahoma. I served in the Oklahoma State Senate for thirteen years, in the lower House of Congress for four years, and at fifty years of age, I achieved my lifelong ambition: I was elected to the United States Senate from Oklahoma. I have served in that capacity since March 4, 1927. Since Oklahoma and Indian Territories became the state of Oklahoma on

November 16, 1907, I have been continuously honoured by the Democrats of my adopted state by nominations—first for State Senate, then for Congress, and later for the United States Senate.

I have told this story, not to brag about my own fleeting accomplishments, which can't possibly interest anyone else. I have told it wholly with the hope that it may give renewed courage and confidence to some poor boy who is now suffering from the worries and shyness and feeling of inferiority that devastated my life when I was wearing my father's cast-off clothes and gaiter shoes that almost dropped off my feet as I walked.

克服自卑心理

15岁时，我经常遭受烦恼、恐惧、自卑的折磨。当时我的身高相对我的年龄来说实在太高了，而且我瘦得像竹竿一样。我身高6.2英尺，而体重只有118磅。虽然我长得这么高，身体却很弱，一直都不能和其他男孩在棒球或田径比赛上竞争。他们嘲笑我，叫我"瘦脸"。我十分忧愁，非常自卑，几乎不敢见人。而我确实也很少与人见面，因为我们的农场离公路很远，四周全都是茂密的树林。我们的住处离公路有半英里远，所以我经常是一连七八天都看不到陌生人，只能看见我的父母和兄弟姐妹。

如果我被动地让这些烦恼和恐惧打击我，那我可能终生都是一个失败者。每一天的每一小时，我总是在担心自己那高瘦虚弱的身体。我无法想其他事情。我的自卑与恐惧如此严重，简直难以描述。我母亲知道了我的感觉。她当过学校老师。她对我说："孩子，你应该去读书。你应该靠你的大脑生活，因为你的身体不好。"

由于父母没有能力送我去读大学，因此我知道自己必须努力奋斗。有一年冬天，我去打猎：铺设陷阱捕捉负鼠、臭鼬、貂和浣熊。到了春天，我把这些兽皮卖了4美元，然后用那些钱买了两头小猪。我先用流质饲料喂养小猪，然后改用玉米。第二年秋天，两只猪卖了40美元。我带了这笔钱，到位于印第安纳州丹维尔市的中央师范学院。我每周的伙食费是1.4美元，房租每周是0.5美元，穿着母亲给我缝制的棕色衬衫（显然，她用棕色布是因为不容易脏）。我穿了一套以前父亲穿的西服——父亲的衣服，我穿着不合身。我脚上穿的那双鞋也是父亲的，同样不合适——那种鞋子两侧有松紧带，你一拉紧，它们就松开，但是父亲那双鞋的松紧带早就没了弹性，加上前端又很宽松，因此，我一走起路来鞋子就会从脚上掉下来。我觉得很难堪，不敢和其他学生往来，所以独自一人关在房间看书。当时，我最大的欲望就是有能力买一些衣服，既合我的身材，又不会让我感到羞耻。

没过多久，发生了几件事，使我克服了忧虑和自卑感。其中一件事不仅给了我勇气、希望和信心，还完全改变了我以后的生活。我简单描述一下这几件事。

第一件：在进入师范学院八周后，我参加了一项考试，获得一份"三等证书"，这样我就可以在乡村公立学校教书。说得更明确一点，这份证书的期限只有6个月，但它可以使别人对我有信心——这是除了母亲之外，第一次有人对我有信心。

第二件：一所位于"快乐谷"的乡村学校的董事会聘请了我，每天的薪水是2美元，或者月薪40美元。这更表明有人相信我。

第三件：领到第一份薪水之后，我从商店里买了衣服，穿上这衣服使我不再觉得羞耻。如果现在有人给我100万美元，我也不会像当初花几美元买那些衣服那么兴奋。

第四件：我生命中真正的转折点——我克服自卑和忧愁的第一次伟大胜利，发生在印第安纳州班桥镇每年举行一次的"普特南郡博览会"上。母亲鼓励我参加一项将在博览会上举行的演讲赛。对我来说，这可是个幻想。我甚至没有勇气当着一个人的面谈话——更不用说面对一群人了。但是，母亲对我的信心几乎令人心酸。她对我的前途期望很高，她是为她的儿子而活的。她的信任使我决定参加比赛。

我选择了我唯一有资格演讲的题目《美国的自由艺术》。老实说，我刚开始准备这次演讲时，并不知道什么是自由艺术。不过，因为我的听众也不懂，所以我将我那份辞藻华丽的演讲词全部背了下来，并对着树木和牛练习了不下一百遍。由于我想在母亲面前好好表现一下，因此我一定是带着深厚的感情作那次演讲的。总之，我得了第一名。

我不禁呆了！听众中间响起一片欢呼。那些曾讥笑我、称我为"瘦脸"的男孩子，现在却拍着我的背说："艾玛，我早知道你能行。"母亲抱着我哭了。

回顾过去，可以看出那次演讲比赛获胜是我人生的转折点。当地报纸在头版刊登了一篇报道，预言我前途无量。

在那次比赛中获胜，使我在当地声名鹊起。更重要的是，这极大地增加了我的信心。现在我很清楚，如果我不是在那次比赛中获胜，恐怕我一辈子也进不了美国参议院，因为它开启了我的视野，使我明白自己具有以前想都不敢想的潜力。不过，最重要的是，我在那场演讲比赛中得到的头等奖，是中央师范学院一年的奖学金。

那时，我渴望多学一点东西。因此，在以后的几年当中，我把时间分为教和学两部分。为了支付我在迪保大学的费用，我当过服务生，看过锅炉，剪过草，当过记账员，暑假还去麦田和玉米田工作，并在公路上挑石子修路。

1896年，我只有19岁，但我已作了28次演说，呼吁人们投票选威廉·詹宁斯·布莱恩当总统。为布莱恩竞选拉选票的经历，使我产生了从政的兴趣。因此，在我进入迪保大学之后，就选修法律和公开演说两门课程。1899年，我代表学校参加了和巴特勒学院的辩论赛。这次比赛在印第安纳波利斯举行，题目是《美国参议员是否应由大众选举》。我还赢得了其他演讲比赛，成为班刊和校刊的总编辑。

在迪保大学获得学士学位之后，我接受柯雷斯·格莱利的建议，去了西南方。我来到一个新地方俄克拉何马州。当基俄瓦、康曼奇、阿帕奇的印第安人保留区开放之后，我也申请到一块土地，并在俄克拉何马州罗顿市开了一家法律事务所。我在州参议院干了13年，在州众下议院干了4年。50岁那年，我终于实现了一生最大的愿望：从俄克拉何马州被选入美国参议院。从1927年3月4日起，我一直担任该职。自从俄克拉何马和印第安区于1907年11月16日合并成为俄克拉何马州之后，我一直获得了该州民主党的光荣提名——先是进入州参议院，然后进入州下议院，最后进入美国参议院。

我讲这些往事，并不是炫耀我小小的成就，因为人们不会感兴趣。我这样做只是希望给那些目前受烦恼和自卑感所苦的可怜小伙子们增添一些勇气和自信心。想当初，在我穿着父亲那身旧衣服和那双走路几乎要脱落的鞋子时，那种烦恼、羞怯及自卑几乎毁了我。

Five Methods I Use to Banish Worry

1. When I was twenty-four years old, my eyes suddenly gave out. After reading three or four minutes, my eyes felt as if they were full of needles; and even when I was not reading, they were so sensitive that I could not face a window. I consulted the best occultists in New Haven and New York. Nothing seemed to help me. After four o'clock in the afternoon, I simply sat in a chair in the darkest corner of the room, waiting for bedtime. I was terrified. I feared that I would have to give up my career as a teacher and go out West and get a job as a lumberjack. Then a strange

thing happened which shows the miraculous effects of the mind over physical ailments. When my eyes were at their worst that unhappy winter, I accepted an invitation to address a group of undergraduates. The hall was illuminated by huge rings of gas jets suspended from the ceiling. The lights pained my eyes so intensely that, while sitting on the platform, I was compelled to look at the floor. Yet during my thirty-minute speech, I felt absolutely no pain, and I could look directly at these lights without any blinking whatever. Then when the assembly was over, my eyes pained me again.

I thought then that if I could keep my mind strongly concentrated on something, not for thirty minutes, but for a week, I might be cured. For clearly it was a case of mental excitement triumphing over a bodily illness.

I had a similar experience later while crossing the ocean. I had an attack of lumbago so severe that I could not walk. I suffered extreme pain when I tried to stand up straight. While in that condition, I was invited to give a lecture on shipboard. As soon as I began to speak, every trace of pain and stiffness left my body; I stood up straight, moved about with perfect flexibility, and spoke for an hour. When the lecture was over, I walked away to my stateroom with ease. For a moment, I thought I was cured. But the cure was only temporary. The lumbago resumed its attack.

These experiences demonstrated to me the vital importance of one's mental attitude. They taught me the importance of enjoying life while you may. So I live every day now as if it were the first day I had ever seen and the last I were going to see. I am excited about the daily adventure of living, and nobody in a state of excitement will be unduly troubled with worries. I love my daily work as a teacher. I wrote a book entitled *The Excitement of Teaching*. Teaching has always been more than an art or an occupation to me. It is a passion. I love to teach as a painter loves to paint or a singer loves to sing. Before I get out of bed in the morning, I think with ardent delight of my first group of students. I have always felt that one of the chief reasons for success in life is enthusiasm.

2. I have found that I can crowd worry out of mind by reading an absorbing book. When I was fifty-nine, I had a prolonged nervous breakdown. During that period I began reading David Alec Wilson's monumental *Life of Carlyle*. It had a good deal to do with my convalescence because I became so absorbed in reading it that I forgot my despondency.

3. At another time when I was terribly depressed, I forced myself to become physically active almost every hour of the day. I played five or six sets of violent games of tennis every morning, then took a bath, had lunch, and played eighteen holes of golf every afternoon. On Friday night I danced until one o'clock in the morning. I am a great believer in working up a tremendous sweat. I found that depression and worry oozed out of my system with the sweat.

4. I learned long ago to avoid the folly of hurry, rush, and working under tension. I have always tried to apply the philosophy of Wilbur Cross. When he was Governor of Connecticut, he said to me: "Sometimes when I have too many things to do all at once, I sit down and relax and smoke my pipe for an hour and do nothing."

5. I have also learned that patience and time have a way of resolving our troubles. When I am worried about something, I try to see my troubles in their proper perspective. I say to myself: "Two months from now I shall not be worrying about this bad break, so why worry about it now? Why not assume now the same attitude that I will have two months from now?"

驱逐烦恼的5个方法

方法一：

我24岁时，视力突然变得很差。看书三四分钟，眼睛就觉得扎满了针一样；即使不看书，眼睛也十分敏感，甚至不敢面对窗口。我去向纽哈芬和纽约市最出色的眼科大夫求医，但收效甚微。

每天下午四点以后，我只能坐在房子里最暗角落的椅子上，等着上床睡觉。我真的吓坏了，害怕自己必须放弃教师职业，去西部当一名伐木工人。

接着，发生了一件怪事，显示了精神意志对肉体疾病的奇迹般的影响。

在那个悲惨的冬天，我的眼睛实在是差到了极点，我应邀为一群大学生作演讲。当时，演讲厅的天花板上悬挂了许多大灯，强烈的灯光刺得我的眼睛疼痛难忍。我坐在台上，等待被介绍上去演讲之前，只能被迫盯着地板。然而，在30分钟的演讲时间里，我完全忘了疼痛，同时可以直接看那儿盏灯却不眨眼。但演讲结束之后，我的眼睛又开始疼痛了。

当时我就想，如果我能专心致志地做某件事——不是短短的30分钟，而是一周的话，也许我就可以痊愈。很明显，心理上的兴奋战胜了肉体上的不适。

后来，我有一次乘船经过大西洋时，又有过一次类似的经历。那一次，我的腰突然痛得很厉害，走不了路。我站直身子，更是痛到了极点。正是在那种情况下，我应邀在甲板上作了一次演讲。当我开始演讲时，所有的疼痛都不见了。我站得笔直，完美地表达自己，讲了一个小时。演讲结束之后，我轻松地走回房间。这时，我以为自己已经痊愈了。但那只是暂时的，腰痛不久又来了。

这些经历使我深深领悟到，一个人的心理状态非常重要。它们教导我，要尽一切可能享受生活的美好。所以，我现在每天都在努力地生活，把每一天都当作我一生中的第一天，同时是最后一天。对于每天这种新奇而冒险的生活，我一直都很兴奋，而一个情绪兴奋的人是永远不会有烦恼的。我很喜欢每天的教学工作，我还写了一本书《教学的乐趣》。对我来说，教学不仅仅是一种艺术或职业，它更是一种爱好。我像画家喜爱绘画、像歌手喜爱唱歌一样喜爱着教学。我每天早上下床之前，只要想到我的学生，心里就充满了无限的喜悦。我一直以为人生成功的最大因素就是"热情"。

方法二：

我发现我可以通过读一本吸引人的书，将烦恼抛除。在我59岁那年，曾经历了相当长时间的精神崩溃。在那段日子里，我开始阅读戴维·威尔逊的伟大作品《卡莱尔传》。这对我的恢复很有用，因为我被深深吸引，忘记了精神上的消沉。

方法三：

还有一次，我十分沮丧，因此我强迫自己每天每小时做一次剧烈的运动。我每天早上都要打五六场激烈的网球，然后洗澡，吃中午饭，下午再打18洞的高尔夫球。星期五晚上，我会一直跳舞跳到凌晨一点。我强迫自己流了许多汗，发现沮丧和忧愁全都随汗水流走了。

方法四：

我很早以前就知道如何避免匆忙，如何避免在紧张的状态下工作。我一直想尝试应用韦伯·克洛斯的哲学。他担任康涅狄格州州长时曾对我说："我有时要同时处理很多工作，我会先坐下来放松，抽根烟，一小时内什么事也不干。"

方法五：

我也知道，耐心和时间能解除我们的烦恼。当我为某事而烦恼时，我就从积极的角度来看待它。我会告诉自己："两个月以后，我就不会再为这事烦恼了。所以，我现在又何必为它烦恼呢？为什么我现在不采取两个月以后我会采取的那种态度呢？"

I Stood Yesterday.I Can Stand Today

I have been through the depths of poverty and sickness. When people ask me what has kept me going through the troubles that come to all of us, I always reply: "I stood yesterday. I can stand today. And I will not permit myself to think about what might happen tomorrow."

I have known want and struggle and anxiety and despair. I have always had to work beyond the limit of my strength. As I look back upon my life, I see it as a battlefield strewn with the wrecks of dead dreams and broken hopes and shattered illusions—a battle in which I always fought with the odds tremendously against me, and which has left me scarred and bruised and maimed and old before my time.

Yet I have no pity for myself; no tears to shed over the past and gone sorrows; no envy for the women who have been spared all I have gone through. For I have lived. They only existed. I have drank the cup of life down to its very dregs. They have only sipped the bubbles on top of it. I know things they will never know. I see things to which they are blind. It is only the women whose eyes have been washed clear with tears who get the broad vision that makes them little sisters to all the world.

I have learned in the great University of Hard Knocks a philosophy that no woman who has had an easy life ever acquires. I have learned to live each day as it comes and not to borrow trouble by dreading the morrow. It is the dark menace of the future that makes cowards of us. I put that dread from me because experience has taught me that when the time comes that I so fear, the strength and wisdom to meet it will be given me. Little annoyances no longer have the power to affect me. After you have seen your whole edifice of happiness topple and crash in ruins about you, it never matters to you again that a servant forgets to put the doilies under the finger bowls, or the cook spills the soup.

I have learned not to expect too much of people, and so I can still get happiness out of the friend who isn't quite true to me or the acquaintance who gossips. Above all, I have acquired a sense of humor, because there were so many things over which I had either to cry or laugh. And when a woman can joke over her troubles instead of having hysterics, nothing can ever hurt her much again. I do not regret the hardships I have known, because through them I have touched life at every point I have lived. And it was worth the price I had to pay.

Dorothy Dix conquered worry by living in"day-tight" compartments.

既然昨天已经度过，今天也不会难熬

我经历过极其严峻的贫困和疾病。有人问我是如何渡过那些难关的，我总是回答说："我已经度过了昨天，今天也不会难熬。我不会让自己去猜想明天将发生什么。"

我深知什么是需要、奋斗、焦虑和失望。我经常会以超乎自己的能力拼命工作。我回顾自己的生活，觉得像是一个战场，它充满了破灭的梦想、残败的希望和残缺的幻想——在那场战斗中，我的获胜机会非常小，我在战斗中全身是伤，手脚残缺，显得苍老了许多。

　　然而，我没有为自己哀怜，也不为过去的烦恼而哭泣，也不嫉妒那些不曾遭遇我这些苦难的女性。因为我确实生活过了，她们只是一种简单的存在。我已饮尽了生活的苦酒，她们只是尝到上面的一层泡沫。我经历的事情，她们永远不会理解。我看到的东西，她们永远不会看到。只有泪水洗净了眼睛的妇人，视野才会开阔。

　　我从这种困苦的环境中学到了一种哲学，而这是那些生活在舒适环境中的女人所学不到的。我学会了珍惜每一天，不必因为担心明天的来到而自寻烦恼。恐惧只会令人懦弱。我将恐惧感从自己身上排除出去，因为经验告诉我，当我害怕的那一刻来临时，我自然而然地会产生勇气和智慧去应对它。那些小小的不快不再对我有任何影响。当你经历过这种极度的不幸之后，即使是仆人服侍不周，或者是厨师弄坏了一锅汤，你也不会再恼怒了。

　　我已经学会不要对人期望太高，因此当有朋友对我不忠，或是有人说我的坏话时，我也不会介意，仍然乐于和他们交往。除此以外，我还学会了幽默，因为让我哭笑不得的事情实在是太多了。而当一个女人遇到烦恼时，如果能不焦急，就能变不利为有利，没有东西可以伤害她了。

　　对于遭遇的困难，我并不遗憾，因为通过这些东西，我可以接触生活的每个层面。这已经值得我为之付出了。

　　多萝西·迪克斯通过生活在今天克服了忧虑。

I Did Not Expcct to Live to See the Dawn

[On April 14, 1902, a young man with five hundred dollars in cash and a million dollars in determination opened a drygoods store in Kemmerer, Wyoming—a little mining town of a thousand people, situated on the old covered-wagon trail laid out by the Lewis and Clark Expedition. That young man and his wife lived in a half-storey attic above the store, using a large empty drygoods box for a table and smaller boxes for chairs. The young wife wrapped her baby in a blanket and let it sleep under a counter while she stood beside it, helping her husband wait on customers. Today the largest chain of drygoods stores in the world bears that man's name: the J.C. Penney stores—over sixteen hundred of them covering every state in the Union. I recently had dinner with Mr. Penney, and he told me about the most dramatic moment of his life.]

Years ago, I passed through a most trying experience. I was worried and desperate. My worries were not connected in any way whatever with the J.C.

Penney Company. That business was solid and thriving; but I personally had made some unwise commitments prior to the crash of 1929. Like many other men, I was blamed for conditions for which I was in no way responsible. I was so harassed with worries that I couldn't sleep, and developed an extremely painful ailment known as shingles—a red rash and skin eruptions. I consulted a physician—a man with whom I had gone to high school as a boy in Hamilton, Missouri: Dr. Elmer Eggleston, a staff physician at the Kellogg Sanatorium in Battle Creek, Michigan. Dr. Eggleston put me to bed and warned me that I was a very ill man. A rigid treatment was prescribed. But nothing helped. I got weaker day by day. I was broken nervously and physically, filled with despair, unable to see even a ray of hope. I had nothing to live for. I felt I hadn't a friend left in the world, that even my family had turned against me. One night, Dr. Eggleston gave me a sedative, but the effect soon wore off and I awoke with an overwhelming conviction that this was my last night of life. Getting out of bed, I wrote farewell letters to my wife and to my son, saying that I did not expect to live to see the dawn.

When I awoke the next morning, I was surprised to find that I was still alive. I can't explain it. I can only call it a miracle. I felt as if I had been instantly lifted out of the darkness of a dungeon into warm, brilliant sunlight. I felt as if I had been transported from hell to paradise. I realized then that I alone was responsible for all my troubles. From that day to this, my life has been free from worry. I am seventy-one years old.

J.C. Penney learned to overcome worry almost instantaneously, because he discovered the one perfect Cure.

我以为活不到明天

（1902年4月14日，一个只有500美元现金的年轻人立志要赚100万美元，他在怀俄明州的克莫勒镇开了一家绸布店——克莫勒是一个只有1000人的矿业小镇，位于以前开发西部所必经的篷车道上。这个年轻人和他的妻子住在商店上面的小阁楼里，用一个装绸布的大木箱做桌子，再用小木箱做椅子。年轻的妻子用毯子裹住婴儿，将他放在柜台底下睡觉，而她站在柜台旁边，帮助丈夫招呼客人。今天，全世界最大的一家绸布连锁店就以这个人的姓名为名——J.C.潘尼百货店——它一共有1600家分店，遍布美国各州。最近，我和潘尼先生共进晚餐，他把他生活中最富戏剧性的经历告诉了我。）

几年前，我经历了一段最痛苦的时光。当时，我既忧虑又绝望——我的忧虑和公司的业务完全没有关系。当时，公司业务十分稳定，而且蒸蒸日上，但我个人做出了一些不明智的举措，导致我于1929年破产。和其他人一样，我遭到了别人的指责，忧虑得无法入睡，终于发展成一种疼痛难忍的疾病，即"带状疱疹"——这是一种突发性的红疹。我向密歇根州巴托卫生局的伊格斯顿大夫求治，他是和我从小一起长大的老朋友。伊格斯顿大夫让我躺在床上，并警告说，我病得十分严重。我接受了一次严格的治疗，但没有什么效果。我的身体越来越虚弱，精神和肉体都开始崩溃，我绝望至极，一丝希望也没有。我活得毫无寄托，认为自己在这世界上没有一个朋友，甚至连家里人也反对我。一天晚上，伊格斯顿大夫给我服了一剂镇静剂，但它的功效很快就消失了，我痛得醒了过来，心想这可能是我生命中最后一个晚上了。我爬起床，给夫人和儿子写了诀别书，说我活不到天亮了。

第二天早上醒来时，我惊异地发现自己仍然活着。我对此无法解释，只能说那是一个奇迹。我觉得自己似乎一下子被人从黑暗的地牢中接到了温暖、明亮的阳光之下，立即从地狱进入了天堂。我恍然大悟，原来所有的烦恼都是自找的。从那时到今天，我的生活中一直没有任何烦恼。现在，我已经71岁了。

J. C. 潘尼学会了几乎瞬间克服忧虑，因为他找到了一种极好的治疗方法。

I Go to the Gym to Punch the Bag or Take a Hike Outdoors

When I find myself worrying and mentally going round in endless circles like a camel turning a water wheel in Egypt, a good physical work-out helps me to chase those "blues" away. It may be running or a long hike in the country, or it may be a half-hour of bag punching or squash tennis at the gymnasium. Whichever it is, physical exercise clears my mental outlook.

On a weekend I do a lot of physical sport, such as a run around the golf course, a game of paddle tennis, or a ski weekend in the Adirondacks. By my becoming physically tired, my mind gets a rest from legal problems, so that when I return to them, my mind has a new zest and power.

Quite often in New York, where I work, there is a chance for me to spend an hour at the Yale Club gym. No man can worry while he is playing squash tennis or skiing. He is too busy to worry. The large mental mountains of trouble become minute molehills that new thoughts and acts quickly smooth down.

I find the best antidote for worry is exercise. Use your muscles more and your brain less when you are worried, and you will be surprised at the result. It works that way with me—worry goes when exercise begins.

锻炼可以消除忧虑

如果发现自己有了烦恼，或者在精神上像埃及骆驼寻找水源那样猛绕圈子转个不停，我就会利用激烈的体能训练来帮助自己驱除这些烦恼。这些活动可能是跑步，或是在乡村徒步远足，或是打半小时沙袋，或是去体育馆打网球。不管是什么体育活动，都会使我的精神为之振奋。

每到周末，我就去做多项运动，例如绕高尔夫球场跑一圈，打一场激烈的网球，或者去阿第伦达克山滑雪。当我的肉体疲倦时，我的精神也会随之得到休息。因此，等我再度回去工作时，我就会神清气爽，充满活力。

在纽约，我上班的地方经常有机会去耶鲁俱乐部健身房，待上一小时。没有任何人会在滑雪或激烈运动时还会烦恼。因为他忙得没时间去忧虑。这时，烦恼的大山很快就变成微不足道的小丘，一个新念头和新行动很容易就能将它"抚平"。

我发现，运动是烦恼的最佳"消毒剂"。烦恼时，多用肌肉，少用大脑，其结果将会令你惊讶。这种方法对我来说极其有效——开始运动时，烦恼就会消失。

I Was "the Worrying Wreck from Virginia Tech"

Seventeen years ago, when I was in military college at Blacksburg, Virginia, I was known as "the worrying wreck from Virginia Tech." I worried so violently that I often became ill. In fact, I was ill so often that I had a regular bed reserved for me at the college infirmary at all times. When the nurse saw me coming, she would run and give me a hypo. I worried about everything. Sometimes I even forgot what I was worrying about. I worried for fear I would be busted out of college because of my low grades. I had failed to pass my examinations in physics and other subjects, too. I knew I had to maintain an average grade of 75-84. I worried about my health, about my excruciating attacks of acute indigestion, about my insomnia. I worried about financial matters. I felt badly because I couldn't buy my girl candy or take her to dances as often as I wanted to. I worried for fear she would marry one of the other cadets. I was in a lather day and night over a dozen intangible problems.

In desperation, I poured out my troubles to Professor Duke Baird, professor of business administration at V. P. I.

The fifteen minutes that I spent with Professor Baird did more for my health and happiness than all the rest of the four years I spent in college. "Jim," he said, "you ought to sit down and face the facts. If you devoted half as much time and energy to solving your problems as you do to worrying about them, you wouldn't have any worries. Worrying is just a vicious habit you have learned."

He gave me three rules to break the worry habit:

Rule 1. Find out precisely what is the problem you are worrying about.

Rule 2. Find out the cause of the problem.

Rule 3. Do something constructive at once about solving the problem.

After that interview, I did a bit of constructive planning. Instead of worrying because I had failed to pass physics, I now asked myself why I had failed. I knew it wasn't because I was dumb, for I was editor-in-chief of The Virginia Tech Engineer.

I figured that I had failed physics because I had no interest in the subject. I had not applied myself because I couldn't see how it would help me in my work as an industrial engineer. But now I changed my attitude. I said to myself: "If the college authorities demand that I pass my physics examination before I obtain a degree, who am I to question their wisdom?"

So I enrolled for physics again. This time I passed because instead of wasting my time in resentment and worrying about how hard it was, I studied diligently.

I solved my financial worries by taking on some additional jobs, such as selling punch at the college dances, and by borrowing money from my father, which I paid back soon after graduation.

I solved my love worries by proposing to the girl that I feared might marry another cadet. She is now Mrs. Jim Birdsall.

As I look back at it now, I can see that my problem was one of confusion, a disinclination to find the causes of my worry and face them realistically.

Jim Birdsall learned to stop worrying because he ANALYZED his troubles. In fact, he used the very principles described in the chapter "How to Analyze and Solve Worry Problems."

我曾是"烦恼大王"

17年前，我在弗吉尼亚州布莱克斯堡军事学院上学时，是人人皆知的"弗吉尼亚烦恼大王"。我的烦恼如此严重，所以经常生病。事实上，由于我常常生病，因此学校的医院经常为我保留一张病床。每当护士看到我又上门时，就会跑上前来为我注射一针。我对任何事情都会忧虑。有时我甚至会忘了自己担心什么。我会担心因为成绩不好而被学校开除，我的物理学和其他科目考试不及格，我知道自己的平均分必须维持在75~84分之间。我还担心自己的健康：急性消化不良、失眠。我担心自己的收入状况。我还会因为不能经常买礼物送给女朋友，或是带她去跳舞而烦恼。我担心她会嫁给另一位军校学生。

我整天整夜地担心各种无形的问题。

绝望之下，我向杜克·巴德教授倾诉了我的烦恼。巴德教授是企业管理学教授。

见巴德教授的那15分钟，对我的健康和幸福的帮助远远超过我在大学四年所学的一切。"吉姆，"他说，"你应该坐下来，面对现实。如果你能把你用于烦恼的一半时间和精力去解决问题，那么你将不会再有烦恼。而你以前只学会烦恼这一项不良习惯。"

他为我订了三项消除烦恼的规则。

第一，准确查明忧虑的究竟是什么问题。

第二，找出问题的真正原因。

第三，立刻采取建设性的行动，以解决问题。

这次会谈之后，我拟定了一些积极的计划。我不再因为物理考试不及格而烦恼，而是反问自己为什么会不及格。我知道那并不是因为我天资愚笨，因为当时我已经当上了校刊的总编辑。

我发现，我之所以考试不及格，是因为我对这门功课没有什么兴趣。而我之所以对它不感兴趣，是因为我认为它对我将来从事工业工程师并没有多大帮助。但是，我现在改变了态度。我告诉自己："如果学院要求我们通过物理考试才能取得学位，我怎么能对他们的智慧产生怀疑呢？"

所以，我又埋头研究物理。这一次，我通过了考试，因为我不再花时间去想物理多么困难，而是专心致志地学习。

我还以打工的方式——例如在学院的舞会上推销果汁——解决了经济困难。我又向父亲贷款，毕业不久便还清了贷款。

我还解决了爱情难题：我向当初担心她会移情别嫁的女子求婚，现在她已经是吉姆·勃德索夫人了。

现在回想起来，我发现我当时的问题在于不愿去寻找烦恼的原因，并勇敢面对它们。

吉姆·勃德索因为分析了他的烦恼而学会了停止忧虑。事实上，他应用的正是"如何分析和解除烦恼"这一条规则。

I Hit Bottom and Survived

I used to be a terrible "worry wart". But no more. In the summer of 1942, I had an experience that banished worry from my life—for all time, I hope. That experience made every other trouble seem small by comparison.

For years I had wanted to spend a summer on a commercial fishing craft in Alaska, so in 1942 I signed on a thirty-two-foot salmon-seining vessel out of Kodiak, Alaska. On a craft of this size, there is a crew of only three: the skipper who does the supervising, a No. 2 man who assists the skipper, and a general work horse, who is usually a Scandinavian. I am a Scandinavian.

Since salmon seining has to be done with the tides, I often worked twenty hours out of twenty-four. I kept up that schedule for a week at a time. I did everything that nobody else wanted to do. I washed the craft. I put away the gear. I cooked on a little wood-burning stove in a small cabin where the heat and fumes of the motor almost made me ill. I washed the dishes. I repaired the boat. I pitched the salmon from our boat into a tender that took the fish to a cannery. My feet were always wet in rubber boots. My boots were often filled with water, but I had no time to empty them. But all that was play compared to my main job, which was pulling what is called the"cork line". That operation simply means placing your feet on the stem of the craft and pulling in the corks and the webbing of the net. At least, that is what you are supposed to do. But, in reality, the net was so heavy that when I tried to pull it in, it wouldn't budge. What really happened was that in trying to pull in the cork line, I actually pulled in the boat. I pulled it along on my own power, since the net stayed where it was. I did all this for weeks on end it was almost the end of me, too. I ached horribly. I ached all over. I ached for months.

When I finally did have a chance to rest, I slept on a damp lumpy mattress piled on top of the provisions locker. I would put one of the lumps in the mattress under the part of my back that hurt most—and sleep as if I had been drugged. I was drugged by complete exhaustion.

I am glad now that I had to endure all that aching and exhaustion because it has helped me stop worrying. Whenever I am confronted by a problem now—instead of worrying about it, I say to myself: "Ericksen, could this possibly be as bad as pulling the cork line?" And Ericksen invariably answers: "No, nothing could be that bad!" So I cheer up and tackle it with courage. I believe it is a good thing to have to endure an agonising experience occasionally. It is good to know that we have hit bottom and survived. That makes all our daily problems seem easy by comparison.

我做过最苦的工作

我以前是个糟透了的"烦恼大王"。不过,我现在不再是了。1942年夏天,我有过一次经历,它消除了我所有的忧虑烦恼——我希望今后也能永远如此。那次经历,使我所有的烦恼相比之下都显得微不足道。

多年以来,我一直希望能在阿拉斯加州的一艘渔船上工作了一个夏天。

因此，1942年夏天，我签约后，上了阿拉斯加州科地亚克的一艘32英尺长的鲑鱼拖网渔船工作。这艘船上只有3名船员：船长负责督导，另一个大副协助船长，剩下那个是日常打杂的水手，这通常由北欧人担任，而我正好是北欧人。由于用拖网捕捞鲑鱼必须配合潮汐进行，因此我经常要连续工作20小时。有一次，我这样工作了一周。我干的是其他人都不愿干的工作：洗甲板、保养机器、在小船舱里用一个烧木材的小炉子做饭。小船舱里马达的热气和恶臭令我作呕。我还要洗碗修船，把鲑鱼从我们的船抛到另一艘小船，将它们送去制成罐头。尽管我穿着长统胶鞋，但两脚总是湿漉漉的，胶鞋里面经常有水，我却没有时间倒水。而上述这些工作跟我的主要工作比起来只能算是游戏，我的主要工作就是所谓的"拉网"——这个工作看起来很简单：你只需要站在船尾，把渔网的浮标和边线拉上来即可。我的工作就是这些。但渔网太重，我想把它拉上来时，却怎么也拉不动。我本想把渔网拉上来，但实际上把船给拉了下去。由于渔网拉不动，我只好用尽全力，沿路拖住不放。我这样做了好几周，累得浑身酸痛，而且一连痛了好几个月。

最后，我好不容易有时间休息时，就在一个临时拼成的柜子上放好潮湿的被褥，倒头就睡。我浑身上下无处不疼，却睡得烂熟，像服了安眠药一样。其实，极度的劳累就是我的安眠药。

我很高兴当初能吃那些苦头，因为它们使我不再烦恼。现在，如果遭遇了困难，我不会再烦恼，会反问自己："埃瑞克森，还有什么比拖网更辛苦的吗？"我总是回答说："不，没有比它更辛苦的！"于是，我振作起来，勇敢接受这项挑战。我认为，偶尔体验一下痛苦是件好事。我很高兴自己能做世界上最辛苦的工作并挺了过来。它使得我日常生活中的所有问题相比之下都显得微不足道。

I Used to Be One of the World's Biggest Jackasses

I have died more times from more different diseases than any other man, living, dead, or half dead.

I was no ordinary hypochondriac. My father owned a drug-store, and I was practically brought up in it. I talked to doctors and nurses every day, so I knew the names and symptoms of more and worse diseases than the average layman. I was no ordinary hypo—I had symptoms! I could worry for an hour or two over a disease and then have practically all the symptoms of a man who was suffering from it. I recall once that, in Great Barrington, Massachusetts, the town in which I lived, we had a rather severe diphtheria epidemic. In my father's drug-store, I had been selling medicines day after day to people who came from infected homes. Then the evil that I feared came upon me: I had diphtheria myself. I was positive I had it. I went to bed and worried myself into the standard symptoms. I sent for a doctor. He looked me over and said: "Yes, Percy, you've got it." That relieved my mind. I was never afraid of any disease when I had it—so I turned over and went to sleep. The next morning I was in perfect health.

For years I distinguished myself and got a lot of attention and sympathy by specialising in unusual and fantastic disease—I died several times of both lockjaw and hydrophobia. Later on, I settled down to having the run-of-mill ailments—specialising on cancer and tuberculosis.

I can laugh about it now, but it was tragic then. I honestly and literally feared for years that I was walking on the edge of the grave. When it came time to buy a suit of clothes in the spring, I would ask myself: "Should I waste this money when I know I can't possibly live to wear this suit out?"

However, I am happy to report progress: in the past ten years, I haven't died even once.

How did I stop dying? By kidding myself out of my ridiculous imaginings. Every time I felt the dreadful symptoms coming on, I laughed at myself and said: "See here, Whiting, you have been dying from one fatal disease after another now for twenty years, yet you are in first-class health today. An insurance company recently accepted you for more insurance. Isn't it about time, Whiting, that you stood aside and had a good laugh at the worrying jackass you are?"

I soon found that I couldn't worry about myself and laugh at myself at one and the same time. So I've been laughing at myself ever since.

The point of this is: Don't take yourself too seriously. Try "just laughing" at some of your sillier worries, and see if you can't laugh them out of existence.

我曾是世界上最大的笨蛋

我比这个世界上任何一个人——包括活的、死的、奄奄一息的——都得过更多的疾病。

我并不是那种普通的抑郁症患者。我父亲开了一家药铺，我从小就在那种环境中长大。每天我都和大夫、护士聊天，所以我比普通人知道更多的疾病名称和病症。尽管我并不是抑郁症患者，但我有时确实有某些病症！我可能因为某种疾病而担心一两个小时，于是在不知不觉中就有了那种疾病的全部病症。有一次，在我居住的马萨诸塞州巴林顿镇，流行相当严重的白喉。我每天都在父亲的药铺里给受传染的病人卖药。接着，我害怕的事情降临到了我身上。我敢肯定我是感染上了。我躺到床上，忧虑万分，结果真的出现了一些标准症状。我请来医生。他给我检查了一遍，说："不错，波希，你已经感染上了。"这使我心情为之一松。得病后，我不再害怕任何疾病了。于是，我翻过身，呼声如雷地睡着了。第二天早上醒来时，我发现自己健康如初。

有好几年，我都成为人们注意和同情的重点，因为我得了一些不寻常的怪病——我曾多次"死"于狂犬病和牙关紧闭症。后来，我又发展到一些更加恐怖的疾病，特别是癌症和肺结核。

现在我可以笑对这一切，但我当时的情景却十分悲惨。我多年来一直心存恐惧，总害怕自己走在坟墓边缘上。例如，到了春天我该给自己买衣服时，我总是问自己："我既然已经知道自己不能再活着穿这些衣服了，为什么还要浪费钱呢？"

不过，我很高兴地告诉你，我已经大有进步：在过去10年中，我甚至连一次都没有"死"过。

我是如何取得进步的呢？那就是对自己这些荒唐的想象大加嘲笑。每当我觉得那些恐怖的病症又降临到我身上时，我就会笑着对自己说："嘿！惠廷，过去20年来，你一次又一次地'死'于一些致命的疾病，但你目前身体健康。一家保险公司最近甚至还同意你为自己买更多的人寿保险。惠廷，难道你不认为，现在正是你嘲笑自己是个大笨蛋的时候吗？"

很快，我就发现如果我能嘲笑自己，就不会有时间去烦恼了。于是，从那以后，我就一直嘲笑自己。

这篇故事的意义是：不要太过严肃地对待自己。对自己一些愚蠢的忧虑，不妨"开怀一笑"，然后看看是否可以将它们笑得不见踪影。

I Have Always Tried to Keep My Line of Supplies Open

I figure that most worries are about family troubles and money. I was fortunate in marrying a small-town Oklahoma girl who had the same background I had and enjoyed the same things. We both try to follow the golden rule, so we have kept our family troubles to a minimum.

I have kept my financial worries to a minimum also by doing two things. First, I have always followed a rule of absolute one hundred per cent integrity in everything. When I borrowed money, I paid back every penny. Few things cause more worry than dishonesty.

Second, when I started a new venture, I always kept on ace in the hole. Military experts say that the first principle of fighting a battle is to keep your line of supplies open. I figure that that principle applies to personal battles almost as much as to military battles. For example, as a lad down in Texas and Oklahoma, I saw some real poverty when the country was devastated by droughts. We had mighty hard scratching at times to make a living. We were so poor that my father used to drive across the country in a covered wagon with a string of horses and swap horses to make a living. I wanted something more reliable than that. So I got a job working for a railway-station agent and learned telegraphy in my spare time. Later, I got a job working as relief operator for the Frisco Railway. I was sent here, there, and yonder to relieve other station agents who were ill or on vacation or had more work than they could do. That job paid $150 per month. Later, when I started out to better myself, I always figured that that railroad job meant economic safety. So I always kept the road open back to that job. It was my line of supplies, and I never cut myself off from it until I was firmly established in a new and better position.

For example, back in 1928, when I was working as a relief operator for the Frisco Railway in Chelsea Oklahoma, a stranger drifted in one evening to send a telegram. He heard me playing the guitar and singing cowboy songs and told me I was good—told me that I ought to go to New York and get a job on the stage or radio. Naturally, I was flattered; and when I saw the name he signed to his telegram, I was almost breathless: Will Rogers.

Instead of rushing off to New York at once, I thought the matter over carefully for nine months. I finally came to the conclusion that I had nothing to lose and everything to gain by going to New York and giving the old town a whirl. I had a railroad pass: I could travel free. I could sleep sitting up in my seat, and I could carry some sandwiches and fruit for my meals.

So I went. When I reached New York, I slept in a furnished room for five dollars a week, ate at the Automat, and tramped the streets for ten weeks—and got nowhere. I would have been worried sick if I hadn't had a job to go back to. I had already worked for the railway five years. That meant I had seniority rights; but in order to protect those rights, I couldn't lay off longer than ninety days. By this time, I had already been in New York seventy days, so I rushed back to Oklahoma on my pass and began working again to protect my line of supply. I worked for a few months, saved money, and returned to New York for another try. This time I got a break. One day, while waiting for an interview in a recording-studio office, I played my guitar and sang a song to the girl receptionist: "Jeannine, I Dream of Lilac Time". While I was singing that song, the man who wrote it—Nat Schildkraut—drifted into the office. Naturally, he was pleased to hear anyone singing his song. So he gave me a note of introduction and sent me down to the Victor Recording Company. I made a record. I was no good—too stiff and self-conscious. So I took the advice of the Victor

Recording man: I went back to Tulsa, worked for the railway by day, and at night I sang cowboy songs on a sustaining radio programme. I liked that arrangement. It meant that I was keeping my line of supplies open—so I had no worries.

I sang for nine months on radio station KVOO in Tulsa. During that time, Jimmy Long and I wrote a song entitled "That Silver-Haired Daddy of Mine". It caught on. Arthur Sattherly, head of the American Recording Company, asked me to make a recording. It clicked. I made a number of other recordings for fifty dollars each, and finally got a job singing cowboy songs over radio station WLS in Chicago. Salary: forty dollars a week. After singing there four years, my salary was raised to ninety dollars a week, and I picked up another three hundred dollars doing personal appearances every night in theatres.

Then in 1934, I got a break that opened up enormous posstibilities. So Hollywood producers decided to put on cowboy pictures; but they wanted a new kind of cowboy—one who could sing. The man who owned the American Recording Company was also part owner of Republic Pictures. "If you want a singing cowboy," he said to his associates, "I have got one making records for us." That is how I broke into the movies. I started making singing- cowboy pictures for one hundred dollars a week. I had serious doubts about whether I would succeed in pictures, but I didn't worry. I knew I could always go back to my old job.

My success in pictures exceeded my wildest expectations. I now get a salary of one hundred thousand a year plus one half of all the profits on my pictures. However, I realize that this arrangement won't go on forever. But I am not worried. I know that no matter what happens—even if I lose every dollar I have—I can always go back to Oklahoma and get a job working for the Frisco Railway. I have protected my line of supplies.

我的补给线永远畅通

　　我认为大部分忧虑都和家庭事务与金钱有关。我幸运地娶了俄克拉何马州一个小镇的女子为妻，她的家庭背景和我的相同，我们的兴趣爱好也大致相同。我们两人都尽量遵守这些"金律"，所以我们的家庭烦恼也降到了最低限度。

　　我通过两种方法使自己的金钱烦恼减到了最低限度：第一，我总是坚持一条原则，对任何事情都要百分之百诚实。如果我向别人借了钱，就必须全部偿还。诚实可以使人免去许多烦恼。

　　第二，每当我开拓一项新事业时，我总会给自己预留后路。军事专家曾指出，作战的第一原则，就是保持补给线的畅通。我认为这项原则同样可以用于个人的"战斗"。例如，我从小生活在得克萨斯州和俄克拉何马州，在那里遭受干旱侵袭时，我才真正领略到了贫穷。我们辛勤劳作。我们太穷了，父亲必须驾着敞篷车，带着交换得来的马匹，到处不停地奔波谋生。我希望找一份比较稳定的工作，所以在一家火车站找了一份差事，在闲暇时学习发电报。后来，我找到另一项工作，在佛里斯科铁路公司当一名轮班员。我经常被派往各处，接替其他生病或休假的火车站站员，或在他们忙不过来时提供支援。这份工作的月薪是150美元。后来，准备开创更美好的前途时，我总觉得在铁路公司工作有经济保障，所以我总是保留了回到那项工作的退路，这就是我的补给线，我从来不会关闭那条路，除非我已建立了更稳定、更可靠的位置。

例如，1928年，当时我就职于佛里斯科铁路公司，被派往俄克拉何马州切尔西市工作。一天晚上，一个陌生人走进火车站办公室发一封电报。他听到我正在弹吉他，唱着牛仔歌曲，就对我说我弹得不错，歌也唱得不错——还告诉我，说我应该去纽约，去电台或戏院工作。我当然觉得他是在奉承我。但当我看到他在电报上的签名时，我几乎惊待了——威尔·罗吉斯。

我并没有立刻去纽约。我把这件事前后仔细考虑了九个月。最后，我得出结论：去纽约，我绝无损失，而且一定会有收获。我有铁路通行证，可以免费乘车。我还可以坐在火车上睡觉，而且可以带一些三明治和水果当一日三餐。

于是，我去了纽约。到达纽约后，我找到一间每周房租5美元并带有家具的房间住了下来，在快餐厅吃饭，在街上流浪了10周，可是一无所获。如果我回去没有工作可干的话，那我一定会急出病来的。我已在铁路公司工作了5年，这意味着我有优先权；但要想保留这项优先权，我不能离职超过90天。而我那时已在纽约待了70天，于是我充分利用我的铁路通行证，立即赶回俄克拉何马州，又回去开始工作，以保证我的补给线不至于中断。我工作了几个月，存了一点钱，又到纽约去碰运气。这一次，我有了新的进展。一天，我在一家录音房等待面试时，弹吉他为那些女接待员唱了一首歌《珍妮，我梦到了紫丁香》。当我正在唱那首歌时，恰巧歌曲的作者纳特·史切克劳特走进办公室。他当然很高兴听到别人唱他的歌曲。于是，他写了一张条子，要我去维克多唱片公司试试。我录了一首歌，但成绩不很理想——说是太生硬了，显得不自然。于是，我接受了唱片公司录音师的劝告，回到图尔萨，白天在铁路公司上班，晚上去当地电台唱牛仔歌曲。我喜欢这种安排，这使我的补给线始终敞开着，因此我没有了烦恼。

我在图尔萨KVOO电台演唱了9个月。在那段时间内，吉米·朗和我合写了一首歌《我的白发父亲》，结果颇受好评。美洲唱片公司老板亚瑟·萨德利甚至要求我灌一张唱片，也获得了成功。我另外灌制了许多唱片，每张50美元，最后终于在芝加哥WLS电台找到了一份演唱牛仔歌曲的工作，薪水为每周40美元。我在那家电台唱了4年，薪水提高到了每周90美元；同时，我每天晚上又在戏院登台表演，另有300美元收入。

1934年，我的机会来了。当时好莱坞的制片商决定拍摄牛仔影片，但他们需要的是一种会唱歌的新型牛仔。美洲唱片公司的老板——同时也是"共和电影公司"的老板之一说："如果你们想找一个会唱歌的牛仔，我的唱片公司里正好有这么一个人。"我就是这样闯进电影圈的。我开始拍牛仔歌曲电影时，每周薪水为100美元。我对拍电影是否能够成功十分怀疑，但我并不担心。因为我知道，我随时可以回到干原来的工作。

我在电影上的成就远远超出了我的期望。我现在的年薪为10万美元，另外加上我所有影片的一半红利。不过，我知道这种情况并不能永远保持下去，但我并不忧虑。我知道，无论发生什么——即使我失去了所有的金钱——我也可以随时回到俄克拉何马，在佛里斯科铁路公司里找到一份工作——我的补给线永远畅通。

When the Sheriff Came in My Front Door

The bitterest moment of my life occurred one day in 1933 when the sheriff came in the front door and I went out the back. I had lost my home at Forest Hills, Long Island, where my children were born and where I and my family had lived for eighteen years. I had never dreamed that this could happen to me. Twelve years before, I thought I was sitting on top of the world. I had sold the motion-picture rights to my novel *West of the Water Tower* for a top Hollywood price. I lived abroad with my family for two years. We summered in Switzerland and wintered on the French Riviera—just like the idle rich.

I spent six months in Paris and wrote a novel entitled *They Had to See Paris*. Will Rogers appeared in the screen version. It was his first talking picture. I had tempting offers to remain in Hollywood and write several of Will Rogers' pictures. But I didn't. I returned to New York. And my troubles began!

It slowly dawned on me that I had great dormant abilities that I had never developed, I began to fancy myself a shrewd businessman. Somebody told me that John Jacob Astor had made millions investing in vacant land in New York. Who was Astor? Just an immigrant peddler with an accent. If he could do it, why couldn't I?… I was going to be rich! I began to read the yachting magazines.

I had the courage of ignorance. I didn't know any more about buying and selling real estate than an Eskimo knows about oil furnaces. How was I to get the money to launch myself on my spectacular financial career? That was simple. I mortgaged my home, and bought some of the finest building lots in Forest Hills. I was going to hold this land until it reached a fabulous price, then sell it and live in luxury—I who had never sold a piece of real estate as big as a doll's handkerchief. I pitied the plodders who slaved in offices for a mere salary. I told myself that God had not seen fit to touch every man with the divine fire of financial genius.

Suddenly, the great depression swept down upon me like a Kansas cyclone and shook me as a tornado would shake a hen coop.

I had to pour $220 a month into that monster-mouthed piece of Good Earth. Oh, how fast those months came! In addition, I had to keep up the payments on our now-mortgaged house and find enough food.

I was worried. I tried to write humor for the magazines. My attempts at humour sounded like the lamentations of Jeremiah! I was unable to sell anything. The novel I wrote failed. I ran out of money. I had nothing on which I could borrow money except my typewriter and the gold fillings in my teeth. The milk company stopped delivering milk. The gas company turned off the gas. We had to buy one of those little outdoor camp stoves you see advertised; it had a cylinder of gasoline; you pump it up by hand and it shoots out a flame with a hissing like an angry goose.

We ran out of coal; the company sued us. Our only heat was the fireplace. I would go out at night and pick up boards and leftovers from the new homes that the rich people were building…I who had started out to be one of these rich people.

I was so worried I couldn't sleep. I often got up in the middle of the night and walked for hours to exhaust myself so I could fall asleep.

I lost not only the vacant land I had bought, but all my heart's blood that I had poured into it.

The bank closed the mortgage on my home and put me and my family out on the street.

In some way, we managed to get hold of a few dollars and rent a small apartment. We moved in the last day of 1933. I sat down on a packing case and looked around. An old saying of my mother's came back: "Don't cry over spilt milk."

But this wasn't milk. This was my heart's blood!

After I had sat there a while I said to myself: "Well, I've hit bottom and I've stood it. There's no place to go now but up."

I began to think of the fine things that the mortgage had not taken from me. I still had my health and my friends. I would start again. I would not grieve about the past. I would repeat to myself every day the words I had often heard my mother say about spilt milk.

I put into my work the energy that I had been putting into worrying. Little by little, my situation began to improve. I am almost thankful now that I had to go through all that misery; it gave me strength, fortitude, and confidence. I know now what it means to hit bottom. I know it doesn't kill you. I know we can stand more than we think we can. When little worries and anxieties and uncertainties try to disturb me now, I banish them by reminding myself of the time I sat on the packing case and said: "I've hit bottom and I've stood it. There is no place to go now but up."

What's the principle here? Don't try to saw sawdust! Accept the inevitable! If you can't go lower, yon can try going up.

当我突然一无所有时

我一生中最悲惨的时刻是在1933年的一天。这天，警长来到我家的前门口，我则从后门溜了出去。我失去了在长岛林山市的家，我的孩子都出生在那里，我和家人在那里住了18年。我从未想到这种事情竟然会降临到我头上。12年前，我认为我处于世界顶端。我的小说《水塔之西》的电影版权以最高价格卖给了好莱坞。我和家人在国外待了两年，去瑞士避暑，在法国南部过冬——过着标准的富翁生活。

我在巴黎住了6个月，写了一本小说《他们必须来巴黎观光》。它后来被改编成电影，由威尔·罗吉斯主演，这也是他的第一部有声电影。他们要求我留在好莱坞为罗吉斯写几部电影剧本，但我还是回到了纽约。我的麻烦从此开始了！

我渐渐认为自己拥有一些尚未开发的潜能，开始幻想自己是一个精明的商人。有一个人告诉我，约翰·嘉科布·亚斯特在纽约投资购买空地而成为百万富翁。亚斯特是什么人呢？他只不过是一个带着口音的移民商贩。如果他能成功，为什么我就不能？我马上就要发大财了！我开始读游艇杂志。

我空有无知的勇气，对房地产却一无所知。我应该如何开始这方面的事业呢？很简单。我抵押了我的房子，然后买下林山一些位置最好的建筑用地。我想保留这块地，直到地价涨到最高时再将它卖掉，去过奢华的生活——我这个人从未卖过巴掌大的一块地。我同情那些在办公室为一点点薪水而忙碌的职员。我告诉自己，上帝并未赋予每个人特殊的创富才能。

经济危机突然像堪萨斯的旋风摇荡鸡笼一样袭击了我。

我每个月必须为那块地支付220美元。唉，那几个月过得真快啊！除外，我还必须为那座被抵押的房子还款，养活一家人。

我十分烦恼，想为杂志社写一些幽默小说。但是，我的幽默小品颇似《旧约》中的哀歌。我没有卖出任何稿子。我写的小说也没人要。我的钱全用光了，除了打字机和我口中的金牙，我没有任何东西可抵押借款。牛奶公司停止为我送奶，燃气公司也关掉了燃气，我只好买了一个广告宣传的露营用的小火炉。它有一个汽油缸，要用手举着，喷出嘶嘶响的火焰，就像发怒的鹅在叫唤。

我们没有煤了，煤炭公司起诉了我们。唯一取暖的东西是那个壁炉。我会在晚上出去，到那些有钱人正在建造的房子附近捡一些废木头……而我本来是想跻身这些有钱人的行列。

我忧虑得难以入睡，经常半夜起床，走上几个小时，直到疲倦入睡。

我不仅失去了我买的那块空地，连我花在上面的全部心血也都付诸东流。银行中止了我的抵押，把我和家人全赶到了大街上。

我们好不容易找到几美元，租了一小间公寓，在1933年的最后一天搬过去。我坐在行李箱上，抬头四处张望。这时，母亲的一句老话涌入我的脑海："不要为打翻的牛奶哭泣！"

但这并不是牛奶，而是我的心血！

我在那里坐了一会儿，然后对自己说："好吧！我已经历过最悲惨的遭遇，而且熬了过去。现在，情况只会好转，而不会变坏。"

我开始想到好的方面，被抵押的房子还在，我的身体依旧健康，还有朋友。一切都可以重新再来。我不再为过去而哀伤，每天重复我过去常听到的母亲说的那句话。

我把精力用在工作上，不再自寻烦恼。渐渐地，我的情况开始改善。对我以前的那段悲惨遭遇，我现在充满了感激：它给了我力量、坚忍和信心。现在我知道什么是最困苦的生活，我还知道天无绝人之路，更知道我们能忍受更多的苦难。现在，遇到小烦恼、焦虑和障碍时，我就会提醒自己当年坐在行李箱上对自己说的话："我已经历过最悲惨的遭遇，而且熬过去了。现在，情况只会好转，而不会变坏。"

这篇故事的规则是什么？不要锯木屑！接受不可避免的事实！如果你的境况已经糟至极点，那就试着往上爬吧！

The Toughest Opponent I Ever Fought Was Worry

During my career in the ring, I found that Old Man Worry was an almost tougher opponent than the heavyweight boxers I fought. I realized that I had to learn to stop worrying, or worry would sap my vitality and undermine my success. So, little by little, I worked out a system for myself. Here are some of the things I did:

1. To keep up my courage in the ring, I would give myself a pep talk during the fight. For example, while I was fighting Firpo, I kept saying over and over: "Nothing is going to stop me. He is not going to hurt me. I won't feel his blows. I can't get hurt. I am going to keep going, no matter what happens." Making positive statements like that to myself, and thinking positive thoughts, helped me a lot. It even kept my mind so occupied that I didn't feel the blows. During my career, I have had my lips smashed, my eyes cut, my ribs cracked—and Firpo knocked me clear through the ropes, and I landed on a reporter's typewriter and wrecked it. But I never felt even one of Firpo's blows. There was only one blow that I ever really felt. That was the night Lester Johnson broke three of my ribs. The punch never hurt me, but it affected my breathing. I can honestly say I never felt any other blow I ever got in the ring.

2. Another thing I did was to keep reminding myself of the futility of worry. Most of my worrying was done before the big bouts, while I was going through training. I would often lie awake at nights for hours, tossing and worrying, unable to sleep. I would worry for fear I might break my hand or sprain my ankle or get my eye cut badly in the first round so I couldn't coordinate my punches. When I got myself into this state of nerves, I used to get out of bed, look into the mirror, and give myself a good talking to. I would say: "What a fool you are to be worrying about something that hasn't happened and may never happen. Life is short. I have only a few years to live, so I must enjoy life." I kept saying to myself: "Nothing is important but my health. Nothing is important but my health." I kept reminding myself that losing sleep and worrying would destroy my health. I found that by saying these things to myself over and over, night after night, year after year, they finally got under my skin, and I could brush off my worries like so much water.

我最大的对手是忧虑

在我的拳击生涯中，我发现"忧虑"比我遇到的任何重量级拳手都更难对付。我知道我必须学会停止忧虑，否则忧虑会削弱我的活力，毁坏我的成就。于是，我给自己草拟了一项制度，以下就是其中的几部分：

第一，为了保持在比赛中的勇气，我总是在比赛时自我打气。例如，当我和佛波比赛时，我不断地告诉自己："没有人打得过我！他伤不了我！他的拳头伤不了我！我不会受伤！不论发生什么事，我一定要勇往直前！"这样不断为自己鼓气，使内心的想法变得主动积极，对我帮助很大，甚至使我不觉得对方的拳头打到了我。在我的拳击生涯中，我的嘴唇曾被击裂，眼睛被打伤，肋骨被打断，佛波有一次还将我打出场外，摔倒在一位记者的打字机上，压坏了打字机。但是，我对佛波的拳头甚至没有任何感觉。只有一次，我真的感觉到了拳击。那天晚上，李斯特·约翰逊一拳打断了我三根肋骨。虽然那一拳伤不了我，但影响到了我的呼吸。我可以坦白地说，除此以外，我从未在比赛中对任何拳击有过感觉。

第二，另一个方法就是不断提醒自己，烦恼毫无益处。我的大部分烦恼都出现在大型比赛之前，也就是我接受训练期间。我经常会在半夜醒来，一连好几个小时辗转反侧，无法入睡。我担心自己会在第一回合被对方打断手，或扭伤脚，或眼睛被严重击伤，这样我就不能尽情发挥攻势了。当我有了这种烦恼时，我总是爬下床，对着镜子，好好训斥自己一顿。我会说："你真是个大笨蛋，竟然会为一些尚未发生而且可能永远都不会发生的事情担心！人生苦短，你的时间只有几年，所以你必须尽情享受。"我又对自己说："你的健康是最重要的。除了你的健康，没有任何东西比它更重要。"我不断提醒自己，失眠和忧虑会损害我的健康。我发现，当我不停地提醒自己这些事时，它们最后终于渗透到我的内心当中了，因此我可以轻易消除所有的烦恼。

I Prayed to God to Keep Me out of an Orphan's Home

As a little child, my life was filled with horror. My mother had heart trouble. Day after day, I saw her faint and fall to the floor. We all feared she was going to die, and I believed that all little girls whose mothers died were sent to the Central Wesleyan Orphans' Home, located in the little town of Warrenton, Missouri, where we lived. I dreaded the thought of going there, and when I was six years old I prayed constantly: "Dear God, please let my mummy live until I am old enough not to go to the orphans' home."

Twenty years later, my brother, Meiner, had a terrible injury and suffered intense pain until he died two years later. He couldn't feed himself or turn over in bed. To deaden his pain, I had to give him morphine hypodermics every three hours, day and night. I did this for two years. I was teaching music at the time at the Central Wesleyan College in Warrenton, Missouri. When the neighbors heard my brother screaming with pain, they would telephone me at college and I would leave my music class and rush home to give my brother another injection of morphine. Every night when I went to bed, I would set the alarm clock to go off three hours later so I would be sure to get up to attend to my brother. I remember that on winter nights I would keep a bottle of milk outside the window, where it would freeze and turn into a kind of ice-cream that I loved to eat. When the alarm went off, this ice cream outside the window gave me an additional incentive to get up.

In the midst of all these troubles, I did two things that kept me from indulging in self-pity and worrying and embittering my life with resentment. First, I kept myself busy teaching music from twelve to fourteen hours a day, so I had little time to think of my troubles; and when I was tempted to feel sorry for myself, I kept saying to myself over and over: "Now listen, as long as you can walk and feed yourself and are free from intense pain, you ought to be the happiest person in the world. No matter what happens, never forget that as long as you live! Never! Never!"

Second, I was determined to do everything in my power to cultivate an unconscious and continuous attitude of gratefulness for my many blessings. Every morning when I awoke, I would thank God that conditions were no worse than they were; and I resolved that in spite of my troubles I would be the happiest person in Warrenton, Missouri. Maybe I didn't succeed in achieving that goal, but I did succeed in making myself the most grateful young woman in my hometown—and probably few of my associates worried less than I did.

This Missouri music teacher applied two principles descried in this book: she kept too busy to worry, and she counted her blessings. The same technique may be helpful to you.

摆脱烦恼的秘诀

我小时候，生活充满了恐惧。母亲患有心脏病，我经常看见她晕倒在地板上。我们都害怕她会死，而且我认为那些失去母亲的小女孩都会被送到位于我们住的密苏里州华林顿镇的卫斯理中心孤儿院。只要一想到被送到那里，我就非常害怕。我还只有6岁时，就经常祈祷："亲爱的上帝，请让我母亲继续活下去，直到我长大了，可以不用去孤儿院。"

20年后，哥哥梅勒受了重伤，遭受极大的痛苦，直到20年后才去世。他不能吃东西，也不能在床上翻身。为了减轻他的痛苦，无论白天或晚上，我每隔3小时必须为他注射一针吗啡。我这样做了两年。那时，我在镇上的卫斯理中心学院教音乐。当邻居们听到我哥哥痛苦得大声呼叫时，就打电话到学院找我，我会立即放下手中的工作，跑回家再为我哥哥注射一针吗啡。每天晚上上床时，我会把闹钟拨到3小时后，以便起床照料哥哥。我记得，一个冬天的晚上，我总是把一瓶牛奶放在窗外，好让它结成冰，变成我最喜欢吃的冰激凌。当闹钟响时，窗外的冰激凌也就成了我起床的另一种动力了。

在这么艰苦的情况下，我采取了两项措施，使自己避免陷入自怜自艾，也免受烦恼和悔恨之苦。第一，我让自己每天忙着教12～14小时的音乐课，因此没有时间去想我的忧虑。而我为自己感到难过时，会一再对自己说："听着，只要你还能走路，还能自己吃饭，身上又没有大病大痛，那你就是这个世界上最快乐的人。千万不要忘记，不管遇到什么困难，只要你还活着，那你就是最幸运的人！不要忘记！"

第二，我决定为我获得的这些幸福培养一种永远感激的态度。我每天早晨醒来时，就会感谢上帝：情况没比以前更糟。我深深感到，尽管我遇到了许多困难，但我仍是密苏里州华林顿最快乐的人。也许我并未成功实现这一目标，但我的确成功地使自己成为这个镇上最知道感恩的年轻女子——而我的同事中可能没有几人会像我这样没有忧虑。

这位密苏里州的音乐教师应用了本书介绍的两条原则：使自己保持忙碌而没有时间去忧虑；对自己的幸福心存感激。这两条原则对你也许同样有用。

I Was Acting like a Hysterical Woman

I had been working very happily in the publicity department of the Warner Brothers studio in California for several years. I was a unit man and feature writer. I wrote stories for newspapers and magazines about Warner Brothers stars.

Suddenly, I was promoted. I was made the assistant publicity director. As a matter of fact, there was a change of administrative policy, and I was given an impressive title: Administrative Assistant.

This gave me an enormous office with a private refrigerator, two secretaries, and complete charge of a staff of seventy-five writers, exploiters, and radio men. I was enormously impressed. I went straight out and bought a new suit. I tried to speak with dignity. I set up filing systems, made decisions with authority, and ate quick lunches.

I was convinced that the whole public relations policy of Warner Brothers had descended upon my shoulders. I perceived that the lives, both private and public, of such renowned persons as Bette Davis, Olivia De Havilland, James Cagney, Edward G. Robinson, Errol Flynn, Humphrey Bogart, Ann Sheridan, Alexis Smith, and Alan Hale were entirely in my hands.

In less than a month I became aware that I had stomach ulcers. Probably cancer.

My chief war activity at that time was chairman of the War Activities Committee of the Screen Publicists Guild. I liked to do this work, liked to meet my friends at guild meetings. But these gatherings became matters of dread. After every meeting, I was violently ill. Often I had to stop my car on the way home, pulling myself together before I could drive on. There seemed to be so much to do, so little time in which to do it. It was all vital. And I was woefully inadequate.

I am being perfectly truthful—this was the most painful illness of my entire life. There was always a tight fist in my vitals. I lost weight. I could not sleep. The pain was constant.

So I went to see a renowned expert in internal medicine. An advertising man recommended him. He said this physician had many clients who were advertising men.

This physician spoke only briefly, just enough for me to tell him where I hurt and what I did for a living. He seemed more interested in my job than in my ailments, but I was soon reassured: for two weeks, daily, he gave me every known test. I was probed, explored, X-rayed, and fluoroscoped. Finally, I was instructed to call on him and hear the verdict.

"Mr. Shipp," he said, leaning back and offering me a cigarette, "we have been through these exhaustive tests. They were absolutely necessary, although I knew of course after my first quick examination that you did not have stomach ulcers.

"But I knew, because you are the kind of man you are and because you do the kind of work you do, that you would not believe me unless I showed you. Let me show you."

So he showed me the charts and the X-rays and explained them. He showed me I had no ulcers.

"Now," said the doctor, "this costs you a good deal of money, but it is worth it to you. Here is the prescription: don't worry.

"Now" —he stopped me as I started to expostulate—" now, I realise that you can't follow the prescription immediately, so I'll give you a crutch. Here are some pills. They contain belladonna. Take as many as you like. When you use these up, come back and I'll give you more. They won't hurt you. But they will always relax you.

"But remember: you don't need them. All you have to do is quit worrying.

"If you do start worrying again, you'll have to come back here and I'll charge you a heavy fee again. How about it?"

I wish I could report that the lesson took effect that day and that I quit worrying immediately. I didn't. I took the pills for several weeks, whenever I felt a worry coming on. They worked. I felt better at once.

But I felt silly taking these pills. I am a big man physically. I am almost as tall as Abe Lincoln was—and I weigh almost two hundred pounds. Yet here I was taking little white pills to relax myself. I was acting like an hysterical woman. When my friends asked me why I was taking pills, I was ashamed to tell the truth. Gradually I began to laugh at myself. I said: "See here, Cameron Shipp, you are acting like a fool. You are taking yourself and your little activities much, much too seriously. Bette Davis and James Cagney and Edward G. Robinson were world-famous before you started to handle their publicity; and if you dropped dead tonight, Warner Brothers and their stars would manage to get along without you. Look at Eisenhower, General Marshall, Macarthur, Jimmy Doolittle and Admiral King—they are running the war without taking pills. And yet you can't serve as chairman of the War Activities Committee of the Screen Publicists Guild without taking little white pills to keep your stomach from twisting and turning like a Kansas whirlwind."

I began to take pride in getting along without the pills. A little while later, I threw the pills down the drain and got home each night in time to take a little nap before dinner and gradually began to lead a normal life. I have never been back to see that physician.

But I owe him much, much more than what seemed like a stiff fee at the time. He taught me to laugh at myself. But I think the really skilful thing he did was to refrain from laughing at me, and to refrain from telling me I had nothing to worry about. He took me seriously. He saved my face. He gave me an out in a small box. But he knew then, as well as I know now, that the cure wasn't in those silly little pills—the cure was in a change in my mental attitude.

The moral of this story is that many a man who is now taking pills would do better to read Chapter 7, and relax.

我曾像个疯女人

我曾在加利福尼亚州的华纳兄弟影片公司宣传部愉快地工作了几年。我是个专栏作家，一个人单独写作，为几家报纸和杂志撰写文章，报道华纳公司的明星动态。

我曾在突然之间获得升迁，被提拔为宣传部副主任。事实上，公司的行政策略有所改变，我被授予了一项重要头衔——行政助理。

这个新头衔使我拥有了一间大办公室、一台私人冰箱和两位秘书，并负责指挥75名撰稿人员、开发人员及无线电人员。我自以为一路顺风，马上买了一套新衣服。我以威严的口气说话，建立起档案制度，作出权威的决定，吃饭也匆匆忙忙。

我觉得华纳公司的整个公共关系政策全部托付在我身上，甚至以为公司的一些大明星，如贝蒂·戴维斯、奥利维尔·哈维兰德、詹姆斯·卡格尼、爱德华·鲁滨孙……全都在我掌握之中。

可是，不到一个月，我就觉得自己得了胃溃疡，甚至是癌症。

我当时的另一项主要工作，是任银幕宣传指导委员会的策划小组组长。我喜欢这个工作，很高兴能在各种会议中和老朋友见面。但这些聚会后来让我害怕，因为每次开完会后，我总是不舒服。我必须经常在回家的半路上将汽车停在路边，好使自己轻松一下，再继续开车。我似乎有许多工作要做，但时间不够。这些工作都很重要，我却难以胜任。

我生来为人诚实——我认为这是我一生中最大的痛苦。我总觉得精神压抑，体重减轻，开始失眠，而且经常觉得疼痛。

于是，我去看了一位著名的内科大夫。一位广告商向我推荐了他，他说这名大夫有许多患者都是广告商。

这位大夫说话简短，只让我告诉他哪里不舒服，以及从事什么工作。他对我的工作似乎比对我的病情更感兴趣，不过我后来发现并不是这样的。接连两周，他给我作了各种检查。最后，他通知我去见他，告诉我检查的结果。

"希普先生，"他说，同时向椅背上一靠，并递给我一支烟，"我们已经作了各种检查。这些检查对你来说是绝对必要的，虽然我第一天为你作了大致的检查之后，就知道你并没有患胃溃疡。

"不过我知道，就你的个性和你目前所从事的工作而言，你是不会轻易相信我的，除非我能向你证明。让我来告诉你。"

于是，他拿来各项检查表及X射线片为我解释，说我并未患胃溃疡。

"听着，"大夫说，"虽然这些会花你不少钱，但是很值。给你的药方是：不要烦恼。"

我正想对他发火，但他制止了我，继续说道："注意听我说：我知道你无法立刻遵照这个药方去做，所以我给你开了一些药。这些药你想服用多少，就放心服用多少。用完了，你再到我这儿来，我会再给你开一些。它们不会对你有害，但能使你经常保持轻松愉快。

"但要记住：你不是非服用不可。你要做的就是抛除烦恼。

"如果你又有了烦恼，那你必须回我这儿来。那时，我可又要向你要一大笔治疗费了。你可愿意？"

我希望能告诉各位，这位医生的话在我身上生效了，我立刻停止了烦恼。然而，这一切并没有发生。我连续服用了好几周的药。而它们确实有效，我立刻觉得好多了。

但是，我觉得服用这些药实在可笑。我已经是一个成年人，几乎和林肯总统一样高，体重也将近200磅，而我还在服用这种白色小药片使自己放松。我觉得自己像个歇斯底里的妇人。当朋友们问我为何服药时，我都不好意思说出真相。慢慢地，我开始嘲笑自己。我说："喂，卡梅龙·希普，你的举止像个大傻瓜。你把自己和你那不起眼的工作看得太重要了。贝蒂·戴维斯、詹姆斯·卡格尼、爱德华·鲁滨孙早在你开始作他们的宣传之前，就已经闻名世界了。假如你今晚突然暴亡，华纳公司和它所有的明星没有你也照样能过下去。艾森豪威尔、马歇尔、麦克阿瑟、吉米·杜立特，虽然他们主持全球的战争，却不必服药。你却必须吞下那些小白药丸，才能使你保持平静，才能干好你的工作。"

我开始不服药，并以此为荣。没过多久，我就把那些药扔进马桶，晚上准时回家，先小睡一会儿，然后吃晚饭。我渐渐开始恢复了正常生活，再也没有去看过那位大夫。

但我欠他的太多了，这远非我那次付的高昂诊费所能比。他教会了我如何放松。但我认为，他真正高明之处在于避免嘲笑我，也没有直接告诉我实际上没有什么好担心的——相反，他郑重地接纳了我，给我留了面子。他只给我一小盒药丸，但他早已知道——而我现在也知道——并不是那些令人发笑的小药丸治好了我，而是我改变了自己的心态。

I Learned to Stop Worrying by Watching My Wife Wash Dishes

A few years ago, I was suffering intensely from pains in my stomach. I would awaken two or three times each night, unable to sleep because of these terrific pains. I had watched my father die from cancer of the stomach, and I feared that I too had a stomach cancer—or, at least, stomach ulcers. So I went to Byrne's Clinic at Petosky, Michigan, for an examination. Dr. Lilga, a stomach specialist, examined me with a fluoroscope and took an X-ray of my stomach. He gave me medicine to make me sleep and assured me that I had no stomach ulcers or cancer. My stomach pains, he said, were caused by emotional strains. Since I am a minister, one of his first questions was: "Do you have an old crank on your church board?"

He told me what I already knew; I was trying to do too much. In addition to my preaching every Sunday and carrying the burdens of the various activities of the church, I was also chairman of the Red Cross, president of the Kiwanis. I also conducted two or three funerals each week and a number of other activities.

I was working under constant pressure. I could never relax. I was always tense, hurried, and high-strung. I got to the point where I worried about everything. I was living in a constant dither. I was in such pain that I gladly acted on Dr. Lilga's advice. I took Monday off each week, and began eliminating various responsibilities and activities.

One day while cleaning out my desk, I got an idea that proved to be immensely helpful. I was looking over an accumulation of old notes on sermons and other memos on matters that were now past and gone. I crumpled them up one by one and tossed them into the wastebasket. Suddenly I stopped and said to myself: "Bill, why don't you do the same thing with your worries that you are doing with these notes? Why don't you crumple up your worries about yesterday's problems and toss them into the wastebasket?" That one idea gave me immediate inspiration—gave me the feeling of a weight being lifted from my shoulders. From that day to this, I have made it a rule to throw into the wastebasket all the problems that I can no longer do anything about.

Then, one day while wiping the dishes as my wife washed them, I got another idea. My wife was singing as she washed the dishes, and I said to myself: "Look, Bill, how happy your wife is. We have been married eighteen years, and she has been washing dishes all that time. Suppose when we got married she had looked ahead and seen all the dishes she would have to wash during those eighteen years that stretched ahead. That pile of dirty dishes would be bigger than a barn. The very thought of it would have appalled any woman."

Then I said to myself: "The reason my wife doesn't mind washing the dishes is because she washes only one day's dishes at a time." I saw what my trouble was. I was trying to wash today's dishes and yesterday's dishes and dishes that weren't even dirty yet.

I saw how foolish I was acting. I was standing in the pulpit, Sunday mornings, telling other people how to live, yet I myself was leading a tense, worried, hurried existence. I felt ashamed of myself.

Worries don't bother me any more now. No more stomach pains. No more insomnia. I now crumple up yesterday's anxieties and toss them into the wastebasket, and I have ceased trying to wash tomorrow's dirty dishes today.

Do you remember a statement quoted earlier in this book? "The load of tomorrow, added to that of yesterday, carried today, makes the strongest falter."… Why even try it?

不要把烦恼叠加在一起

多年来，我因患了严重的胃病而十分痛苦。我每晚会痛醒两三次，无法入睡。我曾见到父亲死于胃癌，我担心自己也会得胃癌——或者至少也是胃溃疡。因此，我去了一家诊所接受检查。胃科专家利尔伽医生用荧光镜和X射线检查了我的胃部。他给我开了一些药帮助我入睡，并向我保证，我并没有得胃溃疡或胃癌，他说我的胃痛是由精神紧张引起的。由于我是牧师，因此他的第一个问题是："你在教堂是不是很忙？"

他问我的我其实早已知道：我总是想做太多的事。除了每个星期天的讲道和主持教堂的各种活动，我还担任了红十字会主席、吉瓦尼斯俱乐部会长；同时，每周还要主持两三次葬礼和各种其他活动。

我在持续压力下工作，永远都无法放松。我总是紧张匆忙地生活着，几乎到了凡事皆烦恼的地步。我一直生活在紧张不安中，因此当然乐于接受利尔伽医生的忠告。我每个星期一都自动休假，同时减少了各种社会工作和活动。

一天，我在清理桌子时，突然产生一个念头，结果证明这个念头极其有效。当时，我正在看抽屉里一大堆以前讲道的旧笔记，以及一些已经过时的备忘录。我将它们全都拿出来，然后扔进了废纸篓里。突然，我停了下来对自己说："为什么你对自己的烦恼不能像对这些旧笔记一样呢？为什么不将昨天的全部烦恼捡出来扔进废纸篓呢？"这个念头立刻起了作用——我顿时觉得肩上的重担减轻了不少。从那天起到今天，我已将它当成一项规则：把我无力解决问题都扔进废纸篓。

接着，有一天，太太在洗盘子，我帮她擦干，我又产生了另一个念头。当时，太太一面洗盘子，一面唱着歌。我对自己说："瞧，你太太多么快乐。我们已结婚18年，而她洗盘子也洗了18年。假如我们结婚时，她就看到她在这期间要洗的盘子堆起来可以装满一个谷仓，一定会吓走任何一个女人。"

然后，我告诉自己："我太太之所以不介意洗盘子，是因为她一次只洗一天的盘子。"我终于找到了我的问题所在——我企图一次洗完今天和昨天甚至尚未使用的盘子。

我发现我的行动多么愚蠢。每个星期天的早晨，我都会站在讲台上，告诉人们如何生活，而我自己一味地紧张、匆忙和烦恼。我对自己感到惭愧。

从此以后，烦恼再也不来打扰我了，胃也不再痛了，而且不再失眠。我现在将昨天的烦恼全揉成一团，然后将它们扔进废纸篓；同时，我开始停止为未来担忧。

你是否还记得这句话："明天的烦恼，加上昨天的烦恼，与今天的合起来，就造成了最沉重的负担。"为什么要这样做呢？

I Found the Answer—Keep Busy!

In 1943 I landed in a veterans' hospital in Albuquerque, New Mexico, with three broken ribs and a punctured lung. This had happened during a practice Marine amphibious landing off the Hawaiian Islands. I was getting ready to jump off the barge, onto the beach, when a big breaker swept in, lifted the barge, and threw me off balance and smashed me on the sands. I fell with such force that one of my broken ribs punctured my right lung.

After spending three months in the hospital, I got the biggest shock of my life. The doctors told me that I showed absolutely no improvement. After some serious thinking, I figured that worry was preventing me from getting well. I had been used to a very active life, and during these three months I had been flat on my back twenty-four hours a day with nothing to do but think. The more I thought, the more I worried: worried about whether I would ever be able to take my place in the world. I worried about whether I would remain a cripple the rest of my life, and about whether I would ever be able to get married and live a normal life.

I urged my doctor to move me up to the next ward, which was called the "Country Club" because the patients were allowed to do almost anything they cared to do.

In this "Country Club" ward, I became interested in contract bridge. I spent six weeks learning the game, playing bridge with the other fellows, and reading Culbertson's books on bridge. After six weeks, I was playing nearly every evening for the rest of my stay in the hospital. I also became interested in painting with oils, and I studied this art under an instructor every afternoon from three to five. Some of my paintings were so good that you could almost tell what they were! I also tried my hand at soap and wood carving, and read a number of books on the subject and found it fascinating. I kept myself so busy that I had no time to worry about my physical condition. I even found time to read books on psychology given to me by the Red Cross. At the end of three months, the entire medical staff came to me and congratulated me on "making an amazing improvement". Those were the sweetest words I had ever heard since the days I was born. I wanted to shout with joy.

The point I am trying to make is this: when I had nothing to do but lie on the flat of my back and worry about my future, I made no improvement whatever. I was poisoning my body with worry. Even the broken ribs couldn't heal. But as soon as I got my mind off myself by playing contract bridge, painting oil pictures, and carving wood, the doctors declared I made "an amazing improvement".

I am now leading a normal, healthy life, and my lungs are as good as yours.

Remember what George Bernard Shaw said? "The secret of being miserable is to have the leisure to bother about whether you are happy or not." Keep active, keep busy!

我找到了答案

1943年，我住进了新墨西哥州阿尔伯克基市的一家军队医院，因为我的肋骨三根折断，肺部穿孔。这发生在夏威夷岛的一次陆战队两栖登陆大演习中。

当时我正准备从小艇跳到沙滩上，碰巧一阵大浪扑来，托起了小艇，我失去了平衡，跌倒在沙滩上。由于摔下来力量很大，我折断了肋骨，其中一根刺进了我的右肺。

我在医院待了3个月之后，经历了一生中最严重的惊吓——医生说我的伤势绝不可能好转。经过谨慎思考之后，我认为是过度的烦恼使我无法康复。我以前的生活活跃且多姿多彩，可这3个月我必须一天24小时躺在病床上，无事可做，只能胡思乱想。想得愈多，就愈烦恼：担心自己是否能恢复以前的地位；担心是否会终身残疾，以及是否还能结婚，过正常的生活。

于是，我要求医生将我安排到隔壁的病房，这是一间被称为"乡间俱乐部"的病房，因为那里的病人几乎可以完全自由活动。

在这个"乡村俱乐部"病房，我对"合约桥牌"发生了兴趣。我用了6周学会这个游戏，和其他伙伴一起搭档，还阅读了一些桥牌书。六周之后，我几乎每天晚上都打桥牌。我还对油画产生了兴趣：在每天下午三至五点，我都在一位老师的指导下学习画画。我的一些作品画得极好，你甚至一眼就可以看出我画的是什么。我还尝试雕刻肥皂和木头，并读了许多有关的书籍，觉得十分有趣。我让自己变得十分忙碌，因此没有时间去担心我的伤势。我甚至花了许多时间阅读红十字会赠送给我的心理学书。到了第三个月末，全体医护人员来向我道贺，说我伤势恢复极佳。那是我自出生以来听见的最甜美的话。我高兴得真想放声大叫。

我在此想说明的一点是，当我无所事事，成天只能躺在床上为将来烦恼时，我没有任何进步。我那只是用烦恼来残害身体，甚至折断的肋骨也难以好起来。但等我专心打桥牌、画画、雕刻，忘记了身体的伤痛时，医生就说我"进步极大"。

我现在过着正常健康的生活，我的肺也和你的一样好。

你是否还记得萧伯纳说过的一句话？"痛苦的根源在于你有空去想自己是否快乐。"活跃起来，让自己忙起来！

Time Solves a Lot of Things

Worry caused me to lose ten years of my life. Those ten years should have been the most fruitful and richest years of any young man's life—the years from eighteen to twenty-eight.

I realize now that losing those years was no one's fault but my own.

I worried about everything: my job, my health, my family, and my feeling of inferiority. I was so frightened that I used to cross the street to avoid meeting people I knew. When I met a friend on the street, I would often pretend not to notice him, because I was afraid of being snubbed.

I was so afraid of meeting strangers—so terrified in their presence—that in one space of two weeks I lost out on three different jobs simply because I didn't have the courage to tell those three different prospective employers what I knew I could do.

Then one day eight years ago, I conquered worry in one afternoon—and have rarely worried since then. That afternoon I was in the office of a man who had had far more troubles than I had ever faced, yet he was one of the most cheerful men I had ever known. He had made a fortune in 1929, and lost every cent. He had made another fortune in 1933, and lost that; and another fortune in 1939, and lost that, too. He had gone through bankruptcy and had been hounded by enemies and creditors. Troubles that would have broken some men and driven them to suicide rolled off him like water off a duck's back.

As I sat in his office that day eight years ago, I envied him and wished that God had made me like him.

As we were talking, he tossed a letter to me that he had received that morning and said: "Read that."

It was an angry letter, raising several embarrassing questions. If I had received such a letter, it would have sent me into a tailspin. I said: "Bill, how are you going to answer it?"

"Well," Bill said, "I'll tell you a little secret. Next time you've really got something to worry about, take a pencil and a piece of paper, and sit down and write out in detail just what's worrying you. Then put that piece of paper in the lower right-hand drawer of your desk. Wait a couple of weeks, and then look at it. If what you wrote down still worries you when you read it, put that piece of paper back in your lower right-hand drawer. Let it sit there for another two weeks. It will be safe there. Nothing will happen to it. But in the meantime, a lot may happen to the problem that is worrying you. I have found that, if only I have patience, the worry that is trying to harass me will often collapse like a pricked balloon."

That bit of advice made a great impression on me. I have been using Bill's advice for years now, and, as a result, I rarely worry about anything.

Times solves a lot of things. Time may also solve what you are worrying about today.

时间可以解决许多问题

"忧虑"使我丧失了十年光阴，而这十年本来应该是年轻人最有收获、最丰富多彩的岁月——18～28岁的时间。

现在，我已经明白，失去这10年不是别人的错，而是我自已造成的。

我对所有的事情忧虑：我的工作、健康、家庭、自卑感。为此，我经常不得不躲避我认识的人。我在街上碰到某位朋友时，会假装没有看见，因为我害怕遭到嘲笑。

我非常害怕见到陌生人——在陌生人面前我就会不自在——因此有一次在两周当中，我接连失去了三个工作机会，只因为我没有勇气对未来的老板说我能干什么。

然后，八年前的一天下午，我征服了一切烦恼——从那时起，我就很少有烦恼了。那天下午，我去了某人办公室。那人似乎没有任何烦恼，而且是我认识的人当中最快乐的一个。他在1929年发了一笔大财，可后来分文不剩。1932年，他东山再起，可又赔光了。然后，在1939年，他又大赚一笔，可又赔光了。他曾多次破产，遭到敌人和债主的逼压。他遇到的烦恼可以使任何人精神崩溃，甚至自杀。

八年前的那天，我坐在他的办公室，对他充满了羡慕，希望上帝将我也改造得像他一样。

在我们谈话时，他把那天早晨收到的一封信递给我，说："你看看这封信。"

那是一封愤怒的来信，提出了一些令人难堪的问题。如果我收到这样一封信，我可要烦死了。我说："比尔，你打算如何回复？"

"噢，"比尔说，"我告诉你一个小秘密。当你下一次碰到令你烦恼的事时，取出一支铅笔和一张纸，详细写下你的烦恼，然后将那张纸放在你右手下方的抽屉里。一两周之后，再取出来看看。如果你第二次阅读时，认为那些事情仍让你烦恼，再将它放回原来的抽屉，再放上一两周。它在那里绝对安全，不会有什么变化。但与此同时，你的烦恼可能会发生许多变化。而且我发现，只要我有耐心，烦恼总会自动消失。"

比尔的忠告给了我极深的印象。我已经使用比尔的忠告许多年了，结果我真的烦恼少多了。

时间可以解决许多问题。时间也许可以解决你今天的烦恼。

I Was Warned Not to Try to Speak or to Move Even a Finger

Several years ago I was a witness in a lawsuit that caused me a great deal of mental strain and worry.

After the case was over, and I was returning home in the train, I had a sudden and violent physical collapse. Heart trouble. I found it almost impossible to breathe.

When I got home the doctor gave me an injection. I wasn't in bed—I hadn't been able to get any farther than the living- room settee. When I regained consciousness, I saw that the parish priest was already there to give me final absolution!

I saw the stunned grief on the faces of my family. I knew my number was up. Later, I found out that the doctor had prepared my wife for the fact that I would probably be dead in less than thirty minutes. My heart was so weak I was warned not to try to speak or to move even a finger.

I closed my eyes and said: "Thy will be done…If it has to come now, Thy will be done."

As soon as I gave in to that thought, I seemed to relax all over. My terror disappeared, and I asked myself quietly what was the worst that could happen now. Well, the worst seemed to be a possible return of the spasms, with excruciating pains—then all would be over. I would go to meet my Maker and soon be at peace.

I lay on that settee and waited for an hour, but the pains didn't return. Finally, I began to ask myself what I would do with my life if I didn't die now. I determined that I would exert every effort to regain my health. I would stop abusing myself with tension and worry and rebuild my strength.

That was four years ago. I have rebuilt my strength to such a degree that even my doctor is amazed at the improvement my cardiograms show. I no longer worry. I have a new zest for life. But I can honestly say that if I hadn't faced the worst—my imminent death—and then tried to improve upon it, I don't believe I would be here today. If I hadn't accepted the worst, I believe I would have died from my own fear and panic.

逃 脱 死 亡

多年前，我曾在一件官司中担当一名证人，结果导致我精神紧张和烦恼。官司结束后，我搭火车回到家，突然病倒，而且病得非常厉害。心脏病！我发现我几乎喘不过气来。

我回家后，医生给我打了一针。当时，我并不是躺在床上——我只能支撑到客厅，再也走不动了。我神志恢复后，发现教区的牧师已经在为我准备最后的洗礼。

我看到了家人脸上的悲伤。我知道我的生命已到了最后时刻。后来，我又发现医生要我妻子面对现实：我可能会在30分钟后死去。我的心脏如此衰弱，医生警告我不得说话，甚至连手指头也不得动弹。

我闭上眼睛，对自己说："该来的，总会来……总会来。"

有了那个想法之后，我似乎全身放松了。我的恐惧消失了，我镇静地问自己，现在可能会发生的最糟糕的事情是什么？嗯，大不了是心脏痉挛，让我疼痛好一阵子，然后一切都过去了。我知道我马上就要去见上帝，永远安息了。

我躺在沙发上，等了一小时，但疼痛并没有再次袭击我。最后，我开始问自己，如果我现在不死，我将对生活作何打算。我决定尽一切努力恢复健康，不再用紧张和烦恼来毁灭自己，要重建自己的力量。

那已是四年前的事了。我的身体恢复得很快，甚至连医生也对我的进步大加赞扬。我不再自寻烦恼，对生命有了新的感受。但是，我必须承认，如果我不是曾经在死亡线上挣扎过，然后努力进步，我不相信我今天还会健在。如果没有接受最糟糕的情况，我相信我会因自身的恐惧和惊慌而死去。

I Am a Great Dismisser

Worry is a habit—a habit that I broke long ago. I believe that my habit of refraining from worrying is due largely to three things.

First: I am too busy to indulge in self-destroying anxiety. I have three main activities—each one of which should be virtually a full-time job in itself. I lecture to large groups at Columbia University. I am also chairman of the Board of Higher Education of New York City. I also have charge of the Economic and Social Book Department of the publishing firm of Harper and Brothers. The insistent demands of these three tasks leave me no time to fret and stew and run around in circles.

Second: I am a great dismisser. When I turn from one task to another, I dismiss all thoughts of the problems I had been thinking about previously. I find it stimulating and refreshing to turn from one activity to another. It rests me. It clears my mind.

Third: I have had to school myself to dismiss all these problems from my mind when I close my office desk. They are always continuing. Each one always has a set of unsolved problems demanding my attention. If I carried these issues home with me each night, and worried about them, I would destroy my health; and, in addition, I would destroy all ability to cope with them.

消除忧虑的良方

忧虑是一种习惯，而我早就打破了这种习惯。我认为我能解除烦恼，主要归功于3项举措。

第一，我太忙，没有时间沉溺于自我毁灭的焦虑之中。我有3项主要活动：在哥伦比亚大学讲课，担任纽约市高等教育委员会主席，又掌管哈泼兄弟出版公司的经济及社会丛书部。每一项活动都是全天性的工作。这3项主要工作，使我根本没有时间去自寻烦恼。

第二，我是一个放得开的人。我放下一项工作去干另一项工作时，会完全抛开以前所想的问题。我发现，变换新的活动可以令人振奋，使我得到休息，神志清醒。

第三，我离开办公桌之后，就让自己把所有的烦恼从大脑中剔除出去。这些问题都是连贯性的，如果我每天晚上都把这些问题带回家，并为它们烦恼，那我的健康就全完了，也将失去解决烦恼的能力。

If I Had Not Stopped Worrying, I Would Have Been in My Grave Long Ago

I have been in professional baseball for over sixty-three years. When I first started, back in the eighties, I got no salary at all. We played on vacant lots, and stumbled over tin cans and discarded horse collars. When the game was over, we passed the hat. The pickin's were pretty slim for me, especially since I was the main support of my widowed mother and my younger brothers and sisters. Sometimes the ball team would have to put on a strawberry supper or a clambake to keep going.

I have had plenty of reason to worry. I am the only baseball manager who ever finished in last place for seven consecutive years. I am the only manager who ever lost eight hundred games in eight years. After a series of defeats, I used to worry until I could hardly eat or sleep. But I stopped worrying twenty-five years ago, and I honestly believe that if I hadn't stopped worrying then, I would have been in my grave long ago.

As I looked back over my long life （I was born when Lincoln was President）, I believe I was able to conquer worry by doing these things:

1. I saw how futile it was. I saw it was getting me nowhere and was threatening to wreck my career.

2. I saw it was going to ruin my health.

3. I kept myself so busy planning and working to win games in the future that I had no time to worry over games that were already lost.

4. I finally made it a rule never to call a player's attention to his mistakes until twenty-four hours after the game. In my early days, I used to dress and undress with the players. If the team had lost, I found it impossible to refrain from criticising the players and from arguing with them bitterly over their defeats. I found this only increased my worries. Criticising a player in front of the others didn't make him want to cooperate. It really made him bitter. So, since I couldn't be sure of controlling myself and my tongue immediately after a defeat, I made it a rule never to see the players right after a defeat. I wouldn't discuss the defeat with them until the next day. By that time, I had cooled off, the mistakes didn't loom so large, and I could talk things over calmly and the men wouldn't get angry and try to defend themselves.

5. I tried to inspire players by building them up with praise instead of tearing them down with faultfinding. I tried to have a good word for everybody.

6. I found that I worried more when I was tired; so I spend ten hours in bed every night, and I take a nap every afternoon. Even a five-minute nap helps a lot.

7. I believe I have avoided worries and lengthened my life by continuing to be active. I am eighty-five, but I am not going to retire until I begin telling the same stories over and over. When I start doing that, I'll know then that I am growing old.

要不是停止忧虑，我早就完了

我在职业棒球界已经63年多了。我首次加入球队时，完全没有薪水。我们在空地上打球，常常被地上的废弃物绊倒。比赛结束后，我们就摘下帽子，传过去向大家收钱。但是，这些钱实在太少了。尤其是我，承担养活寡母及弟弟妹妹的责任。有时，球队为了赚钱，必须做一些逗笑的演出，才能使球赛继续下去。

我有许多可以烦恼的原因。我曾是连续7年都排在最末位的唯一一位棒球队经理，而且曾在8年内输了800场球。经过一连串失败，我愁得吃不下，睡不着。但是，我在25年前就不再烦恼了。我相信，如果不停止烦恼，那么我早就进棺材了。

现在，回忆我漫长的生命历程（我是在林肯总统时代出生的），我认为我能征服忧虑，得益于下面这些方法：

第一，我认为烦恼毫无益处。除了对我的棒球生涯造成威胁，烦恼对我毫无帮助。

第二，我认为烦恼会损害我的健康。

第三，我让自己忙着准备在将来的比赛中获胜，因此没有时间为已经失败的球赛去自寻烦恼。

第四，我给自己定了一个规则：球赛过后24小时内，不得批评球员犯的过错。以前，我总是和球员们一起穿衣、更衣。如果球队在比赛中输了，我总会忍不住批评球员们，而且毫不留情地与他们争论为什么会失败。后来，我发现这样只会增加我的烦恼；而且在其他球员面前批评某位球员，只会使他以后更不愿合作，因为这确实使他大丢面子。因此，既然我没有把握在球赛刚结束时控制自己，那我只好给自己立下一个规则：比赛失败后，绝不立刻和球员见面；一直要等到第二天，才和他们讨论失利问题。到那时，我已经冷静下来，不会扩大错误，而且可以和球员们冷静地讨论事实，球员也不会生气或为自己辩护。

第五，我会赞扬球员们，激励他们，而不是像以前那样总是挑他们的毛病。我想对每个人都说些赞扬的话。

第六，我发现，我身体疲倦时，烦恼就更多。所以，我每天晚上要休息10小时，每天下午还要睡一会儿。即使是5分钟的小睡，对我也大有帮助。

第七，我相信，我不断忙碌，不再受各种烦恼的干扰，因而延长了我的寿命。我已经85岁，但我还不想退休，而是要把同样的故事讲一遍又一遍。那时，我才知道自己确实已经老了。

One at a Time，One at a Time

I discovered years ago that I could not escape my worries by trying to run away from them, but that I could banish them by changing my mental attitude toward them. I discovered that my worries were not outside but inside myself.

As the years have gone by, I have found that time automatically takes care of most of my worries. In fact, I frequently find it difficult to remember what I was worrying about a week ago. So I have a rule: never to fret over a problem until it is at least a week old. Of course, I can't always put a problem completely out of mind for a week at a time, but I can refuse to allow it to dominate my mind until the allotted seven days have passed, either the problem has solved itself or I have so changed my mental attitude that it no longer has the power to trouble me greatly.

I have been greatly helped by reading the philosophy of Sir William Osler, a man who was not only a great physician, but a great artist in the greatest of all arts: The Art of Living. One of his statements has helped me immensely in banishing worries. Sir William said, at a dinner given in his honor: "More than to anything else, I owe whatever success I have had to the power of settling down to the day's work and trying to do it well to the best of my ability and letting the future take care of itself."

In handling troubles, I have taken as my motto the words of an old parrot that my father used to tell me about. Father told me of a parrot that was kept in a cage hanging over the doorway in a hunting club in Pennsylvania. As the members of the club passed through the door, the parrot repeated over and over the only words he knew: "One at a time, one at a time." Father taught me to handle my troubles that way: "One at a time, one at a time." I have found that taking my troubles one at a time has helped me to maintain calm and composure amidst pressing duties and unending engagements. "One at a time, one at a time."

一次只做一件事

几年前，我发现我并不能以逃避忧虑的方式来摆脱忧虑，但我可以改变心态来消除忧虑。我发现我的忧虑不是来自外部，而在我自身。

岁月流逝，我发现时间会自动消除我的大部分忧虑。事实上，我经常发现要记住一周前的忧虑很难。于是，我定下一条原则：绝不为一个问题而烦恼一周。当然，我不可能一次就将一个问题从大脑中清除一周，但我不会让它控制我的思想，或者让问题自行解决，或者我改变心态，让它不再来烦我。

读威廉·奥斯勒爵士的名言对我助益匪浅。他不仅是伟大的医生，还是生活这门最伟大艺术的艺术家。他的一句话对我消除忧虑帮助极大。在一次欢迎晚宴上，他说："我的成就归功于有能力解决今天的问题，尽力干好工作，让将来去照料它。"

在处理烦恼时，我将父亲常对我讲的一只老鹦鹉说的话当作我的座右铭。父亲告诉我，宾夕法尼亚州有一只挂在猎人俱乐部门廊上方笼子里的鹦鹉。每当俱乐部的成员穿过门廊时，这只鹦鹉会一再重复它唯一会说的话："一次只做一件事！一次只做一件事！"父亲教我那样处理我的烦恼："一次只做一件事！"我发现一次处理一件事情有助于我保持平静，承受重压和繁杂的工作。"一次只做一件事！"

I Now Look for the Green Light

From the time I was a small boy, throughout the early stages of young manhood, and during my adult life, I was a professional worrier. My worries were many and varied. Some were real; most of them were imaginary. Upon rare occasions I would find myself without anything to worry about—then I would worry for fear I might be overlooking something.

Then, two years ago, I started out on a new way of living. This required making a self-analysis of my faults—and a very few virtues—a "searching and fearless moral inventory" of myself. This brought out clearly what was causing all this worry.

The fact was that I could not live for today alone. I was fretful of yesterday's mistakes and fearful of the future.

I was told over and over that "today was the tomorrow I had worried about yesterday". But it wouldn't work on me. I was advised to live on a twenty-four-hour program. I was told that today was the only day over which I had any control and that I should make the most of my opportunities each day. I was told that if I did that, I would be so busy I would have no time to worry about any other day—past or future. That advice was logical, but somehow I found it hard to put these darned ideas to work for me.

Then like a shot from out of the dark, I found the answer—and where do you suppose I found it? On a Northwestern Railroad platform at seven P. M. on May 31,1945. It was an important hour for me. That is why I remember it so clearly.

We were taking some friends to the train. They were leaving on *The City of Los Angeles*, a streamliner, to return from a vacation. War was still on—crowds were heavy that year. Instead of boarding the train with my wife, I wandered down the tracks towards the front of the train. I stood looking at the big shiny engine for a minute. Presently I looked down the track and saw a huge semaphore. An amber light was showing. Immediately this light turned to a bright green. At that moment, the engineer started clanging a bell; I heard the familiar"All aboard!" and, in a matter of seconds, that huge streamliner began to move out of that station on its 2,300-mile trip.

My mind started spinning. Something was trying to make sense to me. I was experiencing a miracle. Suddenly it dawned on me. The engineer had given me the answer I had been seeking. He was starting out on that long journey with only one green light to go by. If I had been in his place, I would want to see all the green lights for the entire journey. Impossible, of course, yet that was exactly what I was trying to do with my life—sitting in the station, going no place, because I was trying too hard to see what was ahead for me.

My thoughts kept coming. That engineer didn't worry about trouble that he might encounter miles ahead. There probably would be some delays, some slowdowns, but wasn't that why they had signal systems? Amber lights—reduce speed and take it easy. Red lights—real danger up ahead—stop. That was what made train travel safe. A good signal system.

I asked myself why I didn't have a good signal system for my life. My answer was—I did have one.

No more worrying for me since that day two years ago when I made this discovery. During those two years, over seven hundred green lights have shown for me, and the trip through life is so much easier without the worry of what color the next light will be. No matter what color it may be, I will know what to do.

寻找人生的绿灯

从我还是个小男孩时开始，直到我成年之初，以及在成年阶段，我一直是个"烦恼大王"。我的烦恼太多了，而且千奇百怪。有些是真烦恼，但大部分是胡思乱想。我几乎很少发现自己没有什么事不烦恼的——从那时起，我就担心我是否遗漏了什么东西。

后来，在两年前，我开始了新的生活方式。这种生活方式要求我对自己的过错和极少数美德作自我分析，对自己进行全面了解。这样，我就把所有烦恼的原因弄清楚了。

事实是这样的：我并不只是为今天而活着；我为昨天的错误而后悔，又对将来心存恐惧。

不断有人这样告诫我："今天就是你昨天忧虑的明天。"但是，这句话对我并不管用。还有人建议我，只活在今天。也有人说，今天是我唯一能掌握并好好利用的时间。还有人说，尽量让自己忙碌起来，这样就没有时间去烦恼了。这些说法都很有道理，但我发现很难把它们用到我身上来。

接着，我像从黑暗中突然冲出来一般，终于找到了答案。你知道我是在哪里找到的吗？那是1945年5月31日晚上七点，在西北铁路公司的一个站台上。对我来说那是如此重要的时刻，因此我一直记得一清二楚。

我们当时在送朋友上火车。他们刚度完假，准备搭"洛杉矶市"号快车离开。当时战争还未结束，车站上人潮涌动。我没有和太太一起送朋友上车，而是沿着轨道向火车头走去。我站在那里看闪着亮光的庞大引擎，然后目光移向铁道的前方，发现了一座巨大的信号灯台，当时正好显示的是黄灯。

突然，黄灯变成了绿色。这时，火车鸣起了汽笛，我听见站务人员高喊"全部上车！"接着，几秒钟之后，巨大的列车开始驶出车站，开上了2300英里的旅程。

我的大脑开始旋转——似乎要向我证明什么。我正在经历一次奇迹，一切突然真相大白——原来那位火车司机已经为我提供了我一直在找寻的答案。他只看见一盏绿灯，就开始了漫长的旅程。如果是我在他的位置上，我会希望全程都是绿灯。当然，这是不可能的，但我对生活的期望正是那样——坐在人生的车站里，结果哪儿也去不了，因为我一直想看清楚前面是什么。

我思潮澎湃。那位火车司机并没有为前面旅程中可能遇到的麻烦而忧虑。火车可能会出现延误、故障，但不正是因此而有了信号灯系统吗？黄灯——减速慢行；红灯——前方危险——停车。这可以保证火车安全，因此是一种良好的信号系统。

我问自己，为什么不为自己的生活制定一套良好的信号系统呢？我找到了答案——我本来就有。

我两年前发现这个奥秘之后，就不再忧虑了。在这两年中，我遇到了大约700盏绿灯，使我不必担心下一盏灯是什么颜色，我的人生之旅也更为轻松愉快。不管前面的信号灯是什么颜色，我已经知道怎么办了。

How John D.Rockefeller Lived on Borrowed Time for Forty-five Years

John D. Rockefeller, Sr. , had accumulated his first million at the age of thirty-three. At the age of forty-three, he had built up the largest monopoly the world has ever seen—the great Standard Oil Company. But where was he at fifty-three? Worry had got him at fifty-three. Worry and high-tension living had already wrecked his health. At fifty-three, he"looked like a mummy," says John K. Winkler, one of his biographers.

At fifty-three, Rockefeller was attacked by mystifying digestive maladies that swept away his hair, even the eyelashes and all but a faint wisp of eyebrow. "So serious was his condition," says Winkler, "that at one time John D. was compelled to exist on human milk." According to the doctors, he had alopecia, a form of baldness that often starts with sheer nerves. He looked so startling, with his stark bald dome, that he had to wear a skullcap. Later, he had wigs made—at $500 a piece—and for the rest of his life he wore these silver wigs.

Rockefeller had originally been blessed with an iron constitution. Reared on a farm, he had once had stalwart shoulders, an erect carriage, and a strong, brisk gait.

Yet at only fifty-three—when most men are at their prime—his shoulders drooped and he shambled when he walked. "When he looked in a glass," says John T. Flynn, another of his biographers, "he saw an old man. The ceaseless work, the endless worry, the streams of abuse, the sleepless nights, and the lack of exercise and rest" had exacted their toll; they had brought him to his knees. He was now the richest man in the world; yet he had to live on a diet that a pauper would have scorned. His income at the time was a million dollars a week—but two dollars a week would probably have paid for all the food he could eat. Acidulated milk and a few biscuits were all the doctors would allow him. His skin had lost its color—it looked tike old parchment drawn tight across his bones. And nothing but medical care, the best money could buy, kept him from dying at the age of fifty-three.

How did it happen? Worry. Shock. High-pressure and high-tension living. He"drove" himself literally to the edge of the grave. Even at the age of twenty-three, Rockefeller was already pursuing his goal with such grim determination that, according to those who knew him, "nothing lightened his countenance save news of a good bargain." When he made a big profit, he would do a little war dance—throw his hat on the floor and break into a jig. But if he lost money, he was ill! He once shipped $40,000 worth of grain by way of the Great Lakes. No insurance. It cost too much: $150. That night a vicious storm raged over Lake Erie. Rockefeller was so worried about losing his cargo that when his partner, George Gardner, reached the office in the morning, he found John D. Rockefeller there, pacing the floor.

"Hurry," he quavered. "Let's see if we can take out insurance now, if it isn't too late!" Gardner rushed uptown and got the insurance; but when he returned to the office, he found John D. in an even worse state of nerves. A telegram had arrived in the meantime: the cargo had landed, safe from the storm. He was sicker than ever now because they had"wasted" the $150! In fact, he was so sick about it that he had to go home and take to his bed. Think of it! At that time, his firm was doing gross business of $500,000 a year—yet he made himself so ill over $150 that he had to go to bed!

He had no time for play, no time for recreation, no time for anything except making money and teaching Sunday school. When his partner, George Gardner, purchased a second-hand yacht, with three other men, for $2,000, John D. was aghast, refused to go out in it. Gardner found him working at the office one Saturday afternoon, and pleaded: "Come on, John, let's go for a sail. It will do you good. Forget about business. Have a little fun." Rockefeller glared. "George Gardner," he warned, "you are the most extravagant man I ever knew. You are injuring your credit at the banks—and my credit too. First thing you know, you'll be wrecking our business. No, I won't go on your yacht—I don't ever want to see it!" And he stayed plugging in the office all Saturday afternoon.

The same lack of humor, the same lack of perspective, characterized John D. all through his business career. Years later he said: "I never placed my head upon the pillow at night without reminding myself that my success might be only temporary."

With millions at his command, he never put his head upon his pillow without worrying about losing his fortune. No wonder worry wrecked his health. He had no time for play or recreation, never went to the theatre, never played cards, never went to a party. As Mark Hanna said, the man was mad about money. "Sane in every other respect, but mad about money."

Rockefeller had once confessed to a neighbor in Cleveland, Ohio, that he"wanted to be loved"; yet he was so cold and suspicious that few people even liked him. Morgan once balked at having to do business with him at all. "I don't like the man," he snorted. "I don't want to have any dealings with him." Rockefeller's own brother hated him so much that he removed his children's bodies from the family plot. "No one of my blood," he said, "will ever rest in land controlled by John D." Rockefeller's employees and associates lived in holy fear of him, and here is the ironic part: He was afraid of them—afraid they would talk outside the office and"give secrets away". He had so little faith in human nature that once, when he signed a ten-year contract with an independent refiner, he made the man promise not to tell anyone, not even his wife! "Shut your mouth and ran your business" —that was his motto.

Then at the very peak of his prosperity, with gold flowing into his coffers like hot yellow lava pouring down the sides of Vesuvius, his private world collapsed. Books and articles denounced the robber-baron war of the Standard Oil Company!— secret rebates with railroads, the ruthless crashing of all rivals.

In the oil fields of Pennsylvania, John D. Rockefeller was the most hated man on earth. He was hanged in effigy by the men he had crushed. Many of them longed to tie a rope around his withered neck and hang him to the limb of a sour-apple tree. Letters breathing fire and brimstone poured into his office—letters threatening his life. He hired bodyguards to keep his enemies from killing him. He attempted to ignore this cyclone of hate. He had once said cynically: "You may kick me and abuse me provided you will let me have my own way." But he discovered that he was human after all. He couldn't take hate—and worry too. His health began to crack. He was puzzled and bewildered by this new enemy—illness—which attacked him from within. At first"he remained secretive about his occasional indispositions," tried to put his illness out of his mind. But insomnia, indigestion, and the loss of his hair—all physical symptoms of worry and collapse—were not to be denied. Finally, his doctors told him the shocking truth. He could take his choice: his money and

his worries—or his life. They warned him he must either retire or die. He retired.
But before he retired, worry, greed, fear had already wrecked his health. When Ida
Tarbell, America's most celebrated female writer of biographies, saw him, she was
shocked. She wrote: "An awful age was in his face. He was the oldest man I have
ever seen." Old? Why, Rockefeller was then several years younger than General
Macarthur was when he recaptured the Philippines!But he was such a physical wreck
that Ida Tarbell pitied him. She was working at that time on her powerful book which
condemned the Standard Oil and all that it stood for; she certainly had no cause to
love the man who had built up this"octopus". Yet, she said that when she saw John D.
Rockefeller teaching a Sunday school class, eagerly searching the faces of all those
around him—"I had a feeling which I had not expected, and which time intensified. I
was sorry for him. I know no companion so terrible as fear."

When the doctors undertook to save Rockefeller's life, they gave him three
rules—three rules which he observed, to the letter, for the rest of his life. Here they
are:

1. Avoid worry. Never worry about anything, under any kind of circumstances.

2. Relax, and take plenty of mild exercise in the open air.

3. Watch your diet. Always stop eating while you're still a little hungry.

John D. Rockefeller obeyed those rules; and they probably saved his life.
He retired. He learned to play golf. He went in for gardening. He chatted with his
neighbors. He played games. He sang songs.

But he did something else too. "During days of torture and nights of insomnia,"
says Winkler, "John D. had time for reflection." He began to think of other people.
He stopped thinking, for once, of how much money he could get; and he began to
wonder how much that money could buy in terms of human happiness.

In short. Rockefeller now began to give his millions away! Some of the time
it wasn't easy. When he offered money to a church, pulpits all over the country
thundered back with cries of"tainted money!" But he kept on giving. He learned of
a starving little college on the shores of Lake Michigan that was being foreclosed
because of its mortgage. He came to its rescue and poured millions of dollars into
that college and built it into the now world-famous University of Chicago. He tried
to help the Negroes. He gave money to Negro universities like Tuskegee College,
where funds were needed to carry on the work of George Washington Carver. He
helped to fight hookworm. When Dr. Charles W. Stiles, the hookworm authority,
said: "Fifty cents' worth of medicine will cure a man of this disease which ravages
the South—but who will give the fifty cents?" Rockefeller gave it. He spent millions
on hookworm, stamping out the greatest scourge that has ever handicapped the
South. And then he went further. He established a great international foundation—
the Rockefeller Foundation—which was to fight disease and ignorance all over the

world.

I speak with feeling of this work, for there is a possibility that I may owe my life to the Rockefeller Foundation. How well I remember that when I was in China in 1932, cholera was raging all over Peking. The Chinese peasants were dying like flies; yet in the midst of all this horror, we were able to go to the Rockefeller Medical College in Peking and get a vaccination to protect us from the plague. Chinese and"foreigners" alike, we were able to do that. And that was when I got my first understanding of what Rockefeller's millions were doing for the world.

Never before in history has there ever been anything even remotely like the Rockefeller Foundation: It is something unique. Rockefeller knew that all over the world there are many fine movements that men of vision start. Research is undertaken; colleges are founded; doctors struggle on to fight a disease—but only too often this high-minded work has to die for lack of funds. He decided to help these pioneers of humanity—not to "take them over", but to give them some money and help them help themselves. Today you and I can thank John D. Rockefeller for the miracles of penicillin, and for dozens of other discoveries which his money helped to finance. You can thank him for the fact that your children no longer die from spinal meningitis, a disease that used to kill four out of five. And you can thank him for part of the inroads we have made on malaria and tuberculosis, on influenza and diphtheria, and many other diseases that still plague the world.

And what about Rockefeller? When he gave his money away, did he gain peace of mind? Yes, he was contented at last. "If the public thought of him after 1900 as brooding over the attacks on the Standard Oil," said Allan Kevins, "the public was much mistaken."

Rockefeller was happy. He had changed so completely that he didn't worry at all. In fact, he refused even to lose one night's sleep when he was forced to accept the greatest defeat of his career!

The defeat came when the corporation he had built, the huge Standard Oil, was ordered to pay"the heaviest time in history". According to the United States Government, the Standard Oil was a monopoly, in direct violation of the antitrust laws. The battle raged for time years. The best legal brains in the land fought on interminably in what was, up to then, the longest court war in history. But Standard Oil lost.

When Judge Kenesaw Mountain Landis handed down his decision, lawyers for the defense feared that old John D. would take it very hard. But they didn't know how much he'd changed.

That night one of the lawyers got John D. on the phone. He discussed the decision as gently as he could, and then said with concern: "I hope you won't let this decision upset you, Mr. Rockefeller. I hope you'll get your night's sleep!"

And old John D.? why, he crackled right back across the wire: "Don't worry, Mr. Johnson, I intend to get a nights sleep. And don't let it bother you either. Good night!"

That from the man who had once taken to his bed because he had lost $150! Yes, it took a long time for John D. to conquer worry. He was "dying" at fifty-three—but he lived to ninety-eight!

洛克菲勒的快乐法则

约翰·D. 洛克菲勒在33岁时就赚到了第一个100万美元。43岁时，他建立了世界上前所未有的最大垄断企业——庞大的标准石油公司。但是，当他到了53岁时，情况又怎么样呢？他被烦恼搞惨了，各种烦恼和高度紧张的生活已经破坏了他的健康。这时，他"看起来像个木乃伊"，为他写传记的作家约翰·K. 温克勒说。

洛克菲勒在53岁时患了奇怪的消化性疾病，不仅头发全掉光了，甚至连眼睫毛也一样，只剩下一绺淡淡的眉毛。"他的病情十分严重。"温克勒说，"有段时间，他靠喝人奶维持生存。"根据医生们的说法，他得了"脱毛症"，这种病通常是由过度紧张造成的。他的头光秃秃的，模样很是古怪，他不得不戴上帽子。后来，他定制了一些假发，每顶假发500美元。从此，他就一直戴着这些假发。

洛克菲勒的身体本来十分强健。他从小在农场长大，肩膀又宽又壮，腰杆笔直，步伐稳健有力。

可是在53岁的时候——这正是大多数男人的壮年时期——洛克菲勒却双肩下垂，走起路来摇摇晃晃的。据另一位传记作家佛林说："他照镜子时，看见的是个老头。没完没了的工作、无穷无尽的烦恼、长期的不良生活习惯、经常失眠及缺乏运动和休息，夺走了他的健康，使他挺不起腰来。"虽然他现在成了世界上最富有的人，但他只能吃些连穷人都不屑一顾的食物。当时，他每周收入100万美元，而他每周吃的食物只需要2美元就可以解决，因为医生只允许他吃一些酸牛奶和饼干。他的皮肤早已失去光泽，看起来像是老羊皮包在骨头上。金钱这时候也没有用了，只能为他付医疗费用，使他不至于在53岁就死去。

这是怎么回事呢？忧虑、惊吓、高度紧张的生活！他自己把自己"推"到了坟墓的边缘。洛克菲勒早在23岁时，就全身心地追求他的目标。据他的朋友说："除生意上的好消息，没有任何事情能令他开怀大笑。"当他赚到了一大笔钱时，他会高兴得把帽子摔到地上，开心地跳起舞来。但如果失败了，他会随之病倒。有一次，洛克菲勒在五大湖上托运一批价值4万美元的谷物，但他没有买保险。因为保险费太高了——要150美元。那天晚上，暴风雨袭击伊利湖。洛克菲勒十分担心，怕他的货物遭遇不测。第二天早上，当他的合伙者乔治·加德勒来到办公室时，发现洛克菲勒已在那里，正来回走动。

"快，"他发抖地说："看现在是否还能投保，否则来不及了！"加德勒立即冲到城里，买好了保险；而当他回到办公室时，却发现洛克菲勒的情况更严重了。这时，恰好来了一封电报：货物已经卸下，未受到暴风雨袭击。洛克菲勒这时反而更沮丧了，因为他已经"浪费"了150美元！事实上，他太伤心了，只好回家去躺下来休息。想想看，那时他的公司每年做着50万美元的生意，可是他为150美元而失魂落魄，甚至病倒在床。

他没有时间玩，也没有时间休息，除了赚钱和教堂生活，没有时间做其他事情。当他的合伙人加德勒和其他三个朋友花了2000美元买下一艘二手游艇时，洛克菲勒几乎吓坏了，拒绝搭乘那艘游艇出航。一个星期六的下午，加德勒发现洛克菲勒还在办公室工作，就对他说："走吧，约翰！我们乘船出海吧。暂时忘掉工作，轻松一下！"但洛克菲勒对他怒目而视。"乔治·加德勒，"他警告说，"你是世界上最浪费的人了！你正在破坏你在银行的信用，包括我的信用。将来你会把我们的生意毁掉。不行，我可不乘你的游艇，我永远也不愿见到它！"于是，他整个星期六下午都留在办公室工作。

缺乏幽默感和安全感，这是洛克菲勒一生的特征。几年后，他说："每天晚上，我一定会先提醒自己，我的成功也许只是暂时性的！然后才躺下来睡觉。"

这时，他已经有几百万美元可以支配，但他仍然担心会失去一切财富。怪不得忧虑会拖垮他的身体。他没有时间游玩或娱乐，也从未进过戏院，没打过纸牌，没参加过宴会。正如马克·汉纳所说，他为金钱而疯狂，"他在别的事情上都很正常，唯独为金钱疯狂"。

洛克菲勒曾在俄亥俄州克利夫兰市向一位邻居承认，他"希望有人爱"，但他太冷漠多疑了，很少有人喜欢他。有一次，摩根大发怨言，说不愿和他打交道。"我不喜欢那种人，"他不屑地说，"我不愿再和他有任何往来。"洛克菲勒的亲弟弟对他也深恶痛绝，甚至把自己孩子的棺木从祖坟中移走。他说："在我的亲骨肉之中，不允许任何一个人在约翰控制的土地上安息。"洛克菲勒的职员和同事也很敬畏他。但令人好笑的是,他竟然也怕他们——怕他们在办公室以外随意说话,"泄露公司的秘密"。他对人类天性没有任何信心。有一次,他和一位独立制造商签订了10年合作协议,但他要那位商人保证不告诉任何人,甚至他的妻子。"闭紧你的嘴,努力工作"——这就是他的座右铭。

正当他的事业达到顶峰,他的财富像维苏威火山的金黄色岩浆那样源源不断流入他的保险库时,他的私人世界却崩溃了。许多书和文章都公开谴责标准石油公司不择手段攫取财富的财阀行为——因为它和铁路公司之间的秘密回扣无情地压击垮了所有竞争者。

在宾夕法尼亚产油区,当地居民最痛恨的就是洛克菲勒。被他击败的竞争对手甚至把他的画像挂在树上解恨。他们当中有许多人都恨不得亲手将绳子套在他萎缩的脖子上,将他吊死在酸苹果树上。充满火药气味的信件也如雪花般飞进他的办公室,威胁要他的命。因此,他雇用了许多保镖,以防遭对手杀害。他试图忽视这些仇恨之火。有一次,他曾以讽刺的口吻说:"你们尽管踢我骂我,但我还是按我自己的方式行事。"而他最后还是发现,自己毕竟是一个普通人,无法忍受人们对他的仇恨,也受不了忧虑的侵扰。他的身体开始不行了。这个新的敌人——疾痛——从内部向他发起进攻,令他措手不及,惶恐不安。刚开始,"他试图对自己偶尔的不适保密"。但是,失眠、消化不良、掉头发——这些烦恼和精神崩溃的肉体上的病症无法遮掩。最后,医生只好将惊人的实情告诉他:他只有两种选择:财富和烦恼——或是性命。他们警告他:必须在退休和死亡之间作出抉择。他选择了退休。退休前,烦恼、贪婪、恐惧已经破坏了他的健康。美国著名传记女作家伊达·塔贝尔看见他时,几乎吓坏了。她写道:"他的脸上显示的是可怕的苍老,我从未见过他那样苍老的人。"老人?为什么?洛克菲勒可比当时重新占领菲律宾的麦克阿瑟将军还要年轻几岁呀!但是,他的身体如此衰弱,使伊达·塔贝尔为他深感悲哀。她当时正在撰写她那本有名的著作,揭发标准石油公司的罪恶,她当然不喜欢这个一手建造了这个庞大组织的人。不过,她又说,当她看见洛克菲勒在主日学校教书,焦急搜寻他四周的脸孔时,"我有一种前所未有的感觉。这种感觉与日俱增。我真为他悲哀。我知道,一个人没有知心的伙伴是一件可怕的事。"

医生开始挽救洛克菲勒的性命,他们为他制订了三条规则——这成为他后来奉行不渝的三条规则。这就是:

第一,避免烦恼。在任何情况下都不为任何事情而烦恼。

第二，放松，多做适当的户外运动。

第三，注意节食，随时保持半饥饿的状态。

洛克菲勒严格遵守这三条规则，保住了自己的性命。他退了下来，学打高尔夫球，修整庭院，和邻居聊天，还打牌、唱歌。

然而，他也做一些其他的事情。温克勒说："在那段痛苦的日子和失眠的夜晚，洛克菲勒终于有时间进行自我反省。"他开始为别人着想，一度停止去想还能赚多少钱，并开始思考如何用这些钱换取人类的幸福。

简而言之，洛克菲勒现在开始考虑把数百万财富捐出去。有时这可真不容易。例如，当他准备向一座教堂捐款时，全国各地的传教士一致发出反对的怒吼："腐败的金钱！"但是，他继续捐献。当他获悉密歇根湖岸的一家学院因为抵押权而被迫关闭时，他立刻做出了援助行动，捐出几百万美元给这家学院，将它建设成目前举世闻名的芝加哥大学。他还尽力帮助那些黑人。例如塔斯基吉黑人大学需要一笔基金来实现黑人教育家华盛顿·卡尔文的志愿，洛克菲勒捐出了巨款。他还出资协助消灭钩虫。当著名的钩虫专家史泰尔博士说："50美分的药就可以为一个人治好这种在南方肆虐的病。可谁会捐这些钱呢？"洛克菲勒立即捐了出来。他捐出数百万美元消除了钩虫，解除了曾经使美国南方陷于瘫痪的这种疾病。然后，他又采取了更进一步的行动，成立了一个庞大的国际性基金会"洛克菲勒基金会"，致力于消灭全世界各地的疾病、文盲。

我谨向这一伟大工程致敬，因为洛克菲勒基金会曾救过我一命。我还记得很清楚，1932年，我在中国，当时霍乱蔓延整个北京，农民们大批死去。而在这种恐怖之中，我们仍然能够去洛克菲勒医学院接受预防注射，这才使我们免受感染。那时我才第一次明白，洛克菲勒的百万美元财富对全世界的贡献。

洛克菲勒基金会这种壮举史无前例，全世界也绝无仅有。洛克菲勒深知世界各地有许多有识之士正在进行各种有意义的活动：进行研究工作，建立学校，医生则致力于和某些疾病作斗争，但这些高尚的工作经常因经费短缺而中止。他决定帮助这些人道主义的开拓者，但并不是"将他们接收过来"，而是资助他们一笔钱，帮助他们完成工作。今天，你和我都应该感谢约翰·洛克菲勒先生，因为在他的资助下，人类发现了青霉素和其他多种新事物。你也应该感谢他，因为是他使你的孩子不再因患"脊髓性脑膜炎"而死亡。你更应该感谢他的是，他使我们克服了疟疾、肺结核、流行性感冒、白喉和目前仍在危害世界的其他疾病。

洛克菲勒自己又怎么样了？他把钱捐出去之后，是否已获得了心灵上的平安？不错，他最后终于满足了。"如果人们仍然认为，他在1900年以来因为人们对标准石油公司的攻击而一蹶不振的话，"亚伦·凯文斯说，"那可就大错特错了。"

洛克菲勒十分快乐。他已经完全改变了，不再烦恼。事实上，在被迫接受生命中最大的一次失败时，他甚至不愿失去一个晚上的睡眠。

那次失败是这样的：他一手创建的标准石油公司被政府勒令支付"历史上最重的罚款"。根据美国政府的说法，标准石油公司是一个垄断性企业，直接违反了《反托拉斯法案》。这场官司打了好几年。全美国最顶尖的法律人才全都投入了这场看来似乎永无休止的官司，但标准石油公司最后还是败诉。

在南迪斯法官宣布了他的判决之后，辩方律师担心洛克菲勒无法接受这个坏消息。但他们不知道他已经完全变了。

那天晚上，一位律师打电话给洛克菲勒，尽量委婉地把判决告诉他，然后关切地问："洛克菲勒先生，我希望这项判决不至于让你沮丧，希望你睡个好觉。"

洛克菲勒怎么说的呢？噢，他毫不迟疑地回答："不要担心，约翰逊先生。我本来就想好好睡一觉。希望你也不要不安。晚安！"

这些话竟出自一个曾因损失了150美元而病倒在床的人之口？不错。洛克菲勒花了很长时间才克服了忧虑。尽管他曾"死于"53岁，但他活到了98岁。

Reading a Book on Sex Prevented My Marriage from Going on the Rocks

I hate to make this story anonymous. But it is so intimate that I could not possibly use my name.

However, Dale Carnegie will vouch for the truth of this story. I first told it to him twelve years ago.

After leaving college, I got a job with a large industrial organization, and five years later, this company sent me across the Pacific to act as one of its representatives in the Far East. A week before leaving America, I married the sweetest and most lovable woman I have ever known. But our honeymoon was a tragic disappointment for both of us—especially for her. By the time we reached Hawaii she was so disappointed, so heartbroken, that she would have returned to the States, had she not been ashamed to face her old friends and admit failure in what can be—and should be—life's most thrilling adventure.

We lived together two miserable years in the Orient. I was so unhappy that I had sometimes thought of suicide. Then one day I chanced upon a book that changed everything. I have always been a lover of books, and one night while visiting some American friends in the Far East, I was glancing over their well-stocked library when I suddenly saw a book entitled *Ideal Marriage*, by Dr. Van de Velde. The title sounded like a preachy, goody—goody document. But, out of idle curiosity, I opened it. I saw that it dealt almost entirely with the sexual side of marriage—and dealt with it frankly and without any touch of vulgarity.

If anyone had told me that I ought to read a book on sex, I would have been insulted. Read one? I felt I could write one. But my own marriage was such a bust that I condescended to look this book over, anyway. So I got up the courage to ask my host if I could borrow it. I can truthfully say that reading that book turned out to be one of the important events of my life. My wife also read it. That book turned a tragic marriage into a happy, blissful companionship. If I had a million dollars, I would buy the rights to publish that book and give free copies of it to the countless thousands of bridal couples.

I once read that Dr. John B. Watson, the distinguished psychologist, said: "Sex is admittedly the most important subject in life. It is admittedly the thing which causes the most shipwrecks in the happiness of men and women."

If Dr. Watson is correct—and I am persuaded that his statement, sweeping as it is, is almost, if not wholly, true—then why does civilization permit millions of sexual ignoramuses to marry each year and wreck all chances for married happiness?

If we want to know what is wrong with marriage, we ought to read a book entitled *What is Wrong With Marriage*? by Dr. G. V. Hamilton and Kenneth MacGowan. Dr. Hamilton spent four years investigating what is wrong with marriage before writing that book, and he says: "It would take a very reckless psychiatrist to say that most married friction doesn't find its sources in sexual maladjustment. At any rate, the frictions which arise from other difficulties would be ignored in many, many cases if the sexual relation itself were satisfactory." I know that statement is true. I know from tragic experience.

The book that saved my marriage from shipwreck, Dr. Van de Velde's *Ideal Marriage*, can be found in most large public libraries, or bought at any bookshop. If you want to give a little gift to some bride and groom, don't give them a carving set. Give them a copy of Ideal Marriage. That book will do more to increase their happiness than all the carving sets in the world.

一本书挽救了我的婚姻生活

我恨自己只能用假名来写这个故事。但因为这件事太具有隐私性，所以我不可能使用自己的真名。

但无论如何，卡耐基先生可以为这个故事的真实性作证。我在12年前第一次把我的故事告诉了他。

大学毕业后，我在一家大公司找到了一份工作。5年后，公司派我到太平洋彼岸的远东地区，担任公司驻该地区的代表。在离开美国的前一周，我娶了一位最可爱、最甜蜜的女郎为妻。但对我俩，尤其是对她来说，我们的蜜月既悲伤又失望。当我们抵达夏威夷时，她失望至极。若不是因为她不好意思面对老朋友，并承认婚姻生活的失败的话，她可能早就回美国了。

我们在远东度过了两年不幸的日子。我很不开心，好几次都想自杀。有一天，我偶然看到了一本书，它改变了一切。我一向喜欢读书。一天晚上，我去拜访一些住在远东的美国朋友，在浏览他们藏书丰富的图书室时，我突然看到了一本《理想的婚姻》，作者是韦尔迪博士。从书名来看，这是一本说教式的论文报告。但出于好奇，我将它翻开看了看，结果发现里面讨论的几乎都是婚姻生活中的"性"问题——开诚布公地讨论性问题，却没有任何粗俗之谈。

如果有人告诉我应该去阅读有关"性"的书，我会认为那是对我的侮辱。看那种书？我觉得我甚至可以写一本。但我自己的婚姻如此失败，我决定好好看这本书。所以，我鼓起勇气，问主人是否可以借那本书。现在，我可以说，读那本书其实正是我一生中最重要的一件大事。我太太也读了那本书。那本书使一次濒临破裂的婚姻变得既快乐又幸福。如果我有100万美元，我会买下那本书的版权，印刷之后免费送给所有的夫妇。

我读过著名心理学家沃特逊博士的一段话："性，无疑是人生中最重要的主题。导致绝大多数男女婚姻触礁的，也正是这件事。"

如果沃特逊博士是对的——我也由此得到建议，并且它几乎（即使不是完全）正确的话，我们为什么每年还要让千百万对性无知的年轻人结婚，从而破坏婚姻生活的幸福机会呢？

如果我们希望知道婚姻生活中的问题，我们应该去看看《婚姻的问题》。这是由汉密尔顿博士和麦克高文博士合著的。汉密尔顿博士花了四年时间调查婚姻的问题究竟出在哪里，然后写成这本书。他说："只有最愚蠢的精神病学家才会否认婚姻生活的不美满不是由性生活的不协调造成的。无论如何，如果性生活本身获得了满足，则婚姻生活中其他的许多不美满都好解决。"

韦尔迪博士这本挽救了我婚姻的书在许多大图书馆都能找到，或在书店买到。如果你想送给某对新人礼物，不要送雕塑，就送这本书给他们，它会比雕塑更有助于他们的幸福。

I Was Committing Slow Suicide Because I Didn't Know How to Relax

Up to six months ago, I was rushing through life in high gear. I was always tense, never relaxed. I arrived home from work every night worried and exhausted from nervous fatigue. Why? Because no one ever said to me: "Paul, you are killing yourself. Why don't you slow down? Why don't you relax?"

I would get up fast in the morning, eat fast, shave fast, dress fast, and drive to work as if I were afraid the steering wheel would fly out the window if I didn't have a death grip on it. I worked fast, hurried home, and at night I even tried to sleep fast.

I was in such a state that I went to see a famous nerve specialist in Detroit. He told me to relax. He told me to think of relaxing all the time—to think about it when I was working, driving, eating, and trying to go to sleep. He told me that I was committing slow suicide because I didn't know how to relax.

Ever since then I have practised relaxation. When I go to bed at night, I don't try to go to sleep until I've consciously relaxed my body and my breathing. And now I wake up in the morning rested—a big improvement, because I used to wake up in the morning tired and tense. I relax now when I eat and when I drive. To be sure, I am alert when driving, but I drive with my mind now instead of my nerves. The most important place I relax is at my work. Several times a day I stop everything and take inventory of myself to see if I am entirely relaxed. When the phone rings now, no longer do I grab it as though someone were trying to beat me to it; and when someone is talking to me, I'm as relaxed as a sleeping baby.

The result? Life is much more pleasant and enjoyable; and I'm completely free of nervous fatigue and nervous worry.

紧张就等于慢性自杀

六个月前，我的生活高度紧张。我总是紧张，从不会轻松。我每天晚上下班回到家时，总是忧心忡忡，精疲力竭。这是为什么呢？因为从来没有人对我说："保罗，你正在自杀。为什么不慢慢来？为什么不放松？"

　　每天早上，我总是匆匆起床、吃早餐、刮脸、穿衣服，然后又匆匆开车上班。我紧握方向盘，好像它随时会飞出窗外。我迅速工作，又匆匆赶回家。到了晚上，我甚至匆匆入睡。

　　我这种状况太严重了，因此，我去找了底特律一位著名的精神科专家。他建议我放松，还建议我随时都要想到放松——也就是在工作、开车、吃饭、入睡时，都要想到放松。他说，我正在慢性自杀，因为我不知道如何放松。

　　从那时起，我就开始学习放松。我每天晚上上床时，并不急着入睡，而是先使自己的身体和呼吸放松。现在，我每天早上醒来时会觉得休息充分。这是一大进步，因为我以前每天早上醒来时总觉得疲惫紧张。而现在，我开车、吃饭时也很轻松。为了安全，我驾车时提高了注意力，却不如以前那样紧张。最重要的是，我上班时也能放松。一天当中，我总要将手里的工作停几次，仔细检讨自己是否已经彻底放松了。现在，当电话铃响时，我不再像以前那样急着去接听；有人对我讲话时，我也会使自己轻松得像熟睡的婴儿一样。

　　结果呢？我的生活更轻松愉快了，我完全不再紧张烦恼了。

A Real Miracle Happened to Me

　　Worry had completely defeated me. My mind was so confused and troubled that I could see no joy in living. My nerves were so strained that I could neither sleep at night nor relax by day. My three young children were widely separated, living with relatives. My husband, having recently returned from the armed service, was in another city trying to establish a law practice. I felt all the insecurities and uncertainties of the postwar readjustment period.

　　I was threatening my husband's career, my children's natural endowment of a happy, normal home life, and I was also threatening my own life. My husband could find no housing, and the only solution was to build. Everything depended on my getting well. The more I realized this and the harder I would try, the greater would be my fear of failure. Then I developed a fear of planning for any responsibility. I felt that I could no longer trust myself. I felt I was a complete failure.

　　When all was darkest and there seemed to be no help, my mother did something for me that I shall never forget or cease being grateful for. She shocked me into fighting back. She upbraided me for giving in and for losing control of my nerves and my mind. She challenged me to get up out of bed and fight for all I had. She said I was giving in to the situation, fearing it instead of facing it, running away from life instead of living it.

So I did start fighting from that day on. That very weekend I told my parents they could go home, because I was going to take over; and I did what seemed impossible at the time. I was left alone to care for my two younger children. I slept well, I began to eat better, and my spirits began to improve. A week later when they returned to visit me again, they found me singing at my ironing. I had a sense of well-being because I had begun to fight a battle and I was winning. I shall never forget this lesson…If a situation seems insurmountable, face it! Start fighting! Don't give in!

From that time on I forced myself to work, and lost myself in my work. Finally I gathered my children together and joined my husband in our new home. I resolved that I would become well enough to give my lovely family a strong, happy mother. I became engrossed with plans for our home, plans for my children, plans for my husband, plans for everything—except for me. I became too busy to think of myself. And it was then that the real miracle happened.

I grew stronger and stronger and could wake up with the joy of well-being, the joy of planning for the new day ahead, the joy of living. And although days of depression did creep in occasionally after that, especially when I was tired, I would tell myself not to think or try to reason with myself on those days—and gradually they became fewer and fewer and finally disappeared.

Now, a year later, I have a very happy, successful husband, a beautiful home that I can work in sixteen hours a day, and three healthy, happy children—and for myself, peace of mind!

生活中的奇迹

烦恼已将我完全击败。我的大脑中一片混乱，觉得生活毫无乐趣，精神十分紧张，不但晚上睡不着觉，连白天也无法休息。我的三个孩子都和亲戚住在一起，和我隔得很远。我的丈夫最近刚从军队退役，一个人住在外地，正准备成立一家法律事务所。我认为自己完全感染了战后恢复时期的那种不安全的惶惑情绪。

我的情绪影响了丈夫的事业和我们正常的家庭生活，同时严重影响了我自己的生活。我的丈夫找不到房子，唯一的解决方法就是自己建一栋。现在，万事俱备，就等我恢复健康了。我对这种情况知道得愈多，愈想努力恢复，对失败的恐惧也就愈甚。于是，我对任何事情都怀有一种深切的负罪感。我觉得我再也无法相信自己，觉得自己完全失败了。

在最黯淡无助的时期，是母亲帮助了我，使我永远难忘，终生感激。她鼓励我和生活奋斗。她责怪我消极放弃，失去了对神经和大脑的控制。她让我爬起床去拼搏。她说我这是对生活妥协，不敢直面人生，是在逃避生活。

于是，从那天起，我开始振作起来。到了那个周末，我对父母说他们可以回家了，因为我就要恢复了。那时，我完成了一些几乎不可能的工作：我一个人照顾两个幼小的孩子，睡得很好，食欲也开始好转，精神也大有进步。一周之后，他们再来看我时，发现我正在熨衣服，还哼着歌曲。我有一种富裕满足的感觉，因为我已经展开一场自我战斗，而且正在获胜。我将永远记住这个教训……如果情况似乎很难克服，就勇敢面对它！开始奋斗！永不放弃！

从那时起，我强迫自己工作，让自己沉浸在工作中。最后，我把孩子全部接回家来，和我丈夫一起住在我们新房子里。我知道我可以恢复，使我这个可爱的家庭有一位健康、快乐的母亲。我将全部身心放在了家庭、孩子、丈夫和所有事情上——除了我自己。我太忙了，根本没时间去想自己。就在这时，真正的奇迹出现了。

我越来越强健，每天早上起床时都充满喜悦：富足的喜悦，为新的一天到来的喜悦，生活的喜悦。虽然我偶尔也有沮丧的时候，特别是疲倦之时，但我告诉自己，不必在沮丧的时候想那么多——于是，这种情况逐渐愈来愈少，终于完全消失了。

现在，一年之后，我有了一位非常快乐且成功的丈夫。一个美好的家庭，以及三个健康快乐的孩子——而我自己也快乐安详。

Setbacks

Exactly fifty years ago my father gave me the words I have lived by ever since. He was a physician. I had just started to study law at the Budapest University. I failed one examination. I thought I could not survive the shame so I sought escape in the consolation of failure's closest friend, alcohol, always at hand: apricot brandy to be exact.

My father called on me unexpectedly. Like a good doctor, he discovered both the trouble and the bottle, in a second. I confessed why I had to escape reality.

The dear old man then and there improvised a prescription. He explained to me that there can be no real escape in alcohol or sleeping pills—or in any drug. For any sorrow there is only one medicine, better and more reliable than all the drugs in the world: work!

How right my father was! Getting used to work might be hard. Sooner or later you succeed. It has, of course, the quality of all the narcotics. It becomes habit-forming. And once the habit is formed, sooner or later, it becomes impossible to break one's self of it. I have never been able to break myself of the habit for fifty years.

挫　折

50年前，父亲给了我一句话，从那以后我靠它生活至今。父亲是医生。我刚开始在布达佩斯大学学习法律，有一次考试不及格。我受不了这种羞辱，不想见朋友，并借酒浇愁，手中总是拿着杏味白兰地。

父亲意外地来看我了。就像一位善良的医生，他立即看出了我的麻烦和酒瓶。我承认了为何要逃避现实。

这可爱的老人立即给我开了一个处方。他向我解释说：酒精和安眠药都不能解决问题——任何药物都不能。治疗不幸的药只有一种，世界上比药物更好、更可靠的东西就是——工作。

父亲太对了！投入工作可能很难。但是，你迟早会做到这一点。工作当然拥有所有麻醉剂的功效。它是一种习惯的培养。一旦这种习惯养成，就不可能剔除。我这种习惯就保持了50年。